PACIFIC NORTHWEST PALATE

Pacific Northwest Palate

FOUR SEASONS OF GREAT COOKING

Susan Bradley

Illustrated by Earl Thollander

ARIS BOOKS

ADDISON-WESLEY PUBLISHING COMPANY, INC.

Reading, Massachusetts   Menlo Park, California   New York
Don Mills, Ontario   Wokingham, England   Amsterdam   Bonn
Sydney   Singapore   Tokyo   Madrid   San Juan

Many of the designations used by manufacturers and sellers to distinguish their products are claimed as trademarks. Where those designations appear in this book and
Addison-Wesley was aware of a trademark claim, the designations have been printed
in initial capital letters (e.g., Thermos).

LIBRARY OF CONGRESS CATALOGING-IN-PUBLICATION DATA
Bradley, Susan.
  Pacific Northwest palate.

  "Aris books."
  Includes index.
  1. Cookery, American—Pacific Northwest style.
I. Title.
TX715.2.P32B73 1989   641.59795   89-6965
ISBN 0-201-51764-7
ISBN 0-201-55088-1 (pbk.)

Aris Books Editorial Offices and
Test Kitchen
1621 Fifth Street
Berkeley, CA 94710
(415) 527-5171

Text design by Beth Tondreau Design
Illustrated by Earl Thollander
Cover photograph by Patricia Brabant
Food styled by Robert Lambert
Set in 11 point Garamond No. 3 by Compset Inc., Beverly, MA

1 2 3 4 5 6 7 –VB– 95 94 93 92 91
First printing, September 1989
First paperback printing, January 1991

TO MARY PULLMAN STAHL

For all the joys, culinary and otherwise,
that only you could give.

C O N T E N T S

ACKNOWLEDGMENTS

My heartfelt gratitude goes to the testing team, all graduate students of the Northwest Culinary Academy: Rosalyn Rourke, Lynn Kaplan, Jean Ann Hodges, Pat Sherman, and Lindsay Horton—the remarkable five. There are no recipes in this book that a majority of them did not truly like; the final selections are as much theirs as mine. Without the enthusiasm and involvement of these very special friends, I could not have made it through the development and testing phase of this book. They were, individually and as a group, a constant source of energy, motivation, and encouragement to me. *Muchas gracias, compadres.*

My gratitude goes also to Aris Books founder John Harris for his tenaciousness in getting this book published, for his insightful and detailed editing of the original manuscript, and for following the project from inception to completion with humor, tact, and determination. Without his vision, *Pacific Northwest Palate* would still be a figment of this writer's imagination.

I am grateful to partner, best friend, and husband James Bradley for his unwavering confidence in the merits of this project and in my ability to complete it; and also for his extensive computer knowledge and numerous hours of patient assistance.

My gratitude to my mom, Virginia Mitchell, for typing the entire three hundred pages of the Advanced Certificate Course for the Academy so that I could get back to work on the book, and for encouraging me in my sundry and assorted cooking adventures from age eight to the present day.

And also my sincere appreciation to the following:

Elliot Wolf for his initial enthusiasm and his great help in clarifying and defining the project at hand; Addison-Wesley Senior Production Supervisor Lori Foley for her valuable input on this project and her always cheerful voice on the other end of the line; copy editor Frances Bowles for her masterful editing and fine polishing of my prose; Greg Kaplan of Aris Books for picking up loose ends and tying them neatly together; Larry and Deborah Jaffee of Mr. J. Kitchen Gourmet in Bellevue for providing the kitchen space each week for recipe testing; Lynn Kaplan for her prodigious efforts as Promotions Director of the Academy during its fledgling years and for her encouragement of this project; Lynn Fantozzi for her help in the beginning stages of the testing; Steve Horton, Bob Kaplan, Dr. Michael Leff, Philip Rourke, and Bill Sherman for their gracious company and good humor throughout the testing process; Casey Johnston Yunker for her enormous help in my early teaching days and for her continuing encouragement and support; Carol Lampman, Charlene Howson, and Linda Kelleran for their many years of encouragement; Joshua Bradley and Rachel Bradley, who provide a constant source of perspective and balance; Academy apprentices Karen Anderson, Bonita Atkins, Susan Carter, Laura Crofts, Susan Dewalt, Beverly Dillon,

Lynn Fantozzi, Mitch Harter, Janet Hawley, Karen Hedge, Diane Honeycutt, Lindsay Horton, Sammalee Knox, Penny Kulp, Barbara Manning, Jean Osborne, Pamela Powers, Judy Prindle, Judy Schwab, Lynn Snyder, Shirley Strand, Myrna Torrie, Genie Rognier, and Laura Wilde for their hard work and enthusiasm—always above and beyond the call of duty; and all past and present students of the Northwest Culinary Academy for their interest, enthusiasm, and encouragement.

I wrote this book for two reasons. First to chronicle my progress as I began—eight years ago—to cook predominantly with the local, seasonal foods of the Pacific Northwest. Second, to encourage others to emphasize the fresh, that is, unpackaged, unfrozen, uncanned, gifts of land and sea in their own cooking and to use the seasons in which these gifts are offered as inspirational palettes of color, taste, and texture. (Thus the play on the words *palate,* meaning the sense of taste, as used in the title and *palette* as I am using it here to suggest a range of colors or ingredients that an artist or cook uses in a composition or dish.)

It is a joyful way to eat. Strawberries in the winter are not only out of harmony with the spirit of snow, sleet, and perpetual fog, they are also tasteless. Corn that is more than a few hours off the stalk is not worth eating. Highly perishable mussels "rushed" from East to West Coast are a travesty too unpalatable for words. To eat supremely well, one must eat within the natural, cyclical seasons of the surrounding countryside. That is the premise of this book.

Eating seasonally is not so much a matter of restriction as it is an issue of reorientation. There is nothing like a ten-month absence of raspberries to lift the imagination anew when they do at last offer themselves fully ripened on the bush. Resounding pleasure is what I feel each spring when consuming my first bunch of sweet, succulent asparagus from the Yakima Valley. The eating is the sweeter if you have passed by the tempting, much-traveled asparagus that appears on the grocer's shelves only

minutes after Christmas. I would not trade the expectation and the climactic gustatory reward of the seasonal offerings of my native region for all the pale, seasonless facsimiles in the world. I know that if you proceed likewise, working within the seasons and with the foods of your own region, the expanded enjoyment will prove worth the effort.

However, I am not advocating *total* rejection of all foods grown outside your locale. Perhaps in your case that would mean giving up something indispensible such as apples or even something as inconceivable as all ocean fish if you do not happen to live near one of the coastlines. No one is going to do that. Even within the purist confines of this book, I have allowed some auxiliary ingredients from outside the Northwest region to enter the recipes. I would find it difficult to do without lemons or olives though they certainly do not grow here. The other thing to keep in mind while reading this book is that although the ingredients for the recipes are drawn from the foods of the Northwest region, it is assumed that your own regional ingredients are going to be somewhat—or perhaps significantly—different from mine. Use the ideas as a point of reference. I hope that the recipes themselves will offer inspiration to cooks of all regions. Most of them can easily be adapted to alternate ingredients. Take Dungeness crab for instance. Not everyone can get it. And even if you can get it, it may be ridiculously expensive. Fine. Use the crab of your region instead. Atlantic blue crab or Southern stone crab perhaps. No crab at all?

That, too, is not a problem. Shrimp, crawfish, or lobster will probably work. In the recipe for Crab in Black Bean Sauce on page 224, for instance, mussels or clams are wonderful alternatives. Just keep in mind the basic taste of the ingredient you are replacing. Is it rich, sweet, tart, or nutty tasting? What is the texture like? Is color important? No recipe in this book is so ironclad that you should feel reluctant to play around with it by substituting your favorite regional ingredients for mine.

The idea of regionality has other aspects beyond that of the ingredients used. When I began teaching cooking, nearly fifteen years ago, many talented American cooks were frantically busy acquiring the skills necessary to produce a carbon copy French cuisine. Never mind that our ingredients were not the same. Never mind that all the *haute cuisine* rules and injunctions about what classically—thus legitimately—could go with what were straightjackets to us. You just were not a cook if you could not produce a soufflé, a croissant, or an elaborate six-course dinner with effortless aplomb. Old-time American cuisine was considered decidedly provincial and beneath the developing sophistication of the contemporary American palate. The world *casserole* could be uttered only under one's breath and only to trusted family members who would not divulge our more ignominious culinary predilections to outsiders. We had become snobs. Even worse, we were denying our own American heritage and character and trying to be something we were—for the most part—not.

After gaining some level of mastery over French cuisine, American cooks shot rapid-fire through every other cuisine they could: Italian, Moroccan, Chinese, Indian, Japanese, Spanish. Then, at some magical point of proficiency and understanding, the spell was broken and a great many cooks, in seeming unison, began looking around their own back yards. Increased attention was directed to local foods, to discovering them, growing them, and procuring them. Culinary confidence was beginning to take the place of unthinking compliance with the rules. Cooks were becoming brazen enough to use elements of different cuisines—say, Chinese with French—to create fresh combinations. New attitudes, eclectic, free-wheeling, spontaneous, imaginative, often intellectual, sometimes crazy, and above all fun, shaped the budding new American cuisine.

My own awakening took the form of recognizing that I could never be really credible as a teacher of French cuisine. Even though I had been doing just that for nearly seven years and could turn out and show others how to turn out a multitude of wondrous dishes, something was wrong. I was not French. Nor had I been to France. After making this rather startling personal discovery, I began a food column for the *Eastside Journal-American* entitled "Seasonal Bounty—Northwest Style." I reasoned that, since I was a Northwest native and had been cooking enthusiastically since childhood, this was a topic I could tackle authentically, at firsthand. That was 1982 and the term *North-*

west cuisine was being whispered by only a small handful of cooks.

Culinary miracles have definitely been wrought in the past ten years. An awakening food consciousness has surfaced in the Northwest as it has in much of the rest of America. In this region we have local purveyors of food who take great pride in their products, farmers and fishermen who go to admirable lengths to deliver a perfect harvest, grocers who pay attention to what cooks want, talented chefs working predominantly with Northwest ingredients, a praiseworthy wine industry, writers on food and wine who extoll the virtues of the region at every opportunity, the continuing presence and influence of the Pike Place Market in Seattle, and a discriminating public who, when it comes to eating, knows the best and expects the best. But even more important than all of these, we have what we have always had in this region (a region defined for our purposes as Washington, Oregon, Idaho, British Columbia, and coastal Alaska—though the text focuses primarily on the first two): one of the most incredible land and water formations (combined with ideal soil and a wide range of climates) in the world. Within the confines of Washington and Oregon alone, there are so many different growing conditions that nearly anything can be grown or harvested here. The Northwest region is an ecological wonderland unsurpassed in beauty or abundance.

So now—barely ten years after setting sail on this culinary odyssey—I am frequently asked: Is there a Northwest cuisine? My answer is that what we have in this region is not a Northwest cuisine but rather an emerging Northwest cuisine. The first label implies completion, the second suggests process. We have all the elements necessary for the development of a great regional style and it is likely that this style will have numerous identifiable, cohesive elements in perhaps another twenty-five years. It would take more than a miracle to produce a full-blown cuisine in one—even one very fruitful—decade. French cuisine was first written about by Taillevent in the 1370s. Washington State was admitted to the Union in 1889. Imagine what five hundred years will do for our regional food consciousness. As a cook, would you rather come into a region with a clear-cut, codified cooking style or would you rather be a part of the initial energy that brings that style into being? I hope you choose the latter. That is what this book is all about.

PACIFIC NORTHWEST PALATE

Spring

MARCH • APRIL • MAY

Spring is the season of re-emergence and expectation. The comatose earth slowly awakens with the lengthening daylight hours and the first tentative rays of warming sunshine. This signals the onset of a new and colorful palette of ingredients as well as a lighter, brighter approach to cooking. Gone are the hearty, layered gratins, the deeply flavored stews, the rich casseroles. Simplicity and clear, bright flavors are elements of the spring culinary style. Dishes now have an uncomplicated immediacy of taste. There is not the depth of choice in ingredients that will follow in summer but what is available is long awaited and appreciated all the more because it is so fleeting.

Pale, slender ribs of hothouse rhubarb announce the onset of spring, arriving as early as February in most markets. Nature always seems to know best, as rhubarb happens to offer one of the best and easiest ways to make the transition from hearty to lighter foods. It has a beautiful color and a distinctive flavor and its powerful acidity works to decided advantage with a wide variety of other ingredients, cutting through richness and adding a counterpoint of tang to everything it comes into contact with. In fact there are very few other foods that enhance as wide a range of ingredients as rhubarb does.

Following shortly after hothouse rhubarb are other comestibles that make spring meals distinctive: the brighter, larger ribs of field-grown rhubarb, Yakima Valley asparagus, sweet peas, Pacific shrimp, Pacific halibut, and rainbow trout. Lamb too is important now, though more because of its traditional association with spring than because of any actual seasonality involved. Most Northwest herb gardens rejuvenate themselves by March or April, thus insuring an adequate supply of these most indispensable of seasonings as well.

If you have put away the grill over the winter, pull it back out again, clean it up, and get ready for the mild evenings that can now be enjoyed outside. There is no need in the Northwest to wait anxiously for summer. Spring offers a wealth of opportunity for culinary creativity and gustatory enjoyment. But hurry, this is perhaps our shortest of seasons. Do not let it slip by without getting your fill of rhubarb and asparagus in particular. When they are gone, they are gone.

Because fresh fish figures so prominently in the springtime kitchen, I have included the fish primer, with its basic information on fishing methods, selection, and preparation, in this chapter. This information is equally vital to the understanding of the other types of fish that are central to the remaining seasons. Be sure then to refer back to this section as needed.

In Search of the Perfect Fish

There has been much talk recently about the importance of the way fish is caught and the manner in which it is treated on board. As consumers we have more say now in the basic quality of seafood in our markets. Our voices are being heard because changes are beginning to occur that affect us, the retail customer. For years first-rate seafood restaurants have been setting up their own networks with fishermen. The fish they have been able to buy, fish that have been line-caught, bled and gutted on board, and either frozen or properly chilled before reaching the restaurant, have not been available to the rest of us. Thus, even in a good seafood market where the merchant really cares about his fish, it has sometimes been difficult to get anything worth eating. This is why, I believe, so many people think they do not like fish. They have never tasted fresh fish.

Today a few markets in the Northwest are experimenting with carefully handled line-caught, sometimes frozen, fish that is of superlative quality. More are sure to join in if their customers ask for and are willing to pay for these special fish. It has been a major undertaking to educate the public to the fact that "frozen" is not synonymous with "bad" when it comes to fish. I have been to numerous professional tastings in which fresh and frozen fish were compared and in each case the frozen fish won the blind taste sampling, simply because no so-called fresh fish of even two or three days old (which is much fresher than any of *us* ever get it in the market) can compare to a fish that has been treated well and frozen almost immediately after its demise.

This said, a cook should know the usual ways in which fish are caught so that appropriate questions can be asked at the point of purchase and an intelligent choice made. The methods are known as long lining, gill netting, and seining.

Long lining is an expensive and time-consuming method of fishing, by which long lines with many hooks on each are used to catch the fish individually and keep them apart in the water and on board. The fish are not jostled against one another so much and, best of all, they are often treated with a great deal of pampering and careful attention once they are on board, where they are bled, gutted, and iced immediately. These trolled fish are caught out at sea where they are at their vigorous best. Of course we should expect to pay more per pound for these fish but the eating is so much better the additional expense is well justified.

I assume that everyone understands that gutting is the removal of the viscera or internal organs of the fish. Bleeding is the process by which the blood is drained from live fish as soon as they come over the sides of the boat. An established practice in Norway where only bled fish can be sold as fresh, bleeding has also become common procedure with quality-oriented fishermen in the Northwest. Unbled fish has a mottled appearance; bled fish is very white or uniformly bright in color. More than appearance though, taste and even texture are impaired when the blood of the fish is allowed to remain within its tissues. There are two or three ways of bleeding a fish but one is preferred by experts. The gill plate is lifted with one finger to expose the gills, then a knife is used to make a short jab in front of the collar, between the throat latch and the gills, just forward of the heart. This single cut severs the artery, causing the heart to pump blood out of the circulatory system and onto the deck. In about 10 minutes the blood will have been all pumped out. While this method works well for fish such as Pacific cod, ling cod, rockfish, sablefish, and halibut, extra help is needed with salmon. After the heart has stopped pumping and the salmon has been dressed, this fish is then force-bled with the aid of running water and massage—a time-consuming chore to say the least.

Another basic thing a fisherman can do to improve the quality of the fish is to chill it as quickly as possible to 32 degrees. On-board chilling dramatically delays the onset of spoilage by as much as five to eight days. (Fish spoil three times faster at 40 degrees, seven times faster at 50 degrees and ten times faster at 60 degrees than they do at 32 degrees.) *Rigor mortis,* the natural process of contraction and stiffening after death, can actually be delayed and then prolonged by quick chilling to 32 degrees. For some unknown reason, fish do not decay while in *rigor.* Thus, on-board chilling can produce a fish that tastes as fresh at point of purchase as it would have tasted right out of the water. Incredible!

Gill netting is a commercial fishing method that involves catching quantities of fish by their gills in large vertical nets. This method is used only at the mouths of rivers where fish are returning to spawn. Fish caught by this method are not generally of high quality because they are usually handled in bulk, thrown about, and left uncleaned for an indeterminate time before arriving at the local fish market. (The gill netters who do quickly bleed and gut their fish are the exception.) There is probably nothing more destructive to the taste of fish than its rotting from the inside out; the gastric juices contained in the stomach and intestines are strong and must be removed immediately after the fish is killed. Unfortunately, I have seen ungutted fish aplenty at the point of purchase; some seafood merchants seem oblivious to what is happening to their products as they wait for sale.

Seining is a method of commercial fishing that uses large nets to scoop up the fish close to shore. Fish that are caught in this manner are frequently mistreated and bruised, and taste unpleasant because they are not gutted right away. You can imagine what happens to huge hauls of fish as they are drawn out of the water and thrown on board. Those at the bottom of the heap do not stand a chance of tasting good.

SELECTING FRESH FISH

Your first indicator of the quality of the fish you are about to buy occurs a split second after you enter the door of the retail store. What does the store smell like? If there is a heavy odor of decaying fish, a so-called fishy smell, be immediately on guard. Fresh fish do not smell fishy. They have a clean, sea-brine smell that is in no way unpleasant or strong. Yes, you can ask the merchant if you may smell his fish. He will not think you odd, only knowledgeable. The following points will hold you in good stead when you are selecting a whole fresh fish:

1. Ask the fish merchant which, if any, of the fish he has for sale have been bled, gutted and iced to 32 degrees on board the fishing vessel. If he sneers, shop elsewhere. (When I ask this question and start opening belly flaps and smelling disapprovingly, most merchants run to the back to bring out better specimens for my approval. It is amazing how far a little good information will get you.)
2. The fish must be fully embedded in ice and preferably under refrigeration. Never buy a fish that has even its upper body exposed to room temperature. Always reach down into the ice to select your fish, or better yet, ask the fish merchant to bring you out a few specimens from the back storage refrigerator to choose from. If the merchant balks at this, shop elsewhere.
3. The fish should have a clean, fresh smell. Especially note the smell of the belly cavity, where decay usually begins. If the fish has not been gutted, forget it.
4. The fish should have a moist, glistening overlay of natural fish slime and the scales should be tight and intact. If either of these indicators of quality is not present, the fish has most likely been mishandled and/or stored improperly. Look for another fish. Fillets and steaks are harder to judge; they should look moist and bright colored with no yellowing around the edges and, above all, they should smell good. When possible, have these cut from a whole fish that you have selected.
5. When pressed with your finger, the flesh of the fish should be firm and elastic; it must not feel so soft that your finger leaves an indentation.
6. The eyes of the fish should be bright, clear, and convex in appearance. When a fish ages, the eyes sink into the sockets and become milky and opaque.
7. Check the gills, if they have not been removed, to be sure they are bright reddish. With age, they fade first to pink, then to gray, then to brownish green.

PURCHASING FISH

First of all, fish are *dressed* rather than *cleaned*. There is nothing dirty about fish to clean. The following are the most common ways in which you will be able to purchase fresh fish.

Whole Dressed

In this form the fish is left whole with the scales, viscera, and fins removed. Allow about ¾ pound per person, depending on the kind of fish. (Some fish have smaller bodies and larger heads which affects the proportion of edible meat.)

Pan Dressed

Same as above but with the head removed. Allow about ½ pound per person.

Fillet

This is the lengthwise, boneless cut off each side of the fish. Fillets may be skinned or not. Be sure you specify which you prefer as often the fish merchant will leave the skin on if you say nothing but, "Fillet the fish, please." Allow ⅓ to ½ pound per serving.

Steak

A fish is cut across its width to produce a steak. This can be done with larger, firm-fleshed fish, such as halibut, salmon, cod, or swordfish but is not possible with thin flat fish such as sole or flounder. Allow ⅓ to ½ pound per serving.

Roast

These are cross-section chunks of dressed fish with the backbone left in. Allow ⅓ to ½ pound per person.

STORING FRESH FISH

Fish should always be stored embedded in ice and under refrigeration. If you have far to go after making your purchase at the seafood market, have a cooler loaded with ice in your trunk ready to accept your very perishable fish. Once home, cover the bottom of a deep tray with ice, lay the plastic-wrapped fish on top and cover with more ice. Refrigerate until you are ready to cook.

If the fish is frozen, thaw it slowly in the refrigerator. A large fish can take up to twenty-four hours to thaw.

If you need to freeze a fish (preferably your own just-caught specimen), seal it tightly in plastic wrap, then in heavy-duty foil, and set in the freezer at the lowest possible temperature setting. (It is always desirable to freeze the fish as quickly as possible.) Three to six months is the maximum storage time under these conditions. The sooner you use it, the better the fish will taste; deterioration does take place even while the fish is frozen.

BONING WHOLE ROUND FISH

For culinary purposes there are two types of fish skeletal structures: round fish such as salmon, trout, and striped bass; and flat fish such as flounder, sole, and turbot. Each requires a somewhat different boning method; either can be easily mastered with a little practice. Round fish may be prepared in two ways; filleted and skinned or whole-boned with the head and tail left on. The first method is useful for quick pan sautés, poaching, and steaming; the second provides a pocket for stuffing.

Preparing the Whole Fish

Whether you decide to fillet or whole-bone, these preparation steps need to be attended to first.

1. First the viscera should be removed, preferably just after the fish comes from the water and is bled. To do this, make a shallow cut down the belly from between the gills to the anal opening. The cavity will now come open. Reserve the roe if you wish, then cut away and discard the innards. Remove the gill on either side of the fish by holding it firmly in your hand, then cutting around the membrane and through the point where it joins the body. (When

you are purchasing a fish at the market, these steps should already have been taken.)
2. To scale the fish, hold it firmly by the tail and scrape the scales with a fish scaler, using a brushing motion from tail to head. This will make quite a mess; you may wish to cover your work surface with newspaper. (Your fish dealer will do this for you if you ask.)
3. The fins are next. Simply cut them all off with a large pair of kitchen shears.
4. Wash the fish thoroughly under cold running water, making sure that the interior cavity is completely empty of blood and viscera.

Filleting the Whole Fish

After the basic preparation steps outlined above are completed, the fish may be filleted.

1. Using a very sharp, thin-bladed knife, make a shallow diagonal cut on one side of the fish, skin-side up, just behind the head, going from the top-back of the fish down to the belly on the meaty side of the gill.
2. Turn the fish with its backbone toward you and make a cut just about an inch deep along the top edge (backbone) of the fish from head to tail, grazing the bones with the knife. Continue the cut on one side to the center bone. Be sure you can feel the outline of the bones with your knife.
3. With the knife at a slight angle, begin to cut down along the center bone, using a slicing, sliding motion with the knife.

With your free hand, pull back the flesh so that you can see what is happening. When completed, the entire side of the fish should come off, though it will still be attached at the tail. Sever the attachment.

4. Turn the fish over. Bone the remaining side as already outlined and cut the fillet away at the tail.

5. To skin the fillets, hold each one by its tail skin. With a long, thin, flexible knife, begin a cut separating the skin from the meat at a flat angle. Then hold the skin securely and pull it away from the knife as you continue to cut in a sawing motion down the length of the fillet. If you pull the skin too tightly, the fillet will come away with some of the silvery inner skin still attached; if you don't pull tightly enough, some of the fillet meat will remain with the skin. Do not despair; this comes easily with practice.

6. Run your fingers down the center length of each fillet, first in one direction, then in the other. You should be able to feel the thirty or so tiny bones that have been left. Remove these one by one with tweezers.

Whole-Boning the Fish

After the basic preparation steps outlined above are completed, the fish may be whole-boned.

1. In whole-boning a fish the object is to remove the center bones without severing the head or tail and without slicing through the skin. Open the fish up so that you can see the inside belly cavity. Note the thick bone running down the center of the fish—this is the backbone—and the row of thin bones attached to it on either side—these make up the rib cage.

2. With a sharp, thin knife, make a quarter inch cut on both sides of the backbone, along its entire length, cutting through the row of bones attached to it on each side.

3. Continue cutting down on both sides of the backbone, through another set of smaller, more delicate bones. Stop as you reach the skin; be careful not to cut through that. Both sides of the fish, with the flesh, will fall open and away from the backbone at this point.

4. Slip one finger under the middle of the backbone and lift up and away from the skin. Snip the backbone with kitchen shears where it joins the head and the tail. There will be some short bones left attached to the center skin. Do not worry about these; they will come away later when the cooked fish is skinned.

5. To remove the rib cage bones still remaining on each side of the fish, use the tip of your knife to begin lifting the cut edges of the bones all along the length of the fish. Continue working the blade just under the bones until you reach the end of the belly flap, which is where the bones stop. Lift them out on each side.

6. Run your fingers down the center length of each side, first in one direction, then in the

other. You should be able to feel the thirty or so bones that have been left. Remove these one by one with tweezers. The fish is now ready to season or stuff, as you wish.

Pacific Shrimp

Judging from our retail markets, local shrimp barely exist. We can buy Norwegian shrimp, Mexican shrimp, Ecuadorian shrimp, Indian shrimp, and Gulf shrimp from many states, but Northwest shrimp are not as easy to find. It is not that Northwest waters are not home to a variety of cold-water shrimp; they are. It is rather a problem of world economics combined with the fluctuating health of the Northwest shrimp industry. In the last twelve years, the Northwest has experienced an annual decrease in the number of shrimp available in its waters; from a peak of 180 million pounds from the biggest producer—Alaska—in 1977, to less than forty million pounds in 1985. In other words, by 1985 the Northwest shrimp fishery had collapsed. The causes are not at all clear and marine biologists struggle to understand the complexities of underwater life cycles. The eating habits of large schools of pollock are generally blamed, though. In the meantime, several foreign nations and the fisheries in the Gulf of Mexico have jumped happily to the rescue. America is the biggest consumer of shrimp in the world and, with the Northwest out of the action for nearly a decade, the inevitable was bound to happen. Local purveyors of seafood went elsewhere. In 1986 the shrimp began to come back (where have the pollock gone?) but retailers were used to the cheaper prices and constant supply of Norwegian and other imported shrimp and were reluctant to support the local industry. A fishery that becomes more reliable each year will eventually win them over, I am sure; that and customer demand. In the meantime, outside of a few specialty markets, your best bet for finding fresh Northwest shrimp are the many roadside stands that dot the areas around fishing towns such as Westport.

The sidestripe, coonstripe, brokenback, spot, and pink shrimp all come under the umbrella heading of "cold-water" shrimp and, as such, are members of the *Pandalus* shrimp family. The pink shrimp, which is quite important commercially is divided into the *Pandalus borealis* and the *Pandalus jordoni*. The smaller *borealis* is harvested in the Gulf of Alaska; Washington and Oregon bring in the slightly larger *jordoni*. Both of these fall in a size range of eighty to one hundred per pound. In Alaska and Hood Canal in Washington a considerable quantity of larger spot shrimp are harvested. If tall tales are to be believed these can reach a size of two to the pound (more normally though, these reach a maximum size of eight or nine per pound), and sidestrip shrimp, with a maximum size of fifteen or sixteen per pound.

Do not be confused in the seafood markets by the names shrimp and prawn. In common usage they refer to the same species. The word *shrimp* is generally used to indicate very small, precooked, salad shrimp; *prawn* indicates the larger, usually uncooked, specimens. (Technically, there is a difference: prawns are a freshwater species and none of our salt water shrimp qualifies.)

Season

Shrimp seasons are regulated by the fisheries department and vary, according to the quantities of shrimp, from year to year. Generally though, in Washington and Oregon, fresh shrimp are a spring and summer commodity; in Alaska, shrimp have a winter season as well as a summer season.

Selection

Nothing compares with the taste of just-caught, barely cooked shrimp. Unfortunately this is not what is available to most of us in the markets. Shrimp loses flavor appreciably with each minute it is out of the water; thus the tasteless, disappointing stuff we so often have to eat. Fresh is not always better with shrimp; it depends on how many days it takes the boat to get the haul to shore. If the look and smell of the previously frozen product is better, do not hesitate to buy it instead. The smell of raw shrimp, fresh or frozen, should be clean and briny, even a little sweet, and should

never have a trace of iodine or ammonia, the latter of which indicates the presence of excessive bacteria. (The iodine by the way occurs naturally in shrimp from certain localities. It is not harmful and does not indicate spoilage, but does ruin the taste.) Raw shrimp should look translucent without any dark spots that indicate deterioration. The shrimp should also feel firm. Ask if your merchant will let you sample cooked shrimp before you buy. When purchasing a large quantity (five pounds or more) of shrimp, it is better to buy them solidly frozen, rather than already thawed. Thaw them slowly in your own refrigerator.

Occasionally you will buy shrimp that look and smell fresh but turn to a horrible mush when cooked. This is the fault of a bacterial infection common to shrimp. Unfortunately it cannot be detected when raw. The shrimp are not harmful to eat, but of course you probably will not want to.

Shrimp are available, depending on the season, in several forms:

- Raw with the shell and tail "feathers" left on, but without the head; fresh or frozen
- Cooked whole; fresh or frozen
- Cooked then peeled, without the head and tail (called salad shrimp); fresh or frozen

You will rarely, if ever, see a raw shrimp with the head left on, because even though this portion of the shrimp contains a great deal of flavor it deteriorates rapidly. Small salad shrimp are always processed—meaning cooked and usually peeled—to create a longer shelf life.

Shrimp are very infrequently sold by species name and instead are marketed by size. Size guidelines vary from place to place but generally "jumbo" mean up to fifteen prawns per pound, "extra-large" means sixteen to twenty prawns per pound, "large" means twenty-one to thirty prawns per pound, "medium" means thirty-one to forty prawns per pound, and on down to salad shrimp.

When calculating the quantity to buy, it helps to know that you will end up with a shelled, cooked weight that is just half of the purchased weight; thus if you want one pound of cooked shrimp, buy two pounds raw, un-shelled shrimp.

Preparation

To peel a headless shrimp, hold on to the tail "feathers" to keep them from breaking off and pull off the shell starting at the inside curve where the feelers are. The shell should come away easily. To devein, make a shallow cut along the length of the outside curve to the point where you can see the gut and pull it out with your fingers. The vein on the inside curve is generally much smaller and does not need to be removed. Do not discard the shells or heads if you have them. They contain a lot of flavor and can be used to produce a shrimp-flavored stock or sauce and are also excellent as the fla-voring ingredient for shrimp butter. Freeze them if you cannot get to either of these tasks right away.

To peel a shrimp that still has its head, sim-ply break the head off where it joins the body and complete the peeling as directed above. If the shrimp is cooked and you must remove the gut (not really necessary, especially with smaller shrimp), insert a small knife at the large end of the outside curve and peel off the strip that covers the vein. Pull out the vein with your fingers.

It is sometimes necessary to devein shrimp while leaving the shell on. Make a slit through the shell, remove the vein, pat the shell back in place, and proceed with your recipe.

Cooking

If you can get fresh shrimp right out of the water, break off the heads and boil them for just a minute or so and eat straight away with butter and a little lemon juice—nothing more. They are so good you will not want to doctor them with anything. Otherwise, marinate them before cooking—an hour or more in lemon or lime juice with a bit of olive oil and perhaps a few fresh herbs.

Never, never overcook shrimp. They are wonderful raw, so it is quite enough to cook as little as possible. Cook, regardless of whether you steam, sauté, grill, or stir-fry, just until the shells change color and never so long that the shrimp lose all their flavorful liquid to the pan and curl up like doughnuts.

Pacific Shrimp Recipes

Broiled Shrimp with Basil and Lime, *page 40*

Fresh Fruit and Shrimp Salad with Cilantro, *page 85*

Grilled Shrimp and Scallops with Dill Sauce, *page 86*

Shrimp and Scallop Lasagne, *page 141*

Shrimp and Strawberry Salad with Honey Mint Vinaigrette, *page 33*

Shrimp with Tomatoes, Peppers, and Cream Cheese, *page 123*

Spicy-Fried Shrimp with Herbed Cucumber and Yogurt Sauce, *page 294*

Sweet and Hot Honey-Glazed Shrimp, *page 41*

Pacific Halibut

Pacific halibut is the largest flatfish in the flounder family. It can weigh anywhere from one hundred to three hundred pounds at maturity though small halibut nicknamed "chickens" are sometimes brought in at five to ten pounds. Eighty percent of the sixty million pounds of halibut (including Atlantic halibut) harvested annually is made up of Pacific halibut; most are caught in the Gulf of Alaska during short sporadic spurts during spring and summer. Halibut is taken by longliners with extremely efficient circle hooks. The fish is generally well treated on the boats but, because of the massive quantities harvested at one time, the processing and distribution link in the chain can be severely stressed. The difficulties created by having to handle so much fish cause the quality to vary by the time the halibut reaches the consumer. Pacific halibut is very lean; a piece weighing three and a half ounces contains only ninety-seven calories. The flesh is firm with large snow-white flakes and a delicate, slightly sweet flavor. The cheeks are prized for their similarity in taste and texture to crab.

Season

The season, regulated by the fisheries department, usually begins by the end of April and continues on and off through the end of September. May and June are the strongest months.

Selection

Since home-cooks cannot usually buy halibut whole, they are at a disadvantage in the marketplace. The fish is available in pre-cut steaks, chunks, cheeks, and segments of fillets. About the only way to judge the quality of a headless, skinless piece of fish is to smell it. If there is anything at all fishy about the aroma, find another fish. A good market and a merchant you can trust are essential when so much of the evidence has been destroyed.

Storage

Refer to the guidelines listed in Storing Fresh Fish, page 6.

Preparation

Halibut is usually pan-ready. Just dip it in cold water, dry with paper towels, and cook it.

Cooking

The fish is excellent poached, as this method preserves its moisture. Because it is so firm it also takes well to steaming, grilling, broiling, baking, and frying. It makes an excellent *se-viche,* is a particularly good fish to use cold in salads, and works wonderfully well with a wide variety of sauces and marinades. Pacific halibut can appropriately be used in any recipe calling for sole or flounder.

Pacific Halibut Recipes

Baked Halibut with Parmesan Mayonnaise, *page 42*

Braised Halibut with Mint Mayonnaise, *page 42*

Marinated Grilled Halibut with Cilantro-Lime Butter, *page 43*

Rainbow Trout

One of the Northwest's mysterious spring rituals involves migratory hordes of diehard fishermen, returning en masse to the dozens of beautiful lakes that dot the mountains, valleys, and hills of Washington, Oregon, and Idaho. As an adolescent I had the opportunity to view this lunacy at close range. We lived on the shores of one of the tiny lakes (no motor-boats allowed) that was yearly stocked with a good supply of rainbow trout. On opening day, beginning at the ungodly hour of 3:00 A.M., the winding country road down to the lake was jammed with cars, trailers, and boats. I watched with malicious expectation as each group of fishermen attempted to launch its craft. Those who did not know the lake, which on our end was composed primarily of peat, would take a few steps into the water and promptly sink into thigh-high mud. All that trouble for a few trout, which I am embarrassed to say I took very much for granted in those days. Now I am willing to pay dearly in the market for what was once abundantly free.

Today nearly every state in the Union farms trout, but Idaho's Magic Valley boasts more trout farmed per square mile than anywhere else in the world. All by itself, Idaho supplies over half of the United States market. Rainbows are the primary farm crop though many other varieties of trout are available to those who are willing to fish for their supper. In the Northwest one of the best of these is the pink-fleshed cutthroat trout. Regardless of variety, it is important to take your fish from very cold waters. Otherwise they tend to be flabby and taste muddy; this applies to farm-raised trout as well. (Diet is equally important.) Just as with all other fish, trout should be bled, gutted, and iced immediately for best quality. A fisherman without an ice-filled cooler may as well pick raspberries for his supper.

Season

Available year-round but best in the colder months of winter and early spring.

Selection

Farm-raised rainbows usually weigh less than a pound; those weighing between six and ten ounces are the most desirable. They are normally available whole but you may also find boneless fillets and kited (opened out and boned), hot-smoked trout.

Use the guidelines listed in Selecting Fresh Fish (page 5) when you are purchasing farm-raised trout. Do not expect them to look just like their wild cousins. Farm-raised trout are usually olive-drab in color rather than black-speckled and the customary red rainbow band

that should run from head to tail is often rather faded and perhaps nonexistent. No matter, the fish will still taste good if they are firm, smell fresh, and have an overlay of "just-caught" slime.

Storage

Refer to the guidelines listed in Storing Fresh Fish, page 6.

Preparation

Avoid scaling trout, as this damages the fish's ability to take a coating which is recommended in many forms of preparation.

Cooking

In selecting a recipe to use with trout remember that the fish has a medium-high fat content (a three-and-a-half-ounce serving contains 154 calories and is 6.8 percent fat and 20.7 percent protein). Therefore it takes equally well to poaching, steaming, baking, broiling, grilling, and frying. The only treatments it does not like are braising and stewing. Trout is flaky rather than firm or meaty and will fall apart in the stew pot. Because the flavor of trout is both delicate and distinctive, it is a fish best treated with simplicity and restraint in the kitchen. Do not overpower it with intense combinations of flavors or textures.

Rainbow Trout Recipes

Boned Rainbow Trout with Salmon Mousse and Sauce Beurre Rouge, *page 44*

Fillet of Trout with Chili Mint Chutneys, *page 48*

Wannacut Lake Trout with Toasted Hazelnuts, *page 49*

Wheat Germ-Fried Fillet of Trout with Fresh Herbs, *page 47*

Northwest Lamb

Idaho, Oregon, and Washington states combined produce over seven hundred thousand lambs annually (this is a conservative figure published by the United States Department of Agriculture; the individual states claim more). Idaho is the eighth largest producer in the nation and Oregon the tenth largest. All the lamb from Idaho and Oregon is shipped *live* to Washington, California, or Colorado for processing. Then the lamb is shipped all around the country with no indication of where it originally came from. This state of affairs is unfortunate. Consumers would appreciate knowing where their lamb has been raised because the raising makes a definite difference. In the Northwest, lambs are often produced from a crossing of white-faced ewes from several different types with the black-faced Suffolk ram. The offspring, which no longer have their parents' white or black faces are appropriately called "smut-faced" lambs. Crossbreeding produces a lamb that matures rapidly, making it possible to market the lamb just as it is being weaned or at least is still eating grass. Because of the grassy plains in much of the Northwest, our lambs do not need auxiliary feed such as corn. Thus grass-fed lamb is a distinctive Northwest product.

When it comes to determining when a lamb should be brought to market age is not as important as is weight. Beginning at around four months, lambs are screened for fat content. An experienced eye can tell if a lamb is ready by the way the wool lies over the back; wrinkling indicates a lack of the necessary fat. Lamb that is selected for processing will generally weigh between 105 and 125 pounds, though the restaurant trade is reputed to prefer larger lambs of about 135 pounds because of their larger, plate-filling chops, ribs, etc. Though a cut-off age of one year is often quoted as the point where lamb is no longer legally lamb, at the processing plants the inspectors from the

United States Department of Agriculture are not interested in birth certificates. Instead they check what is called the break-joint, which is comparable to our wrist. If it will break, the meat is stamped lamb, if not, it is mutton. With some animals, the break test can be safely passed at fifteen months. So there is no way of telling in the market how old the animal is, though the smaller animals are generally younger. Hot-house lamb, produced from a different, stubby, small-bodied sheep reaches its prime condition in just eight weeks. No major producer grows this type of lamb in the Northwest as the main markets for it are in the East, especially New York, and in California, especially in San Francisco and Los Angeles.

The phrase "spring lamb" does not mean anything in the Northwest. Most lambs are born between January and March and are not harvested until August, September, and October, making "fall lamb" a more appropriate label. This said, what is called "year-round lamb" can be bought with confidence as the many different climate zones in the Northwest make a continuing supply of fresh lamb a reality. But cultural heritage and custom play a big part in eating patterns and for many of us lamb is a "spring" meat. I have included it in the spring chapter partly for this reason but also because it goes so well with many other ingredients of spring, such as rhubarb and fresh mint.

Season

Year-round, but especially August through October.

Selection

Look for firm flesh and snowy-white fat. The ends of the bones should be red, moist, and porous. The fat should be dry and firm to the touch. "U.S.D.A. Choice" lamb is high-quality lamb that is available at most retail markets. "U.S.D.A. Prime" cuts are also sporadically available; these have more fat marbling. The merchants do not usually charge more for prime cuts because they get them incidentally.

Preparation

If your piece of lamb is not covered with a thin layer of fat, brush it lightly with corn oil before using any of the dry-heat cooking methods. Look for the paper-thin covering found over the fat of all lamb. This is called the fell and should be removed from smaller cuts to prevent shrinkage or distortion. Larger cuts such as the leg benefit if the fell is left in place; it helps retain the shape. Lamb also benefits from overnight marinades, either wet or dry, with an exuberance of herbs, spices, lemon juice, and olive oil.

Cooking

Because lamb today is bred especially for tenderness, most cuts can be cooked by the so-called dry-heat methods, roasting, grilling, broiling, and sautéing, all of which use heat without moisture. The tougher cuts of the breast, shank, and shoulder (blade chops and round bone chops are best cooked by moist-heat methods, slow braising, or stewing). In either case lamb is better cooked at a constant low to moderate heat, which prevents it from drying out. Basting, though promoted by many food writers, actually leaches juice from all meat and should be done sparingly (especially with the smaller cuts). Perhaps all one needs is just a bit of butter near the end of the cooking time to glaze the surface of a roast.

A distinctively flavored meat, lamb has a natural affinity with many herbs, especially thyme, savory, marjoram, oregano, and mint. Rosemary and dill are also good seasonings in moderation, as are spices such as cinnamon, ginger, and cloves, fresh and dried fruits, and garlic, shallots, and onions. Lamb lends itself to sweet or sweet-and-sour sauces and chutneys. It is at home with zippy calamata olives as well as bland foods such as potatoes and dried beans. Lamb may be served hot or cold but not tepid. Except where braising or stewing are called for, most cuts of lamb will be at their succulent, flavorful best if left rare (at an internal temperature of 140 degrees) or at the very most, medium-rare (150 degrees). The internal temperature of a large roast will continue to rise a bit after you take the meat from the oven, so compensate by taking it out when it is a few degrees short of the temperature you want.

Northwest Lamb Recipes

Grilled Lamb Chops with Fresh Thyme and Rhubarb Chutney, *page 54*

Herb-Marinated Grilled Leg of Lamb with Mint Aioli, *page 51*

Asparagus

In the Northwest, spring for me officially begins when asparagus from the Yakima Valley arrives in the markets of western Washington. It does not matter if the weather is doing its best to defeat the spirit with unseasonal rains and cold snaps. Where there is asparagus, there is hope—and a promise. Sunshine, and lots of it, is just around the corner. Of course I am not the only one who looks forward to this event with such relish; hundreds of adventurous foragers head for eastern Washington come the first of April to gather the first tender

shoots as they emerge along the irrigation ca-
nals and streams where they grow wild as
weeds. I have seen burlap bags filled to burst-
ing with the results of these expeditions. It
really sets the mind reeling. Could you keep
your family interested in eating asparagus all
the way to the bottom of the bag? Of course
you are going to freeze a lot of the booty, but
even so . . .

Since I am always very busy at the beginning of asparagus season feeding the wood-
burning stove the hourly meal of split cedar
and maple that the weather still demands, I
have as yet failed to make the easterly trek with
my comrades. Therefore I content myself, be-
side the toasty fire, with stacks of cookbooks
searching for new and interesting ways to cook
the crop when it finally arrives at the Pike
Place Market. I never jump the gun and buy
the asparagus from Mexico or California that is
in the market much earlier. Why? Well, it just
does not taste as good and, though our marvelous soil conditions and moist environment
in the Northwest do contribute considerably to
the taste of our asparagus, the uninteresting
taste of southern asparagus is probably due
more to the fact that this vegetable deteriorates
rapidly when exposed to temperatures above
32 degrees (a distinct possibility when it is
shipped over long distances) than to any inherent lack of breeding.

Season

Mid-April through June.

Selection

When purchasing fresh asparagus, local or otherwise, look for stalks that are a rich green in
color with closed, compact tips. The stalks
should be tender but very firm. Stalks that
have large, woody, white bases should be
passed over. The spears should be at least two-
thirds green. As to which is better—the pencil-thin asparagus or the chubbier asparagus—
even the experts disagree, so take your choice.
In my opinion they both taste wonderful when
freshly picked. The thinner asparagus certainly
looks elegant and, as a bonus it does not require peeling; it is perfectly tender from tip to
toe. Chubby asparagus must be peeled. If you
do not peel the asparagus, from the bottom up
to the start of the tip, it will take longer for
the stalk to cook than the tip. If you overcook
the tip to compensate for the stalk, you have
ruined the best part. So, though peeling is tedious, peel you must. Once the peel is removed, the asparagus is entirely edible and
will cook evenly regardless of the method
you use.

Preparation

The practice of snapping off asparagus at the
point it becomes tender is wasteful, to say the
least. When you take the time to peel, no more
than an inch to an inch and a half need be
trimmed from the base of each stalk.

Cooking

Over the past few seasons I have tried every method known for cooking these delectable stalks. It seems that the easiest is also the best. Rather than bother with a special asparagus steamer or any other make-shift assemblage—purportedly to hold the asparagus in an upright position so that the tips do not overcook while the stalks become tender—I simply use a good-sized, uncovered stockpot filled with gently boiling water. The asparagus can then be dropped in separately or tied loosely in a bundle for easier removal. If you own a spaghetti cooker—a large pot fitted with a perforated insert—use it. The insert makes it easy to remove and drain the stalks. Otherwise, remove the asparagus with slotted spoons or tongs. They should then be drained on a towel-lined wire rack for a few seconds before being sauced or used in a recipe. In most cases asparagus takes between four and eight minutes to cook once the water boils again. It should never be taken beyond the tender-crisp point. If it is, the olive-drab color will advertise all too clearly that it has been overcooked.

Asparagus Recipes

Asparagus Salad with Vinaigrette Chinoise, *page 32*

Curried Asparagus Soup with Lemon, *page 36*

see also Recipe Notes, *which follow*

RECIPE NOTES

Though I collect my asparagus at the Pike Place Market rather than in the wild hinterland of eastern Washington, I always buy more than a rational person should—just because the season is so short; only six weeks or so from mid-April to the end of May. I absolutely must have my fill of asparagus during those few fleeting weeks. Unfortunately, what I consider enough is not what my family considers sane and reasonable. To circumvent their displeasure I have eagerly sought out and developed recipes over the years that show asparagus off in a variety of ways, all quite different from one another.

The following are rough sketches rather than full-blown recipes, although proportions are indicated when I feel you might need them. These ideas assume that you have had your fill of warm asparagus with melted butter and lemon juice and slightly chilled asparagus with Dijon-flavored vinaigrette, the two universal favorites.

ASPARAGUS FRITTERS WITH SPICY VINAIGRETTE

Blanch trimmed and peeled asparagus until barely tender, refresh under cold running water and drain on paper towels. Cut diagonally into 2-inch lengths, dip into flour, then in beaten egg, then in fresh white bread crumbs, and set on a wax-paper-lined cookie sheet. Refrigerate until ready to serve. Deep fry in hot (350°) corn oil until golden and drain on paper towels. Serve with a hot vinaigrette (page 202) spiked with garlic and paprika, or a mustard-flavored mayonnaise (see Basic Mayonnaise, page 347).

ASPARAGUS PARMESAN

Sprinkle freshly grated Parmesan cheese, lemon juice, and melted butter over whole, blanched, warm asparagus. Broil briefly to melt the cheese and serve.

ASPARAGUS GRATIN

Arrange whole, blanched, warm asparagus in a gratin dish. Cover with a thin mornay sauce, sprinkle with grated cheese and buttered bread crumbs, and bake at 425° for 15 to 20 minutes, until the sauce is lightly browned and bubbling.

ASPARAGUS COMPOSÉE

Arrange whole, blanched, cold asparagus, thinly sliced prosciutto, sliced hard-boiled eggs, and sliced tomatoes on individual salad plates. Drizzle on a Dijon-flavored vinaigrette (page 359), and garnish with minced parsley, minced dill pickles, and minced onion.

ASPARAGUS TIMBALES

Combine in the bowl of a processor 1 pound peeled, trimmed, blanched asparagus, cut into 1-inch pieces with 2 eggs, ½ cup cream, ½ teaspoon nutmeg, and salt and pepper to taste. Purée. Pour the custard into buttered, individual 5- to 6-ounce custard cups or timbale molds. Place in a *bain-marie* and fill with enough simmering water to reach two-thirds up the sides of the molds. Cover loosely with a sheet of foil. Bake at 375° for 20 to 30 minutes. Carefully unmold and serve, with melted butter or Lemon Beurre Blanc (page 361), as a first course.

ASPARAGUS AND ONION SOUP

Sauté 2 cups chopped onions in 4 tablespoons unsalted butter until soft. Add 4 cups chicken stock and bring to a simmer. Add 1 pound trimmed, peeled asparagus stalks, reserving the tips for later, to the simmering liquid and cook gently until the asparagus is tender, about 30 minutes. Purée the soup and return to a clean saucepan. Add the reserved asparagus tips. Simmer until tender but still firm. Season to taste with salt and white pepper.

CHILLED ASPARAGUS WITH HORSERADISH SAUCE

Serve whole, blanched, chilled asparagus with a horseradish sauce made by lightly whipping heavy cream and adding finely grated horseradish, drops of fresh lemon juice, salt, and a pinch of sugar.

FRESH PASTA WITH MONTRACHET AND ASPARAGUS

Boil 2 cups heavy cream briefly to thicken just slightly. Add 3 ounces Montrachet (mild goat cheese) and stir to melt. Add ½ pound blanched asparagus tips, warm briefly, and toss with a pound of cooked fresh pasta. Season quickly with coarse salt and freshly ground black pepper and serve.

FRESH PASTA WITH BLUE CHEESE, CHICKEN, AND ASPARAGUS

Melt 2 tablespoons unsalted butter, add a few tablespoons of finely minced shallots, and cook for 30 seconds. Add 1 pound of julienned chicken breast and sauté until barely white. Add a pound of trimmed, peeled, blanched, asparagus cut on the diagonal, and salt and black pepper to taste. Add a cup of cream, about ¼ pound nicely flavored blue cheese, and red hot pepper flakes to taste. Cook just until the cheese melts, then toss with about ¾ pound of cooked fresh pasta. Serve with grated Parmesan cheese on the side.

HOT FRIED ASPARAGUS WITH SESAME OIL

Heat a little corn oil in a large skillet or wok and add a large pinch of crushed red pepper flakes. Heat briefly and add 1 pound of trimmed, peeled, 1-inch diagonally cut, blanched asparagus and toss to heat and coat with oil. When hot, drizzle on a little sesame seed oil. Salt and pepper to taste.

HOT ASPARAGUS WITH HAZELNUT VINAIGRETTE

Make a standard vinaigrette (2 tablespoons white wine vinegar to 6 tablespoons corn oil), season it well with salt and pepper and add 2 tablespoons finely chopped toasted hazelnuts.

Let sit for several hours, until the vinaigrette takes on a hazelnut flavor. Strain and drizzle over trimmed, peeled, whole, blanched, hot asparagus and top with ½ cup toasted, skinned, chopped hazelnuts.

GRILLED SALMON WITH ASPARAGUS SAUCE

Cook 1 pound of trimmed, peeled, sliced asparagus in a large quantity of boiling water until quite tender. Drain and purée with 4 tablespoons butter. Reduce 2 cups of cream by half, then add the puréed asparagus, whisking to blend. Season to taste with salt, pepper, and lemon juice; serve hot with mesquite-grilled salmon steaks.

Rhubarb

I have loved rhubarb for as long as I can remember. As children, my brother and I would pilfer it from between the pickets of the deteriorating white fence that separated our yard from the neighbor's. We thought of it as high mischief but as I look back now on our shenanigans, I realize that no one else wanted that rhubarb. Too bad really because the only way we were able to eat it (without being found out) was raw—and behind a prickly mass of bushes to boot. No one made rhubarb pie when I was growing up, and certainly no one

made rhubarb mousse, rhubarb parfait, rhubarb crisp, or rhubarb strawberry daiquiris. Those were the bad ole days. Even though I have a lot of enthusiasm for this highly acidic fruit cum vegetable (on July 17, 1947, the United States customs court of Buffalo, New York, officially declared rhubarb to be a fruit, not a vegetable, because of the way it is used in American households), I realize others may have to be led gently to the trough. Perhaps I can arouse regional pride by telling you that Washington state produces 90 percent of the nation's supply of hothouse rhubarb and over 50 percent of the fresh field rhubarb. But if that doesn't do it, try thinking of it as an incredibly versatile cooking fruit; its special tartness is a perfect foil for all forms of sugar. I particularly like it with maple syrup (another spring crop, albeit from Vermont and Canada), brown sugar, and honey. It also has a natural affinity for many of nature's other fruity-spicy flavors, such as strawberry, orange, lemon, grapefruit, fresh ginger, and cloves. Also anything toasty (such as wheat germ, hazelnuts, walnuts, and oatmeal), anything creamy (such as ice cream, cheesecake, and custard), and as I have recently discovered, cinnamon, especially cinnamon-hot as in those little red candies that are so addictive. It is effective as an ingredient in sauces and chutneys meant to accompany sweet meats such as pork, ham, and sausage, and also turkey, chicken, and yes, even lamb. With all this going for it, and the fact that it is the first fresh crop of the Northwest spring, why do we not eat more of it? Perhaps cooks just do not know what to do with rhubarb after they have made the one or two obligatory pies. This we should remedy. Armed with the following basic information, a bevy of quick recipes, and the many rhubarb-centered recipes in this chapter, your own rhubarb horizons will I hope be expanded. Try it, you'll like it!

Season

Hothouse rhubarb begins appearing in February, and the field crop arrives in late April. Local rhubarb is available through June only.

Selection

Fresh rhubarb should be firm, crisp, and tender. It will snap crisply if bent; it should not be limp or flabby. Rhubarb is at its best when young and slender, no more than 1 inch thick. By the time the stalks are thick and green the fruit has become coarse and too acid. Early hothouse rhubarb has smaller leaves and the stalks are lighter pink and less acidic. Later the rhubarb tends toward rosy red and has quite a bit more acid. I have noticed that in some years the rhubarb appears mottled. I suspect this has to do with the rain; it doesn't seem to affect the taste at all. Rhubarb leaves are highly toxic, containing oxalic acid. They are usually removed by the growers. If they are not be sure to finish the job yourself.

Preparation

Rhubarb does not need to be peeled (it should never be so old and coarse as to have noticeable strings) because peeling removes most of its valuable nutrients. Just clean it and completely trim and discard the leaves along with an inch or so of the base.

Cooking

When creating your own rhubarb recipes, keep in mind that the fruit contains a good deal of liquid. Cut the rhubarb into chunks or dice and cook it, covered, over very low heat without any water at all for between ten and twenty minutes, depending on whether you want some chunkiness or a mush. This fruit disintegrates easily. Another thing to consider, especially if you are developing new recipes, is that the gorgeous color you see when you buy rhubarb may pale when you cook it and that it will certainly be paler if you combine the cooked rhubarb with a lot of cream, egg whites, and so forth. Rhubarb soufflé is a ghastly muddy pink, though it tastes wonderful; rhubarb mousse is a barely perceptible shell-pink. This frustrates me considerably. The best effect is gained by using rhubarb sauce, which is a brilliant red, over and around the other ingredients. Otherwise you must compensate with some other coloring agent, strawberries perhaps, or in a savory sauce, to-

mato paste, brown sauce, or even a bit of caramelized sugar. No, you may not use red food
coloring; that is cheating.

Rhubarb Recipes

RECIPE NOTES

If I could make but one point in this chapter
on spring it would be to suggest that you buy
lots of rhubarb while it is in season and put it
up. It is a wonderfully versatile fruit to have
around. Simply make a sauce of it, sweetened
or not, by cooking it alone in a covered saucepan for about 20 minutes. Cool and freeze in
1-cup containers. Then many of these recipe
notes will be possible for you even in the dark
of winter.

SWEET RHUBARB SAUCE

Sprinkle 1 cup sugar over 1 pound diced rhubarb and let sit for an hour. Cook slowly, uncovered, until tender and falling apart. Sauce
may be thickened if desired with a tablespoon
of cornstarch mixed with an equal amount of
cold water or simply by reducing it down to
the desired consistency. This sauce may be flavored with fresh ginger, cinnamon, cloves,
lemon, orange, or grapefruit zest and juice.

RHUBARB HONEY SAUCE

Combine 1 pound diced rhubarb with 6 tablespoons honey and the zest of a lemon in a
saucepan and cook slowly, stirring, until the
rhubarb is a mush. Process and put through a
strainer if desired.

RHUBARB MINT SAUCE

Complete Sweet Rhubarb Sauce (above) and
add ¼ cup minced fresh mint after it has
cooled slightly. Wonderful with lamb.

SAVORY RHUBARB DEGLAZING SAUCE

Combine 1 cup diced rhubarb and 2 tablespoons brown sugar and let sit for an hour.
Add ¾ cup chicken, veal, or beef stock and
cook, uncovered, until the rhubarb is disintegrating. Deglaze a pan that has been just used
to sauté chicken, chops, or steaks with 1 cup
stock. Add the rhubarb and sugar mixture.

Whisk and cook until thickened. Strain and season with the zest of an orange, minced thyme, and salt and pepper to taste.

RHUBARB SORBET

Combine 2 cups of Sweet Rhubarb Sauce (page 24), Rhubarb Honey Sauce (page 24), or Rhubarb-Cinnamon Hot Sauce (page 65) and 1 cup of orange juice. Process in an ice cream machine until almost set. Beat 2 egg whites to soft peaks and blend into the fruit slush. Continue processing until set. Freeze and eat within a few hours.

RHUBARB CRISP

Beat 1 egg, add 4 teaspoons flour and 1 cup sugar and continue to beat. Stir in 3 cups diced rhubarb and spread into a buttered 9- by 9-inch baking dish. Mix ¼ cup each brown sugar, flour, oatmeal, and chopped walnuts, along with 1 teaspoon baking powder and 2 tablespoons melted butter. Sprinkle over the top of the rhubarb mixture. Bake at 350° for 40 minutes.

RHUBARB COBBLER

Mix 6 cups rhubarb and 1 cup sugar and spread into a 9- by 9-inch buttered baking pan. Whip ½ cup cream and fold it into a mixture of 1¼ cups flour, 1½ teaspoons baking powder, and 6 tablespoons sugar. Spoon on top of the rhu-

barb. Bake at 375° for 40 minutes or until golden brown on top. Serve with whipping cream or ice cream.

RHUBARB STRAWBERRY PARFAIT

Combine 1 cup strawberries with 6 tablespoons sugar and let sit for half an hour. Fold the strawberry and sugar mixture into Sweet Rhubarb Sauce (page 24) or Rhubarb Honey Sauce (page 24). Soften vanilla ice cream slightly and layer the ice cream and the rhubarb and strawberry mixture into parfait glasses. Serve immediately or freeze to set.

RHUBARB MOUSSE

Combine 1 cup Sweet Rhubarb Sauce (page 24), Rhubarb Honey Sauce (page 24), or Rhubarb-Cinnamon Hot Sauce (page 65) with 1 package gelatin softened in ¼ cup cold water and heat to dissolve gelatin. Cool to room temperature. Whip 2 cups cream together with the cooled rhubarb and gelatin mixture until light and fluffy. Whip 2 egg whites until soft peaks form, then add 2 tablespoons sugar and continue whisking to stiff peaks. Fold into the rhubarb and cream mixture. Refrigerate for 2 hours or more to set.

RHUBARB SYRUP

Bring a mixture of 3 cups sugar and 2 cups water slowly to a boil, being sure that the sugar is completely dissolved and the liquid clear before boiling. Add 2 pounds diced rhubarb and continue simmering until the rhubarb is very tender, about 15 minutes. Purée in a processor or put through a food mill. Refrigerate and use within a few weeks or freeze. This syrup is refreshing when made into an Italian soda with soda water and crushed ice, as a French *kir* (combine, to taste, with white wine or champagne), or mixed with an equal quantity of orange juice, topped with soda.

CRUMPETS WITH RICOTTA AND RHUBARB SAUCE

Mix 2 tablespoons *thick* Sweet Rhubarb Sauce (page 24) or Rhubarb-Cinnamon Hot Sauce (page 65) into ½ cup ricotta and spread on 4 toasted, buttered crumpets. Top each with a little more rhubarb sauce. Wonderful for breakfast or a snack.

RHUBARB-OATMEAL BAR COOKIES

Cut ½ cup butter into 1 cup brown sugar and blend in a mixture of 1½ cups flour, 1 teaspoon cinnamon, and 1 teaspoon baking soda. Add 1½ cups oatmeal and 1 tablespoon orange juice and mix lightly. Pat half the crumb mixture into a buttered 9- by 13-inch baking dish. Top evenly with 2 cups *thick* Sweet Rhubarb Sauce (page 24) or Rhubarb-Cinnamon Hot Sauce (page 65) and sprinkle on 1 cup chopped walnuts. Sprinkle on the remaining half of the crumbs and pat evenly in place. Bake at 350° for 25 to 30 minutes. Cool and cut into bars.

Cornmeal Fritters with Beer and Buttermilk

Makes 4 dozen; serves 8 to 12 as an appetizer.

Lighter than most cornmeal fritters, these have a delightfully crunchy exterior. Although cornmeal fritters (also known as hush puppies) are traditionally served as an accompaniment to fried catfish, they go equally well with trout or halibut and make wonderful cocktail fare served with a coarse-grained mustard or a fresh herb-flavored mayonnaise.

Gluten flour is used in this recipe because cornmeal has no gluten (the protein strands in flour that cause it to stretch when moistened) at all and will make the hush puppies heavy if used without the extra help of a gluten-rich flour. Gluten flour is available in health food stores.

½ cup whole wheat flour
½ cup gluten flour
1 cup fine yellow cornmeal
2 teaspoons baking powder
1 teaspoon baking soda
1 teaspoon coarse salt
½ teaspoon freshly ground black pepper
½ cup minced green onion tops
2 large cloves garlic, minced
½ to ¾ teaspoon cayenne pepper, to taste
1 teaspoon crumbled thyme
1 teaspoon crumbled oregano
½ cup beer
½ cup buttermilk
1 egg, lightly beaten
Corn oil for deep frying

Combine the flours, cornmeal, baking powder, and baking soda. Stir in the salt, pepper, green onions, garlic, cayenne, thyme, and oregano.

Mix the beer, buttermilk, and egg together and pour over the dry ingredients. Mix together lightly and quickly; the batter will be lumpy.

Heat the oil in a deep sauté pan or deep-fryer to 350° and maintain this temperature. Drop the batter by teaspoonsful (keep the hush puppies small) into the hot oil and fry for about 3 to 5 minutes, turning halfway, until well browned on the outside and cooked through. Drain on paper towels and serve right away while hot. (These do not reheat well.)

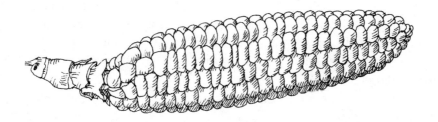

◀🐟◀ ◀🐟◀ ◀🐟◀ ◀🐟◀ ◀🐟◀ ◀🐟◀ ◀🐟◀ ◀🐟◀ ◀🐟◀ ◀🐟◀

Rainbow Trout Paupiettes with Red and Yellow Peppers

Serves 6.

Here is a visually stunning first course salad of rolled, poached trout seasoned with a trio of peppers, ginger, green onions, garlic, and sesame oil. Chilled and coated with an herb-infused crème fraîche, the rolled batons, or paupiettes as they are called, are presented on individual beds of curly endive surrounded by lightly sautéed red and yellow sweet peppers. Though this dish sounds complicated, it is not difficult to make, especially if you have your fish merchant fillet the trout for you. Everything can be done well in advance except the sautéing of the sweet peppers and the final assembly. In fact, because it takes time to set the crème fraîche and to cool the paupiettes, you need to begin this dish the day before you plan to serve it.

This dish also works well as a main course. Double everything except the sauté of peppers and bed of curly endive.

Crème Fraîche (page 357)

SEASONING

    2 teaspoons minced garlic
    2 teaspoons minced fresh ginger
    2 tablespoons minced green onion
    1 teaspoon sesame oil

1 teaspoon red pepper flakes
1 teaspoon black peppercorns
1 teaspoon dried green peppercorns

3 medium-sized fresh rainbow trout,
    filleted and skinned (each weighing
    about 1 pound; about 14 inches in
    length whole or 10 inches filleted)
Coarse salt
Fresh Ginger Vinaigrette (page 360)
1 tablespoon minced parsley
1 tablespoon minced green onions
2 tablespoons corn oil
2 red bell peppers, cored, seeded, and
    cut into ¾-inch dice
2 yellow bell peppers, cored, seeded,
    and cut into ¾-inch dice
1 head curly endive, cleaned, torn into
    pieces, and put into an airtight
    plastic bag to crisp in the
    refrigerator

One day ahead make the Crème Fraîche.

To make the seasoning, mash together the garlic, ginger, green onion, and sesame oil. Set aside. In a mortar and pestle or spice grinder grind the red pepper flakes and black and green peppercorns together finely. Reserve.

Brush the 6 trout fillets on the inside flesh (not the skin side) with the mixture of garlic, ginger, green onions, and sesame oil, using about 1 teaspoon each. Sprinkle each with coarse salt and the finely ground pepper to taste. Roll up lengthwise, with the seasoning on the inside, and wrap tightly in plastic wrap, twisting the ends to secure them. (Only a microwave-safe plastic wrap such as Saran Wrap will do here; other plastic wraps may disintegrate in the boiling water.) Refrigerate.

Bring a large sauté pan two-thirds full of water to a bare simmer. Lower the paupiettes into the barely simmering water and poach gently for 2 minutes. Remove from the heat, cover and let cool to room temperature. (This method is called scotch poaching and though it takes some time it insures perfectly cooked, moist fish.) Remove the paupiettes from the water when they have reached room temperature, wipe dry with paper towels, and refrigerate still wrapped in the plastic. (If you are in a hurry, poach the trout in barely simmering water for exactly 10 minutes per inch of thickness, remove, and proceed.)

Prepare the Fresh Ginger Vinaigrette and reserve.

Whisk the green onions and parsley into the prepared crème fraîche. Season to taste with salt. Remove the paupiettes from the refrigerator, remove the plastic wrap, and dry with paper towels. Lay the paupiettes on a wire rack and carefully pour the crème fraîche over each one to coat it. Refrigerate. Just before serving, arrange the curly endive on individual salad plates and carefully—so as not to disturb the coating—place 1 paupiette in the center of each.

Heat the corn oil and lightly sauté the bell peppers just to heat through; they should still be crunchy. Season with the ground peppercorn trio and toss with Fresh Ginger Vinaigrette. Surround each paupiette with a ring of peppers. Serve immediately so your guests may enjoy the contrast of hot and cold. To serve as a main course, arrange 2 paupiettes per person opposite each other on the curly endive and position the sweet peppers in between to resemble spokes of a wheel.

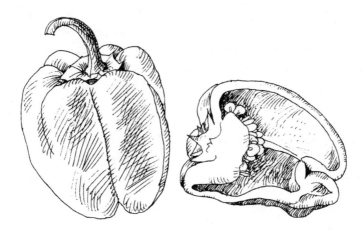

Wild Rice and Cornmeal Waffles with Smoked Salmon Mousse

Serves 8 to 10.

The crunchy texture given by the cornmeal and wild rice easily transports these waffles from the breakfast table to the dinner table as an elegant first course. The addition of a salad of spring greens complements both the waffles and the mousse, cutting through some of the richness. You may use any waffle iron here, but the batter needs to be poured on the griddle in a round shape so that wedge-shaped pieces can be cut after cooking. If you are fortunate enough to own a Danish waffle iron with a circular pattern of five hearts, the individual heart shapes make an amusing and pretty presentation.

WAFFLES

1 cup flour
½ cup gluten flour
½ cup fine yellow cornmeal
½ cup cooked wild rice (follow package directions for cooking)
½ teaspoon baking soda
1 teaspoon baking powder
Pinch salt
Pinch freshly ground black pepper
1 teaspoon sugar
¾ cup buttermilk
2 tablespoons corn oil
3 egg yolks
3 egg whites
⅛ teaspoon cream of tartar (optional)

MOUSSE

1 cup unsalted butter, chilled and cut into chunks
½ pound boneless, skinned, cold-smoked salmon, well chilled and cut into chunks
1 teaspoon fresh lemon juice
½ teaspoon coarse salt (or to taste)
Freshly ground black pepper

VINAIGRETTE

4 teaspoons fresh lemon juice
2 teaspoons white wine vinegar
2 teaspoons minced parsley
2 teaspoons minced fresh marjoram
1 teaspoon sugar
Coarse salt
Freshly ground black pepper
6 tablespoons olive oil
2 teaspoons small capers

SPRING GREENS

1 head radicchio, cleaned, torn into bite-sized pieces, and chilled
1 head butter lettuce, cleaned, torn into bite-sized pieces, and chilled
2 cups mixed baby leaves of dandelion greens, sorrel, and watercress
Sunflower seed sprouts (optional)

To make the waffles, combine the flour, gluten flour, cornmeal, cooked wild rice, baking soda, baking powder, salt, pepper, and sugar. Mix together the buttermilk, corn oil, and egg yolks. Beat the egg whites in a copper bowl with a balloon whisk just until stiff peaks are formed. (If you are using a glass or stainless steel bowl with a mixer, you will need to add the cream of tartar to help to stabilize the egg whites; you may not get quite the volume with this beating method but it is perfectly acceptable.)

Quickly and lightly fold the wet ingredients into the dry mixture, then gently and swiftly fold in the egg whites.

To make the mousse, whip the butter in a processor until very light, but do not let it warm. Add the chunked salmon and blend again until very light. Add the lemon juice and salt and pepper to taste and blend to incorporate. Put into a pastry bag fitted with a ½-inch fluted tip. Pipe the mousse into 8 to 10 individual ⅛-cup ramekins, mounding each one nicely. You may have a little mousse left over; it freezes well. Refrigerate the ramekins, covered lightly with plastic wrap until 1 hour before serving. Then remove from the refrigerator and let them warm to room temperature.

Make the vinaigrette by combining the lemon juice, white wine vinegar, parsley, marjoram, sugar, and salt and pepper to taste. Stir to dissolve the sugar and salt thoroughly, then whisk in the olive oil. Taste and adjust the seasoning if necessary. Add the capers. Reserve.

Just before serving, heat a round or heart-shaped waffle iron and spray the surfaces with a vegetable spray. Make the waffles, using about ⅓ cup of batter for each one. Cook until nicely browned, remove, and keep warm in the oven while you are finishing the others. (You may make the waffles a few hours ahead, cool them on a wire rack, then seal in plastic wrap at room temperature. Reheat, uncovered, in a 350° oven to recrisp.)

Combine the radicchio and butter lettuce and toss with the vinaigrette. Arrange on one side of 8 to 10 individual plates. Scatter on a few of the sunflower seed sprouts, which look like tiny green flowers, if you are using them.

To serve, put the ramekins filled with mousse in the center of the plates. Cut the hot waffles into wedges and arrange on the free side. Serve right away with small cheese knives so that your guests can spread the mousse on the waffles.

Asparagus Salad with Vinaigrette Chinoise

Serves 4.

This is a very easy salad to make and delicious with just a suggestion of heat from the red pepper flakes. The only thing to be careful about is not overcooking the asparagus, which should still be bright green and have plenty of crunch. This is wonderful preceding Chinese Steamed Salmon with Ginger, Garlic, and Black Beans (page 122). Check the Asparagus primer (page 17) for trimming tips and remember, if you buy thick asparagus, you will have more waste than you will with the thinner variety—in other words, purchase more of the thick asparagus than the one pound specified here to compensate for the loss in trimming.

> 1 pound thin asparagus, ends trimmed
>   and stalks peeled to the tip if thick
> Half a head red-leaf lettuce

VINAIGRETTE CHINOISE

> ¼ cup rice wine vinegar
> 2 tablespoons soy sauce
> ½ teaspoon sugar
> ¼ teaspoon dried red pepper flakes
> 3 tablespoons corn oil
> 4 teaspoons sesame seed oil
> Coarse salt

GARNISH

> 1 teaspoon unsalted butter
> ¼ cup raw sunflower seeds
> 1 tablespoon diagonally sliced green
>   onion; green part only

Slice the asparagus on a long diagonal at 2-inch intervals. Blanch in a large pot of boiling water for about 4 minutes, until just tender-crunchy. Drain, refresh under cold running water, then dry carefully with paper towels.

Whisk together the rice wine vinegar, soy sauce, sugar, red pepper, corn oil, sesame seed oil, and salt to taste. Toss with the asparagus. Cool, cover, and refrigerate for several hours or overnight if desired.

Melt the butter in a small sauté pan and stir-fry the sunflower seeds until golden brown. Remove and reserve.

When ready to serve, toss the asparagus and vinaigrette again, arrange on red lettuce leaves on individual salad plates, and top with toasted sunflower seeds and sliced green onions.

Shrimp and Strawberry Salad with Honey Mint Vinaigrette

Serves 4 for lunch or 6 as a first course.

I was lunching with friend Lynn Kaplan one afternoon at the Crêpe de Paris in downtown Seattle when she ordered the salad that was to become the point of departure for this recipe. At the Crêpe de Paris, the salad is composed of perfectly cooked sweet shrimp and tart grapefruit wedges. Here Northwest strawberries work perfectly to offset the richness of the shrimp.

A chiffonnade is a very fine lengthwise shred. With very narrow chives you need do nothing but cut them on a long diagonal; cut fatter chives lengthwise into thin shreds.

> 1 pound medium-large fresh shrimp
> (24 to 36 shrimp)
> ¼ cup water
> 2 slices lemon
> 2 heads Belgian endive, the leaves
> separated
> 2 cups perfect strawberries, sliced
> lengthwise
> ½ cup fresh mint leaves
> ¼ cup chiffonnade of chives
> Zest of 1 lemon, blanched for 2
> minutes in boiling water
> Honey Mint Vinaigrette (recipe
> follows)

Steam the shrimp in a covered sauté pan with the water and lemon slices until they are just cooked through (they will turn bright pink). Do not overcook them. Remove, peel, and devein along the outside curve, leaving the tails on.

Arrange 3 endive leaves on each individual salad plate in a spokelike fashion. Position two shrimp on each leaf. Arrange the sliced berries in between the leaves and garnish with mint leaves. Scatter the chiffonnade of chives and the lemon zest over the top.

Drizzle the dressing evenly over each salad and serve right away.

Honey Mint Vinaigrette

> 1 tablespoon sherry vinegar
> ½ teaspoon coarse salt
> Freshly ground black pepper
> 2 teaspoons minced fresh mint leaves
> 1 clove minced garlic
> 1 tablespoon pear blossom honey (or
> another fragrant honey; wild
> huckleberry or blackberry are also
> good), warmed
> 3 tablespoons olive oil

Combine the vinegar, salt and pepper to taste, mint, and garlic and whisk to dissolve the salt. Add the honey and oil and whisk until emulsified. Use right away or refrigerate and whisk again just before using.

Baby Red Potato, Snow Pea, and Prosciutto Salad

Serves 8.

Everyone enjoys a good potato salad but the perennial favorite can become boring when its components are everlastingly predictable. This version has several lively differences; no mayonnaise for one thing, fresh herbs for another, and a decided Italian leaning. Be sure to get the smallest, firmest Red Pontiac potatoes you can find. Small White Rose potatoes will also work here but do not be tempted to use brown-skinned Russet Burbank potatoes—they turn to glue when you steam them.

2 pounds baby red "new" potatoes

1 pound snow peas, cut widthwise on a slight diagonal into ¼-inch strips

¼ pound prosciutto, very finely sliced, then cut into 1½-inch julienne

¼ pound provolone cheese, sliced, then cut into 1½-inch julienne

DRESSING

1 cup sour cream

¼ cup lemon juice

¼ cup julienned basil leaves

1 tablespoon fresh minced thyme

2 teaspoons sugar

Tabasco sauce

Coarse salt

Freshly ground black pepper

GARNISH

4 thin slices prosciutto, cut in half widthwise and formed into cones

Several extra snow peas

Scrub the potatoes and steam them over simmering water, covered, until just tender, about 20 minutes. Remove from the pan and let cool. Do not peel.

Bring a large saucepan full of water to a boil and immerse the peas for 30 to 60 seconds only. Remove and refresh under cold running water; drain well.

Quarter the cooled potatoes and combine with the peas, prosciutto, and provolone.

Whisk together the sour cream and lemon juice and add the basil, thyme, sugar, Tabasco sauce, and salt and pepper to taste. Toss this dressing with the other ingredients. Chill until 30 minutes before serving. Remove from the refrigerator, let warm just a bit, then gently toss and arrange on a colorful serving platter. (If the dressing appears too thick, sprinkle the salad with a few teaspoons of milk and toss to loosen.) Arrange 4 prosciutto cones on each end of the salad with several snow peas tucked between.

Smoked Chicken and Cracked Wheat Salad

Serves 8.

A marvelous salad with a variety of interesting textures and tastes. The smoky quality of the chicken, Chinese mushrooms, and walnuts goes well with the sweet red bell pepper and cracked wheat, the latter treated in the same manner as couscous to produce light, fluffy, separate grains. This is great for the buffet table and may easily be made a day or two in advance.

> 1 cup coarsely cracked wheat
> ½ cup dried black mushrooms (of the small Chinese type, not Japanese shiitakes)
> ½ pound smoked chicken (or turkey) breast, skinned and boned, cut into ¼-inch julienne
> ¾ cup lightly toasted, chopped walnuts
> 3 green onions, thinly sliced on the long diagonal (should resemble a julienne cut)
> 1 small red bell pepper, cored, seeded, and cut into ¼-inch julienne
> 1 cup peeled and julienned jicama
> Fresh Ginger Vinaigrette (page 360)

GARNISH
Green onion brushes

Prepare the cracked wheat according to directions for couscous on page 356.

Pour boiling water over the mushrooms and soak them for 30 minutes. Drain, remove the stems, and slice.

Combine the chicken, mushrooms, walnuts, green onions, red pepper, and jicama in a mixing bowl and dress lightly with Fresh Ginger Vinaigrette. Chill thoroughly before serving.

To make green onion brushes, cut the green part of the onion lengthwise in several places and put into ice water. The edges will curl. Use to garnish the salad immediately before serving.

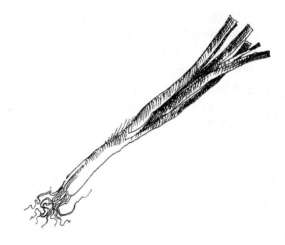

Curried Asparagus Soup with Lemon

Serves 4 to 6.

This is very much a concept recipe and is meant to be interpreted as you like with any number of single vegetables or combinations of vegetables. Curry powder is only one of many possibilities for seasoning. Fresh herbs provide a wonderful alternative when available, as they increasingly are these days, even in supermarkets. I have tried squash, carrots, pumpkin, cauliflower, potatoes, broccoli, onion, and combinations thereof in this soup. All are tasty. When using orange vegetables, try substituting fresh lime juice and slices of lime for the lemon specified here. (For example, see following recipe for Curried Butternut Squash Soup with Lime.)

Dried herbs and spices, and most particularly curry powder, should always be cooked in butter or oil before being incorporated into any dish. This process mellows their initial raw taste while bringing out the fullest possible flavor.

1 pound fresh asparagus
5 cups chicken stock
4 tablespoons unsalted butter
1 teaspoon good-quality curry powder
   (Madras brand is excellent)
4 tablespoons flour
¾ cup cream or half-and-half
   Coarse salt
   Freshly ground white pepper
1 tablespoon fresh lemon juice

GARNISH
   Thin lemon slices

Trim and peel the asparagus if it is thick. Cut off the asparagus tips and reserve. Cut the stalks into ½-inch lengths.

Cook the asparagus tips in boiling water for 3 minutes, until just tender-crisp. Drain, refresh, and reserve. Cook the asparagus stalks in chicken stock until tender, about 15 minutes. Purée the asparagus stalks in a processor with a little of the chicken stock. Set aside.

Melt the butter, add the curry powder, and blend in the flour. Cook for at least 2 minutes, whisking constantly. Add the puréed asparagus and stock, bring to a boil, and whisk until the soup thickens.

Add the cream or half-and-half and the asparagus tips. Heat through but do not boil after this point. Adjust the final flavor, adding drops of lemon juice and salt and pepper to taste.

Serve hot, garnished with thin slices of lemon.

CURRIED BUTTERNUT SQUASH SOUP
WITH LIME

Following the preceding recipe, substitute 1 pound peeled, seeded, and chunked butternut squash for the asparagus and lime juice and slices of lime for the lemon.

Fresh Ginger Consommé with Sorrel Chiffonnade

Serves 4 to 6.

This soup is light, refreshing, and elegant. Because it is so straightforward, the end result depends entirely on a well-flavored homemade stock. Follow the master recipe for Chicken Stock with the addition of veal if possible. The veal neck bones give the stock the perceptible gelatinous quality characteristic of consommé. (However, the basic Chicken Stock is quite acceptable.) If you do not have a garden, fresh sorrel may be difficult to obtain. Spinach or watercress leaves may be substituted, along with a little extra lemon juice. Serve the consommé in shallow clear glass or white porcelain bowls for the best effect.

> 6 cups Chicken Stock with Veal (page 346)
> 1½ tablespoons fresh ginger, peeled, cut into paper-thin disks, then into a very fine julienne
> 1 tablespoon garlic, cut into paper-thin disks, then into a very fine julienne
> 2 teaspoons coarse salt or to taste
> 1 teaspoon fresh lemon juice or to taste
> ¾ cup finely shredded sorrel leaves, stacked neatly and cut, crosswise, very finely

To prepare the chicken stock pour it through a very fine strainer lined with professional-quality (tightly woven) cheesecloth. Do not press on the bits and pieces that remain in the cloth. Thoroughly degrease the stock by pouring it through a bottom-pouring degreaser (available in kitchenware stores) or by chilling and then lifting the hardened fat off the top.

To get a sparkling clear liquid almost as transparent as clarified stock, pour the strained and defatted stock through a strainer lined with flat-bottomed drip coffee filters. (It is important to use this type of coffee filter, as the cone-shaped varieties I have tried are not porous enough.)

Put the stock into a saucepan and bring to a simmer. Add the ginger, garlic, and salt and lemon juice to taste. Simmer gently for just 2 minutes. Just before serving, stir in the shredded sorrel. Simmer for 30 seconds and serve.

Baby Clam and Spinach Soup with Pepper Bacon

Serves 4 to 6.

This is a wonderful, satisfying soup, reminiscent of a clam chowder but lighter and more subtly flavored. It combines the distinct flavor of fresh clams with delicate undertones of spinach and just enough bacon. Choose the very tiny clams when they are available. If you cannot get them small enough, chop the large ones.

Be careful with the wine. Those described as "soft" or "semi-dry" are too sweet for use here. If you are unsure, use a good dry vermouth.

> 4 strips lean bacon (preferably pepper-
>   flavored)
> 1 medium-sized onion, chopped
> 2 cloves garlic, minced
> 1 bunch fresh spinach, stems removed
>   and chopped
> 4 pounds small clams, cleaned (2 to 3
>   cups when shelled)
> 4 cups very dry white wine
> 2 tablespoons unsalted butter
> 2 tablespoons flour
> 1 cup cream
>   Coarse salt
>   Freshly ground black pepper
>   Lemon juice

Sauté the bacon over medium-low heat until crisp. Remove from the pan and drain on paper towels. Add the onion to the fat remaining in the pan and sauté slowly until tender, about 15 minutes. Stir in the garlic. Add the spinach to the sauté pan and cook slowly until it has wilted, about 3 minutes. Set aside.

Place the clams in a large saucepan, add the wine, cover, and bring to a boil. Simmer for 5 to 6 minutes, just until the clams open their shells. Remove the opened clamshells immediately with a slotted spoon and continue steaming the remaining shellfish. Remove the clams from their shells once they are cooked and reserve. There should be 2 to 3 cups in all. (If the clams are large, chop them.)

Strain the cooking liquid through a very fine strainer lined with cheesecloth into a saucepan. (Occasionally the liquid from the clams will be very dark, excessively salty, and virtually unusable. If this happens, substitute chicken stock or canned clam nectar. Reduce the liquid by about half, tasting to make sure that the raw alcohol flavor has disappeared. If it has not, keep simmering. You should end up with 4 cups of liquid; add bottled clam nectar or juice (or even chicken stock) if you are short.

In a large saucepan, melt the butter and add the flour. Cook and whisk constantly for 2 to 3 minutes without browning. Slowly pour the hot stock into the pan and bring to a boil. Add the sautéed onion, garlic, and spinach and the clams. Pour in the cream and heat through. (If the soup is held too long, the bright green spinach will turn darker in color. If you must prepare the recipe ahead, add the spinach and onion mixture just before serving.) Season to taste with salt, pepper (use extra if you are not using pepper-flavored bacon), and drops of lemon juice.

VARIATION

This soup may also be puréed before the cream is added and oysters may be used instead of clams.

Broiled Shrimp with Basil and Lime

Serves 4 to 6 as a main course.

Fresh shrimp marinated in a tangy herb-infused vinaigrette and then quickly broiled are perfect for the first outdoor dining opportunities of spring. The recipe will serve four to six people but when I really feel like treating myself and someone special, I prepare the whole batch for just the two of us. This makes an exciting first course as well as a main dish. Do not be tempted to grill the shrimp. The smoky quality of wood charcoal competes with the clear vibrant taste they should have here.

MARINADE

¼ cup fresh lime juice (2 limes
  should do it)
1 teaspoon coarse salt
1 teaspoon brown sugar
½ teaspoon coarsely ground black
  pepper
2 tablespoons minced fresh basil
2 to 4 large cloves minced garlic
½ cup cold-pressed olive oil
2 pounds fresh raw shrimp, peeled
  and deveined (page 11), with
  the tails left on

GARNISH

Finely shredded basil

To make the marinade, combine the lime juice, salt, brown sugar, pepper, basil, and garlic. Make sure that the salt and sugar are dissolved, then stir in the olive oil.

Toss the peeled and deveined shrimp gently with the prepared marinade, lay them out flat in a glass baking dish, pour the remaining marinade over, and leave at room temperature for 1 hour, turning them over at the halfway point.

Remove the shrimp from the dish and push them onto metal skewers. Broil for about 6 minutes in all, depending on the size of the shrimp, turning the shrimp a couple of times in the process. (The shrimp will turn bright red as they cook; do not overcook or they will be tough.) Brush the shrimp with the remaining marinade while cooking to keep them moist and glistening.

Remove from the oven and arrange on a colorful platter. Scatter the shredded basil over the top and serve hot.

Sweet and Hot Honey-Glazed Shrimp

Serves 4.

During the winter I occasionally whip up a little drink consisting of whiskey, lemon juice, honey and boiling water that has the miraculous ability to relieve coughs and sore throat symptoms. I do not remember where this tonic originally came from, but I have grown quite fond of its particular combination of flavors. Here they are transposed in spring to spicy, fiery shrimp that make either a first or main course dish. In the latter case it is wonderful served with Basmati Rice Pilaf with Onions and Yogurt (page 333). I particularly like using snoberry honey (made from the nectar of snoberry bushes and star thistle that grow on the high flat farmland between Cle Elum and Ellensburg) in this recipe because it has a bright, lemony flavor, but other fragrant, tangy honeys will work too. You may wish to alter the amount of cayenne to the heat level you prefer; this amount is medium-hot. This will not cure the common cold; for that you need the tonic.

4 tablespoons unsalted butter
¼ cup minced shallots
½ teaspoon tumeric
½ teaspoon cardamom
½ teaspoon cinnamon
¼ teaspoon cayenne pepper
¼ teaspoon mace
1 large clove minced garlic
1 tablespoon lemon zest (from 2 medium-sized lemons)
¼ cup lemon juice (from 2 medium-sized lemons)
¼ cup whiskey
2 pounds fresh raw shrimp, shelled and deveined (page 11), with tails left on
1½ tablespoons snoberry honey
Coarse salt

Melt the butter in a sauté pan and add the shallots, tumeric, cardamom, cinnamon, cayenne, and mace. Cook slowly until the shallots soften.

Add the garlic, lemon zest, lemon juice, whiskey, and shrimp. Cook on high heat, uncovered, turning often, until the shrimp turn bright red. If there is still more than 2 tablespoons of liquid left in the pan, remove the shrimp with a slotted spoon and keep warm while you reduce the liquid to a syrup.

Add the shrimp back to the pan if you have removed them and drizzle on the honey. Salt to taste. Toss to melt the honey and to coat the shrimp evenly. Serve on a colorful platter.

Baked Halibut with Parmesan Mayonnaise

Serves 4 to 6.

Coating a fish fillet or steak with mayonnaise during part or all of its cooking time will keep it moist. A very easy dish, this is great for an impromptu supper.

> 2 or 3 large halibut steaks, 1-inch thick, and cut in half lengthwise
> Coarse salt
> Freshly ground black pepper
> Lemon juice

MAYONNAISE TOPPING
> ¼ cup unsalted butter, softened
> ¼ cup Garlic Mayonnaise (page 348)
> ½ cup grated Parmesan cheese
> 2 tablespoons very finely sliced green onion
> Dash Tabasco sauce

Season the halibut with salt and pepper, place in a glass baking dish, and sprinkle with lemon juice.

Combine the butter, Garlic Mayonnaise, Parmesan, green onion, and Tabasco. Set aside.

Bake the steaks at 450° for 6 to 8 minutes, until just about done. Remove from the oven and spread the tops and sides of the steaks with the Mayonnaise Topping. Broil for 2 to 3 minutes, until steaks are done and the topping is lightly browned.

Braised Halibut with Mint Mayonnaise

Serves 4.

This treatment for fresh fish could not be easier, yet the results are perfectly delicious. The wine and mayonnaise keep the fish extra moist.

> 2 or 3 large halibut steaks, 1-inch thick, cut in half lengthwise
> Coarse salt
> Freshly ground black pepper
> 1 cup very dry white wine or Vermouth
> 1 cup Mint Mayonnaise (page 348)

Season the halibut steaks with a light sprinkling of salt and lots of pepper. Lay them out in a baking dish and pour the wine into the bottom of the dish. Spread the mayonnaise on the top and sides of the steaks to seal in the juices.

Bake at 425° for 8 to 10 minutes per inch of thickness. Most of the wine will have evaporated, leaving the fish moist and succulent.

Lift each steak carefully from the baking dish with a slotted spatula, position on dinner plates, and serve right away.

Marinated Grilled Halibut with Cilantro-Lime Butter

Serves 4 to 6.

Here is an example of what you can do with a classic French technique (that for beurre blanc*) and a variety of international flavorings. In the basic recipe the halibut steaks are first marinated in an aromatic blend of soy sauce, sesame oil, fresh ginger, garlic, and red pepper, then simply grilled, and served with a* beurre blanc *flavored with lime zest and juice, cilantro, more ginger, more garlic, and more red pepper. The white flesh of the fish and the vivid green of the sauce make a wonderful combination. The flavor of the sauce is deepened by the inclusion of fish stock in the initial wine and vinegar reduction. Other firm-fleshed fish, such as salmon, tuna, swordfish, black cod, or shark may also be used. Roasted, peeled, and julienned red peppers make a striking accompaniment.*

2 or 3 large halibut steaks, 1-inch thick, and cut in half lengthwise

MARINADE

¾ cup Kikkoman soy sauce

⅜ cup sesame oil

2 tablespoons minced fresh ginger

4 large cloves garlic, minced

¼ teaspoon crushed red pepper

½ cup dry white wine

½ cup fish fumet (page 346)

2 tablespoons rice wine vinegar

CILANTRO-LIME BUTTER

4 cloves garlic, minced

1 tablespoon minced fresh ginger

½ cup packed cilantro leaves

1 teaspoon lime zest

½ cup unsalted butter

2 tablespoons lime juice

Pinch crushed red pepper

Coarse salt

Freshly ground black pepper

Lay the halibut steaks in a single layer in a glass baking dish. Combine the marinade ingredients and pour over the fish. Leave at room temperature to marinate for 1 hour or refrigerate for 2 to 3 hours. Turn the steaks once or twice during this time to make sure the marinade is evenly penetrating the flesh.

To make the sauce, reduce the white wine, fish fumet, and rice wine vinegar together in a small saucepan until they are barely more than a syrup. Set aside. Using a processor, purée the garlic, ginger, cilantro, and lime zest. Add the butter in chunks and purée until smooth.

With the machine running, drizzle in the lime juice and the crushed red pepper. Season to taste with salt and pepper and refrigerate.

Prepare the barbecue, preferably with mesquite charcoal, and oil the grill. Pat the steaks dry, oil both sides lightly with corn oil, and lay them carefully on the grill. Cook for about 4 minutes per side, basting with the marinade if the fish appears to be drying out.

While the steaks are cooking, reheat the reduction of wine, fumet, and vinegar. Off the heat, add all of the cold flavored butter and swirl with a wooden spoon to emulsify. Give the pan a little more heat if necessary to incorporate the butter, but do not allow the butter to boil or it will separate from the sauce.

Remove the steaks from the grill, create a half swirl on each of 4 to 6 plates with the Cilantro Lime Butter (by pouring a pool on one side and tipping the plate to achieve something like an S-shape), and place the fish on top. Arrange the suggested julienne of red bell pepper in the remaining open space or simply position a slice of lime and a sprig of cilantro there instead.

MARINADE VARIATIONS

The first marinade option eliminates the Chinese overtones, while the second is distinctly Indian in origin; in both cases change the lime zest and juice in the butter sauce to lemon and proceed.

Variation 1

Combine ½ cup lemon juice, 4 large cloves minced garlic, 1 tablespoon minced fresh ginger, 1 teaspoon lemon zest, 4 tablespoons light olive oil, and coarse salt and freshly ground black pepper to taste.

Variation 2

Combine ½ cup lemon juice, 2 tablespoons light olive oil, 2 tablespoons minced onion, 4 cloves minced garlic, 1 tablespoon minced ginger, 2 to 3 hot green chilies, seeded and minced, 1 teaspoon turmeric, and coarse salt and freshly ground black pepper to taste.

Boned Rainbow Trout with Salmon Mousse and Sauce Beurre Rouge

Serves 4.

A very dramatic dish, this looks more difficult than it actually is. Have your fish dealer remove the bones from the fish, leaving the head and tail on. Try it accompanied by tiny, steamed new potatoes, a few stalks of barely cooked asparagus, and a garnish of sautéed mushroom caps.

POACHED TROUT

    4 small trout (10 inches long or
        weighing about 12 ounces),
        dressed and boned with the heads
        and tails left on and the skin
        casing intact
    Coarse salt
    Freshly ground black pepper
    Fresh minced chives

SALMON MOUSSE

    ½ pound fresh salmon, skinned,
        boned, cut into 1-inch
        chunks, and kept very cold
    1 egg white, very cold
    1 tablespoon cognac or brandy
    ½ to ¾ cup cream, very cold
    Coarse salt
    Freshly ground white pepper

SAUCE BEURRE ROUGE

    1 tablespoon unsalted butter
    3 tablespoons minced shallots
    3 tablespoons minced mushrooms
    1 teaspoon tomato paste
    ½ cup dry red wine
    ½ cup fish stock
    8 tablespoons unsalted butter, cold and
        cut into chunks

Season the cavities of the trout with salt, pepper, and fresh chives. Refrigerate the trout while preparing the poaching liquid and the mousse.

To poach the fish, assemble a baking dish large enough to hold the four fish without curling them and enough aluminum foil to cover it. Fill the dish two-thirds full with water and bring to a simmer on top of the stove. Ten minutes before poaching the fish, put the covered baking dish into a 375° oven to heat.

To make the salmon mousse, coarsely chop the very cold salmon, in a processor, using the steel knife. Add the egg white and continue processing for a few seconds. With the machine running, slowly pour in the brandy and then the ½ cup cream. The mousse should be light but with enough body to hold its shape when scooped up with a spoon. Add more cream if necessary. Season to taste with salt and freshly ground pepper. Put the mousse into a pastry bag fitted with a ¾-inch plain tip.

Pipe or, if you do not have a pastry bag, spoon the salmon mousse into each trout. You should be able to close the trout without excess mousse oozing out. Wrap each trout rather tightly with microwavable plastic wrap and secure the ends with bag ties. Lay the fish in the barely simmering water (which should now stop simmering; 180°, well beneath a simmer, is the ideal temperature for poaching fish), cover with foil, and bake at 375° for 10 minutes for every inch of thickness. Thus if the fish is 1½ inches thick with its mousse stuffing, you will need to poach it for 15 minutes. When done, the flesh will be opaque and will just pull away from the bone. The salmon mousse will appear set.

Prepare the sauce while the trout are baking. In a small saucepan, melt the 1 tablespoon butter, add the shallots and mushrooms, and sauté for several minutes until the vegetables soften. Add the tomato paste, red wine, and fish stock. Reduce to a syrupy consistency. Remove from the heat and add the remaining 8 tablespoons of chunked butter. Stir to emulsify, using more heat if necessary. A *beurre blanc* (in this case a *beurre rouge* because of the red wine) is meant to be warm, not hot; the sauce will separate and liquefy if heated even to the simmer.

Remove the trout from their poaching water and carefully peel away the plastic wrap. Arrange the fish side by side on a heated serving platter or on individual dinner plates. Then carefully and quickly peel off the uppermost layer of skin. To do this, make a shallow cut through the skin from backbone to belly flap

just behind the collar, then make another shallow cut along the length of the backbone, then another from backbone to belly flap just in front of the tail. All you are doing here is outlining the area you intend to strip. Peel the skin off. With the knife carefully scrape off the small amount of dark flesh along the center line.

Strain and pour the sauce over each trout just before serving. This sauce does not hold well (unless put into a warmed wide-mouthed Thermos—in which case it will hold for up to 5 hours), so you will need to coordinate the arrival of the fish with it. You may wish to finish the reduction step and then reheat the sauce slightly and whisk in the butter after the fish has been taken from the oven.

Wheat Germ-Fried Fillet of Trout with Fresh Herbs

Serves 4.

I grew up eating whole trout, carefully picking out all the bones myself—so now to be able to have an entirely edible, boneless fillet is wonderful beyond words. I'm sure your guests will appreciate it too. It is not all that difficult to fillet trout yourself, but any fish merchant worth his salt will do it for you. This is such a lovely early spring dish and is especially good accompanied by a generous arrangement of pencil-thin asparagus, the fresher the better. Balsamic vinegar has a special mellowness and sweetness that is in particular harmony with wheat germ. If you do not have it, a good sherry vinegar or white wine vinegar will also work; you may need to add a pinch of brown sugar to the sauce for balance if using either of these.

 2 medium-sized trout, filleted and
     skinned (4 boneless fillets)
    Coarse salt
    Freshly ground black pepper
 ¼ cup raw (not toasted) wheat germ
 4 tablespoons unsalted butter, chilled
 1 clove garlic, minced
 1 tablespoon balsamic vinegar
 1 tablespoon lime juice
 ¼ cup unsalted fish fumet (page 346) or
     homemade chicken stock (page
     345)

 ½ cup cream
 1 tablespoon each minced fresh chives,
     thyme, and parsley

GARNISH
    whole thin stalks and ½-inch slices
       of chives

Check the trout fillets for bones by running your fingers down their length, first in one direction, then in the other. Remove the bones with tweezers.

Dry the trout fillets with paper towels, season with salt and pepper, then dredge in wheat germ to coat both sides evenly and well.

Melt 4 tablespoons of the butter in a large sauté pan. When it is hot, but not browning, lay in the fillets, being careful not to crowd them. If necessary, sauté the fish in two batches. Shake the pan to keep the fillets from sticking and cook for about 1 or 2 minutes per side. Turn and brown the other side. Remove from the pan and keep warm.

Wipe the sauté pan clean with paper towels. Melt 1 tablespoon butter and add the garlic. Cook to soften but do not brown. Then add the balsamic vinegar, lime juice, and fish fumet; reduce slightly. Add the cream and reduce until slightly thickened. Whisk in the herbs, remove from the heat, and swirl in the remaining 4 tablespoons butter so that it forms a creamy emulsion. (Too much heat will cause the butter to separate from the sauce.) Season to taste with salt and pepper.

To serve, cover the bottoms of individual plates with sauce. Arrange one fillet on each plate and garnish with 2 chive stalks. Arrange a small mound of sliced chives on the sauce and serve.

Fillet of Trout with Chili Mint Chutneys

Serves 4.

This is an easy dish to prepare. The only thing you can do wrong is to overcook the trout. The trout is coated lightly with cornmeal and garam masala, *sautéed, and served with two versions of an Indian-style chutney. The result is pure ambrosia. I have specified trout here, though halibut works wonderfully well too; they are both springtime fish. Remember when you are substituting one fish for another, that fish in general are more alike than different. With this recipe for instance, ling cod, black cod, or catfish would each be deliciously appropriate in its season. The important thing is that the fish be absolutely fresh.*

Garam masala is an Indian spice mixture that *varies considerably from one cook to another but generally consists of cardamom, cinnamon, cloves, black pepper, cumin, and coriander. You may buy this mixture at Indian markets (there is one, the Souk, in the Pike Place Market in Seattle) or make your own following the recipe on page 358.*

Chili Mint Chutneys (recipe follows)

¼ cup flour
¼ cup fine cornmeal
1 teaspoon *garam masala* (optional)
2 whole trout, filleted and skinned
Coarse salt
Freshly ground black pepper
1½ tablespoons unsalted butter
1½ tablespoons corn oil

GARNISH
Mint leaves

Prepare the Chili Mint Chutneys first, according to the recipe that follows, to allow time to chill. To prepare the trout, combine the flour, cornmeal and optional *garam masala*. Sprinkle the trout with salt and pepper on both sides and dip them into the cornmeal mixture to coat lightly and evenly.

Heat the butter and corn oil until hot but not smoking. Add the fillets and brown nicely on each side. This must not take longer than 5 minutes in total or the fish will be overcooked. (Generally fish requires just 10 minutes of cooking time per inch of thickness, regardless of cooking method.)

Remove the fillets to individual warmed serving plates and place a small ramekin of each of the chutneys alongside. Garnish with mint leaves.

Chili Mint Chutneys

Makes about 1½ cups.

1 cup loosely packed fresh spearmint
    leaves, chopped
1 seeded green chili pepper, chopped
3 tablespoons chopped mild red onion
1 teaspoon fresh ginger
½ teaspoon sugar
1 tablespoon lemon juice
1 tablespoon cold-pressed olive oil
    Coarse salt
¼ cup unflavored yogurt

Combine the spearmint, green chili pepper,
red onion, ginger, sugar, lemon juice, olive
oil, and salt to taste. Divide the mixture in
half and blend yogurt into one portion. Cover
each and chill.

Wannacut Lake Trout with Toasted Hazelnuts

Serves 4.

*This variation of trout meunière is one of the best
and simplest dishes I know. Lightly floured whole
trout are fried in butter until just cooked, then finished with lemon juice and toasted hazelnuts. This
dish is best done with small fish because they are
easier to turn and also so that each person can be
presented with the entire trout in all its crusty, flavorful glory. Baby "new" potatoes, steamed, then
drizzled with melted butter, sprinkled with grated
Parmesan cheese, and broiled for a minute or two
are an ideal accompaniment. Wannacut Lake is one
of the many beautiful little lakes in Washington
State that are stocked yearly with rainbow trout by
the Department of Fish and Game.*

4 small trout
    Coarse salt
    Freshly ground black pepper
1½ teaspoons each minced fresh
    tarragon and parsley
1 cup flour
16 tablespoons (½ pound) unsalted
    butter
    Juice of 2 lemons
1 cup hazelnuts, toasted, skinned
    (page 291), and chopped

GARNISH
    Lemon wedges
    Minced fresh tarragon and parsley,
    mixed together

Pat the trout dry with paper towels and season
the interior cavity with salt, pepper, and the
mixed fresh herbs.

Combine salt and pepper to taste with the
flour on a plate and dredge the whole trout
lightly to coat the outside.

Melt 2 tablespoons of the butter in a sauté pan large enough to hold 2 of the trout. When the butter is foaming but not browning, add the 2 trout. Cook for about 5 minutes on each side over medium heat. The surfaces should be crusty brown and when pierced with a fork the flesh should just barely pull away from the central bone. Remove the trout to an oblong heated serving platter, cover and keep warm in a 200° oven. Proceed with the remaining 2 fish, using 2 additional tablespoons butter. Remove from the pan to the serving platter with the other fish; cover and keep warm while completing the sauce.

Deglaze the skillet with the lemon juice, scraping up any bits and pieces clinging to the pan. Add the hazelnuts, remove from the heat, and whisk in the remaining 12 tablespoons butter to form an emulsion with the lemon juice. (If you use too much heat, the butter will melt and separate from the sauce rather than emulsify.) Season to taste with salt and pepper and pour over the trout. Garnish with wedges of lemon and a sprinkling of mixed fresh herbs.

Herb-Marinated Grilled Leg of Lamb with Mint Aioli

Serves 12 to 14.

This is a versatile main course. It lends itself as well to elegant entertaining as to having the gang over for a summertime grill. Ask your butcher to bone the leg for you when you purchase it, or if you are a glutton for punishment, refer to Julia Child and Company, *by Julia Child, for photographs and a good description of the boning and butterflying process. In either case you will be left with a rather awkward looking slab of meat. However, once roasted and sliced, it looks as good as it tastes.*

For an excellent accompaniment, try a garlicky potato and fennel bulb gratin or sautéed potato cakes with parsley and chives. Grilled baby vegetables, such as zucchini, eggplant, garlic, red and green bell peppers, summer squash, and green beans are also wonderful with this.

7 pounds leg of lamb, boned (the bones can be saved for stock)
1 medium onion, minced
1 bunch parsley, minced
¼ cup cilantro, minced
1 tablespoon ground cumin
1 tablespoon coarse salt
1 tablespoon freshly ground black pepper
½ cup olive oil
Juice of 2 lemons (about ½ cup)
Mint Aioli (recipe follows)

Slice through the largest lobes of the meat, making long 1½-inch-deep cuts, then flatten it to give the roast an even thickness so that the entire piece will cook at the same rate.

Combine the remaining ingredients to make the marinade. Place the lamb, fat-side down, in a large baking dish and pour the marinade over it. Seal with plastic wrap and refrigerate overnight.

Remove the lamb from the refrigerator 2 hours before you plan to grill it. Scrape most of the marinade off the lamb. Put the marinade through a strainer, and push on it with the back of a large wooden spoon to collect as much of the liquid as possible. Set aside. Dry the lamb with paper towels. After the roast has been marinated overnight, take several long wooden skewers and push them lengthwise through the meat in 2 or 3 places, then push the meat in slightly from each end to give the roast a more compact shape. It will still look rather odd.

Using an open, oiled barbecue, grill the lamb over prepared mesquite charcoal (page 363), about 5 inches from the coals, turning and basting with the marinade occasionally to prevent scorching. The roast should test 145°

with an instant-read thermometer when it is ready to come off the grill. Remove to a platter and let rest 10 minutes before carving. During this time the temperature should reach 150°, which means that the roast is medium-rare. Lamb cooked beyond this point loses much of its full and delicate taste and tends to toughen. (During the winter you may wish to use the oven. Roast on a rack at 450° for 10 minutes, then turn the heat down to 350° and continue roasting for 30 to 40 minutes until the lamb reaches 145°.)

Carve the roast on the diagonal in ½-inch-thick slices. The roast comfortably serves 12 to 14 guests. For fewer people, purchase half a leg (the butt end is best) and treat it in the same manner. Serve with Mint Aioli on the side.

Aioli

Makes 1½ cups.

An exciting, garlicky mayonnaise from the south of France, aioli has been called, among other things, "the butter of Provence," "the soul of the south," and "the cream of the sun." In Provence, feast days are often celebrated with a huge aioli platter (called le grand aioli *or* aioli monstre*) on which a dozen or so cooked vegetables and poached seafoods are arranged around a central dish of aioli. It is a perfect dish for informal summer entertaining. The intense colors and powerful flavors bring the gaiety of Provence to your own table. Aioli is also used with another famous dish from the south of France—a seafood soup-stew called* bourride. *Aioli is used to enrich and thicken the broth, and is served alongside as a sauce.*

> 4 to 6 large cloves garlic, mashed and finely minced
> 2 to 4 tablespoons lemon juice
> Coarse salt
> Freshly ground white pepper
> 2 egg yolks
> 1½ cups light olive oil (or use half olive oil and half corn oil)

Combine the garlic, lemon juice, salt, pepper, and egg yolks. Whisk by hand until thick and sticky. Add the oil, drop by drop, whisking all the while, until all of the oil is incorporated and the sauce has thickened. Taste and adjust the flavor with salt, pepper, and drops of lemon juice.

To make aioli in a processor use 1 whole egg in place of the 2 egg yolks and proceed, as outlined above, using the steel blade.

VARIATIONS

Basil Aioli

Add ½ cup tightly packed fresh basil leaves, minced, to the completed aioli and whisk. Or add the whole leaves to aioli made in the processor and purée.

Mint Aioli

Add 1 cup tightly packed fresh mint leaves, minced, to the completed aioli and whisk. Or add the whole leaves to aioli made in the processor and purée.

Sauté of Rabbit with Fennel Seed, Pancetta, and Garlic

Serves 4.

This dish is delicious with rabbit but it works equally well with chicken. Commercially grown, domesticated rabbit fryers are very tender and do not need the lengthy marination that is usually necessary for wild rabbit. A creamy, rich, and subtly colored sauté, this dish is best served with a crisp mélange of sweet red and green bell peppers or something similarly colorful.

Pancetta is the Italian equivalent of bacon. It is not smoked, just lightly salted, lightly spiced, and rolled up tightly into a salami shape. The slices will stick together when you shred them, but the pieces will separate when they are cooked.

> Flour
> Coarse salt
> Freshly ground black pepper

> 1 rabbit, cut into serving-sized pieces and dried well with paper towels
> 2 tablespoons unsalted butter
> 2 tablespoons corn oil
> 1 large onion, diced
> 2 teaspoons fennel seed
> 4 ounces very thinly sliced *pancetta,* cut into ¼-inch shreds
> 4 cloves minced garlic
> 1 cup dry white wine
> 2 egg yolks
> ½ cup cream
> 1 tablespoon fresh minced thyme
> 1 tablespoon freshly minced marjoram
> 2 tablespoons lemon juice
> Coarse salt
> Freshly ground black pepper
> 4 tablespoons unsalted butter (optional)

GARNISH
> 2 tablespoons minced Italian parsley

Season the flour with salt and pepper and dredge the rabbit pieces, shaking off any excess flour. Heat the butter and oil in a sauté pan and add the rabbit. Do not overcrowd the pan or the meat will steam rather than brown. Sauté briskly to brown all sides. Remove the rabbit from the pan and set aside.

Add the onion, fennel seed, and *pancetta* to the sauté pan and cook slowly until the onions are tender. Add the garlic and stir to combine. Deglaze the pan with the wine, reduce by half,

and add the rabbit back to the pan. Cover and cook slowly for 30 minutes or until the rabbit is fully tender. Remove the rabbit to a warm serving platter and keep warm. Leave the juices in the pan.

Mix the egg yolks with the cream, thyme, and marjoram. *Off the heat,* stir a little of the hot pan juices into the egg-yolk mixture to warm it up, then whisk the egg yolks back into the pan juices, tilting the pan to gather the sauce into a pool. Season to taste with salt, pepper, and drops of lemon juice. Use a little more heat if necessary to thicken the sauce slightly, whisking all the time. Do not let the sauce boil or the egg yolks will turn granular. Whisk the optional butter into the sauce slowly to emulsify it.

To serve, pour the sauce over the rabbit and sprinkle with parsley.

Grilled Lamb Chops with Fresh Thyme and Rhubarb Chutney

Serves 6.

These plainly grilled lamb chops may be marinated overnight to infuse them with the flavor of fresh thyme. But this is not absolutely necessary if you are in a hurry. The Rhubarb Chutney can be made days

in advance, so this recipe makes a quick and easy main-course supper dish.

> 6 thick lamb chops (1½ to 2 inches thick)
> 1 tablespoon minced fresh thyme
> 2 tablespoons cold-pressed olive oil
> Rhubarb Chutney (recipe follows)

GARNISH
> Sprigs of thyme

Sprinkle the lamb chops on both sides with the thyme, arrange in a glass baking dish, drizzle with olive oil, cover, and refrigerate overnight.

When ready to cook, bring the chops to room temperature, then grill over a prepared bed of flavorful wood charcoal such as mesquite (page 363) for about 13 minutes per side, or until the internal temperature of the lamb reaches 145° (medium-rare).

Serve hot off the grill with a ramekin filled with Rhubarb Chutney; garnish with sprigs of thyme.

Rhubarb Chutney

Makes about 1 cup.

When fresh rhubarb season arrives in the Northwest, I enjoy having this chutney on hand. It goes well, hot or cold, with lamb and with pork, turkey, and game birds. Do not peel the rhubarb; it is not necessary. Just trim off an inch or two of the greenish bottom and the side shoots with leaves before chopping.

Do be careful when seeding and chopping the hot peppers. Keep your face back and away from the fumes and wear rubber gloves if your hands are at all sensitive.

> 2 tablespoons balsamic vinegar
> ¼ cup honey
> 2 tablespoons orange juice
> 2 cups diced fresh rhubarb
> ½ cup currants
> ¼ teaspoon cinnamon
> 1 teaspoon peeled and minced fresh ginger
> 2 hot serrano or jalapeño chili peppers, split, seeded, and minced
> ¼ cup fresh spearmint, minced

Cook the vinegar, honey, and orange juice together briefly until reduced to a thick syrup. Add the rhubarb, currants, cinnamon, fresh ginger, and chili peppers. Cook until the rhubarb is tender but not mushy. Adjust the taste if necessary by adding a little more honey, then stir in the mint and serve hot or cold.

Roast Tenderloin of Pork with Rhubarb Sauce

Serves 4.

The sweet flavor of pork has a natural affinity for acidic fruit flavors, such as that of this rhubarb and orange sauce, and for spices such as cinnamon and allspice, used here in a distinctive marinade. The key to this dish is in not overcooking the pork; it should still be nicely rosy in the center, very juicy and tender. It is quite safe to eat it this way and much preferable to the dried-out, stringy stuff we are so often served. Accompanied by a Garniture of Baby Vegetables (page 57), this dish is striking with its rosy medallions of pork, deep ruby sauce, baby white beans, tiny sweet and sour onions, and miniature squash.

DRY MARINADE
> 2 teaspoons coarse salt
> ½ teaspoon freshly ground black pepper
> ½ teaspoon cinnamon
> ½ teaspoon crumbled thyme
> ¼ teaspoon allspice
> 2 cloves garlic, puréed
> 2 whole pork tenderloins (preferably weighing about 9 ounces each and measuring about 9 inches long)
> 1 cup trimmed, diced rhubarb
> 2 tablespoons brown sugar
> 2 cups homemade chicken stock (page 345)

2 tablespoons unsalted butter

2 tablespoons corn oil

2 tablespoons balsamic vinegar
  Zest of 1 orange

1 teaspoon fresh minced thyme
  Sprigs of thyme

To make the marinade, combine the salt, pepper, cinnamon, thyme, allspice, and garlic. Rub this dry marinade into the surface of the tenderloins, cover with plastic wrap and refrigerate overnight. When ready to cook, pat the pork dry and bring to room temperature.

Combine the rhubarb and brown sugar and leave for 1 hour. Add ¾ cup of the chicken stock and cook until the rhubarb is very soft and actually disintegrating.

Heat the butter and oil in a sauté pan and brown the tenderloins nicely on all sides, turning as necessary. Drain off the fat and add the vinegar and ¼ cup of the stock to the pan to deglaze. Cover and braise slowly (just a bubble on the surface) for 15 to 20 minutes until the internal temperature of the pork reads 145°. (Pork is judged safe to eat at 137° but it is advisable to cook it somewhat beyond this point to be sure.)

When the pork is done, remove from the pan and keep warm for a few minutes. Raise the heat and add the remaining 1 cup stock and the rhubarb and sugar mixture. Whisk and cook until thickened; the sauce should just coat a wooden spoon. Strain into a small saucepan and add the orange zest and thyme. Keep warm.

Cut the tenderloins into ¾-inch slices, arrange on one side of 4 individual warmed dinner plates, and pour the sauce under and around. If using, arrange the Garniture of Baby Vegetables on the remaining side of each plate and accent with sprigs of fresh thyme.

Garniture of Baby Vegetables

Here is a medley of interesting little vegetables to accompany pork, ham, lamb, game birds, and beef. I like to present plates on which the vegetables are as important as the meat and there are no obligatory potatoes, rice, or noodles to fill people up. These go particularly well with Roast Tenderloin of Pork with Rhubarb Sauce, page 55.

Baby White Beans with Fresh Herbs

Makes about 6 cups.

Beans are such a delight to eat, I do not understand why they are not more common in the American diet. Soaking the beans before cooking them, though not absolutely necessary, much improves their flavor, texture, appearance, and digestibility. The soaking water should be discarded, the beans rinsed and cooked in fresh water, and then drained again. In discarding the soaking and cooking liquid you will not lose much of the vitamin content of the beans and you will dispose of the element that is thought to interfere with the digestibility of protein.

Of the two methods given for soaking and cooking the beans, the first and more traditional method results in the best appearance; the second is quicker. These directions reflect recent findings that if the beans are brought to a boil before being soaked, they are even more digestible. Though one pound of beans may be excessive for your immediate needs, it seems pointless to cook less—they make great leftovers. Use them as a main ingredient in composed salads, soups, stews, or gratins, or on their own as an accompaniment to meat or poultry. The small white navy beans specified here are firmer than the larger Great Northern beans and keep their shape better when cooked.

1 pound dried small white navy beans
6 cups homemade chicken stock (page 345)
1 medium-sized onion, halved
4 cloves garlic, peeled, left whole, but mashed slightly
4 tablespoons cold-pressed olive oil
1 tablespoon coarse salt
2 tablespoons lemon juice
1 tablespoon fresh minced thyme
1 tablespoon fresh minced parsley
1 tablespoon fresh minced oregano
Coarse salt
Freshly ground black pepper

Traditional Soaking Method
Wash the beans carefully, removing any debris or foreign material. Add the rinsed beans to 10 cups of boiling water. Boil for 2 minutes, remove from the heat, cover, and soak for 12 hours.

Quick Soaking Method
Follow the directions given above but soak for only 1 to 4 hours.

Drain and rinse the soaked beans. Put them into a large pot along with the chicken stock, onion, garlic, 2 tablespoons of the olive oil, and salt. Simmer gently, partially covered, until tender but not falling apart, about 40 minutes. Remove from the heat and drain off any unabsorbed liquid. Remove the onion and garlic.

Carefully, so as not to break or mash the beans, fold in the remaining 2 tablespoons olive oil, lemon juice, thyme, parsley, oregano, and salt and pepper to taste. Serve hot, or let cool and use as a base for other dishes. (This recipe may be made ahead and reheated, in which case add the herbs just before serving so that they will be fresh looking and bright green.)

Sweet and Sour Glazed Baby Onions

Makes 4 small portions.

Buy the smallest onions you can find, preferably those less than three-quarters of an inch in diameter. They are usually marketed as pearl onions. The easiest way to peel them is to drop them into a pot of boiling water for one minute, remove, and strip or push off the papery skin under cold running water. Trim the root, leaving just enough of it to keep the onions intact while they cook. If you are using larger onions, they will take quite a bit longer to cook. Boil them with their skins on until they are done, then proceed with the recipe.

These are lovely with roast turkey and cranberry sauce, with pork, ham, duck, and sausages.

2 tablespoons unsalted butter
2 tablespoons white wine vinegar
2 teaspoons sugar
1 pound small pearl onions, peeled and dried well with paper towels
¼ teaspoon ground fennel seeds
¼ teaspoon ground coriander

Melt the butter in a sauté pan, add the vinegar and sprinkle on the sugar. Stir over low heat to dissolve the sugar, then raise the heat to high and add the onions. Sprinkle on the fennel and coriander and cook for about a minute, until the onions are tender but still somewhat firm and glazed with the sugar syrup. (These may be made ahead and slowly reheated.)

Steamed Miniature Squash

Makes 4 small portions.

In the summer it is often possible to find tiny squash in a variety of colors and types. Little round patty pans, green zucchini, yellow crookneck, and all the unusual varieties found in backyard gardens make beautiful vegetable garnishes and are a delight to eat. Try to buy summer squash that are no larger than a golf ball if round and no longer than four inches if oblong. Be sure that the squash are very firm and unblemished. Steaming is all that is necessary to bring out their best. I would not want to mask anything this delicate with other compelling flavors.

1 pound tiny young squash, minimally
    trimmed
Lemon juice
Coarse salt
Freshly ground black pepper

Steam the squash over boiling water until tender but still firm, about 3 to 5 minutes. Remove, drizzle with a small amount of lemon juice, and sprinkle with salt and pepper to taste. Serve immediately.

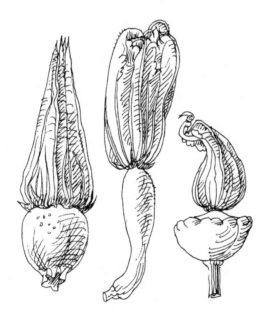

Smoked Black Cod Ravioli with Baby Leeks and Chive Cream

Makes about 60 ravioli; serves 8 to 10 as a first course.

This dish is heavenly. Anything and everything is used these days as fillings for ravioli. Smoked fish in particular has a natural affinity for pasta. This rich sauce, with its concentration of fish fumet and cream, ties the two together nicely. Very little smoked fish, the best of which can be quite expensive, need be used to produce a full and extravagant flavor. The black cod must be cold-smoked. In the Northwest this is called nova-style or lox. These terms can mean something quite different in other parts of the country, however. If you cannot find cold-smoked black cod (which is produced by the Port Chatham Packing Company in Seattle), cold-smoked salmon is equally delicious.

FILLING

1 pound fresh, skinless, boneless black cod or salmon, cut into pieces and kept very cold

4 ounces skinned, cold-smoked black cod or salmon, cut into pieces and very cold

1 egg white, very cold

¾ to 1¼ cups cream, very cold

Coarse salt

Freshly ground black pepper

1 tablespoon lemon juice

PASTA

3-egg recipe of Speckled Herb Pasta dough (page 364) kneaded and ready to roll

CHIVE CREAM

2 tablespoons butter

¼ cup finely chopped shallots

2 cloves garlic, finely minced

2 cups fish fumet (page 346) or 1 cup clam nectar or juice and 1 cup dry white wine

1 cup cream

¼ cup finely sliced chives

Coarse salt

Freshly ground white pepper

Fresh lemon juice

GARNISH

2 tablespoons unsalted butter

2 tablespoons chicken stock (or water)

1 pound very small leeks, cleaned and trimmed of all but the palest green

Using a processor with a steel knife, purée the very cold fresh cod and smoked cod together until smooth. Add the egg white and process for a few seconds more. With the machine running, pour the cream through the feed tube, using enough to lighten the mousse but still enabling it to hold its shape on a spoon. (The quantity of cream will vary from time to time. If the mousse begins to look curdled, you are adding too much cream. Stop.) Season to taste with salt, pepper, and lemon juice.

Using the fresh pasta dough, shape, fill and dry the ravioli as directed on page 365.

To make the sauce, melt the butter and add the shallots and garlic. Sauté for a few minutes to soften. Add the fish fumet and reduce by a little more than half. Add the cream and reduce again to thicken lightly, down to 1¼ cups or so. Stir in the chives. Season with salt, pepper, and drops of lemon juice.

Bring a large pot of water to a boil and add the ravioli; regulate the heat so that a constant low simmer is maintained. Test after about 8 to 10 minutes. The pasta should be tender with just a touch of chewiness. Carefully remove with a slotted spoon and shake to drain slightly.

While the pasta is cooking, melt the remaining 2 tablespoons butter, add the chicken stock and the trimmed leeks, and braise slowly until the leeks are just tender, about 5 minutes. Season to taste with salt and pepper.

Cover the bottoms of 8 heated pasta bowls with equal portions of the sauce, leaving a little to coat the cooked ravioli lightly, and arrange ravioli on top (5 to 7 ravioli per person). Garnish with a few baby leeks on the side of each plate.

VARIATION

For another first course no one is likely to forget, make a triple batch of ravioli, each with a different cold-smoked fish—black cod, salmon, and sturgeon, for instance. Flavor the black cod mousse with fennel seed, the salmon mousse with dill weed, and the sturgeon mousse with lemon juice and capers. Serve them together in heated pasta bowls with the Chive Cream suggested above or a simple unsalted butter and garlic sauce. Freeze the extra ravioli for another occasion.

Ricecakes with Italian Parsley and Fontina

Makes 6 rice cakes.

These wonderful, light and cheesy morsels are novel for lunch (I would serve two per person in this case) and interesting for a first course. Do attempt to get Italian fontina—called fontina d'Aosta; *its taste and melting quality are unsurpassable. A good Swiss cheese, such as Swiss Emmenthal or Swiss or French Gruyère, will work wonderfully well.*

4 tablespoons unsalted butter
1 medium-sized onion, diced (about 1 cup)
3 cloves garlic, minced (about 1½ teaspoons)

1 cup long-grain white rice
2 cups homemade chicken stock (page 345)
½ cup minced flat-leaf Italian parsley
2 tablespoons minced fresh oregano
2 tablespoons minced fresh chives
1 egg, lightly beaten
1¼ cups grated Italian fontina (*fontina d'Aosta*)
   Coarse salt
   Freshly ground black pepper
   Flour for dredging
2 eggs, lightly beaten
2 cups fine dry bread crumbs made from 1 loaf Swedish rye bread without caraway seeds
2 tablespoons corn oil

GARNISH
   Whole chives and lemon wedges

Melt 2 tablespoons of the butter in a saucepan and cook the onion slowly until softened, about 10 minutes. Add the garlic and stir. Add the rice and stir to coat evenly with butter. Cook without browning for 2 to 3 minutes.

Pour in the stock, cover tightly, and simmer gently for 20 minutes, until the rice is tender and has absorbed all of the liquid. Remove from the heat and stir in the parsley, oregano, and chives. When the mixture has cooled somewhat, stir in the egg and 1 cup of the fontina. Season to taste with salt and pepper.

Form the rice mixture into patties about 3 or 4 inches in diameter and ½ inch thick. Dip each one into flour, brush off the excess, dip into egg to coat evenly, then coat all sides with a thick layer of bread crumbs.

Put the patties on a wire rack to dry for 30 minutes. Melt the remaining butter with the oil and sauté the cakes, being careful not to overcrowd the pan, until nicely browned on both sides. Remove to a heated serving platter and keep warm while finishing the rest of the cakes.

When all the cakes are sautéed, sprinkle them with the remaining ¼ cup fontina and broil for a minute until the cheese melts. Serve garnished with whole chives and lemon wedges.

Rhubarb-Strawberry Sorbet

Serves 6 to 8.

Here is a brick-red sorbet with the mingled flavors of rhubarb and strawberry, which just happen to have a natural affinity for each other. The brown sugar lends a subtle caramel taste.

4 cups rhubarb, trimmed of all leaves
  and diced
1 cup brown sugar
2 cups strawberries, sliced
  Zest of 1 orange, finely grated
2 tablespoons Grand Marnier or other
  orange-flavored liqueur

Combine the rhubarb and brown sugar and let sit for 1 hour. In a heavy pan, bring the rhubarb and sugar to a simmer and cook until tender, about 20 to 30 minutes. Puree the mixture in a processor with the strawberries, orange zest, and liqueur. (Or put them all through a food mill.) Put through a fine sieve. Chill thoroughly.

Put the mixture into an ice cream machine and follow the manufacturer's instructions for freezing. When frozen, serve right away or keep frozen for up to several hours. (Ice crystals tend to develop after this time.)

Serve with crisp, delicate cookies if desired.

Crimson Rhubarb Mousse with Strawberry-Gin Sauce

Makes 6 servings; 1½ cups sauce.

Perhaps the best thing about this recipe is all the fun you will have comparing and deciding which gin to use. Gin is a natural enhancement for fruit flavors and is often preferable to brandy.

3 cups diced rhubarb
½ cup brown sugar
1 package unflavored gelatin
¼ cup Tanqueray or other
  distinctively juniper-flavored
  gin, such as Gilbey's or
  Beefeater (Sir Robert Burnett's
  or Boodles gin are even more
  intense)
2 cups cream
2 egg whites
¼ cup sugar

STRAWBERRY-GIN SAUCE
2 cups strawberries, hulled
4 to 5 tablespoons sugar, depending on
  the sweetness of your berries
¼ cup lemon marmalade, the type
  with shreds of lemon rather
  than chunks
2 tablespoons Tanqueray gin

Sprinkle the sugar over the rhubarb and let sit for 1 hour. Put into a saucepan, cover, and simmer gently for 15 minutes or so, until fully tender and quite thick. Purée in a processor.

Soften the gelatin in the gin for 10 minutes. Combine with the rhubarb and heat to dissolve the gelatin. Set into an ice-water bath (a large bowl filled halfway with ice and a couple of cups of water). Cool until cold to the touch, but do not allow the gelatin to set.

With an electric mixer, combine the cream and rhubarb mixture. Whip until fluffy and light. Do not overwhip or the cream will break down.

Beat the egg whites until soft peaks form. Add the sugar and continue beating until stiff peaks have formed. Carefully fold the egg whites into the rhubarb and cream mixture. Turn the mousse into a clear glass, 6-cup, straight-sided soufflé dish or into individual 1-cup soufflé dishes and refrigerate for 2 hours or more. (Or if you would like the mousse to look like a soufflé, spoon it into a 4-cup soufflé dish fitted with a lightly oiled foil collar. When the mousse has set, it will be an inch or so above the top edge of the dish.)

To make the Strawberry Gin Sauce, purée the strawberries and sugar together in a processor. Strain through a fine sieve and reserve. Warm the marmalade just to melt. Combine the marmalade, the gin, and the puréed strawberries, mixing well. Chill thoroughly.

Serve each portion of mousse topped or surrounded with sauce or pass the sauce separately.

Hazelnut-Maple Cheesecake with Rhubarb-Cinnamon Hot Sauce

Serves 8.

This recipe is really trans-seasonal. Rhubarb and maple syrup are early spring foods and hazelnuts are available in the fall. If you make the sauce in quantity in the spring and freeze it, you will be able to make this dessert year-round. The maple syrup used here is real maple syrup—not the awful sugar-water sold as maple syrup in the grocery store. The incomparable flavor is well worth the extra expense. Do not be tempted to use one of the more expensive ricotta cheeses here—I'm speaking of the non-emulsified, "gourmet" ricottas. They do not have enough body for this cheesecake. This recipe was created by Rosalyn Rourke, a friend and member of the recipe testing team.

> Hazelnut Biscotti and Praline Pastry
>   (page 66)
> 1 package unflavored gelatin
> 1 cup real maple syrup
> 15 ounces firm ricotta cheese (such as
>   Precious or Frigio brands, or most
>   of those sold in grocery stores)
> 1 cup cream, whipped to soft peaks
> Rhubarb-Cinnamon Hot Sauce
>   (recipe follows)

Press the Hazelnut Biscotti and Praline Pastry onto the bottom of an 8-inch springform pan.

Soften the gelatin in ½ cup of the maple syrup for 10 minutes. Warm the syrup until the gelatin dissolves or "clears." Use a processor or mixer to smooth the ricotta, then add the maple syrup and gelatin mixture and the remaining ½ cup maple syrup. Blend well.

Fold the whipped cream gently into the ricotta mixture. Pile into the prepared pastry-lined springform pan. Chill for several hours or overnight until firm.

Just before serving, remove the sides of the springform pan and spread 1 cup chilled Rhubarb-Cinnamon Hot Sauce over the top, being careful not to dribble any down the sides; there should be three distinct layers: crust, cheesecake, and topping.

Rhubarb-Cinnamon Hot Sauce

Makes 2 cups thick sauce.

There was so much agony and ecstasy with this sauce in the testing stages, I will tell you a little bit about its development. I wanted to combine rhubarb with the taste of those addictive red-hot candies kids are always chomping on and began by thinking I could get it with cinnamon and something hot such as Tabasco sauce. That combination did not work but al-most immediately a member of the testing team suggested cinnamon oil from the drug store. We added a drop to start with and nothing happened, so we added another drop, and another, until we had used the whole bottle. The sauce tasted pretty good. Shortly we discovered that the intensity of the cinnamon oil more than quadruples over time. The sauce was inedible the next day. After much trial and error, we finally got it right. The result is a wonderful and versatile sauce. Of course you must like the taste of those little red candies to enjoy it as much as I do. This sauce is thick, actually more of a topping; there are also directions for thinning it out.

1 pound trimmed, chopped
    rhubarb (about 4 large
    stalks)
1 cup sugar
⅛ to ¼ teaspoon cinnamon oil (start
    with the lesser amount, see
    how you like the taste after a
    day of refrigeration, then
    add more if necessary)

"Sweat" the rhubarb, covered, over low heat in a heavy saucepan until the liquid is released, from 10 to 20 minutes. Add the sugar and cook, uncovered, until most of the water has evaporated, from 20 to 30 minutes. The sauce should be very thick and smooth. Remove from the heat and add the cinnamon oil. The sauce may be served hot or cold.

To make a thinner sauce, add an equal amount of water to the sauce to give it a pouring consistency.

Hazelnut Biscotti and Praline Pastry

Makes a 10-inch pastry shell.

A cookie crust with a difference, this pastry has lots of flavor, texture, and pizzazz. Consider using it if you happen to have the biscotti and praline on hand; otherwise it is a lot of work. The shredded, unsweetened coconut obtainable at health food stores is much closer in taste and texture to fresh coconut. However, the grocery store variety will work in this recipe.

    1½ cups ground Hazelnut Biscotti
        (page 67)
    ½ cup Rosalyn's Hazelnut Praline
        (page 67)
    ½ cup shredded coconut
    ¼ cup unsalted butter, melted

Mix everything together, crumble onto the bottom of a buttered 8- to 10-inch springform pan, and pat to an even thickness. That's it: no muss, no fuss. Use this as a base for your favorite cheesecake.

Chocolate-Hazelnut Pastry, Quick and Easy

Makes one 10-inch pastry shell.

The recipe for Hazelnut Biscotti and Praline Pastry requires you to make your own biscotti and praline before you can begin the pastry. I know that there are possibly one or two of you who will not do this, no matter how marvelous the taste. Here is another pastry to make instead then. This one is quite good in its own right and, best of all, is quick and easy. For the cookie crumbs I would recommend Ferrara Bruti e Buoni chocolate hazelnut cookies, which are available at DeLaurentis in Seattle and Bellevue, or you might use any other crisp, dry chocolate cookie of your choice.

    1½ cups (about 16 cookies) best-quality
        chocolate-hazelnut cookie crumbs
    ½ cup roughly chopped toasted,
        skinned hazelnuts
    ½ cup shredded coconut
    ¼ cup unsalted butter, melted

Mix all the ingredients together, crumble into the bottom of an 8- to 10-inch springform pan, and pat out evenly.

Rosalyn's Hazelnut Praline

Makes 4 cups.

> ½ cup unsalted butter
> 1¼ cups sugar
> 4 cups lightly toasted, skinned
>   hazelnuts (page 291)

Melt the butter and sugar together in a sauté pan. When sugar has dissolved and starts to bubble, add the nuts. Cook, stirring, until medium brown; pour out onto a buttered baking sheet. When the mixture is cool, chop coarsely in a processor. Store in an airtight plastic container in the freezer. Use as a topping for dessert mousse, ice cream, and custard.

VARIATION

Walnut Praline
Use walnuts instead of hazelnuts; do not bother to skin them.

Hazelnut Biscotti

Makes about 30 cookies.

These are so, so good. I could eat them forever. They are the specialty of Rosalyn Rourke, who is a friend and member of the testing team. They have no relationship whatsoever to the stale, rocklike Italian biscotti cookies offered in specialty food stores. The texture, which is supposed to be firm but not unchewable, comes from baking the cookies twice, once in a lozenge shape and once cut in individual cookies. They make full use of our wonderful Northwest hazelnuts and are just great with a rich, dark cup of coffee or espresso. These are flavored with cinnamon rather than the more usual anise seed.

> 1 cup sugar
> ½ cup unsalted butter, melted
> 2 to 3 teaspoons cinnamon, to taste
> 2 tablespoons vanilla extract
> 1 teaspoon coarse salt
> 3 eggs
> 1 cup coarsely chopped hazelnuts
> 2¾ cups flour
> 2 teaspoons baking powder
>   Powdered sugar

In a processor, or mixer, blend the sugar with the butter, cinnamon, vanilla, and salt. Blend in the eggs, one at a time, until the mixture is light and fluffy. Add the nuts.

Combine the flour with the baking powder and sift together. Stir into the sugar and butter

mixture. After the dough is well blended, chill for at least 2 to 3 hours.

Shape the dough with your hands into lozenge-shaped loaves that are about 1 inch thick, 2 inches wide, and as long as your baking sheet. Place on the greased baking sheet and bake at 350° for 25 minutes, or until golden brown.

Remove from the oven and let cool. Then cut the loaves into diagonal slices about 1 inch thick. Lay the slices cut-side down on a cookie sheet and return to the oven for 5 to 10 minutes or until lightly toasted. Sprinkle with powdered sugar. Stored in an airtight container; these will keep a long time.

Souffléd Omelet with Rhubarb-Cinnamon Hot Sauce

Serves 4.

A light, fabulously delicious cross between an omelet and a soufflé, this is the perfect instant dessert—especially if you have the rhubarb sauce prepared ahead. For this recipe you will need individual gratin dishes or other small shallow baking dishes.

1⅓ cups Rhubarb-Cinnamon Hot Sauce
(page 65)

6 eggs, separated
2 tablespoons flour
1 teaspoon vanilla extract
1 tablespoon lemon juice
¼ teaspoon cream of tartar (optional)
½ cup sugar
 Powdered sugar in a sieve

Thin the rhubarb sauce just a little, using 2 to 3 tablespoons water.

Beat the egg yolks with the flour, vanilla, and lemon juice. Beat the egg whites separately until foamy, preferably in a copper bowl with a balloon whisk. If you use a mixer, add the cream of tartar. Continue beating at a faster pace until soft peaks are obtained, then gradually incorporate the sugar, beating continuously to the stiff peak stage. (When you dip a spatula into the mixture, then slowly lift it out and turn straight up, the egg whites will hold their shape stiffly but will not appear clumpy.) Gently fold the egg whites into the egg yolks.

Butter each of 4 individual gratin dishes and divide the rhubarb sauce among them, spreading to cover the bottoms evenly. Scoop, or put into a pastry bag and pipe, the soufflé mixture onto the top of each.

Bake at 350° for 15 to 20 minutes, until puffed and golden. You may need to broil them briefly at the end to get an attractive brown top. Remove from the oven and sieve powdered sugar over the top. Serve immediately before the soufflés have a chance to deflate.

Summer

JUNE • JULY • AUGUST

Although summer is the season that every good cook should relish most because of its glorious diversity and abundance of vegetables, fruits, and fish, it is instead a time of conflict. Yes, the salmon is beautiful, but, no, I do not want to be in the kitchen preparing it. Since this most perfect of Northwest seasons is much too fleeting to spend any of it indoors unnecessarily, I recommend—for the health and welfare of all inhabitants—that a general fund be set up to provide every cook in this region with an outdoor kitchen. I will gladly act as chairperson for this initiative should anyone care to support it.

Until we can get this project going, however, compromise is in order. The creative possibilities are too ripe to squander carelessly, but time must also be spent in the garden, on the sailboat, and on those tennis courts. In other words, whatever cooking is going to take place in June, July, and August must be quick and easy. In summer, I use the early morning hours for most of my dinner preparations. Clean it, cut it, get all the auxiliary ingredients ready, and sometimes even cook it. The grill out on the deck is ever at the ready. Fortunately the perfection of the basic ingredients at this time of year asks only the simplest of treatments.

What is necessary are frequent trips to the local farmers' markets that spring up all over Washington and Oregon in summer, outings to fields where you can pick raspberries and strawberries for a song, and trips to the numerous herb farms that dot the countryside. This is the time to meet the producers. The Pike Place Market in Seattle, usually one of the best places to meet local growers, is unfortunately a zoo right now. Shopping for an evening meal here can be a feat of endurance that requires one to creep along the walkways, at a rate of about one inch in five minutes, wedged in by thousands of gawking tourists. If you must shop at the Market, arrive at 8:00 A.M. before the vendors are officially open for business and you will do much better.

The local ingredients I focus on for the summer are salmon, scallops, Dungeness crab, broccoli and cauliflower, Walla Walla sweet onions, fresh herbs, raspberries, blueberries, caneberries, stone fruit, and strawberries. All of them are at their peak.

Pacific Salmon

Salmon are anadromous: they are spawned in fresh-water streams and rivers, spend their adult lives hundreds of miles out to sea, and then return to their birthplace to spawn their own offspring and die. Salmon are harvested either by longliners, who fish offshore waters with long lines to hook-catch the fish, mostly king and coho or silver salmon; by seiners, who fish close to shore by enclosing a net around and under the school of fish (catching mostly pink, sockeye or red, and chum salmon); or by gillnetters who fish near the mouths of rivers for all species of salmon, catching the fish by their gills in the webbing of the nets. It pays to know the differences among these three methods, as salmon (like most other commercially caught fish) is subject to much abuse and mishandling between the sea and your local seafood market.

The best tasting fish are those that are line-caught and individually handled. The premium quality fish are bled, gutted, and iced on board. An experienced handler will spend as much as 15 minutes on each fish, completing this process properly. Removing the viscera and blood gives a much whiter appearance and far cleaner taste to these fish than to those left ungutted. Fresh salmon should be dressed (gutted) as soon as possible to prevent the enzymes contained in the stomach from breaking down the belly walls and causing what is called belly burn, discoloration and a rancid smell.

After being dressed, fresh salmon should be held at 32 degrees, which will give it a shelf life of up to two weeks under the best conditions. Sometimes carefully handled fish are frozen at sea and, because of special handling procedures, will actually taste far better than so-called fresh fish that has been handled in bulk. If you have access to premium quality frozen fish, do not hesitate to buy. You may purchase the best salmon you have ever eaten.

Season

Usually, but the seasons vary from year to year, fresh king salmon is available from April to October, coho from May to November, sockeye from May to September, and chum from May to December. From December through March the salmon comes from Alaska as the Northwest salmon fishing season is closed.

Selection

Since salmon, except for the larger specimens of kings, is so often available whole, take advantage of the fact and look for all the signs of quality mentioned in the section on Selecting Fresh Fish (page 5). Always check to see if the fish has been gutted; refuse to buy whole fish that are still carrying around their innards. These are surely suffering from belly burn. (Even good seafood markets will sell them to you this way if you are not paying attention.) Also check the scales on the surface of the fish;

they should be intact. Too many missing scales indicates a roughly handled, mistreated, or aging fish. A prime specimen will have a glistening overlay of natural slime, iridescent silvery sides, and a white belly. If the salmon is dull or dark, it was caught too close to its spawning grounds, well after it had depleted its body fat and lost most of its good flavor.

Preparation

If the fish was not prepared for the pan at the market for you, check the section on Boning Whole Round Fish (page 7) for all the particulars of dressing, filleting, skinning, and whole-boning.

Cooking

Food journalists are prone to repeat the popular tenet, "Cook salmon in the simplest way possible." I take exception. It's true that salmon has a very distinctive taste and needs little embellishment to be truly wonderful. Even so, its powerful taste makes it a perfect candidate for assertive embellishments; it can hold its own in their presence. I love the oriental-style marinades and sauces that include fresh ginger, garlic, crushed red pepper, black beans, soy sauce, sesame oil, and the like because the flavors of both fish and sauce enhance without diminishing each other. Bright, acidic sauces—those made with lemon, capers, sorrel, tomatoes, and fruit vinegars—work well

too because they cut through some of the fish's inherent richness. Or you can amplify the richness with unctuous sauces made of butter, cream, crème fraîche, sour cream, or hazelnuts, for the opposite effect. Salmon lends itself to just about all the standard cooking methods because of its firm flesh and relatively high fat content. Depending on the cut you choose, you can poach, bake, broil, grill, sauté, braise, or steam it, all to good effect.

PACIFIC SALMON SPECIES

On the West Coast, five species of salmon are harvested, accounting for more than ninety percent of the salmon sold in the United States. Most come from Alaska and the next sizable quantities are netted off the shores of British Columbia and then Washington State respectively. Each species has its own appearance, taste, and nomenclature. Where two names are noted, either is commonly used.

King or Chinook

The finest and the largest of Pacific salmon, king salmon, are the first fresh salmon in the Northwest markets in the spring, often arriving as early as April. Kings are normally marketed as king salmon, although other names such as spring salmon, tyee salmon, or blackmouth salmon (usually applied to small, immature kings caught by sport fishermen) also appear occasionally. Kings may also be marketed under names that reflect either their river of origin (the Columbia River bordering Washington and Oregon, the Rogue River in Oregon, and the Copper and Yukon Rivers in Alaska are all noted for kings) or the color of their flesh. There are both red kings and white kings. Color is not an indicator of quality in this species, but because consumers do not always understand this, white kings often cost forty percent less than red kings, although they taste just as good. Kings usually weigh between five and thirty pounds, the larger fish reputed to be the best tasting. The oil content in this species—11.6 percent fat—is the highest of all salmon types, making it a particularly good fish for smoking.

Sockeye or Red

Named for its desirable deep red flesh, this species is also called blueback salmon. Sockeye runs start as early as the beginning of June and extend through the end of July. Dressed weight is normally between three and five pounds. Sockeyes are firm textured, fine flavored, have a gorgeous color, and a fat content of around 9 percent. Even though this species is normally taken by gill net and seine fisheries, it holds up better than other species do to mishandling. Sockeyes are also noted for their river of origin; British Columbia's Frazer and Thompson Rivers being two of the best known and appreciated for their sockeye runs.

Coho or Silver

These are also called redskins. They begin to appear in the markets shortly after king salmon has made its debut, usually in May. Cohos vary in market size from between two and four pounds in June and early July, to between six and twelve pounds in August, September, and October. In July and August look for ocean-caught longlined cohos weighing over five pounds. The larger specimens are the better textured. Cohos coming out of the net fisheries in fall vary in quality. These fish have particularly strong digestive acids and when left uncleaned for even short periods deteriorate rapidly. Check the stomach cavities for belly burn. A coho in fresh water ready to spawn has pink or red skin, thus the name, redskin. These are inferior in quality and should be avoided. Farm-raised baby cohos are sometimes available but they taste more like trout than salmon. Fat content in cohos is around 5.7 percent.

Chum

Also known as dog salmon, keta, and silverbright, industry grades for this species in order of quality are silverbright, semibright, and dark. These last two grades should definitely be avoided. As chums near the fresh-water rivers of their birth, they darken and show vertical streaking. The amount of oil in the flesh and its color are directly related to the skin color. Chum is a late-run salmon taken by the net fisheries from late September through November. Bright chums are pink fleshed, taste good, and are not as expensive as some of the other salmon species. At 4.4 percent, the fat content is quite a bit lower than that of other salmon species.

Pink

The smallest and the most abundant species of Pacific salmon is almost always sold as pink salmon. It may also be called humpback or humpie on occasion. Pinks are landed later in the summer, primarily by seiners and gillnetters. Marketed at two to three pounds, pinks have a very low tolerance of mishandling and very limited shelf life. Pinks are inexpensive, but are rarely a good value because of their quality. When good, they are a fair eating fish. Their fat content is low for salmon at 4.8 percent.

Pacific Salmon Recipes

Boned Rainbow Trout with Salmon Mousse and Sauce Beurre Rouge, *pages 44*

Chinese Steamed Salmon with Ginger, Garlic, and Black Beans, *page 122*

Double Salmon Saucisson, *page 118*

Fillet of Salmon with Sorrel Cream, *page 117*

Salmon in Parchment with Corn, Walla Walla Sweets, and Tomatoes, *page 116*

Pacific Sea Scallops

A small but steady scallop fishery exists on the coast between Oregon and Alaska. The local product, the Pacific sea scallop or weathervane scallop as it is also called, is available either fresh or frozen most of the year. The supply varies from year to year according to the whims of nature and the depletion of stocks by humans. The small Oregon bay scallop and more recently a local rock scallop, sold as. the pink singing scallop, are also obtainable fairly regularly.

Season

Year-round.

Selection

The pink singing scallop is sold in the shell and preferably alive, though sometimes it is difficult to tell whether they are alive or not, because scallops, unlike other bivalves, do not always keep their shells tightly closed. They will often be sitting on ice at the seafood store fully agape and apparently lifeless. If you pass your hand just over the top of the batch, they should move; if they do not, pass them by. Live fish tanks are preferable for scallops and even so they have an extremely short shelf life—just five days from sea to demise. In the tank, select scallops with tightly closed or almost closed shells. When in doubt, I use my nose. If the smell is not clean and sweet, the scallops should not be purchased or eaten. Select each scallop individually. Do not just scoop and hope for the best. If the scallops have already been shucked, look for very white, moist, sweet smelling nuggets. Do not hesitate to ask the fish dealer for a good, close whiff of his product. Fresh shelled scallops are not always better. Scallops hold up to freezing very well, so select whichever looks and smells the best.

Storage

Scallops should be eaten as soon as possible. If shucked, they may be kept in a plastic bag on ice for two to three days if very fresh. If live and in the shell, keep them on ice, covered with a wet towel, for one day at most. If you suspect that your live scallops have died on you, do not immediately despair. Remove them from the shell and store as you would shucked scallops, remembering that the roe—actually roe (or coral, which is orange) and testes (which are white) as most scallops are hermaphrodites—deteriorates more rapidly than does the muscle itself.

Preparation

Peel off the small coarse attachment from each shucked scallop. This is tough when cooked and will mar the succulence of the scallops. If the scallops are whole, scrub the shells with a stiff brush.

Shucking

Use an ordinary small paring knife. Insert the blade between the scallop shells to separate them. Run the blade inside one shell to cut the muscle. Break the hinge open and discard the freed shell. Run the knife under the scallop to free it from the remaining shell. Scallops are delicious eaten whole but with larger ones, you may wish to separate the adductor muscle, the white nugget that most people think of as a scallop, from the rest. To do this, detach the white and orange roe from the grayish viscera that surrounds it. Discard the viscera. The roe is edible and most people who have tried it consider it the best part of the scallop and at least as good as the adductor muscle.

Cooking

Steam open whole, live scallops as you would clams and mussels. Scallops have very thin shells so they take almost no time to open—only about one minute. Remove the scallops as they open; overcooking toughens them and ruins their taste. This rule about overcooking extends as well to shucked scallops. This bivalve is high in water content, and when cooked too long, all the natural, sweet tasting juice is forced from the tissues, producing a tough, rubbery, tasteless morsel. Scallops are perfectly wonderful raw, so I attempt always to err on the side of undercooking, leaving a small core of translucency in the center. Depending on the method used and the intensity of heat, one to three minutes of cooking time will suffice.

Pacific Scallop Recipes

Bay Scallops and Leeks in Orange Cream, *page 125*

Fettuccini with Scallops, Mushrooms, and Cream, *page 126*

Scallops and Shrimp Gratinée, *page 124*

Dungeness Crab

Few seafood delicacies draw such unanimous praise as our own Pacific Coast Dungeness crab. Named after the town of Dungeness on the Olympic Peninsula where it was first commercially harvested, this large, hardshell crab has gained international approval and an uncontested reputation. Its delicate, faintly sweet flavor and succulent texture make it the most popular of the West Coast crabs.

Season

Dungeness crab is generally available year round. The Alaska fisheries supply Dungeness during summer and early fall; Pacific Northwest commercial crabbers concentrate their efforts during late fall and early winter. To Northwest sport crabbers, summer offers the most abundance because commercial vessels are not monopolizing the waterways. The only time that Dungeness crab should be avoided is shortly after annual moulting or shedding of their shells. This event, which can occur at any time of the year, allows the crab to grow as much as half an inch in size before a new soft shell is formed. During its soft-shell phase, the crab's meat is soft, stringy, and underdeveloped; unlike the Atlantic blue crab, Dungeness crab is not eaten with its shell in the soft-shell phase. Some seafood stores, such as Jack's Fish Spot in Pike Place Market and various oriental markets in Seattle's Chinatown, have live crab tanks. Of late, some supermarkets have also installed live tanks for crab and lobster.

Selection

Dungeness crab can be purchased already cooked, although I do not recommend it. Who knows how old the crab is? Also, notice how scummy and smelly the water gets in the seafood markets that offer to cook the crab for you. The quality of the water affects the taste of the crab. It is much better to buy a live crab, kill it, gut it, and then cook it immediately in fresh salted water.

When buying live Dungeness crab, look for a fully active specimen. It is said that foam or bubbles around the mouth of a crab indicates it has started to die; pass these over for better looking specimens. Dungeness crabs usually weigh between 1½ and 3½ pounds.

Storage

Handled with care and kept sufficiently cool and damp (50 degrees), crabs will remain alive for twenty-four hours or more. If refrigeration space or temperature is inadequate, a cold garage or outdoor deck may be used. Keep the crabs contained, of course, but give them some freedom of movement. Damp toweling will provide the necessary moisture.

Killing and Cleaning

Among the ranks of devoted crab connoisseurs, heated debate continues about the best way to cook the fresh crustaceans. Traditionally the live crabs are plunged into rapidly boiling seawater to kill and cook them simultaneously. The crabs are then cooled in cold water for a few minutes and cleaned. The alternate method calls for killing and cleaning the crabs before boiling them.

To settle the question, for myself at least, I tried both ways and compared the results. The second method has several unexpected and decided advantages. The cleaned crabs require much less space in the cooking pot, something to be considered when a large number of crabs is being cooked. Less odor escapes from the cooking pot, which makes the process more pleasant when you are using your home kitchen and not cooking over an open fire on the beach. The cleaning process itself is easier and less messy. But, most notably, the taste, and the appearance of crabs cleaned before being cooked, is infinitely improved. The meat is appetizingly white and has a clear vibrancy of taste. Crabs cooked in the traditional manner taste slightly off by comparison and the juices give the body meat an unsavory yellow tinge.

This process is not as difficult or as barbarous as you might think. Certainly it is more humane than dropping the live creatures into boiling water. At least death is instantaneous. Crabs bought from a tank at the seafood market will usually be wrapped in newspaper. If they are, just pull the paper away from the midsection of each crab, leaving the claws fully bound. Dispatch as described below, then unwrap the crabs.

1. Grasp the crab shell from the rear between your thumb and fingers. In this position, the crab will have difficulty reaching you with its pincers.
2. Lay the crab on its back on a sturdy cutting surface with its eyes away from you (so that you feel better).
3. Using a heavy sharp knife, position the cutting edge along the midsection.
4. Tip first, plunge the blade quickly down and through the midsection, killing the crab instantly. (A little bit of leg movement is normal at this point. Be assured, the crab is dead and in no pain if you have been assertive with the plunge.)

5. Grasp the five legs on one side of the body with your hand while holding the hard shell and the remaining leg sections down and pull them up and toward you. If you are pulling in the right direction, the legs, along with the adjoining honeycombed body section will be easily disengaged from the shell.

6. Remove the legs from the other side. You now have two crab halves.

7. Discard the shell and the innards.

8. Holding half of the crab at a time, sharply shake it downward, over the ocean or into the sink, to discard any innards attached to the body sections.

9. Turn each half over and tear off the feathered gills and any spongy matter clinging to the main body section.

Cooking

The crab may now be used in any recipe calling for raw crab meat (and quickly too as the raw meat deteriorates rapidly) or simply boiled in the following manner.

1. Fill a large pot barely half full with salted fresh water and bring to a boil. Use about ⅓ cup of salt to every 2 gallons of water. Clean seawater may also be used.

2. Drop the crab halves into the rapidly boiling water, cover, and regulate the heat so that the water continues to boil but does not run over the sides of the pan. Cook for 12 minutes.

3. Remove the crab halves with tongs and cool in ice water very briefly. Using a stiff-bristled brush, scrub the midsections to remove any ocean scum still remaining. When the crab is quite cold, put it into a large plastic bag, seal, and refrigerate for up to three days until ready to use.

Dungeness Crab Recipes

Birch Bay Crabcakes, *page 127*
Dungeness Crab in Black Bean Sauce, *page 224*
Dungeness Crab-Stuffed Petrale Sole, *page 223*
Ellen's Famous Dungeness Crab Dip, *page 103*

Broccoli and Cauliflower

Broccoli and cauliflower are two vegetables I am never without during any season. They are part of the summer harvest in the Northwest but have become all-season vegetables for many of us—always available and usually good. Unlike other more perishable vegetables, corn and asparagus for instance (the sugars of which convert so rapidly to starch), these two travel and keep reasonably well. And they are incredibly versatile.

Broccoli and cauliflower can usually be treated in the same way and are thus often interchangeable in recipes.

I am always dismayed to see shoppers with packages of frozen cauliflower and broccoli in their carts when the fresh vegetables are so constantly available and so easy to prepare—not to mention being so much better to eat. They are nearly instant foods, as the following selection and preparation guide shows.

BROCCOLI

Season

Mid-June through September.

Selection

Broccoli should have tight blue-green florets and firm stalks without any visible splits through the core. Avoid broccoli that is yellowing or has a loosely bunched head. Also avoid limp-looking heads.

Storage

Peeled broccoli becomes dry when stored; peel as close to cooking time as possible, then store in a plastic bag. Store unpeeled, unwashed broccoli in a perforated plastic bag.

Preparation

Cut each whole stalk of broccoli where the stalk branches into smaller stems. Separate the smaller stems by cutting between them, then cut each one in half if the pieces are more than bite-sized. To insure even cooking, peel the stems. Insert a paring knife under the skin at the stem base and pull up and off. Continue all the way around each stem. Peel the remaining main stem likewise and cut it into manageable pieces. Rinse under cold running water.

Cooking

Blanch florets in boiling water, uncovered, for 3 to 4 minutes; larger, whole stalks for 4 to 5 minutes. Steaming will take about twice as long. Test the broccoli once or twice while it is cooking. If you are not using it immediately, drain and refresh the broccoli under cold running water as soon as it is *al dente*. Do not let it cook too long or it will lose its beautiful color and turn mushy.

Tips

- Broccoli will turn olive-green if cooked with an acid such as wine or lemon juice or if cooked in a covered pot.
- Peeled stems and trimmed florets will cook in approximately the same amount of time.
- To reheat cold, cooked broccoli, immerse it in boiling water until just heated through.
- The main stem can be cut into a julienne shred to make an interesting sauté or stir fry.

CAULIFLOWER

Season

July through September.

Selection

Look for crisp, firm, creamy white heads. Avoid cauliflower with brown spots. Check to see if the brown spots have already been trimmed from the head and avoid these heads as well. Cauliflower is well past its prime when it starts to brown and will smell and taste strong when cooked. Also avoid granular-looking heads or heads with spreading clusters.

Storage

Cauliflower should not be stored long. Refrigerate in a perforated plastic bag when raw; cauliflower needs oxygen. Cooked cauliflower loses its wonderful texture when refrigerated for any length of time. Either raw or cooked, it will develop a strong unpleasant smell if left too long in the refrigerator.

Preparation

Remove the center core of the cauliflower by cutting a two-inch conical wedge from its base. This cut should also remove most of the exterior green leaves. Break or cut the cauliflower into bite-sized florets and trim the stem end of each piece. In whole cauliflower, make the wedge cut shallow enough to leave the cau-

liflower intact. Soak upside-down in acidulated water to remove any insects; swish around vigorously.

Cooking

Florets will take between three and six minutes to cook when boiled, six to ten minutes when steamed. Whole heads will normally take ten to fifteen minutes of blanching time or fifteen to twenty minutes of steaming. To sauté cauliflower florets, start them in hot butter or oil, then reduce the heat to low, cover the pan, and "sweat" for three to five minutes.

Tips

- For an absolutely white head, blanch the cauliflower, adding 1 or 2 tablespoons lemon juice or 2 tablespoons milk to the water.
- Use unsalted water for blanching cauliflower; salt darkens it.

Broccoli and Cauliflower Recipes

Deep-Fried Cauliflower with Garlic and Vinegar Sauce, *page 244*

Iced Cauliflower Soup with Apricot Cream, *page 115*

Layered Vegetable Purée with Yakima Valley Gouda, *page 325*

Steamed Vegetable Mosaic, *page 134*

Summer Vegetable Stir-Fry with Garlic, Ginger, and Walnuts, *page 134*

Walla Walla Sweet Onions

The Walla Walla sweet onion is not actually all that sweet; it has a twelve percent sugar content, regular onions have an eight percent sugar content. Rather, it is mild, lacking the sulfurous compounds that lend pungency and sharpness to other varieties of onion. A product of Corsican seed stock (said originally to have come from Italy), transplanted to the sandy soils of the Walla Walla Valley by a Frenchman, then subjected to many years of selective breeding by the Italian immigrants farming the valley, the Walla Walla sweet onion of today is truly a horticultural marvel. Larger and earlier than regular golden-skin onions, Walla Walla sweets can be eaten raw out of hand and are superb for hamburgers and salads. They are not, however, the best all-around onion. The water content is extremely high, making them difficult to store for any length of time. Their mildness and juiciness also make them particularly unsuitable for sautéing, because they turn to soup in the pan and become bland with prolonged cooking.

Season

Mid-June through mid-August.

Selection

Walla Walla sweets are usually in good condition, but do look for firm specimens without any apparent bruising. Also shop at a market with high turnover and if possible select onions that feel cold to the touch. Time and heat work against these very perishable onions.

Storage

These onions are so moist that they spoil easily. The best you can do is to keep them separate from one another, perhaps wrapped individually in paper, in a cool, dry area such as a garage.

Preparation

Just skin them. I find this easiest to do under hot running water that loosens the skin enough so that the point of a paring knife can be slipped under at the shoot end. Pry the skin off in two or three large pieces. Or if you prefer, drop the onions into boiling water for fifteen seconds, remove, flush with cold water, then slip the skins off.

Cooking

Why bother? These onions are so good raw that there is no point in contending with their many disadvantages when cooked. If you must do something to use up your fifty-pound bag of Walla Walla sweets, try them pickled, marinated, in chutneys or relishes, or in salads. If you want them hot, try them combined with other vegetables in a quick stir-fry. This cooking method works because there is not enough time for the moisture to escape. If you really like onions, eat them out of hand, like apples.

Walla Walla Sweets Recipes

Petrale Sole with Walla Walla Sweets and Granny Smith Apples, *page 221*

Salmon in Parchment with Corn, Walla Walla Sweets, and Tomatoes, *page 116*

Summer Vegetable Stir-Fry with Garlic, Ginger, and Walnuts, *page 134*

Fresh Herbs

Summertime would not be the same in the Northwest without an abundance of fresh herbs. Gardens are overflowing with mint, lemon verbena, tarragon, purple sage, and rosemary, all so easy to grow and mostly perennial too. Not everyone has a large garden space to dedicate to culinary necessities but even a couple of half whiskey barrels filled with fertile, well-aerated soil will produce enough for most kitchens. (If you are growing your own, be sure to nip back or remove stalks that are about to flower. When the plant goes to seed production, foliage growth slacks off.) If gardening is out of the question, grocery stores now have a fairly regular supply of the basics, though they can be ridiculously expensive.

Fresh herbs give such a bright immediacy of taste to otherwise simple dishes that I find them absolutely indispensable for summertime cooking. My favorites, those I love to eat and find most useful in the kitchen, are highlighted in the Recipe Notes below. Bay leaf is not listed, even though it grows well in the Northwest, because the leaves need to be dried before being used. Chervil I do not bother with; it tastes like a cross between parsley and tarragon and I always have plenty of those two on hand.

Season

Many herbs burst forth in early spring; some come on a little later. Most will continue through the first serious frost, usually in October; but some, such as sorrel, rosemary, and mint will produce at least some foliage all winter long.

Selection

Herbs should look as though you have just picked them from the garden. Look for dry, bright, bushy, and sprightly specimens.

Storage

Keep herbs in the refrigerator in tightly sealed plastic bags. Do not rinse them with water until you use them.

Preparation

Rinse and dry just before using. Many herbs need to be stripped from their main stem before being thrown into the pot. If the stem bends easily, it can probably be chopped with the leaves; if it does not, discard it or use it on the grill fire for aromatic smoke.

Cooking

When cooking with fresh herbs, be sure to add them to the dish near the end of the cooking time. The fresh taste and beautiful color disappear completely with prolonged cooking.

In converting a measurement for dried herbs to fresh, use at least three times as much of the fresh herb.

Herb Recipes

Aioli—Basil and Mint Variations, *pages 52–53*
Chilled Mussels with Basil Mint Vinaigrette, *page 210*
Country Autumn Herb Soup, *page 216*
Fresh Ginger Consommé with Sorrel Chiffonnade, *page 37*
Fresh Herb Gnocchi with Tomatoes and Parmesan, *page 139*

Garlic Soup with Sage Leaves and Herb Profiteroles, *page 218*
Garniture of Baby Vegetables, *page 57*
Grilled Lamb Chops with Fresh Thyme and Rhubarb Chutney, *page 54*
Herb-Marinated Grilled Leg of Lamb with Mint Aioli, *page 51*
Hot Sauced Clams with Fresh Thyme, *page 228*
Lacy Zucchini Herb Fritters with Jack Cheese, *page 104*
Tomato Mint Salad with Creamy Herb Dressing, *page 215*
Wheat Germ-Fried Fillet of Trout with Fresh Herbs, *page 47*
see also Recipe Notes, *below*

RECIPE NOTES

BASIL

BASIL AIOLI

Add a generous quantity of fresh basil to a batch of aioli (page 52).

- Make it thick and spread a ¼-inch layer on a fillet of petrale sole, sockeye salmon, or ling cod. Bake until the fish is just done. The sauce lubricates and flavors the fish.
- Thin the aioli somewhat with chicken stock or cream and use it to dress a cold pasta salad.

▲▟▀▲▟▀▲▟▀▲▟▀▲▟▀▲▟▀▲▟▀▲▟▀▲▟▀▲▟▀▲

• Serve the aioli with an assortment of chilled blanched vegetables and poached fish. This is one of the best summertime meals in the world.

PESTO

To make pesto, which can be used for more than adorning pasta, purée 2 packed cups fresh basil leaves, ¾ cup cold-pressed olive oil, ¼ cup pine nuts, walnuts, or hazelnuts, and 4 cloves garlic in a processor until fairly smooth. Add 1 cup grated Parmesan cheese and pulse-chop just to blend. Season to taste with salt and black pepper.

• Swirl it into fresh Yakima Corn Chowder (page 114).
• Add it to a blended mixture of goat cheese and cream cheese and spread on toasted French bread. Heat through.
• Thin it somewhat with oil if necessary and swirl it through a cornbread batter before baking.
• Top an omelet with small dollops of pesto and crumbled feta cheese.

CHILLED MUSSELS WITH BASIL MINT VINAIGRETTE

Steam and chill a few pounds of mussels. Make Basil Mint Vinaigrette (page 210). Pile the mussels in their shells on a platter and drizzle the vinaigrette over them. Marinate for an hour or more.

FUSILLI WITH TOMATOES, BASIL AND ITALIAN FONTINA

Peel, seed, and cut into large dice a few room-temperature tomatoes. Mix with shredded basil, minced garlic, good olive oil, shredded fontina cheese, and salt and pepper to taste. Toss with hot fusilli (corkscrew-shaped pasta) cooked *al dente*.

ROASTED RED PEPPER SALAD WITH BASIL

Roast, peel, and seed several red bell peppers. Cut into lengthwise strips. Toss with a handful of finely shredded fresh basil and Lemon Garlic Vinaigrette (page 359).

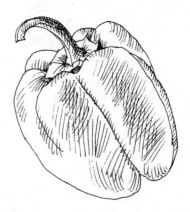

CHIVES

CHIVE BLOSSOM OMELET

Add 2 tablespoons combined minced parsley, chives, and tarragon to 2 to 3 lightly beaten eggs and make an omelet. Pour a little melted butter over the finished omelet and sprinkle with the petals of chive blossoms. Garnish the plate with whole blossoms.

CHIVE BUTTER

Cream ½ cup unsalted butter and add ½ cup minced chives. Season to taste with salt and pepper. Use this butter on potatoes, fish, shellfish, and corn-on-the-cob, or swirl it through bacon-flavored corn or clam chowder.

TOMATO CHIVE COULIS

Braise peeled, seeded, and diced tomatoes in a little unsalted butter and dry red wine until most of the moisture evaporates. Sprinkle on minced chives and finish with a few more tablespoons of butter. Season with salt and pepper to taste. Use as a base for sautéed chicken breasts.

MUSTARD CHIVE BUTTER

Blend ½ cup unsalted butter and add ¼ cup minced chives, ¼ cup minced parsley, 2 tablespoons Dijon mustard, and black pepper to taste. Use about a tablespoon of flavored butter for each serving of grilled poultry, veal, or fish.

CILANTRO

CILANTRO MAYONNAISE

Make 1 cup of mayonnaise using lime juice instead of lemon juice. Add 1 cup of cilantro leaves and purée. Use as the binder for a curried rice and seafood salad.

FRESH FRUIT AND SHRIMP SALAD WITH CILANTRO

Arrange prepared bite-sized pieces of orange, pineapple, banana, and papaya around the outside edges of a salad plate. Heap a small handful of freshly boiled, peeled shrimp in the center and sprinkle with minced cilantro. Drizzle the salad with Honey Lime Vinaigrette (page 359).

CHICKEN CILANTRO SOUP

Strain thoroughly or clarify a good homemade chicken stock and heighten the taste with a few tablespoons of lemon juice and a sprinkling of minced cilantro.

DILL

CARROT VICHYSSOISE WITH DILL

Make a vichyssoise-type soup with half potatoes and half carrots, using a good chicken stock as a base. Chill and finish with heavy cream, freshly grated nutmeg, and minced dill.

MUSTARD DILL SAUCE

Combine equal quantities of sweet, grainy mustard and sour cream and add a generous quantity of fresh dill (about ¼ cup minced dill to 2 cups sauce). This sauce is wonderful with gravlax (salt, sugar, and dill-cured salmon) and cold-smoked fish of all types.

GRILLED SHRIMP AND SCALLOPS WITH DILL SAUCE

Marinate shrimp and scallops for 1 hour in fresh lemon juice, then skewer. Brush with melted butter and grill lightly. Meanwhile, make a lemon-dill *beurre blanc* by reducing ¼ cup lemon juice and 2 tablespoons chopped shallots to a syrup. Over low heat whisk in 12 tablespoons butter and add 1 tablespoon minced dill leaves. Pour the sauce over the cooked brochettes.

GARLIC

WHOLE BAKED GARLIC

As odd as this sounds to people who have not tried it, baked garlic is sweet, earthy, and absolutely delicious. Remove the outer layer of papery skin from several whole heads, leaving the cloves attached to one another. Drizzle the heads with butter and a little chicken stock and bake at 350° for 1 hour, basting as needed. When done, the garlic should be soft enough to be squeezed out of the skins like a paste. Serve as a vegetable accompaniment to grilled meats.

LINGUINI WITH OIL AND GARLIC

Gently heat ¼ cup good olive oil and sauté 6 sliced cloves of garlic until golden. Add ¾ cup chicken stock. Boil 1 pound pasta *al dente* and drain. Put onto a serving platter and pour on the garlic sauce; sprinkle with 1 cup minced parsley and an additional 2 to 6 cloves minced garlic and toss. Grate black pepper and Parmesan cheese over the top. (You may have to hibernate for a few days after eating this, especially if you use the additional raw garlic, but it will seem a small inconvenience for the pleasure of so much flavor.)

GARLIC CONFIT

Separate several heads of garlic without peeling them. Combine with a few sprigs thyme, a few sprigs marjoram, a couple of bay leaves, and 2 cups clarified butter or light olive oil. Cook slowly for 30 minutes until tender. Remove the cloves from the fat and cool. Peel and slice them ⅛-inch thick. Use with chopped tomatoes and minced parsley, minced marjoram, and lemon zest as an accompaniment to fish fillets.

MINT

FRESH MINT RELISH

This may be the Indian equivalent of Mexican salsa. It has much the same consistency and is used extensively in Indian cuisine. Chop 3 cups mint leaves, 2 seeded green chili peppers, and half a small onion. Add 1 teaspoon minced fresh ginger, 1½ teaspoons sugar, 1½ teaspoons lemon juice, 3 tablespoons olive oil, and kosher salt to taste. Serve with vegetable or seafood fritters.

MINT PILAF

Melt 2 tablespoons unsalted butter and lightly sauté 2 chopped green chili peppers, ¼ teaspoon cloves, and ½ teaspoon cinnamon. Add 2 cups long-grain white rice and 2 cups chicken stock. Cover and cook gently for 20 minutes. Uncover and fold in 1 cup minced fresh mint leaves and ½ cup grated fresh coconut (or unsweetened grated coconut from a health food store).

MINT MEATBALLS

Flavor raw meatball mixture with minced mint, garlic, and fresh minced ginger.

SALADE NIÇOISE WITH MINT

A sprinkling of minced mint adds extra sparkle to this classic salad.

OREGANO

TOMATO OREGANO HOT SAUCE

Combine 2 cups peeled, seeded, and chopped tomatoes, a small chopped onion, 3 seeded and chopped jalapeño peppers, and 3 tablespoons minced oregano. Season to taste with kosher salt and black pepper. Serve cold with warm tortilla chips.

STUFFED MUSHROOMS WITH OREGANO

Flavor a mixture of bread crumbs, sautéed minced garlic and mushroom stems, minced parsley, grated mozzarella, grated Parmesan, and olive oil with a generous quantity of minced oregano. Stuff mushroom caps and bake.

PARSLEY

CREAM OF PARSLEY SOUP

To make a standard 6-cup, *roux*-based soup that may be flavored in a number of ways and with a variety of fresh herbs, melt 3 tablespoons butter, add 3 tablespoons flour, and cook this *roux* together without browning it for at least 2 minutes. Slowly whisk in 4 cups chicken stock and 2 cups cream and continue to whisk the mixture while bringing it to a simmer. For a Cream of Parsley Soup, add 1 tablespoon minced savory and 2 cups minced parsley. Heat through and sprinkle with grated nutmeg.

FILLET OF SOLE WITH PARSLEY

Bread sole fillets and sauté in butter. Just before the fish is done, sprinkle with minced parsley and drizzle with lemon juice.

ROSEMARY

PIZZA MARINARA WITH ROSEMARY

Press pizza dough into a pizza pan and spread evenly with a rosemary-scented marinara sauce. Arrange anchovy fillets in a spoke pattern on the top and space pitted, halved calamata olives around. Arrange rings of green pepper, capers, minced rosemary, and strips of mozzarella cheese on top. Bake.

ROSEMARY-BAKED POTATOES

Cut new potatoes into $\frac{1}{2}$-inch slices and toss with olive oil and kosher salt. Spread out on a baking sheet, sprinkle with minced rosemary, and bake until done.

GREEN BEANS WITH ROSEMARY

This is one of my favorites and is wonderful served with potato gnocchi. Toss cooked green beans with a little olive oil flavored with minced rosemary, minced garlic, and kosher salt and black pepper to taste. May be served hot or chilled.

ROSEMARY BISCUITS

Add minced rosemary to your favorite biscuit or muffin recipe.

WHOLE TROUT WITH ROSEMARY AND FENNEL

Sprinkle the cavity of a trout with kosher salt, black pepper, and minced rosemary. Lay the fish on a piece of buttered foil. Slowly sweat slices of fennel bulb in butter until tender. Tuck a sprig of rosemary into the cavity of the fish and another on top. Arrange the fennel over the fish and drizzle with 1 tablespoon dry white wine. Seal the foil and bake the fish until just done.

SAGE

SAGE CORNBREAD

Flavor buttermilk cornbread with minced sage.

FRIED SAGE

Dredge large sage leaves lightly with flour, then deep-fry for 1 minute. Drain on paper towels and sprinkle with sugar and kosher salt to taste. Use as a garnish.

SORREL

SORREL MAYONNAISE

Blanch 3 cups sorrel for 3 minutes, drain, squeeze out moisture, and chop. Add to 1 cup homemade mayonnaise along with 2 tablespoons minced parsley and 2 tablespoons minced green onion.

TARRAGON

TARRAGON VINAIGRETTE

Combine ¼ cup white wine vinegar, 2 table-spoons minced tarragon, and 1 tablespoon each minced parsley, minced dill leaves, minced chives, and Dijon mustard. Add ¾ cup corn oil and ¼ cup best-quality olive oil and blend.

THYME

COLD-SMOKED SALMON WITH CREAM CHEESE AND THYME

Cream ½ pound cream cheese, 2 tablespoons minced thyme, 1½ tablespoons lemon juice, and kosher salt and white pepper to taste. Divide among ½ pound cold-smoked salmon fillets and roll them up from the short side. Chill and cut into ⅜-inch slices.

TAGLIATELLE WITH PROSCIUTTO AND THYME

Sauce boiled tagliatelle noodles with a combination of butter, reduced cream, shredded prosciutto, minced thyme, Parmesan cheese, and salt and pepper to taste.

GREEK SALAD WITH THYME

Arrange calamata olives, sliced red onions, feta cheese, and sliced tomatoes on individual salad plates. Dress with thyme-scented Lemon Garlic Vinaigrette (page 359).

BUTTERNUT SQUASH PURÉE WITH THYME

Flavor puréed butternut squash with minced thyme. Serve with roasted or grilled meat.

Raspberries

If, in mid-July, you find yourself huddled near the warmth of a wood-burning stove, dismally eyeing the rain through a nearby window and consoling yourself with a bowl of perfect red raspberries floating in cream, you are in one of two places, Washington or Oregon. Only in the Northwest do such extraordinary contradictions occur.

Raspberries, both the red and black varieties, grow best and most prolifically in areas blessed with relatively cool summers. California, with all its glorious sunshine, does not produce berries of the quantity or quality of those that come from the two Northwest states. Washington and Oregon together produce nearly ninety percent of the nation's supply of these highly prized, highly praised berries. Most are the superb red Willamette and Meeker varieties (the latter keeps better). And only on the West Coast, from British Columbia to California, are fresh raspberries—of whatever variety or quality—readily obtainable at moderate cost. Highly perishable, raspberries are air-freighted across the country but the resulting price is prohibitive. A typical retail customer on the East Coast will have difficulty even finding fresh raspberries, let alone affording them.

Even for those of us fortunate enough to live here, raspberry season is regrettably short; although in recent years growers have managed to extend the season into September by planting late-bearing varieties. But because the later berries are considerably more expensive, the best course is to eat as many raspberries as possible during the peak of the season. When the season does end, as all good things must, you may be satiated and ready to move on to blueberries and blackberries.

Season

Too short! Too short! Red raspberries are at their peak from mid-June to mid-August, depending on the weather. Black raspberries are available for most of July. The late-bearing red varieties that are increasingly available can extend the season to mid-September.

Selection

The best raspberries are picked right from the bush at one of the numerous farms in Washington and Oregon where you may pick your own. Pick up a yearly farm guide from your local library. Otherwise shop at a market with high turnover. These berries do not keep well, exposed as they usually are to 70° temperatures. Choose raspberries that look bright, plump, and are uniformly shaped. Stained containers indicate mashed or mushy berries. Watch out for the rain in July; all berries are susceptible to mold when wet.

Storage

Refrigerated immediately upon purchase without washing, raspberries will keep for several days. Drape lightly with plastic wrap or enclose in their container in a paper bag. Do not seal tightly or moisture will form and cause the berries to mold. Left at room temperature, they will barely keep for forty-eight hours.

Preparation

Rinse raspberries gently with cold water. Drain first in a sieve, then on paper towels and do it so, so gently as the berries will fall apart if you are at all rough.

Cooking

Raspberries should be cooked briefly, if at all, to preserve their bright, fruity taste and ravishing color. The seeds are easy to remove: just push the berries through a sieve or put them through a food mill.

Raspberry Recipes

Glazed Ginger Coeur à la Crème with Raspberry Chambord Sauce, *page 148*

RECIPE NOTES

RASPBERRY SOUR CREAM GRATIN

Mound raspberries in individual gratin dishes. Sprinkle with brown sugar to taste. Cover with sour cream, sprinkle generously with brown sugar, and broil very briefly just to begin melting the sugar. A small propane torch does a tidy job of glazing the top; don't laugh, it's a great little tool.

RASPBERRY CUSTARD GRATIN

Proceed as in the above example but use a vanilla-flavored custard sauce rather than the sour cream and white sugar instead of brown.

RASPBERRY VINAIGRETTE

Combine 2 tablespoons raspberry vinegar, 3 tablespoons raspberry jam, 2 teaspoons Dijon mustard, and 3 tablespoons corn oil. Season to taste with kosher salt and plenty of freshly grated black pepper. Use on fruit salads and for glazing grilled chicken breasts.

RASPBERRY JEWEL CHEESECAKE

Top your best cheesecake with fresh whole berries, arranged in concentric circles. Glaze with melted raspberry jelly (or strained raspberry jam) flavored with a little Framboise or Grand Marnier liqueur. If using the latter, you might also want to flavor the crust with orange zest.

RASPBERRY SWIRL CHEESECAKE

Purée raspberries and put them through a strainer to remove the seeds. Bring to a simmer and add a small quantity of cornstarch mixed with a little cold water; bring back to a full simmer, whisking. You want just enough cornstarch thickener to create a raspberry sauce of about the same consistency as the cream cheese mixture. Pour the warm purée into a partially cooked, but not set, cheesecake in a swirling pattern. If the cheesecake is just beginning to set, it will hold the raspberry purée without absorbing it. Continue baking the cheesecake until just set.

RASPBERRIES WITH BALSAMIC VINEGAR

This combination may sound strange but is good nonetheless. Steep a split vanilla bean in balsamic vinegar for several hours and remove.

Then sprinkle the flavored vinegar and plenty of freshly ground black pepper over fresh raspberries.

RASPBERRIES AND CRÈME BRULÉE

Prepare Crème Brulée (page 366) and, just before serving, pour Raspberry Chambord Sauce (page 145) on individual dessert plates, mound a portion of the Crème Brulée in the center, and surround it with whole berries.

RASPBERRY COBBLER

Arrange 6 cups raspberries in a buttered 8- by 10-inch gratin dish. Cut 8 tablespoons unsalted butter into a mixture of 1 cup brown sugar, ¾ cup flour, ½ teaspoon ground coriander, ¼ teaspoon cloves, and ¼ teaspoon white pepper. Sprinkle this mixture over the berries without mixing the two together. Bake at 350° for 35 to 40 minutes, until the top is crisp and golden. Serve warm with vanilla ice cream.

Blueberries

Though blueberries are indigenous to America and were among the first fruits encountered by the early settlers, the blueberry industry is relatively new in Washington and Oregon, having begun about twenty-five or thirty years ago. Although the industry is steadily growing, many farmers are reluctant to grow blueberries because it takes too long to get a blueberry field into full and profitable production. A study conducted by Washington State University in 1980 states that the average blueberry crop does not bear productively until it has been in the field for nine years, at the end of which time the grower would be $9,000 an acre in the red. Blueberry plants are nurtured in nurseries for three years before being planted out and most bushes take between ten and fifteen years to reach maximum production. Consequently the growth that is taking place in the industry is limited to the more established growers, most of whom started in the blueberry business in a small way. Even so, Washington State is still third in the nation in blueberry production. The flavor of blueberries depends on acidic soil and cool summers; the Northwest region has plenty of both.

Blueberries are a natural convenience food, requiring no pitting, no peeling, no coring. They are ready to use just as they are and may be popped into the mouth one by one, served with cream, or added to any number of baked goodies. Their color is ravishing; the deep purple-black contrasts irresistibly with strawberries, raspberries, and melon.

Season

From mid-July through September.

Selection

Blueberries can be light or dark blue with a silvery sheen but they should have no reddish tinge when they are fully ripe. They must be fully ripe before being picked. They will not continue to ripen on their own at home. Berries should appear clean and dry. Avoid berries that are soft, watery, dull in color, shriveled, or mushy.

Storage

Always refrigerate blueberries, unwashed and well sealed with plastic wrap. If they are very fresh, they will last for seven to fourteen days.

Preparation

Nothing to do but rinse.

Cooking

I enjoy this berry much better when its flavor is released by a little heat. Many berries suffer at least somewhat with cooking, but not the blueberry. It becomes another entity altogether, richer, fuller, more complex. Throw it into your favorite muffin, pancake or quickbread recipe, or make a sauce, pudding, jam or pie of it. This is a very versatile berry.

Blueberry Recipes

Blueberry Ginger Cheesecake, *page 152*
Blueberry Lemon Gratin, *page 151*
Toasted Hazelnut Blueberry Crumble, *page 150*

Caneberries

No region in America is as blessed with caneberries as is the Northwest. A kaleidoscope of vibrant jewel-toned morsels, ripening in quick succession all summer long, is something we all look forward to with great expectation. Few things taste more seductive, more indulgent, than ripe caneberries. But just what, precisely, is a caneberry? It is a berry that grows on a leafy cane. Caneberries are easy to identify; each one consists of a cluster of small, juice-filled sacs held together by delicate filaments or a soft core. All types of blackberries qualify, from loganberries, boysenberries and marionberries to evergreen blackberries; as do red and black raspberries. These are all commercially grown in western Washington and Oregon and for the adventurous there are more varieties

growing along roadsides, coastal bluffs, and mountain paths: salmonberries, thimbleberries, Himalayan blackberries, dewberries, olallie blackberries, tayberries, and black caps to name only a few. Many of these wild varieties are also available in season from local farmers at the Pike Place Market in Seattle. Some of the more commonly available varieties of blackberry are covered here. Raspberries are extolled in their own section.

BLACKBERRY VARIETIES

Boysenberry

A very large, deep maroon blackberry with large seeds. The flavor is tart and aromatic; the texture is medium-firm. Makes a great pie.

Evergreen Blackberry

A medium-sized, glossy, purple-black berry, with large seeds. The flavor is mild and low in acid. Because of this, these are best combined in pies with brighter tasting berries. A generous squeeze of fresh lemon juice also helps. Texture is firm.

Loganberry

A medium-sized, deep-red blackberry with a high acid flavor. Because of the tartness, loganberries are best combined with sweeter berries for pies or jam. Texture is soft when fully ripe.

Marionberry

A longish, medium-sized blackberry—dark red to black in color with medium-sized seeds. An aromatic berry with a lot of flavor, it has a nice balance of acid to sugar, and a medium-firm texture. Great for pies.

Olallie Blackberry

A medium to large blackberry, slimmer than the boysenberry but nearly the same deep maroon color. When fully ripe, olallies are sweet and full-flavored.

Black Cap

A cross between a raspberry and a wild mountain blackberry that looks like a tiny black raspberry. Available seasonally at Pike Place Market.

Tayberry

A recent cross between the raspberry and the blackberry, with the best traits of each parent. Local growers at Pike Place Market supply these delectable berries in season.

Season

Seasons for caneberries overlap considerably and, depending on the weather, can begin anywhere from mid-June for loganberries, mid-

July for marionberries, to mid-August for evergreen blackberries. Seasons usually last from four to six weeks.

Selection

Caneberries are extremely perishable. Buy them very, very fresh or pick them yourself. Berries should be plump with a bright, clean appearance. Overripe berries are generally dull in color, mushy, and oozing juice. Avoid underripe berries as well; these have green, pale or off-color drupelets (the individual compartments that constitute the berry). Berries that have their green caps intact were picked before reaching maturity. If you are picking them yourself, layer them in shallow containers; never stack them more than four inches deep.

Storage

Refrigerate immediately after buying or picking them. Do not rinse them and cover the berries only lightly with paper or perforated plastic to prevent moisture from accumulating. Some cooks like to lay the berries out singly on paper towel-lined cookied sheets, covered with plastic wrap. I think that the less you touch them the better. Under the best conditions, berries will keep for only one or two days.

Preparation

Caneberries have the most flavor at room temperature, so you might think of removing them from the refrigerator an hour before serving. Rinse with cold water just before eating and drain very gently on paper towels.

Cooking

Little or no cooking is best although many blackberry varieties make fine pies; just be sure to taste the variety you have and balance its flavor with sugar, lemon juice, or other sweeter or tarter berries if necessary. In using a cornstarch thickener when making pie, it is difficult sometimes to compensate accurately for the juiciness of a particular batch of caneberries. It really does not matter that your pie is a little runny; it will taste good.

Caneberry Recipes

Mint Soufflé with Huckleberry Sauce, *page 154*

Tangy Lime Soufflé with Blackberry Lime Sauce, *page 153*

see also Raspberries, *pages 89–92*

Stone Fruits

A stone fruit is defined by Webster's as a *drupe;* a drupe in turn is defined as a "fleshy fruit, such as a peach, plum or cherry, usually having a single hard stone that encloses a seed." To these examples we can add apricots and nectarines. *Tree-ripened* is a phrase that has real meaning in the Northwest. Because most of the stone fruits are produced in relatively small quantities (when compared with production in California) and sold locally to the fresh market, they are generally left on the tree until full maturity is reached. Even cherries, of which more are produced in Washington than anywhere else in the nation, are left to ripen on the tree, shipping considerations aside. Because grocery stores typically rely on out-of-state growers (who must pick the fruit before it ripens so that they can ship it), many people are genuinely surprised when they first taste a tree-ripened stone fruit. Fortunately local growers abound and, with the various farm guides that are published each year and made available through the library system, are easy to find. A jaunt to the eastern realms of Washington and Oregon, where most of the production takes place, provides a great excuse for a lovely one-day excursion, and is well worth the effort.

The terms *clingstone, semifreestone,* and *freestone* are used to describe how easily the stone can be removed. In clingstone fruit, the flesh adheres so tenaciously to the stone that it has to be cut away, thus ruining the appearance. Semifreestone varieties can be cut in half along the seam line, then twisted open to reveal one half holding the stone. Usually the stone is then easily removed with the tip of a paring knife. In freestones, the stone is easily slipped away from the flesh with the fingers or a knife after the fruit has been cut in half.

Ripening

Stone fruits that are not completely ripe can be brought to perfection at home by enclosing them (spread out singly, not on top of one another) in a paper bag. The resulting concentration of released ethylene gas will promote fast and uniform ripening. Check the bag every day and then refrigerate ripened fruit to keep it in perfect condition.

APRICOTS

Season

Mid-July through mid-August.

Selection

The Moorpark, Perfection, Rival, Goldrich, Tilton, and Patterson varieties are all grown commercially in the rich, volcanic valleys of eastern Washington. Grocery stores do not always indicate which variety is being sold, so ask and get to know the subtle differences in flavor of the many types. The Moorpark is perhaps the richest tasting, the Perfection the most intense, and the Rival the most delicately balanced and mildest. Apricots must be left to ripen to a certain magic point on the tree. Otherwise they will not continue the process in the fruit bowl at home. They will shrivel and shrink instead. Ripe apricots are beautifully golden and quite soft; gentle pressure with your thumb should meet with little resistance.

Storage

Apricots should be left out at room temperature until they are fully ripe, that is, soft but not mushy. Store ripe apricots in the refrigerator in a sealed plastic bag for no longer than two days.

Preparation

For most recipes, the thin, velvety skin is not removed. But if you need to do this, immerse the apricots in boiling water for twenty to thirty seconds, remove and put into cold water, then slip off the skins. Cut in half with a small paring knife and remove the stone.

Cooking

Apricots are delicious raw and cooked. Cook them very briefly unless you want a mush or a purée; they are soft to begin with.

CHERRIES

Season

Of the sweet cherries the Bings ripen first and are followed shortly by the Lamberts. The sweet cherry season extends from mid-June through July. Pie cherries are usually available from the first of July through mid-August.

Selection

Many varieties of sweet cherries are grown in the Northwest. The most important commercially are the Lambert and the Bing. Both are big, full-flavored cherries, the Lambert having a more intense taste, a little more acid tang, a firmer texture, and a more elongated shape. Other sweet cherries include Deacons, Burlats, Rainiers, Chinooks, Black Tartarians, Vans, and Republicans. Sour cherries, or pie cherries as they are usually called, are grown on both sides of the Cascade mountains and are easiest to find at local farms and roadside stands and at Pike Place Market. Cherries are fully ripe when they are picked so ripeness is not usually a problem at selection time. Look for plump, firm, and shiny cherries with the stems attached. Pass over cherries with open cuts, bruises, or shriveling stems.

Storage

Refrigeration with a high humidity setting is best for cherries but they should not be stored wet. Store them, unwashed in a plastic bag. The flavor will be more complex if the fruit is eaten at room temperature, so remove cherries from the refrigerator an hour or so before serving.

Preparation

Nothing to do but remove the pit—for which a cherry pitter is a necessity.

Cooking

Sweet cherries are best eaten raw or at most just gently warmed. Pie cherries need to be sweetened and fully cooked.

NECTARINES

Season

Mid-August through mid-September.

Selection

A nectarine is simply a smooth-skinned peach. It is usually a bit smaller and has a sweeter taste and a more distinctive aroma. Commercial varieties include Redgold, the most common, Early Sun Grand, Flavortop, Fantasia, Freedom, Sunglo, and Supreme Red. When selecting nectarines, choose firm, plump specimens that yield slightly to the touch along the seam line. Hard, soft, or shriveled fruit should be passed over. Nectarines will shrivel rather than ripen off the tree if they are picked prematurely. Unlike some other fruits, nectarines and peaches stop developing sweetness once removed from the tree. Use your nose; a sweet smell indicates ripe and luscious tasting fruit.

Storage

Nectarines will soften, without getting any sweeter, in two or three days if left at room temperature. If they are already ripe, store in the coldest part of your refrigerator, sealed in a plastic bag.

Preparation

Nectarines can be peeled in the same way as peaches if desired, though their skin is not fuzzy and is not objectionable for most dishes. To pit, cut the fruit in half along the seam. Open, pulling one side away from the stone, then lift the stone out with the point of a paring knife. This works if the nectarine is very ripe; if it is not, the stone clings mercilessly. Then, I find it easiest to cut the fruit in wedges off the stone. Sprinkle cut nectarines with lemon juice to prevent discoloration.

Cooking

Nectarines are good raw or fully cooked.

PEACHES

Season

Early July for Early Redhavens to early October for Standard Elbertas and J. H. Hales.

Selection

There are many, many varieties to choose from: Early Redhaven, Standard Redhaven, Flavorcrest, Regina, Redglobe, Roza, Suncrest, Flamecrest, Hale, Early Elberta, Angelus, Standard Elberta, and J. H. Hale are among the more common. Regardless of variety, peaches should be firm, plump, well-formed, and slightly soft along the seam. Hard, soft, green, bruised, or shriveled fruit should be avoided.

Storage

Peaches should be stored at a cold temperature with high humidity. Refrigerate sealed in a plastic bag. Cut peaches should be coated with lemon juice, sealed in plastic wrap, and refrigerated to prevent discoloration.

Preparation

To remove the fuzzy skin, submerge whole peaches in boiling water for twenty to thirty seconds, remove, put into cold water to stop the heat from cooking the peach, then slip off the skin.

Cooking

Peaches are great raw or cooked. If the peach is not quite ripe, poaching in a sweetened liquid softens the fruit to succulence.

PLUMS AND PRUNES

Season

Plums and prunes ripen from early August through early September.

Selection

Plums range in color from green, to yellow, to red, to purple, to black. The Friar, the President, the Empress, and the Yakima are the most important commercially but the delectable Damson and Green Gage plums are also available from small growers. Prunes are a type of European plum with an extra-high sugar content. The Italian prune plums are commercially most important. Ripe plums and prunes should yield at the stem end to gentle pressure. There should however be no brownish discoloration or shriveling.

Storage

Put plums into a plastic bag and store in the refrigerator. If they are very firm, leave them at room temperature for no more than a day to soften.

Preparation

Plums have skins of varying tenderness and tartness but it is best to leave the skin on when cooking to show off the best color and flavor. Remove the pit by cutting the plum in half along the seam line, then slip the paring knife under the pit and pry it away from the flesh. If the plum is ripe, this should be easy to do.

Cooking

In general, all plums other than prune plums are best eaten raw; prune plums cook beautifully. Poaching plums to complete tenderness takes between seven and ten minutes.

Stone Fruit Recipes

Chinese Barbecued Duck, Peach, and Toasted Walnut Salad, *page 214*

Iced Cauliflower Soup with Apricot Cream, *page 115*

Spiced Peach Crunch, *page 150*

Strawberries

If you ask ten people at random to name their favorite berry, eight of them will say, "strawberries of course." Who is to argue? In the height of Northwest strawberry season, it is hard to imagine anything tasting better than these juicy, incredibly sweet, powerfully flavorful berries. They are simply remarkable. But what of the berries shipped to our markets from elsewhere in early spring and even midwinter? The name for these should be changed from strawberry, which is very misleading, to mirageberry. They look like strawberries, but when you put them in your mouth they disappear without eliciting any response from the taste buds. Strawberries seem to benefit most from the cooler climate of the Northwest. Our local varieties are chosen not so much for their durability in shipping but for their flavor. They are usually not as large or as glamorous looking as out-of-state strawberries but their intense red color is a near guarantee that they were picked fully ripe and will taste as nature intended.

Season

Commercial strawberry growers have timed their selections to ripen at about the same time that kids are released from school, thus insuring themselves an adequate supply of pickers. So the commercial season begins around the first of June, depending on the weather, and ends in mid-July. Gardeners can extend the season considerably by planting continual and late-bearing varieties.

Selection

Northwest strawberry varieties are more perishable than those shipped in from out of state. They are very juicy and will turn to mush if handled roughly. Look for bright red berries with no signs of oozing. Avoid shriveled berries or any with dry, browning stems. The fragrance of ripe berries should be discernible. Pick them yourself if at all possible or buy them from a local grower. Above all, make sure that you are purchasing Northwest berries. Grocery stores sometimes carry California berries even when local berries are available.

Storage

Refrigerate strawberries, covered with plastic wrap, as soon as you get them home. Do not wash or hull them. If they are very fresh, they will keep from three to five days.

Preparation

Rinse strawberries under cold running water, then remove the stem and hull in one operation. The easiest way I have found to do this is to use a curved grapefruit knife. Insert the knife along the edge of the stem, then change the angle somewhat and lift it out along with the stem and hull.

Cooking

There is strawberry jam and strawberry sauce and even strawberry soup, but if you really want strawberries at their best, eat them raw.

Strawberry Recipes

Shrimp and Strawberry Salad with Honey Mint Vinaigrette, *page 33*
Strawberry-Gin Sauce, *page 63*
Rhubarb-Strawberry Sorbet, *page 63*
Crimson Rhubarb Mousse with Strawberry-Gin Sauce, *page 63*
Rhubarb-Strawberry Parfait, *page 25*
see also Recipe Notes, *below*

RECIPE NOTES

FRESH STRAWBERRIES:
FRENCH METHOD

On each individual serving plate, arrange two small custard cups, one containing ice water, the other 1 tablespoon pure maple syrup. Position a handful of fresh strawberries (uncleaned and unhulled) around the edge of the plate. Guests then grasp each berry by its stem, swish in water to clean, dip in syrup, and eat.

FRESH STRAWBERRIES: AMERICAN METHOD

Arrange fresh strawberries, cleaned but not hulled, on an attractive platter or in a clear glass bowl. Accompany the berries with separate bowls of granulated sugar and sweetened sour cream. Guests help themselves from the communal bowls. Strawberries may also be served in this way with brown sugar and crème fraîche.

STRAWBERRY CRÈME BRULÉE

Serve Crème Brulée (page 366) with crushed fresh strawberries.

STRAWBERRIES IN WINE

Steep whole berries in champagne, red wine, port, or sherry. Serve with a spoon.

STRAWBERRIES WITH ORANGE

Sweeten ripe berries with orange juice to taste, add a splash of dark rum and a teaspoon of grated orange peel.

STRAWBERRIES AND HONEY

Serve berries drizzled with a flavorful wild honey.

CHOCOLATE STRAWBERRIES

Dip whole berries into tempered dark chocolate and let them dry. Grasp the stems to eat. Or serve whole berries with chocolate fondue.

STRAWBERRIES WITH LIQUEUR

Serve whole berries, hulled or unhulled, sprinkled with a few tablespoons of Grand Marnier, Triple Sec, Cointreau, Amaretto, Framboise, or Crème de Cassis Liqueur, or cognac. Sweeten the berries first with sugar if needed.

STRAWBERRY FOOL

Sweeten 1 pint sliced strawberries to taste with sugar. Make a strawberry purée following the directions for the strawberry variation of Raspberry Chambord Sauce on page 145, using a strawberry liqueur, such as Framboise, or Grand Marnier liqueur instead of the Chambord. Whip 1 cup cream to soft peaks and sweeten with 2 tablespoons powdered sugar. Stir in 2 tablespoons Grand Marnier liqueur, then gradually beat in 1 quart of French vanilla ice cream, beating until the mixture is fluffy but not melted. Freeze for half an hour or more. In tall parfait glasses, alternate layers of strawberry purée, fresh sliced strawberries, and the ice cream mixture, ending with sliced berries. Serve immediately.

Ellen's Famous Dungeness Crab Dip

Serves 4.

I hesitate to include this in a collection of seasonal recipes relying strictly on fresh, unprocessed ingredients, but it is so good! I always eat more than my share when my mother-in-law, Ellen Bradley, offers it at her seaside home in Birch Bay, Washington. Where she lives, the crab cannot get any fresher. Her husband, Frank, takes his boat out into the bay each morning to check the crab pots, then brings in the catch to specially built underwater holding cages, thus assuring an abundant supply all summer long.

Though crab must be impeccably fresh to produce the desired result here, the other ingredients are supermarket staples. Make lots; everybody loves this.

8 ounces cream cheese
2 tablespoons cocktail sauce
2 tablespoons red pickle relish
1 cup fresh Dungeness crab meat
　　Crostini (slices of French bread
　　　　brushed with olive oil and freshly
　　　　minced garlic and toasted on both
　　　　sides)

Whip the cream cheese until light, fluffy, and smooth. Mix in the cocktail sauce and relish. Fold in the crab meat. Serve with crostini.

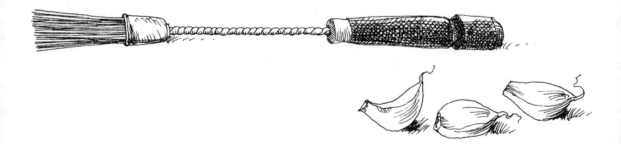

Lacy Zucchini Herb Fritters with Jack Cheese

Makes about 2 dozen fritters.

Fritters make such fine appetizers that I have developed a treasure trove of variations over the years. This one has a few more herbs than usual and a good measure of cheese.

1 cup flour
¾ cup plus 2 tablespoons cold chicken
    stock
2 eggs
1 teaspoon coarse salt
½ teaspoon black pepper
6 small zucchini (about 1½ pounds),
    ends trimmed, then shredded
½ cup minced parsley
¼ cup minced fresh mint
¼ cup minced fresh chives
½ cup grated Monterey Jack cheese
¼ cup grated Parmesan cheese
    Corn oil for deep-frying

Combine the flour, stock, eggs, salt, and pepper in a small bowl and whisk to smooth.

In a large bowl, combine the zucchini, parsley, mint, chives, and both cheeses. Add the batter and mix well.

In a deep saucepan or deep-fryer, heat at least 2 inches of corn oil to 350°. Spoon the batter by tablespoonfuls into the oil in a sweeping motion to create a thinish lacelike fritter and fry until golden brown, about 1½ minutes. Remove with a slotted spoon and drain on paper towels. Serve right away.

Marinated Garden Salad

Serves 8 to 12.

This five-bean salad is always popular at casual summertime picnics and hamburger feeds. Its kaleidoscope of color and tangy sweetness makes even those who avoid vegetables come back for more.

½ cup dried white navy beans
½ cup dried black beans
1 cup fresh wax beans
1 cup fresh green beans, cut into 1-
  inch lengths
1 cup fresh shell or fava beans
1 medium-sized mild onion (preferably
  a Walla Walla sweet), cut into ½-
  inch dice
1 medium-sized green bell pepper,
  cored, seeded, and cut into ½-
  inch squares
1 medium-sized red bell pepper, cored,
  seeded, and cut into ½-inch
  squares
1 medium-sized zucchini, stemmed
  and cut into ½-inch cubes
1 cup apple cider vinegar
2 cups sugar
½ cup corn oil

Wash the dried white and black beans carefully, removing any unsavory bits and pieces of bean or foreign material. Add the rinsed beans to 10 cups of boiling water. Boil for 2 minutes,

remove from the heat, cover, and soak for between 1 and 12 hours (the longer the soak, the better the final appearance of the beans).

Drain and rinse the soaked beans and put them into a large pot with enough water to cover. Simmer gently, partially covered, until tender but not falling apart, about 40 minutes. Remove from the heat and drain off any unabsorbed liquid. Cool.

In a large pot of boiling water, blanch the various fresh beans separately until just tender-crisp. Remove with a wire skimmer as they are done and refresh under cold water.

In a large mixing bowl, combine the cooked and cooled dried beans with the fresh beans and gently toss in the onion, green and red bell pepper, and zucchini.

In a saucepan, mix the cider vinegar with the sugar and oil and bring to a simmer. Remove from the heat, let the mixture cool a bit, then pour it over the salad. Season to taste with salt and pepper and marinate the salad in the refrigerator overnight. This salad will keep for several days. Toss gently just before serving.

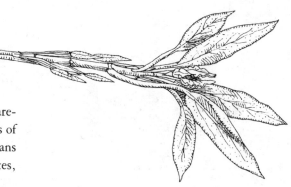

Baby Reds with Oregon Blue and Bacon

Serves 6.

Here is a potato salad with a difference. On a hot evening it makes a satisfying light meal; rich and creamy with some real flavor. Or take it on a picnic outing.

2 pounds baby red potatoes
½ pound bacon
1 medium-sized onion, chopped
¼ cup (2 ounces) Oregon Blue cheese, finely crumbled
¼ teaspoon cayenne pepper
½ teaspoon freshly ground black pepper
Coarse salt
Approximately 1 cup Green Onion Mayonnaise (page 348)
Lemon juice (optional)

Steam the potatoes until done. Cool, then halve or quarter them, depending on their size, to yield bite-sized chunks.

While the potatoes are steaming, sauté the bacon in a skillet until evenly crisp. Remove to paper towels to drain and pour off all but 3 tablespoons of the bacon fat. Sauté the onion in the fat for 5 minutes or so, just to sweeten and soften a bit.

In a large bowl, combine the cooled potatoes, crumbled bacon, onions with bacon fat, and the cheese. Toss gently to combine, then sprinkle on the cayenne, black pepper, and salt to taste.

Fold the mayonnaise (you may not need to use all of it) gently into the potato mixture with a rubber spatula and season to taste with more salt, pepper, and lemon juice if needed. Chill for an hour or two before serving.

Cold-Smoked Salmon, Potato, and Green Bean Salad

Serves 4 to 6.

Another potato salad with a difference. This is modeled after the Spanish potato salad called ensaladilla rusa *as described by Penelope Casas in her illuminating book,* The Foods and Wines of Spain. *In order for the salad to hold its shape properly, be sure that each ingredient is thoroughly dried and that the mayonnaise is quite thick.*

1 pound Red Pontiac, "new" potatoes, peeled and diced
1 tablespoon olive oil
2 tablespoons lemon juice
¼ pound cold-smoked salmon, chopped (high quality hot-smoked salmon may also be used)
1 cup sliced green beans, blanched until tender-crisp, then dried with paper towels
1 red bell pepper, roasted, cored, and diced, then dried with paper towels
2 thinly sliced green onions
2 tablespoons minced fresh dillweed
2 tablespoons small capers, drained
½ cup thick homemade mayonnaise flavored with mustard and lemon
Coarse salt
Freshly ground black pepper

Put the potatoes in a pan, cover with water, and bring to a boil. Cook until just tender. Remove, drain well, and dry with paper towels. Toss the warm potatoes with olive oil and lemon juice.

Combine the potatoes with the cold-smoked salmon, blanched green beans, red bell pepper, green onions, dillweed, and capers. Mix in the mayonnaise. Season to taste with salt and pepper. Chill thoroughly.

Scoop out onto a large platter and shape the sides into an oval. Flatten and smooth the top by running a rubber spatula back and forth over the surface to expose the mosaic of vegetables just underneath the mayonnaise.

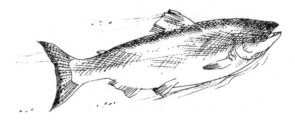

Italian Sausage, Red Pepper, and Couscous Salad

Serves 6 to 8.

Making couscous is perhaps something of a chore but the result is certainly worth the effort (see page 356). Precooked couscous grain may be used here. Just follow the directions on the package. If you have a cherry pitter, use it to remove the olive pits or try a quick and easy trick I picked up by watching a chef through the window at Campagne in Pike Place Market: hit each olive lightly with a mallet, then simply pry out the pit with your fingers. This recipe may be made a day ahead.

COUSCOUS

1 cup cracked wheat
1 tablespoon unsalted butter
½ teaspoon coarse salt

1 pound best-quality hot Italian
    sausages, pricked well
1 cup homemade chicken stock
    (page 345)
2 medium-sized red bell peppers,
    cored, deribbed, and cut into
    ¼-inch dice
1 medium-sized green bell pepper,
    cored, deribbed, and cut into
    ¼-inch dice

2 or 3 green onions, thinly sliced
½ cup minced parsley
½ cup calamata olives, pitted,
    halved, and quartered
    lengthwise
½ cup premium green olives,
    pitted, halved, and slivered
    lengthwise
2 tablespoons small capers, drained

VINAIGRETTE

3 tablespoons white wine vinegar
½ teaspoon coarse salt
    Freshly ground black pepper
2 cloves minced garlic
1 teaspoon Dijon mustard
4 tablespoons cold-pressed olive oil
5 tablespoons corn oil

Prepare the cracked wheat, butter and salt according to couscous directions on page 356. Cool completely.

In a large skillet, begin cooking the pricked sausage in the chicken stock, turning the sausage occasionally. When the stock has evaporated, the sausage should have released enough of its own fat to start browning. Turn the sausages and brown until they are well glazed on all sides and are cooked through, about 10 minutes. (To get an even glaze on the sausages, drain the fat, add 2 more tablespoons stock to the pan and then shake the pan to roll the sausages in the deglazing liquid.) Drain on paper towels and cool.

Slice the sausages into ¼-inch thick disks and combine them with the cooled *couscous,* red and green bell peppers, green onions, parsley, calamata olives, green olives, and capers.

Prepare the vinaigrette by whisking salt and pepper to taste into white wine vinegar. When the salt has dissolved, add the garlic, mustard, olive oil and corn oil and whisk to emulsify. Pour the vinaigrette over the salad and toss gently to combine. Chill for at least 1 hour, toss again to distribute the ingredients evenly and serve.

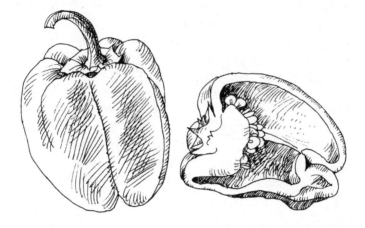

Iced Cucumber Soup with Fresh Mint

Serves 4 to 6.

There is something incredibly refreshing about the taste and smell of fresh cucumbers. Combined with mint, they make a delicious soup, especially good on a hot day. If you have spearmint in your garden, use it, though the fuzzy apple mint has perhaps the finest flavor. For this soup, the mint must be fresh rather than dried.

3 tablespoons unsalted butter
1 medium onion, minced
1 garlic clove, minced
3 medium cucumbers, peeled, seeded, and finely chopped
3 tablespoons flour
2 cups homemade chicken stock (page 345)
2 tablespoons minced fresh mint
1 cup half-and-half
1 cup unflavored yogurt
  Coarse salt
  Freshly ground white pepper
  Fresh lemon juice

GARNISH
   Thinly sliced cucumber with skin

Melt the butter in a large saucepan and sauté the onion and garlic over medium-low heat until softened but not browned, about 20 minutes.

Add the chopped cucumber and cook slowly for 10 minutes. Stir in the flour and continue to cook for 2 minutes.

Add the stock and bring the soup to a simmer. Reduce the heat and simmer until the cucumber is well softened, about 15 minutes, stirring occasionally to keep the bottom of the pan from scorching.

Purée the soup in a processor. Pour into a bowl, let it cool to room temperature, then add the fresh mint. Cover and chill.

Just before serving, stir in the half-and-half and yogurt and combine well. Season to taste with salt, pepper, and drops of lemon juice. Garnish each serving with a slice of cucumber. Serve well chilled.

Honey Tomato Bisque with Basil and Marjoram

Serves 4 to 6.

What better combination than Northwest honey, vine-ripened tomatoes, fresh herbs, and cream? Unlike many other cream of tomato soups, this one has all of the texture left in—to good effect. As for the honey, there are so many local varieties to choose from, I'll leave it to you. But use a good quality, raw, unfiltered honey. Choose from Oregon huckleberry or cherry blossom, or Washington wild blackberry, pear blossom, or snoberry, to name only a few of those available. Note that even though heavy cream is more stable than half-and-half or milk when it is boiled, it may react by curdling if a lot of acid is present; thus, just to be safe we do not boil the cream in a soup like this one. Cornbread or cornsticks are very good with this soup.

4 tablespoons unsalted butter
1 medium-sized onion, finely diced
2 large shallots, minced
2 cloves garlic, minced
4 tablespoons flour
2 pounds vine-ripened tomatoes, peeled, seeded, and diced, with their liquid (or an equal quantity of good-quality canned tomatoes)
2 cups homemade chicken stock (page 345)

1 tablespoon raw, unfiltered honey
1 cup cream
2 tablespoons fresh basil, finely shredded
1 tablespoon fresh marjoram, minced
Coarse salt
Freshly ground black pepper
1 green onion, green part only, minced
1 tablespoon Italian parsley, minced

GARNISH
Cold sour cream
Finely shredded basil
Finely shredded green onion

Melt the butter in a large, nonreactive saucepan and add onions and shallots. Cook slowly, partially covered, until tender but not brown, about 15 minutes. Add the garlic and continue to cook, stirring, for an additional minute. Sprinkle on the flour and cook for 2 to 3 minutes, stirring constantly.

Add the tomatoes, chicken stock, and honey. Cook slowly for an additional 15 minutes, then add the cream. Heat through but do not boil. Stir in the fresh basil and marjoram. Season to taste with salt and pepper.

Stir in the green onion and parsley just before serving. Garnish each bowl with a dollop of cold sour cream and a sprinkling of shredded basil and green onion.

Red Bell Pepper and Fennel Soup

Serves 6.

A late summer soup when the seasons for fennel and red bell pepper happily coincide. The combination is bright in color and taste; a real winner.

1 medium-sized fennel bulb (3 cups chopped)
2 tablespoons olive oil
1 large onion, chopped (2 cups chopped)
2 teaspoons minced garlic
6 red bell peppers, cored, seeded, deribbed, and chopped (8 cups chopped)
4 cups homemade chicken stock (page 345)
  Coarse salt
¼ teaspoon cayenne pepper, or more to taste
  Freshly ground white pepper
2 teaspoons lemon juice

GARNISH
    Sprigs of fennel leaves

To prepare the fennel, trim the stalks off at the point at which they meet the bulb. Remove any dry or pulpy outer layers. Cut in half through the core and remove the core with a small paring knife. Roughly chop the remain-ing fennel. Tear off a handful of the feathery leaves and reserve for the garnish.

Heat the olive oil in a large saucepan or stovetop casserole and "sweat" the onions over medium-low heat until well softened but not browned. Stir in the garlic, red bell pepper, and chopped fennel and continue cooking for about 5 minutes without browning.

Add the chicken stock, bring to a simmer, and cook until the vegetables are very tender. Put through a food mill, return to a clean pot and season to taste with salt, cayenne, white pepper, and lemon juice. Heat just to a sim-mer. Do not try to keep hot for a long time or the fresh taste will be lost.

To serve, garnish each bowl with a sprig of fennel leaves.

RED BELL PEPPER AND
FENNEL GAZPACHO

Red Bell Pepper and Fennel Soup is so tasty hot that I could not resist adding a cold variation. Here the soup is chilled and then mixed with diced cucumber, red bell pepper, and apple.

Red Bell Pepper and Fennel Soup (see above)

GARNISH
1 medium-sized cucumber, peeled, seeded, and diced

1 medium-sized red bell pepper, cored,
    seeded, deribbed, and diced
1 Granny Smith apple, halved, cored,
    and diced

ACCOMPANIMENT
    Crostini (page 103)

Thoroughly chill the soup, increasing the seasonings a bit because it is to be served cold.

    Just before serving, stir in the diced cucum-
ber, bell pepper, and apple. Garnish with fennel leaves as above. Accompany each bowl with
a few crostini.

Corn and Chili Pepper Soup

Serves 6.

*This is one of my favorite summertime corn chowders.
It is spicy, creamy, and rich with the sweetness of
corn just off the cob. If you like cilantro, you might
include a swirl of Cilantro Butter just before serving. Otherwise leave as is or use Parsley and Chive
Butter instead. Fresh corn is essential; the soup just
does not taste the same when made with canned or
frozen corn. I am always very careful when I make
this soup to preserve the color of the chili and bell
peppers. Their vivid green diminishes with time, so
if you must make the soup ahead, sauté a little extra*

*bell pepper at the last minute and stir it in to
brighten the soup.*

2 tablespoons unsalted butter
1 medium onion, chopped
4 ears fresh corn (3½ cups kernels)
1 green bell pepper, seeded and chopped
3 jalapeño peppers, seeded and chopped
1 pound tomatoes, peeled, seeded, and
    chopped
3 cups homemade chicken stock (page
    345)
1 cup cream

GARNISH
    Cilantro Butter, page 362 (optional)
    or Parsley and Chive Butter, page
    362 (optional)

Melt the butter in a soup pot and cook the
onion over medium-low heat until softened
but not browned.

    Holding the corn upright use a small paring
knife to scrape the kernels from the cob with
brisk downward strokes.

    Add the corn, bell pepper, chili peppers,
and tomatoes to the onion mixture and cook
briefly, about 2 minutes. Pour in the chicken
stock and simmer lightly just long enough to
meld the flavors but not so long as to lessen
the color of the vegetables, about 3 minutes.
Pour in the cream, bring just to the simmer,
and season to taste with salt and pepper.

    Serve with a dollop of Cilantro Butter or
Parsley Chive Butter if desired.

Yakima Corn Chowder

Serves 6 to 8.

This delectable, creamy chowder came about when I lived for a few years in the inland, desert climate of the Yakima Valley and discovered the sublime pleasure of corn rushed from the garden to a kettle already boiling in the kitchen. With a surplus of corn and a shortage of clams, this soup was the inevitable result.

Fresh corn is really essential for this recipe; frozen corn seldom has the delicate sweetness necessary.

> ½ pound bacon
> 2 large onions, chopped (1½ pounds)
> 1½ pounds (10 to 12) small Red
>   Pontiac "new" potatoes, scrubbed
>   and diced
> 6 cups homemade chicken stock (page
>   345)
> 2 medium-sized carrots, peeled and
>   diced
> 2 medium-sized celery stalks, diced
> 4 ears fresh corn (3½ cups kernels)
> 2 cups cream (or half and half)

GARNISH
>   Parsley Mint Butter, page 362

In a soup pot, sauté the bacon until crisp. Remove, drain on paper towels, and crumble. Leave 4 tablespoons bacon fat in the pot. Add the onions to the bacon fat and cook slowly until softened but not browned, about 20 minutes.

Add the potatoes and the stock, cover partially, and simmer gently until the potatoes are almost tender, about 15 to 20 minutes. Add the carrots and celery and cook gently for 4 to 5 minutes, until just tender-crisp. Add the cooked bacon, simmer gently for 3 minutes, then add the corn and cook for another 2 minutes.

Pour in the cream and reheat gently without bringing to a boil. Season to taste with salt and pepper.

Top each serving with a teaspoon or so of softened Parsley Mint Butter, swirling the butter around a bit to create a colorful pattern.

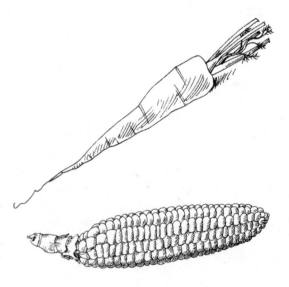

Iced Cauliflower Soup with Apricot Cream

Serves 6 to 8.

The subtle, elusive taste of this soup is often surprising because it is not distinctively of cauliflower. The rich purée is tempered by the sharpness of the apricots in the garnish.

> 2 pounds cauliflower, trimmed and broken into small florets (1½ medium-sized heads; 1 pound after trimming)
> 2 tablespoons unsalted butter
> 2 tablespoons best-quality Indian curry powder
> 1½ cups homemade chicken stock (page 345)
> 1½ cups cream
> 1 teaspoon coarse salt, or to taste
> Freshly ground white pepper
> 2 teaspoons lemon juice, or to taste

APRICOT CREAM
> 2 or 3 fresh, very ripe apricots
> ½ cup cream, lightly whipped
> Thin shreds of lemon zest

Put the cauliflower into a large pot of boiling water and simmer, uncovered, for 10 to 15 minutes, until quite tender. Drain. Purée the cauliflower in a processor or put through a food mill.

In a large saucepan, melt the butter and add the curry powder. Cook without browning for 2 minutes. Pour in the chicken stock and bring to a boil. Add the cauliflower purée and simmer slowly for 2 to 3 minutes to marry the flavors. Remove from the heat and cool.

Stir in the cream, season to taste with salt, pepper, and lemon juice and chill thoroughly. Once the soup is well chilled, taste again and adjust the salt and other seasonings.

To make the garnish, drop the apricots into simmering water for 15 seconds, remove with a slotted spoon, and slip off the skins under cold running water. Pat dry, then cut the apricots into halves, removing the stones. Purée in a processor, sweeten just slightly with sugar if the apricots are not deliciously sweet on their own, then fold the purée (you should have ¼ cup) into the lightly whipped cream. Put the Apricot Cream into a pastry bag fitted with an ⅛-inch plain tip.

To serve, pipe each bowl of soup with a spiral pattern of Apricot Cream, then draw the dull side of a knife through the circular pattern in several radiating spokes. Garnish each bowl with a few strands of lemon zest.

Salmon in Parchment with Corn, Walla Walla Sweets, and Tomatoes

Serves 6.

Except in the occasional French restaurant of elevated stature, this parchment paper treatment is seldom used. But why not, since the procedure is both easy and effective? The fish and vegetables cook in their own delicious steam, with all the flavor trapped inside the paper. The presentation is both elegant and practical as each portion is arranged before cooking. Just position each package on a plate with steamed baby new potatoes, roasted potato wedges, or buttery pasta on the side and at the table snip each packet with a long cross. Your guests will take it from there.

1½ pounds skinless salmon fillet
    Apple Cider Honey Vinaigrette
      (recipe follows)
    Parchment paper
1 large ear fresh, sweet corn
1 medium-sized Walla Walla sweet
    onion, chopped
3 medium tomatoes
4 tablespoons chopped fresh mint
2 tablespoons chopped fresh tarragon

GARNISH
    12 tarragon leaves

Cut the salmon fillet on the diagonal into 12 thin slices. Arrange in a glass baking dish. Make the Apple Cider Honey Vinaigrette and pour it over the salmon. Cover the dish with plastic wrap and refrigerate for 1 to 2 hours.

In the meantime cut 6 sheets of parchment paper each to measure 12 by 18 inches. Lightly butter each on one side only and fold in half (butter to the inside) so that they now measure 12 by 9 inches.

Remove the kernels from the cob of the corn and blanch, together with the chopped onion, in boiling water for 1 minute, then drain. Skin, seed, core, and chop the tomatoes (you should have about 15 ounces).

When the salmon is ready, position 2 slices against the inner fold of each piece of parchment, keeping the slices somewhat away from the edges. Sprinkle with salt and pepper and some of the chopped mint and tarragon. Divide the tomatoes, corn, and onions evenly among the parchment rectangles, covering the fish slices. Season again lightly with salt and pepper and lay a couple of whole tarragon leaves on top of the vegetables along with some of the remaining vinaigrette.

To encase the salmon and vegetables, make a diagonal fold at one open corner and continue making one fold over the other all the way around the packet, leaving a small opening at the last fold. The packet will be almost oval in shape. Insert a narrow straw into the opening and blow into it to inflate the packet with air. Make the last fold tightly so that the air does not escape.

Put the packets on baking sheets and bake at 425° for 10 minutes.

To serve, lift each packet off the baking sheet with a wide spatula and position on a dinner plate. The packets are opened at the table.

Apple Cider Honey Vinaigrette

2 tablespoons apple cider vinegar
¼ teaspoon coarse salt
1 teaspoon Dijon mustard
1 tablespoon fragrant honey
2 cloves minced garlic
6 tablespoons corn oil
   Freshly ground black pepper

Combine the cider vinegar and salt. When the salt has dissolved, whisk in the mustard, honey, garlic, oil, and pepper in that order.

Fillet of Salmon with Sorrel Cream

Serves 6.

This dish takes only minutes to prepare and offers the contrasting richness of the salmon and the lemony acidity of the sorrel. Sorrel can be hard to find but it is easy to grow—tuck a couple of four-inch plants into your garden somewhere and you will have it on hand nearly year-round.

1½ pounds skinless salmon fillet (a
   long narrow fillet from a
   smallish fish)
2 cups fish fumet (page 346)
1 cup dry white wine
1 cup cream
6 ounces fresh sorrel, stems
   removed, then shredded (about
   2 cups)
4 tablespoons unsalted butter, cut
   into several chunks
   Coarse salt
   Freshly ground black pepper
   Lemon juice (optional)
   Flour for dredging
2 to 3 tablespoons unsalted butter

GARNISH
   A handful of small sorrel leaves

Cut the salmon fillet on a slight diagonal into 12 slices of equal width (or if the fillet is rather thick, cut the slices vertically). Season with salt and pepper and hold for a moment.

In a saucepan, combine the fish fumet and wine and reduce the mixture to half a cup. Pour in the cream and boil for a minute or two until it begins to thicken. Stir in the sorrel and cook for a minute more. Remove from the heat, let the boil subside, then stir in 4 tablespoons butter, all at once, to form a creamy emulsion. (If too much heat is used, the butter will melt, separate, and rise to the top of the sauce. If the butter does not disappear completely, use a little more heat, but be careful.) Season to taste with salt, pepper, and drops of lemon juice if desired. Hold the sauce in the top part of a double-boiler over hot but not simmering water or put into a warmed wide-mouthed Thermos while preparing the salmon.

Dredge the salmon fillets lightly in flour. Heat 2 tablespoons butter in a nonstick skillet and sauté the fillets, a few at a time, for about 1½ minutes per side, adding the remaining 1 tablespoon butter if necessary. Remove to a warmed platter as they finish and keep warm while completing the rest.

To serve, cover the bottom of 6 plates with an equal amount of sauce and place 2 overlapping fillets on top. Garnish each plate with a couple of small sorrel leaves or shreds of sorrel if small leaves are unavailable.

Double Salmon Saucisson

Serves 6 to 8.

A seafood saucisson or sausage is a wonderful concept and much easier to make than its appearance would suggest. A basic seafood mousse—a purée of firm-fleshed fish (salmon in this case, but you can also use fresh, raw trout, Pacific whiting, scallops, or shrimp) lightened with egg whites and cream—is rolled in microwavable plastic wrap and poached to set the collagen proteins in the fish. It is imperative that the fish be fresh, not frozen, or the collagen proteins will not set properly. For the same reason everything to do with the mousse must be thoroughly cold.

The unmolded sausage is firm and easy to slice and may be served hot or cold. Cold, it is a perfect main course for the summer buffet table. Surround it on a platter with a colorful assemblage of barely poached baby vegetables, such as carrots, summer squash, tiny red and white new potatoes, and sugar snap peas and serve it drizzled with Lemon Basil Sabayon. Best of all everything can be done well in advance.

ᴧ🦢ᴧ🦢ᴧ🦢ᴧ🦢ᴧ🦢ᴧ🦢ᴧ🦢ᴧ🦢ᴧ🦢ᴧ🦢ᴧ🦢ᴧ🦢ᴧ

1 pound skinned, boned, fresh salmon, cut into 1-inch chunks and kept very cold (purchase 3 steaks to be sure to have enough)

2 egg whites, kept very cold

¾ to 1¼ cups cream, kept very cold

1 tablespoon combined minced basil, parsley, chives, and tarragon

Coarse salt

Coarsely ground black pepper

½ pound skinned, thinly sliced cold-smoked salmon (often called nova-style or lox)

GARNISH

Thin shreds of lemon zest

Finely shredded fresh basil

Garniture of Blanched Summer Vegetables (recipe follows)

Lemon Basil Sabayon (recipe follows)

Using the steel knife of a processor, finely chop the very cold fresh salmon chunks. With the machine running, drop one egg white at a time through the feed tube and process to a thoroughly amalgamated purée. Everything must remain very cold. (Place the bowl with its blade and the seafood mixture in the refrigerator for 30 minutes if you feel they are warming at all.)

With the machine running, slowly pour in ¾ cup of the cream through the feed tube. Stop the machine and check the consistency of the mousse. It should be light but definitely have enough body to hold its shape when lifted with a spoon; add more of the remaining cream if necessary. The exact amount of cream will vary from time to time. Just stop adding cream when the mixture reaches the stage just described. Blend in the minced fresh herbs and salt and pepper to taste.

Lay out a 15-inch sheet of microwavable plastic wrap (other types may not work properly and may even disintegrate in the poaching liquid) on the countertop and position a row of barely overlapping slices of cold-smoked salmon down the length; the slices are overlapped in the same manner as they are when you purchase them, but not as closely. (If the smoked salmon is thicker than ⅛ inch, you will need to lay a piece of plastic wrap on top and pound it lightly with a mallet to flatten.) Spoon the salmon mousse lengthwise evenly down the center of the slices, then wrap the slices around and over the top of the mousse. Roll the *saucisson* up tightly in the plastic wrap, twist the ends, and secure with bag ties or string. The finished roll should be 2½ inches in diameter and about 9 inches long. Refrigerate while preparing the poaching water.

Select a deep sauté pan or fish poacher large enough to hold the *saucisson* and fill it two-thirds full with water. Bring to just beneath a simmer, about 180°, and lay the wrapped *saucisson* into the water. Poach at this temperature or just slightly above for 10 minutes per inch of thickness or for a total of 25 minutes if your *saucisson* is 2½ inches in diameter. Remove from the water and let the mousse cool on a towel. (Or you can "Scotch poach" the mousse. Maintain a visible simmer for 2 minutes after you have added the *saucisson,* remove the pan from the heat, cover tightly, and let it sit until the water reaches room temperature. Then remove the *saucisson.* The mousse will always cook perfectly with this method.) Refrigerate still wrapped in the plastic. To this point, everything can be done 1 or even 2 days ahead.

A few hours before serving, unwrap and slice the saucisson into ¾-inch rounds and arrange, slightly overlapping, in two rows along one side of a large serving platter. Cover with plastic wrap and refrigerate while preparing the Garniture of Blanched Summer Vegetables and the Lemon Basil Sabayon.

When ready to serve, arrange the poached vegetables on the open side of the platter as artistically as possible, then drizzle the sauce over the slices of mousse or serve it alongside. Scatter the garnish of lemon zest and basil shreds over the top.

Garniture of Blanched Summer Vegetables

Makes 2½ pounds vegetables.

The vegetables suggested here are those usually available in the market at this time of year. You can use almost any vegetable you like as long as it is small and pretty. Look for contrast in shape and color. This may seem to be an excessive quantity of vegetables for six people but they are meant to be an important part of the meal, not merely a minor accompaniment.

½ pound baby carrots
½ pound baby summer squash
½ pound baby Red Pontiac "new" potatoes
½ pound baby White Rose potatoes
½ pound sugar snap peas

VINAIGRETTE
2 tablespoons white wine vinegar
Coarse salt
Freshly ground black pepper
6 tablespoons olive oil

Peel the carrots but leave them whole together with 2 inches of their green tops cut on the diagonal. Clean the squash under cold running water, leaving the trimmed stems attached. Scrub the potatoes thoroughly. Clean and stem the sugar snap peas.

Steam the carrots, squash, and potatoes until each is just tender; the carrots and squash should still be slightly crunchy. Refresh under cold running water and let them cool to room temperature. Blanch the sugar snap peas in a large quantity of boiling water until just tender-crisp, then refresh under cold running water to cool. The cooking times will vary with each of these vegetables, depending on their size. Watch closely and taste from time to time. There is nothing worse than mushy vegetables.

Drain, pat dry and seal in separate groups in plastic bags. Refrigerate until ready to arrange with the salmon *saucisson*. These vegetables may be prepared a day ahead of time.

Just before arranging the vegetables, mix the ingredients for the vinaigrette, seasoning to taste with salt and pepper, and coat the vegetables lightly. The arrangement of salmon mousse and vegetables may be done several hours before serving. Sauce with Lemon Basil Sabayon just as you are serving.

Lemon Basil Sabayon

Makes about 2½ cups.

Strictly speaking, a sabayon sauce is a frothy custard sauce consisting of egg yolks, sugar, and some type of wine that may be served hot or cold. Here I have stretched the meaning of the word a bit to encompass a savory sauce that is made in the same way but without the sugar. It is light and airy and is particularly good with cold seafood or poultry mousse for which you sometimes want a sauce that drapes rather than a thicker sauce such as mayonnaise.

> 2 teaspoons minced shallots
> 1 clove garlic minced
> 1 tablespoon white wine vinegar
> 1 cup homemade chicken stock (page 345)
> 1 cup dry white wine
> 6 egg yolks, whisked to blend
> 2 teaspoons lemon juice
>   Coarse salt
>   Freshly ground white pepper
> 2 teaspoons lemon zest
> ¼ cup shredded basil

Combine the shallots, garlic, vinegar, chicken stock, and white wine in a saucepan and reduce by half.

Add ¼ cup of the hot reduction slowly to the egg yolks, whisking furiously all the while. Add the remainder of the reduction, continuing to whisk, then pour the sauce back into the pan and cook over low heat, whisking constantly, until thickened and foamy. The sauce should coat a wooden spoon nicely when it is done. (Do not let the sauce rise above 170°; it will curdle irretrievably at 180°.)

Stir in the lemon juice and season to taste with salt and pepper. Cool, cover, and chill. Just before using, whisk a bit and blend in the lemon zest and shreds of basil.

Chinese Steamed Salmon with Ginger, Garlic, and Black Beans

Serves 3 to 4 as a main dish.

I cannot imagine an easier or more succulent way to prepare impeccably fresh fish. Because the process is so straightforward and simple, you must obtain the freshest fish possible. If you have just caught one yourself, all the better. Just about any type of fish may be used, except very oily species such as mackerel or sardines. Try fresh trout, sole, rockfish, or cod, preferably whole, but steaks or fillets will also work.

2 pounds whole fresh salmon, gutted, scaled, and with the head left on
1 teaspoon coarse salt
1 tablespoon minced fresh ginger
2 cloves garlic, minced
2 tablespoons minced black beans
2 green onions, minced
2 tablespoons soy sauce
2 tablespoons dry sherry
Pinch sugar
½ teaspoon sesame seed oil
Coarse salt

Rinse the salmon and pat it dry. Make diagonal slashes ¾ of an inch apart from the center back to belly flap on both sides, cutting almost to the bone. Measure the fish at its thickest point. (If using steaks or fillets, clean them well of extraneous matter and pat dry. Remove any "free bones" from steaks with a pair of tweezers but leave the backbone and any attached bones and skin in place.)

Pat the salt into the meat of the fish both inside and out, top and bottom, being sure to get the seasoning into the slashes.

Arrange the fish on a heatproof serving platter that will fit inside a long fish poacher, allowing at least an inch of clearance space around the platter. Raise the steamer rack well above the boiling water in the poacher, remembering that the lid must close securely as well. (In my fish poacher, canning jar rings work for this purpose.)

Mix the rest of the ingredients, open each gash, and pour and push some of the flavoring inside. Pour the remaining flavoring evenly over the fish.

Fill the poacher to within ½ an inch of the insert with water, cover, and bring to a full boil.

When water is fully boiling, uncover the poacher, remove the rack, position the platter with the fish on top, and carefully lower them both back into the poacher. Cover and return to a medium, not furious, boil. Steam for 10 minutes per inch of fish thickness. Make sure that the water in the poacher does not entirely evaporate; carefully add more boiling water if necessary. (When you lift the lid for any reason, lift it almost straight up with a slight angle away from you. Bring the lid straight over and wipe the underneath with a towel. This will keep the steam from burning you and prevent the water that has condensed on the bottom of the lid from pouring back onto your fish.) The fish is done when it turns opaque at its thickest point. It should just flake with a fork.

Remove the poacher from the heat and uncover. Let the steam dissipate a moment, then lift the plate out. Notice how the juices of the fish have mingled with the flavoring ingredients to create a lovely light sauce on the plate. Serve right away.

Shrimp with Tomatoes, Peppers, and Cream Cheese

Serves 6.

This dish may be made with any number of soft or soft and crumbly cheeses; just be sure that the cheese you choose complements the shrimp without overwhelming its taste. Excellent quality feta may be used if it is not too strong, or a mild blue-veined or goat cheese. If you do decide to use cream cheese as specified here, it is worth the effort to procure a first

rate, non-emulsified cream cheese. It makes the grocery store stuff seem rubbery and synthetic by comparison.

2 pounds large shrimp, shelled and deveined, with tails left on
4 tablespoons fresh lemon juice
2 tablespoons olive oil
1 medium-small onion, diced (to measure 1 cup)
4 cloves garlic, minced
1 red bell pepper, cored, deribbed, and diced
1 pound very ripe tomatoes, skinned, cored, and diced
1 cup dry white wine
1 green bell pepper, cored, deribbed, and diced
½ teaspoon crushed red pepper
¼ cup minced parsley
¼ cup minced fresh basil
  Coarse salt
  Freshly ground black pepper
¼ pound best-quality cream cheese (or other soft or soft and crumbly cheese), cut into ½-inch cubes

Drain and pat the shrimp dry. Sprinkle with lemon juice and let them marinate while preparing the sauce.

Heat the olive oil in a skillet and cook the onions slowly to soften without browning. Add the garlic, red bell pepper, tomatoes with their juice, and white wine and simmer until the sauce is very thick; there should be no visible moisture remaining. Add the green bell pepper, crushed red pepper, parsley, basil, and salt and pepper to taste.

Again pat the shrimp dry, then arrange with the cream cheese in a large gratin dish or into 6 individual baking dishes, sprinkling on a little salt and pepper. Spoon the sauce over.

Bake at 350° for about 25 minutes until the shrimp are just cooked through and the sauce is bubbling hot.

Scallops and Shrimp Gratinée

Serves 8 as a first course or 4 as a luncheon dish.

A rich, rich dish but oh so good. I like it best as a first course in the smaller portion specified here. But it makes a lovely luncheon main dish as well; just accompany with an assertively dressed salad to counterpoint the richness.

1 cup dry white wine
1 cup or more of water (to barely cover scallops and shrimp)
2 tablespoons minced shallots
Freshly ground black pepper, to taste
Coarse salt, to taste

Half a bay leaf
¾ pound small scallops, fibrous attachments removed
¾ pound shrimp, peeled, deveined, and cut into pieces the size of the scallops

SAUCE
3 tablespoons unsalted butter
4 tablespoons flour
½ cup cream
2 egg yolks mixed with ¼ cup cream
Fresh lemon juice to taste
Tabasco sauce
8 tablespoons grated Gruyère (or other Swiss-style) cheese

Heat the wine, water, shallots, pepper, salt, and bay leaf in a large saucepan. This seasoning liquid should not be boiling; a small bubble or two on the surface is fine. Add the scallops and shrimp and cook, covered, for 2 to 3 minutes. Scallops and shrimp are tough and rubbery when they are overcooked, so be careful. Remove the scallops and shrimp from the cooking liquid and set aside. Reduce the stock to 1 cup to intensify its flavor.

To make the sauce, melt the butter and add the flour. Whisk together until foamy. Cook this *roux* for 2 minutes. Pour in the cream and stock and whisk to smooth out the sauce. Bring to a simmer, stirring, and cook for 4 minutes without allowing it to color. Remove from the heat. Add a little of the hot sauce to the egg yolk and cream mixture, then pour back into the sauce, whisking all the time. Cook for 1 minute but do not bring anywhere near a simmer; egg yolks curdle as they near 185°. Thin down with a little more cream if necessary. Add a little lemon juice and Tabasco to taste. Strain the sauce if necessary (if it is lumpy). It should be fairly thick.

Butter 8 small or 4 large scallop shells (or use gratin dishes of a similar size). Blend two-thirds of the sauce with the scallops and shrimp and spoon the mixture into the shells. Spoon a little more sauce over the shellfish and sprinkle each with at least 1 tablespoon of grated cheese. Dot with bits of butter. Bake for 10 to 15 minutes in a 375° oven. Broil briefly to brown the cheese lightly.

Bay Scallops and Leeks in Orange Cream

Serves 6.

I tried a dish with this name in a Seattle restaurant some time ago, attracted by a combination of ingredients that sounded lovely. When the dish arrived, there was not a leek in sight and no discernible taste of orange; just unthickened, barely seasoned cream as a sauce. So, after some playing around at the stove, here is the dish as I had expected. Larger scallops may also be used if desired.

To clean a leek, split it lengthwise and wash it, root down, under cold running water. Be sure to open up each layer of the stalk and flush with water as leeks are frequently filled with mud. Trim off the root and cut the leaves off at the point at which the light green stalk begins to turn a darker green. Discard the dark green end. The white and light green parts of the leek are edible and will cook to a melting tenderness.

> 1 pound leeks, cleaned, trimmed, cut
>   in half lengthwise, then cut into
>   ½-inch slices (2 heaping cups)
> 4 tablespoons unsalted butter
> ½ cup fish stock or bottled clam juice
> 2 tablespoons shallots, chopped
> 1 clove garlic, minced
> 1½ pounds small bay scallops,
>   connective muscles removed,
>   rinsed, and drained
> ½ cup dry white wine
> ¼ cup orange juice

ORANGE CREAM

> 2 tablespoons Grand Marnier, or other
>   orange-flavored, liqueur
> Zest of 1 orange
> ½ cup cream
> Coarse salt
> Freshly ground white pepper

GARNISH

> Several chives, cut into 1-inch
>   lengths on the long diagonal

Blanch the leeks in a saucepan with 2 table-spoons of the butter and the fish stock until tender, about 10 minutes. Remove, drain, squeeze lightly to extract excess liquid, and dry with paper towels. Reserve the poaching liquid.

Heat the remaining 2 tablespoons butter in a sauté pan and add the shallots and garlic. Stir and cook briefly without coloring. Add the scallops, wine, and orange juice. Bring to a bare simmer and cook for 1 or 2 minutes only, until scallops are barely done. Remove the scallops with a slotted spoon and keep them warm in a heated serving dish.

To make the sauce turn the heat up, add the liqueur, the poaching liquid from the braised leeks, and the orange zest. Reduce until only a thick, slightly syrupy mixture remains. Pour in the cream and simmer briefly until slightly thickened. Season to taste with salt and pepper.

Combine the scallops with the sauce, heat for a few seconds only, and return to a warm serving dish or to individual plates.

Sprinkle with chives and serve.

Fettuccini with Scallops, Mushrooms, and Cream

Serves 4 to 6.

In this quick and easy pasta main course, two colors of fettuccini are used for visual interest. Peeled, de-veined shrimp can replace the scallops on occasion. Fresh chanterelle or oyster mushrooms are wonderful here if you can get them. When using either of these, add a few tablespoons of chicken stock to the initial sauté to prevent them from absorbing all the butter and then sticking to the pan.

6 tablespoons unsalted butter
2 tablespoons minced shallots
2 cloves garlic, minced
½ pound small mushrooms, trimmed and cut in half
1 cup cream
Coarse salt
Freshly ground black pepper
Lemon juice
1 pound small scallops, fibrous muscle attachments removed
½ pound fresh spinach fettuccini
½ pound fresh egg fettuccini
½ cup grated Parmesan

GARNISH
Additional grated Parmesan

Melt 4 tablespoons of the butter in a sauté pan and cook the shallots slowly until softened but not browned. Add the garlic and mushrooms and continue cooking until they release their juices and most of the liquid evaporates. Add ½ cup cream and reduce slightly to thicken. Season to taste with salt, pepper, and drops of lemon juice. Add the scallops to the sauce 2 to 3 minutes before serving and heat just until cooked through. Adjust the seasoning if necessary.

Meanwhile bring a large pot of generously salted water to a full boil and drop in the pasta. Boil for 2 to 3 minutes, until just tender. Drain.

Heat a large pasta serving bowl containing the remaining 2 tablespoons butter and ½ cup cream. When the pasta is done, add it to the serving bowl and toss to coat with butter and cream. Add half the sauce along with the Parmesan and toss again. Pour the remaining sauce on top of the pasta and serve immediately with additional Parmesan if desired.

Birch Bay Crabcakes

Makes 6 to 8 cakes.

Since for me fresh crab means summertime when the commercial crabbers have left Birch Bay in northern Washington (my favorite crab haunt), I like to combine the sweet, succulent meat with fresh summer herbs—parsley, chives, and tarragon—to produce this Northwest version of the Maryland classic. Here the directions specify three-inch patties, but you might also like to try smaller, one-inch cakes to serve as appetizers. The freshest Dungeness crab produces the best cakes.

1 pound fresh, cooked Dungeness
    crabmeat
1 cup dried bread crumbs
¼ cup minced parsley
¼ cup minced fresh chives
2 tablespoons minced fresh tarragon
½ teaspoon cayenne pepper
    Black pepper
    Coarse salt
2 eggs
1 tablespoon Dijon mustard
    Flour for dipping
    Egg for dipping
    Untoasted wheatgerm for dipping
2 tablespoons unsalted butter
2 tablespoons corn oil
    Homemade Mayonnaise (page 347)

Combine the crab, bread crumbs, parsley, chives, tarragon, cayenne, black pepper, and salt to taste in a large bowl. Beat the eggs with the mustard in a small bowl, then drizzle them over the crabmeat mixture and toss to distribute. Taste again for seasoning and adjust if necessary.

Form into 3-inch patties that are about ¾-inch thick. Dredge in flour, pat off the excess, then dip in egg, letting the excess run back into the bowl. Finally dredge to coat all sides in wheat germ. Place on a fine-meshed wire rack in the refrigerator to set up for at least 1 hour.

Melt the butter and oil in a heavy sauté pan and sauté the cakes until nicely brown on both sides, about 5 to 8 minutes in all.

Serve hot with homemade mayonnaise for dipping.

Breast of Chicken Stuffed with Goat Cheese, Basil, and Mint

Serves 10.

This main course is wonderful for casual summertime picnics and buffets. The chicken breasts are boned and halved, then flattened and covered with a thin slice of prosciutto and a layer of creamy basil- and mint-flavored goat cheese. (The goat cheese— chèvre—is expanded and mellowed with puréed ricotta, so you may wish to use a cheese that is a little stronger tasting than those you normally prefer.) The rolled, stuffed breasts can be prepared up to a day prior to poaching and refrigerated. I normally arrange these in a slightly overlapping fashion on one side of a large basil-lined tray with crispy blanched vegetables arranged on the other side and a container of aioli positioned just off center.

½ pound ricotta cheese (thick, emulsified type)
¼ pound creamy goat cheese
½ cup tightly packed fresh basil leaves, minced
¼ cup tightly packed fresh mint leaves, minced
2 cloves garlic, finely minced or put through a press
Juice of 1 small lime
Coarse salt
Freshly ground black pepper
5 whole chicken breasts
Coarse salt
Freshly ground black pepper
Juice of half a lime
10 very thin slices prosciutto
Aioli (page 52) and/or Rouille (page 349)

Mix the ricotta, goat cheese, basil, mint, and garlic until blended. (Do not put into a processor as this makes the mixture too thin.) Add the lime juice and season to taste with salt and pepper. Refrigerate to firm.

Bone, skin, and separate the chicken breasts, removing the tendon on the underside of each. Lay the suprêmes between sheets of wax paper and pound lightly with a rolling pin to thin them somewhat. Salt and pepper the top side of each suprême and squeeze a few drops of lime juice on each one.

Position a suprême, top-side down, on a 1-foot length of microwavable plastic wrap, such as Saran Wrap. Lay a slice of prosciutto on top, then place a heaping tablespoonful of filling in the center, spreading evenly but keeping it away from the edges. Roll the suprême from the short side into a loose bundle. Place the suprême on the edge of the plastic wrap and tightly roll them up together. Twist one end of the roll with a bag tie. Before closing the other end with a second tie, push the suprême toward the closed end, making a uniform,

tight sausage. Repeat with the remaining suprêmes.

Arrange the bundles together in a deep baking dish. Pour boiling water over them to
cover and poach in a 350° oven for 15 minutes.

Remove the sausages from the oven and the
water and put them on a clean dish towel.
Open one end and let drain. Cool to room temperature, seal tightly, and chill thoroughly.
Unwrap, cut each breast into ½-inch thick
slices, and arrange on a platter lined with fresh
basil leaves. Tuck in a few pansy or nasturtium
flowers for color if you have them. Serve with
aioli and/or rouille.

Grilled Breast of Chicken with Cold Hazelnut Spaghettini

Serves 4.

*I enjoy the contrast of textures, temperatures, and
tastes of this recipe. The marinated chicken breasts
are served hot off the grill over a cold pasta salad
tossed with a rich and flavorful hazelnut butter
sauce. The pasta salad is also good by itself and
makes a satisfying simple supper served along with
a stir-fry of a few of your favorite summertime vegetables.*

MARINADE
½ cup fresh lemon juice
Zest of 2 lemons
¼ cup Dijon mustard
¼ cup minced fresh herbs (any
    combination of rosemary, thyme,
    basil, mint, oregano, or parsley)
1 teaspoon coarse salt
Freshly ground black pepper
2 whole chicken breasts, halved,
    boned, and skinned

HAZELNUT SAUCE
6 tablespoons hazelnut butter (available
    in gourmet markets)
4 tablespoons lemon juice
1 clove garlic, minced
2 tablespoons soy sauce
¼ teaspoon cayenne pepper
¼ cup chicken stock
¼ cup minced parsley or mint
2 tablespoons coarse salt
1 tablespoon corn oil

½ pound spaghettini

GARNISH
Zest of 1 lemon
2 tablespoons chopped, well-toasted,
    skinned hazelnuts
Whole sprigs of fresh herbs

Combine the marinade ingredients and rub directly onto the chicken breasts. Put the breasts into a glass baking dish, cover with plastic wrap, and marinate for 2 to 4 hours in the refrigerator (or overnight if that is easier).

Prepare the grill, preferably with peach-wood, mesquite, or some other high-quality fragrant charcoal.

While the grill is heating, prepare the Hazelnut Sauce. Blend the hazelnut butter in a processor, adding the lemon juice, garlic, soy sauce, cayenne, chicken stock and parsley or mint. Process just to combine.

Bring a large pot of water (at least 1 gallon) to a vigorous boil. Add 2 tablespoons salt and 1 tablespoon oil. Drop in the pasta and boil for about 5 minutes, until just *al dente*. Drain and cool completely under cold running water. Drain again thoroughly, patting dry lightly with paper towels, then toss with the Hazelnut Sauce. Chill briefly, for 15 minutes or so. (If

made ahead—which is perfectly fine—toss to redistribute the sauce, then leave the pasta at room temperature for 15 minutes or so to take the chill off.)

Pat the breasts thoroughly dry, removing any herbs and lemon rind still clinging to the surface. Brush all the surfaces with oil and grill 3 inches from the flame for 3 to 5 minutes per side. When just done and still definitely juicy at the center, remove from the grill and slice each breast section against the grain diagonally into 4 or 5 slices.

Mound a portion of the pasta on each of 4 cold plates and arrange the grilled, sliced chicken breast on top of each. Strew additional lemon zest over the top, along with chopped hazelnuts and garnish with sprigs of fresh herbs. Serve right away so that there is a temperature difference between the pasta and the chicken.

Spicy Chicken Suprêmes with Sweet Peppers and Calamata Olives

Serves 2 to 4.

Chicken breast suprêmes (the individual halves of a boneless, skinless chicken breast) are a boon for the busy cook. So easy and quick to prepare, they are also nutritious, lean, and low in calories. In this recipe, a marinade is spiked with lime juice, garlic, chili pepper, cilantro, and cumin to flavor the suprêmes. Served over a bed of multicolored bell peppers dotted here and there with glistening black olives, this dish is as satisfying to look at as it is to eat. The flavor of the chicken is "tied" to the bell pepper sauté with a few tablespoons of chicken stock reduction.

MARINADE

    Zest of 1 lime
  2 tablespoons lime juice
  1 teaspoon coarse salt
  4 cloves garlic, minced
  1 jalapeño chili pepper, minced (1
      tablespoon)
  1 tablespoon minced cilantro
  1 teaspoon freshly ground cumin
  ⅛ teaspoon cayenne pepper
  2 tablespoons olive oil
  2 whole chicken breasts, halved, boned
      and skinned

  1 cup homemade chicken stock (page
      345)
  1 red bell pepper, halved, cored and
      cut into ½-inch-wide strips
  1 green bell pepper, halved, cored and
      cut into ½-inch-wide strips
  1 yellow bell pepper, halved, cored and
      cut into ½-inch-wide strips
  1 clove garlic, minced
  ¼ cup calamata olives, pitted and
      quartered
  3 tablespoons olive oil
    Coarse salt
    Freshly ground black pepper

GARNISH
    Wedges of lime
    Sprigs of cilantro

Combine the ingredients for the marinade, dissolving the salt in the lime juice before adding the olive oil, and rub it directly onto the chicken breasts. Put the breasts into a glass baking dish, cover with plastic wrap, and marinate for 2 to 4 hours in the refrigerator (or overnight if that is easier).

Prepare the grill, preferably with peachwood, mesquite, or some other high-quality fragrant charcoal.

Meanwhile, reduce the chicken stock to 2 to 4 syrupy tablespoons. Reserve.

Prepare the bell peppers, garlic and olives and have ready. (An easy way to pit olives is to whack each one with a mallet so that the pit may easily be slipped out with your fingers.)

Pat the breasts dry thoroughly, removing any lime zest still clinging to the surface. Brush all surfaces with oil and grill 3 inches from the flame for 3 to 3½ minutes per side, depending on how hot the charcoal is. When just done and still definitely juicy at the center, remove from the grill.

About 3 or 4 minutes before the chicken is done, heat the remaining 3 tablespoons olive oil until quite hot and then rapidly sauté the bell pepper mixture, adding the garlic just 30 seconds short of finishing, along with the chicken stock reduction and the olives. Season to taste with salt and pepper.

To serve, mound the peppers on an oval platter and arrange the chicken on top, being sure to have the peppers visible here and there. Garnish with wedges of lime and sprigs of cilantro.

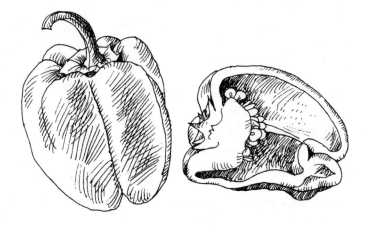

VEGETABLE PATCH

Steamed Vegetable Mosaic

Serves 4.

This very simple dish takes advantage of whatever is fresh at the market. Steaming is a vital technique in vegetable cookery because it retains the nutritional content. The vegetables may be cleaned, cut, wrapped in plastic, and refrigerated for a day if necessary.

¼ pound broccoli, broken into florets, stems peeled and cut into 2-inch diagonal slices
¼ pound carrots, peeled and cut into 2-inch diagonal slices
¼ pound zucchini, stems removed and cut into 2-inch diagonal slices
¼ pound cauliflower, cut into florets
2 tablespoons unsalted butter, melted
1 tablespoon fresh lemon juice
Coarse salt
Freshly ground black pepper
½ cup finely shredded Parmesan cheese

Arrange the vegetables in a mosaic pattern in a bamboo steamer, leaving space here and there and around the edges for the steam to work its way through. Fill a large wok with water so that it clears the bottom of the steamer by 1 inch. Bring the water to a boil, place the steamer on top, cover with its lid, and steam for about 15 minutes, until the vegetables are tender but still somewhat crunchy.

Remove the steamer from the wok and set it on a large serving platter. Quickly lift the lid and drizzle the vegetables with butter and lemon juice. Season well with salt and pepper. Top with cheese and set the lid back in place to encourage the cheese to melt a bit. Bring the bamboo steamer with its platter to the table and serve right away.

Summer Vegetable Stir-Fry with Garlic, Ginger, and Walnuts

Serves 4.

This Chinese-inspired vegetable dish lends an interesting flavor to any number of straightforward entrées such as grilled chicken, roast pork, or poached fish. I use it often, choosing seasonal vegetables that are as fresh as possible and offer contrasts of color and texture. The dish may also be made with just one type of vegetable.

1½ pounds assorted summer vegetables, such as broccoli, cauliflower, red, green, or yellow bell peppers, zucchini, green beans, Walla Walla sweet onions, wild mushrooms, snow peas, sugar snap peas, or carrots

4 tablespoons corn oil

2 teaspoons minced garlic

2 teaspoons minced fresh ginger
Coarse salt

1 tablespoon soy sauce

1 teaspoon rice wine vinegar

1 teaspoon sugar

½ cup homemade chicken stock (page 345)

2 teaspoons cornstarch

1 teaspoon sesame seed oil

¼ cup walnuts, lightly toasted

Cut the chosen vegetables into attractive and uniformly sized pieces. A julienne cut may be used for some vegetables; others are better cut diagonally or in a large dice. Firm vegetables, such as cauliflower, green beans, broccoli, and carrots need to be blanched in boiling water for 1 minute, drained, and dried before being used.

Heat the oil in a large, heavy sauté pan. Add the garlic and ginger and toss in the hot oil for a few seconds only. Do not brown. Add the vegetables and toss to coat each piece in oil. This will take 10 seconds or so. Sprinkle on a little salt.

Add the soy sauce, rice wine vinegar, sugar and half of the stock. Cover the pan and cook for 2 to 4 minutes, just until the vegetables are crunchy-tender.

While the vegetables are steaming, mix the cornstarch with the remaining chicken stock.

Uncover the pan and add the sesame oil, then the cornstarch mixture to the pan. Tip the pan, collecting the sauce on one side. Whisk to blend and make sure that the sauce actually boils so as to activate the cornstarch. Toss the vegetables to coat each one with sauce. Sprinkle the walnuts on top and serve right away.

Zucchini Gratin with Garlic, Tomato, and Italian Fontina

Serves 8.

This dish is something like lasagne except that zucchini replaces the pasta. It is also very good without the tomato sauce topping. In this case individual gratins can be made, turned out onto plates, and surrounded with briefly sautéed chopped tomatoes and fresh basil.

Italian fontina (Fontina d'Aosta) is absolutely irresistible—rich, creamy, and marvelously flavored—but it usually requires a trip to a cheese shop. Northwest Gouda or Jack cheese, a Swedish fontina, or any similar white cheese that melts well may be substituted if necessary.

TOMATO SAUCE

- 1 tablespoon olive oil
- 1 medium-sized onion, peeled and chopped
- 2 cloves garlic, finely minced
- 1 teaspoon basil
- ½ teaspoon oregano
- 1½ pounds peeled, chopped, juicy ripe tomatoes with their juice (or one 28-ounce can)
- 1 teaspoon sugar, optional
- Coarse salt
- Freshly ground black pepper

GARLIC CREAM SAUCE

- 4 large heads garlic, separated and peeled
- 2½ cups homemade chicken stock (page 345)
- 5 tablespoons unsalted butter
- 5 tablespoons flour
- 3 cups milk
- 4 to 6 tablespoons olive oil
- 6 medium-small zucchini (about 1½ pounds), ends trimmed and sliced into ¼-inch thick disks
- 1 teaspoon dried basil, finely crumbled
- Flour for dredging
- 2 cups grated Italian fontina (or other similar white cheese that melts well)

To make the Tomato Sauce, heat the olive oil and add the onion. Cook slowly until the onion begins to soften, about 15 minutes. Add the garlic, basil, and oregano and cook for 5 minutes longer without browning the garlic. Add the tomatoes with all of their juice and simmer slowly, uncovered, for 30 to 45 minutes, until the sauce is thick and most of the visible liquid has evaporated. Taste and adjust the flavor with sugar if needed (to offset excess acidity), salt, and pepper. Set aside.

To make the Garlic Cream Sauce, put the peeled garlic cloves into a small saucepan with the stock and simmer slowly until very soft, about 30 to 40 minutes. Remove the very soft garlic with a slotted spoon and reduce the stock to 2 tablespoons. Purée the garlic with the stock and set aside. In another saucepan, melt the butter and add the flour; cook together without browning for at least 2 minutes. Pour in the milk, whisking all the time and bring to a simmer. Whisk in the garlic purée and the reserved stock and simmer slowly for 10 minutes, being sure not to scorch the bottom of the pan. Season to taste with salt and pepper and put through a very fine strainer. Lay a piece of plastic wrap directly on the surface of the sauce to keep it from crusting and set aside.

Heat 2 tablespoons olive oil in a skillet. Dry the zucchini slices with paper towels, sprinkle with dried basil, salt and pepper, then dredge lightly in flour. In batches, fry quickly until golden on each side and remove to drain on paper towels. Add more oil as needed.

Butter a 9- by 12-inch gratin dish, pour a little of the Garlic Cream Sauce on the bottom, then arrange a single layer of zucchini, slightly overlapping. Drizzle with more of the sauce and sprinkle with cheese. Continue layering the zucchini, sauce, and cheese, reserving ½ cup of the cheese for the top.

Top the casserole with a ½-inch layer of Tomato Sauce, sprinkle with the remaining cheese, and bake at 350° for about 50 to 60 minutes, until heated through (an internal temperature of 150°).

Zucchini and Eggplant with Mediterranean Tomato Sauce

Serves 8.

The tomato sauce here has much to recommend it; the usual sweet-mellow taste is altered considerably by the addition of capers, green olives, crushed red pepper, and lots of herbs. (Dried herbs are used here because of the lengthy cooking time.) Generally I serve this as a hearty vegetarian main course but it is also appealing, in smaller portions, as a first course. If you cannot find the slim Japanese eggplant, use the globe variety.

MEDITERRANEAN TOMATO SAUCE

1 tablespoon olive oil
1 medium-sized onion, peeled and chopped
2 cloves garlic, finely minced
1 teaspoon dried basil
½ teaspoon dried oregano
1 teaspoon fennel seeds, pulverized
¼ teaspoon crushed red pepper flakes
1¾ pounds peeled, diced juicy ripe tomatoes with their juice (or one 28-ounce can)
2 tablespoons capers
¼ cup chopped green olives
½ cup dry white wine
1 teaspoon sugar (optional)
Coarse salt
Freshly ground black pepper

3 medium-small zucchini, ends trimmed and cut into ¼-inch cubes or slices
1 medium-small Japanese eggplant, ends trimmed and cut into ¼-inch cubes or slices
6 tablespoons olive oil
1 teaspoon dried basil, finely crumbled
1 teaspoon dried oregano, finely crumbled
1 teaspoon dried marjoram, finely crumbled
1 cup grated Parmesan cheese
1 cup grated fontina cheese

To make the Tomato Sauce, heat the olive oil in a stovetop casserole and add the onion. Cook slowly until the onion begins to soften, about 15 minutes. Add the garlic, basil, oregano, fennel, and crushed red pepper and cook for 2 minutes longer. Add the tomatoes with all of their juice, capers, green olives, and wine. Simmer slowly, uncovered, for 45 to 60 minutes, until the sauce is thick and most of the visible liquid has evaporated. Taste and adjust the flavor with sugar if needed (to offset excess acidity), salt, and pepper. Set aside.

Sprinkle the eggplant and zucchini with basil, oregano, and marjoram. Heat the olive oil in a skillet and sauté the vegetables until softened slightly, about 10 minutes.

Combine the Parmesan and fontina, then layer with zucchini and eggplant in a 9- by 12-inch gratin dish, reserving ½ cup of the cheese. Top the casserole with Tomato Sauce and sprinkle with the remaining cheese.

Bake at 350° for about 40 minutes or until heated through.

Fresh Herb Gnocchi with Tomatoes and Parmesan

Serves 10 to 12.

Gnocchi are tender little Italian dumplings made from a wide variety of starchy mixtures. In this recipe ricotta cheese and flour hold together an abundance of fresh herbs. In using all of the bunches of spinach, sorrel, and watercress specified here, this recipe produces enough gnocchi to fill two 9- by 12-inch gratin dishes. Cut the formula in half and make a nice little salad with the remaining leafy greens if you wish.

Tomato Sauce with Fennel Seed
   (recipe follows)
2 tablespoons unsalted butter
1 bunch spinach, stemmed (½ pound
   stemmed leaves)
1 bunch sorrel, stemmed (½ pound
   stemmed leaves)
1 small bunch watercress (4 ounces
   trimmed leaves)
½ cup chopped parsley
3 tablespoons chopped fresh tarragon
¼ cup chopped fresh chives
¼ cup chopped fresh mint
2 cups (15-ounce carton) well-drained
   ricotta cheese
4 eggs
2 cups flour
1½ cups grated Parmesan cheese

Coarse salt
Freshly ground black pepper
Freshly grated nutmeg
2 tablespoons corn oil

Be sure to make the Tomato Sauce first and set it aside.

To make the gnocchi, melt the butter in a large skillet and add the spinach, sorrel, and watercress. Heat slowly, encouraging the greens to wilt evenly by turning the mass over occasionally. Once wilted, continue to cook until most of the liquid has evaporated, pressing down with the back of a wooden spoon to force out as much liquid as possible. Remove from the heat, let cool, then squeeze out any remaining moisture with your hands.

Put the cooked greens into the bowl of a processor fitted with the steel knife and add the parsley, tarragon, chives, mint, ricotta, eggs, flour and 1 cup of the Parmesan. Process to purée, scraping down the sides of the bowl once or twice. Season to taste with salt, pepper, and nutmeg.

Lightly coat your work surface with flour and form the mixture, ½ cup at a time, into long, ½-inch thick ropes, using more flour as needed. Cut the gnocchi at 1-inch intervals and set on wax paper to hold. (Or, form the gnocchi as if they were quenelle, using two spoons of equal size. To do this, scoop up a spoonful of the mixture with one spoon then scrape the other spoon directly underneath the mixture. Now the dumpling is on the second spoon. Repeat this procedure three or four times, coming from the same direction each time, and the dumpling will take on an even oval shape. This is very easy to do once you get the hang of it. With this method the gnocchi can be dropped from the spoon directly into the water. To make a batch at one time, pat each dumpling lightly with flour and place on a floured surface while making the rest.)

Bring a large pot of water and 2 tablespoons oil to a bare simmer. Drop the gnocchi gently into the water, a couple of dozen at a time, and cook for 15 minutes. Do not boil them rapidly or they will fall apart. Remove with a slotted spoon and set on a clean, tightly woven dish towel. Continue until all the gnocchi are cooked.

Drizzle a little of the sauce on the bottom of two 9- by 12-inch gratin baking dishes. Arrange the gnocchi in one layer, drizzle with the remaining sauce, and sprinkle with the remaining Parmesan. Bake at 350° for 15 to 20 minutes, until heated through.

Tomato Sauce with Fennel Seed

Makes about 4 cups.

This recipe makes a thick, puréed tomato sauce with the mild licorice flavor of fennel seed. You can amplify the flavor with a final splash of Pernod, a licorice-flavored apéritif. This is a good all-around tomato sauce that may be used in any number of dishes; try it in lasagne or over steamed cauliflower with a little Parmesan on the side.

> 2 tablespoons olive oil
> 1 medium-sized onion, peeled and chopped
> 2 cloves garlic, finely minced
> ½ teaspoon fennel seeds
> 2 pounds peeled, chopped, juicy ripe tomatoes with their juice
> 1 teaspoon sugar, optional
> Coarse salt
> Freshly grated black pepper

Heat the olive oil and add the onion. Cook slowly until the onion begins to soften, about 15 minutes. Add the garlic and fennel seed and cook for 5 minutes longer.

Add the tomatoes with all of their juice and simmer slowly, uncovered, for 30 to 45 minutes, until the sauce is thick and most of the visible liquid has evaporated. Taste and adjust the flavor with sugar (to offset the acidity), salt and pepper. Put through a food mill (or leave chunky if you like).

Shrimp and Scallop Lasagne

Serves 8.

A multicolored layering of fresh pasta, creamy scallops and shrimp, basil-flavored ricotta, and deep red tomato sauce. Each of the flavors comes through bright and clear, producing both separate and combined effects that are subtly enticing to the palate; a lovely dish for entertaining. (This recipe is more manageable if the pasta and tomato sauce are made ahead; even so it is a rather lengthy affair—but worth it, worth it!)

If fresh basil is not available, one or two tablespoons thawed, frozen pesto may be substituted. Or a combination of finely chopped fresh parsley and green onion may be used or one of finely chopped fresh parsley and a teaspoon of dried basil.

¾ pound small fresh shrimp, peeled, deveined (reserve the shells), and cut into pieces

¾ pound small Oregon scallops, tough muscles on sides removed and reserved

4 cloves garlic, finely minced

1 tablespoon shallots, finely minced

2 tablespoons parsley, finely minced

1 cup dry white wine

1 cup fish fumet (page 346); or ½ cup homemade chicken stock (page 345) and ½ cup bottled clam juice

4 tablespoons unsalted butter

6 tablespoons flour

1 cup cream (or half-and-half)

Few drops Tabasco sauce

Coarse salt

Freshly ground white pepper

Beurre manié—2 tablespoons butter kneaded together with 2 tablespoons flour (optional)

1 tablespoon corn oil

1 teaspoon coarse salt

4 thin sheets of fresh egg pasta, each approximately 9 by 13 inches

Small handful fresh basil, finely chopped

1 cup ricotta cheese

1 tablespoon unsalted butter

½ pound Monterey Jack cheese, grated

½ cup freshly grated Parmesan cheese

2 cups Homemade Tomato Sauce (recipe follows)

Purée the shrimp shells in a processor and combine with the removed scallop muscles, garlic, shallots, parsley, and white wine in a small nonreactive saucepan. Reduce slowly to ¼ cup. Put through a fine strainer, pressing against the solids with the back of a spoon to extract all the flavor. Reserve.

Bring the fish stock to a bare simmer; add the shrimp and scallops. Cook for a few seconds only, just long enough to allow some of the seafood's natural juices to be released but not long enough to cook through. (The shrimp should just barely be turning pink and the scallops should still be translucent in the center.) Remove from the stock with a slotted spoon and set aside to cool in a bowl.

Make a *velouté* sauce, melt the butter, add the flour, and cook together without browning for at least 2 minutes. Add the fish stock, cream, and reduced shrimp shell essence. Bring to a simmer, whisking all the time. Add any juices that have collected in the bowl of shrimp and scallops. If the sauce does not seem quite thick enough to hold the lasagne layers together, keep it at a simmer and add bits of the *beurre manié* to thicken it a little more. The thickness of this sauce varies from time to time depending on the amount of juice collected from the shellfish. The sauce should be smooth and creamy; if you get lumps that cannot be removed by whisking, put the sauce through a strainer. Remove from the heat, cool slightly, then pour over the shrimp and scallops. Taste the sauce and adjust the flavor with salt, pepper, and drops of Tabasco. Place a piece of plastic wrap directly on top to keep a crust from forming.

Cut the sheets of pasta a full ¾ inch smaller than the baking dish you plan to use. Bring a large pot of water to a boil, add the oil and a teaspoon of salt. Add the pasta, 1 or 2 sheets at a time, and cook for just 2 to 3 minutes. Remove from the water and run under cold water to stop the cooking. Leave the sheets in cold water for a minute or two until ready to assemble the dish.

While the pasta is cooking, purée the basil, 1 tablespoon at a time, with the ricotta in a processor. Taste, adding more basil if desired, and salt and pepper to taste.

Butter a large baking dish (approximately 8½ by 13½ inches in size). Lift a sheet of pasta from its cold water bath and wipe off excess water with your hands. Put in one sheet of pasta (or slightly overlapping strips of pasta if sheets are unavailable), distribute half the seafood sauce evenly over the top, sprinkle with Parmesan, then add a layer of Monterey Jack and the second sheet of pasta. With a spoon, evenly dollop on all of the ricotta and basil mixture. Top with Monterey Jack and Parmesan, then the third sheet of pasta. Layer on the remaining seafood sauce evenly; then sprinkle on the last of the Monterey Jack and Parmesan. Top with the fourth and last pasta sheet, then carefully seal the surface with all of the Fresh Tomato Sauce. The dish may be covered and refrigerated at this point until ready to bake. Allow 15 minutes extra baking time if refrigerated.

Cover the baking dish with foil and bake in a 350° oven for 15 minutes. Uncover and continue baking for 15 to 20 minutes more, just until the lasagne is bubbling nicely and the cheeses have melted. (Shrimp and scallops become tough and chewy when overcooked, so be careful.) Remove the lasagne from the oven and let it rest for 5 minutes before cutting. Cut into 8 portions to serve.

Homemade Tomato Sauce

Makes about 6 cups.

Because tomatoes are without sufficient taste much of the year and will not produce a really flavorful sauce, it is much better to buy good quality, sun-ripened tomatoes in the can during the off-season to make tomato sauce. This particular version is chunky with onions, garlic, and tomatoes and resembles nothing available commercially.

- 2 tablespoons olive oil
- 2 medium-sized onions, peeled and chopped
- 4 cloves garlic, finely minced
- 2 teaspoons basil
- 1 teaspoon oregano
- 2 cans (28 ounces each) good quality, peeled tomatoes, chopped (reserve all the juice)
- 1 to 2 teaspoons sugar
  Coarse salt
  Freshly grated black pepper

Heat the olive oil and add the onions. Cook slowly until the onions begin to soften, about 15 minutes. Add the garlic, basil, and oregano and cook for 5 minutes longer.

Add the tomatoes with all of their juice and simmer slowly, uncovered, for 1 to 1½ hours, until the sauce is thick and most of the visible liquid has evaporated. Taste and adjust the flavor with sugar if needed (to offset the acidity), salt, and pepper.

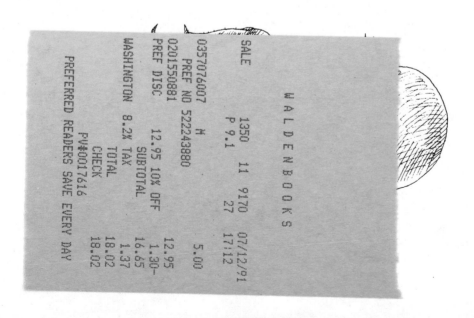

Jewelled Raspberry Tart with Toasted Hazelnut Pastry

Serves 6.

There is something quintessential about this straightforward fresh raspberry tart. The simple elements in coming together become more than the sum of their parts; a truly wonderful taste experience. The tart must, however, be served soon after it is assembled. At most, it will tolerate the refrigerator for two hours or so.

> A 9-inch Toasted Hazelnut Pastry
>   shell, fully baked (page 147)
> 4 ounces cream cheese, very cold
> 1 cup cream, chilled
> 1 teaspoon finely grated lemon zest
> 2 tablespoons powdered sugar
> 2 tablespoons Chambord French
>   raspberry liqueur
> ¾ cup red raspberry jelly
> 2 cups raspberries, rinsed and gently
>   dried on paper towels

Prepare the Toasted Hazelnut Pastry tart shell.

In a mixer (not a processor—it makes the mixture much too thin), blend the cream cheese until very smooth. Add the lemon zest and powdered sugar. Blend again. With the machine running, pour the cream slowly onto the cream cheese and blend until soft peaks are formed. (Yes, a mixture of cream cheese and cream can be whipped.) Add 1 tablespoon liqueur and blend lightly.

Melt the raspberry jelly, remove it from the heat and add the remaining 1 tablespoon liqueur. With a pastry brush, glaze the cooled pastry shell with a thin coating of jelly.

Put the whipped cream mixture into the pastry shell and smooth.

Dip the raspberry bottoms, one at a time, into the still very warm jelly. Arrange the berries on top of the whipped cream mixture in concentric circles until the entire surface of the tart is covered. Using a pastry brush, glaze each berry and the white areas between the berries with jelly. The tart should resemble a shimmering jewel.

Refrigerate for 1 to 2 hours and serve, cut into wedges.

Raspberries and Cream with Toasted Walnut Tiles

Serves 6.

This intensely flavored dessert captures the bright, exotic essence of fresh raspberries. Combined with Raspberry Chambord Sauce, whipped cream and toasted walnut pastry, the effect is both simple and sublime.

12 3- by 4-inch Toasted Walnut Pastry
Tiles (page 146)
1 cup Raspberry Chambord Sauce,
recipe follows
1½ cups cream
2 tablespoons powdered sugar
1½ pints fresh raspberries

GARNISH
6 perfect raspberries

Prepare the Toasted Walnut Pastry Tiles and the Raspberry Chambord Sauce.

Whip the cream with powdered sugar until soft peaks form. Remove ½ cup of whipped cream to a pastry bag fitted with a ½-inch star tip. Refrigerate until ready to use.

Add the raspberries to the Raspberry Chambord Sauce and combine gently.

To assemble, lay one Toasted Walnut Pastry on each of 6 dessert plates. Top each pastry with an equal portion of the whipped cream.

Spoon on the raspberries and sauce, again equally dividing the mixture. (The liquid sauce will form a pool around the pastry.) Top each dessert with another tile. Pipe a large whipped cream star onto each pastry top and place 1 perfect berry in the center. (The whipped cream should be firm enough and deep enough to hold the berry.) Serve immediately.

Raspberry Chambord Sauce

Makes 2 cups.

This elegant sauce brings out all the sparkling flavor of raspberries at their peak and is wonderful with any number of simple desserts, such as rich vanilla ice cream, tart lemon custard, brown sugar-glazed peaches, and especially Glazed Ginger Coeur à la Crème (page 148). The strawberry variation is also wonderful.

2 cups fresh raspberries, cleaned
4 to 6 tablespoons sugar (depending on
the sweetness of the berries)
¼ cup red currant jelly
2 tablespoons Chambord French
raspberry liqueur

Purée the raspberries and sugar together in a food processor. Strain through a fine sieve. Reserve.

Put the red currant jelly into a saucepan over medium heat and warm just to melt, whisking until smooth. Remove from the heat and add the liqueur.

Combine the jelly mixture and the puréed raspberries and mix well. Chill thoroughly.

STRAWBERRY VARIATION

Use strawberries rather than raspberries and strawberry liqueur or a good gin rather than Chambord. You might also want to add a few drops of lemon juice.

Toasted Walnut Pastry

Makes one 9-inch pastry shell or twelve 3- by 4-inch pastry tiles.

Of all the various dessert pastries I do, this is my favorite. The flavor of toasted walnuts is incomparable and the pastry itself, rich with egg yolk and sweet butter, is meltingly tender and crisp at the same time. The hazelnut variation is equally good.

> ¼ cup walnuts
> 1½ cups flour
> 5 tablespoons unsalted butter, cut into pieces and frozen
> 4 tablespoons shortening, chilled
> ½ cup powdered sugar
> 1 egg yolk, lightly beaten
> 2 tablespoons ice water

Arrange the walnuts in a shallow pan and toast in a 275° oven for 20 to 30 minutes, until fragrant and lightly browned. Do not overcook or the walnuts will taste bitter. Remove from the oven and cool.

Using a processor, pulse the nuts, flour, and sugar together until finely chopped. Add the frozen butter and shortening and pulse until very fine and evenly mixed.

Whisk the egg yolk and water together well. Pour this liquid evenly over the top of the flour and butter mixture then pulse a few times just until the dough begins to mass together. Add a few more drops of water if necessary but do not overmix. The pastry should be malleable but not too wet.

Remove the pastry dough from the workbowl and flatten it between 2 pieces of plastic wrap. Refrigerate the dough for 2 hours before rolling it out (or freeze it for 45 minutes.)

Using a pastry cloth and rolling pin cover, roll out the dough to a 12-inch circle or square. Line a 9-inch removable-bottom tart pan with the circular pastry or cut the square pastry into 3- by 4-inch rectangles or "tiles" and put them on a baking sheet.

Refrigerate the rolled pastry dough for 30 minutes. Prick the pastry shell evenly with a fork and line the dough with aluminum foil, filling the foil with pie weights, dried beans or rice. Prick each of the pastry rectangles evenly in a decorative pattern with a fork.

Bake the pastry in a 375° oven for about 20

minutes, until nicely browned. (Remove the foil and pie weights from the pastry shell after 10 minutes and continue baking.) Cool on a wire rack.

HAZELNUT VARIATION

Substitute hazelnuts for walnuts. After they are toasted, rub the hazelnuts in a clean dish towel to loosen and remove the papery skin. Discard the loose skin and do not worry about what remains on the nuts, they will not come uniformly clean.

Raspberries with Champagne Sabayon

Serves 4 to 6.

A simple, elegant, and very pretty blend of fresh raspberries with a light champagne custard. Serve with crisp, lemon-scented cookies and the remaining champagne.

    4 cups fresh raspberries
      Superfine sugar to taste

CHAMPAGNE SABAYON
      4 egg yolks
      ⅓ cup sugar
      ¾ cup champagne
      2 tablespoons Chambord French
         raspberry liqueur

Combine the raspberries with sugar to taste and chill.

To make the sabayon, combine the egg yolks and sugar in the top of a double boiler (or in a heavyweight saucepan if you never curdle your egg yolks). Off the heat, whisk until foamy. Add the champagne and whisk constantly over barely simmering water (or low heat) until thick and creamy. Remove from the heat and add the liqueur.

Fold the sauce into the raspberries and serve hot in tall parfait glasses.

RASPBERRY GRATIN WITH CHAMPAGNE SABAYON

Serves 4 to 6.

Make the Champagne Sabayon as above and chill. Arrange the sweetened berries in individual gratin dishes, cover with chilled Champagne Sabayon, top with a heavy sprinkling of white or brown sugar, and broil very briefly just to glaze the sugar.

Glazed Ginger Coeur à la Crème

Serves 6 to 8.

This creamy dessert cheese may be served with any of the fresh berries and any simple crisp cookie, but this combination with an intense raspberry sauce in addition to fresh raspberries is especially nice. The beautiful heart-shaped mold made especially for this purpose is, if not essential, a pleasure to have. The perforated bottom is meant to allow the cheese to drain though I have found there is little, if any, drainage with this particular recipe. This dessert needs to be put together at least the evening before you intend to serve it.

Stem ginger is available in small, celadon-glazed pottery containers from oriental grocery stores. Or use candied ginger (found in the oriental section of the grocery store) if you like.

- 2 cups grocery-store ricotta (Precious or Frigio brands for instance; you do not want a more expensive ricotta without stabilizers for this; it is too loose)
- 2 cups cream cheese (with or without emulsifiers)
- 2 cups cream
- 6 tablespoons powdered sugar
- 2 tablespoons slivered stem ginger in syrup (do not use the syrup) or slivered candied ginger

Raspberry Chambord Sauce (page 145)
2 cups fresh raspberries

Make sure that the ricotta, cream cheese, cream, mixing bowl, and beaters are all very cold.

In a mixer (do not use a food processor for this—it thins the mixture beyond redemption), purée the ricotta and cream cheese together until very smooth, stopping to scrape the sides of the bowl once or twice. Then, pour the cream in slowly while continuing to whip. Add the slivered ginger and powdered sugar as the cream begins to thicken. Whip only until nicely thick.

Spoon the cheese into a damp cheesecloth-lined heart-shaped porcelain mold (or 4 individual molds) and bring the cheesecloth in over the top to cover the cheese lightly. Put the mold on a rack over an edged plate and refrigerate overnight to allow the whey to drain.

To serve, uncover the cheese, turn it upside-down onto a chilled platter, remove the mold and carefully pull away the cheesecloth. Surround with Raspberry Chambord Sauce and serve with Triple Pepper Cookies (page 149) and fresh raspberries.

VARIATION

This dessert is also wonderful with fresh strawberries and the strawberry sauce described on page 146.

Triple Pepper Cookies

Makes about 6 dozen cookies.

I still remember my first bite of this remarkable cookie. A plate of innocent looking, subtly aromatic ginger cookies was offered. I nibbled one and thought, ah yes, this is very nice—and then, without warning, my entire mouth was on fire. I put the cookie down but found myself retrieving it only a second later. As I quickly learned, these are not only hot, they are also addictive. The original recipe comes from my Finnish mother-in-law, Ellen Bradley. She makes them using only one pepper—white— and calls them Swedish pepparkakor. They are a tradition for the entire Bradley family during the Christmas season but I find them just as wonderful the rest of the year. They are excellent served with Glazed Ginger Coeur à la Crème (page 148), with ice creams and sorbets, and with fresh raspberries or strawberries and crème fraîche.

If you would prefer to be cautious, cut the combined peppercorn measurement in half the first time around. The best way to grind the peppercorns is to use a little spice or coffee mill that is kept only for spices. A mortar and pestle will also work but the pink peppercorns are a bit soft to grind thoroughly in this way.

1 cup unsalted butter, at room temperature
1½ cups sugar
1 egg, beaten

2 tablespoons dark corn syrup
Juice and zest of 1 orange
3¾ cups flour
1 teaspoon ground cinnamon
1 teaspoon ground cloves
1 teaspoon ground ginger
2 teaspoons ground cardamom
2 teaspoons freshly ground white peppercorns
1 teaspoon freshly ground black peppercorns
1 teaspoon freshly ground pink peppercorns
2 teaspoons baking soda
1 teaspoon coarse salt

In a mixer, cream the butter and sugar thoroughly. Add the egg and beat until fluffy. Add the corn syrup, orange juice, and orange zest. Blend well.

Sift the flour together with all of the spices, the baking soda, and the salt. Add this mixture gradually to the cookie batter and blend just to incorporate. Cover the dough with plastic wrap and refrigerate overnight or longer. (Do not eliminate or rush the refrigeration; it is very important to the taste.)

Roll the dough out *very thinly* on a floured pastry cloth with a cloth-covered rolling pin. Cut out shapes with cookie cutters. Arrange on a lightly greased cookie sheet (preferably an air-cushioned cookie sheet) and bake at 375° for 8 to 10 minutes. "Watch, watch," as Ellen says—these cookies color and burn easily. Cool on wire racks. Once cool, these cookies will keep perfectly well for 2 to 3 weeks in an airtight tin or jar. They may also be frozen, wrapped well in heavy-duty foil or in freezer bags, for up to 2 months with no ill effects.

Spiced Peach Crunch

Serves 6.

This dessert is quickly assembled and offers a pleasant contrast between the baked peaches and the crunchy topping that is just right when you have a hankering for peach pie but not the time to make one.

> 5 slightly firm peaches, skinned,
>   pitted, and cut into ½-inch slices
> ¼ cup peach brandy or regular brandy
> ½ cup sugar
> ½ cup brown sugar
> ½ teaspoon freshly grated nutmeg
> ½ teaspoon cinnamon
> ½ cup flour
> ¼ cup toasted wheat germ
> ½ cup unsalted butter
>   Vanilla ice cream or Crème Fraîche
>   (page 357) (optional)

Arrange the peaches in a shallow 1-quart baking dish and sprinkle on the peach brandy.

Combine the dry ingredients, including the spices, and cut in the butter with a pastry cutter until the mixture resembles a fine meal. Sprinkle this mixture evenly over the peaches. Do not mix the two together.

Cover the baking dish with foil and bake at 350° for 30 minutes. Uncover and continue baking for another 30 minutes, or until nicely browned and bubbling.

Let the dessert cool for 10 minutes or so and serve hot with vanilla ice cream or crème fraîche.

Toasted Hazelnut Blueberry Crumble

Serves 8.

As good as this old-fashioned dessert is with fresh blueberries, it is also delicious with cherries, blackberries, or peaches. Adjust the sugar measurement to compensate for varying degrees of sweetness. Need I suggest ice cream as an accompaniment?

> 6 cups blueberries
>   Zest of 1 lemon
>   Juice of 1 lemon (about ¼ cup)
> 2 tablespoons sugar
> 2 tablespoons brown sugar
> 4 tablespoons cornstarch

6 tablespoons unsalted butter
¼ cup flour
¼ cup brown sugar
½ cup sugar
6 tablespoons chopped, toasted
   hazelnuts

GARNISH
   Whipped cream or crème fraîche
   (optional)

Combine the blueberries, lemon zest, lemon juice, regular sugar and brown sugar in a mixing bowl. Sprinkle on the cornstarch and mix in. Butter a 9- by 12-inch gratin dish with 1 teaspoon of the butter and put the berries inside.

Cut the butter into the flour and the remaining two sugars until well incorporated. Mix in the nuts.

Sprinkle the topping over the blueberries, being careful not to mix the two together.

Bake at 350° for 50 to 60 minutes. The topping should be brown, set, and crispy. Serve hot or cold with whipped cream or crème fraîche.

Blueberry Lemon Gratin

Serves 6 to 8.

The contrast of cold mousse and hot, caramelized topping is quite pleasing here. Lemon and blueberries have an affinity. Blackberries are also delicious in this recipe.

LEMON MOUSSE
   5 eggs, separated
   ⅔ cup sugar
   ¾ cup lemon juice
   1 cup cream
   2 teaspoons lemon zest

BERRIES
   4 cups blueberries
   ⅓ cup sugar

TOPPING
   4 tablespoons sugar

In the top of a double boiler off the heat, whisk the egg yolks for several minutes with ⅓ cup of the sugar until thick and pale. Set the mixture over barely simmering water, add the lemon juice, and stir slowly until the mixture coats a wooden spoon. Be careful not to overcook or you will curdle the egg. If you notice any graininess, stop and set the pan immediately into a bowl of ice water to cool, whisking furiously all the while.

Remove from the heat, put the pan into a bowl of ice water (if you have not done so already), place a piece of plastic wrap directly over the top, and chill.

Beat the egg whites in a copper bowl with a balloon whisk to stiff peaks, incorporating the remaining ⅓ cup sugar slowly at the soft-peak stage.

Whip the cream to soft peaks, then fold into the chilled custard base along with the lemon zest. Fold in part of the egg whites to lighten the mousse, then the rest as quickly and gently as possible.

Toss the blueberries with ⅓ cup sugar. Spoon half of the mousse on the bottom of a gratin dish, top with the berries, then evenly cover with the rest of the mousse. Chill thoroughly for 2 to 3 hours.

Just before serving, sprinkle the remaining 4 tablespoons sugar over the top of the gratin and broil briefly to melt and caramelize it. Serve right away.

Blueberry Ginger Cheesecake

Serves 8.

This updated version of blueberry cheesecake was evoked from a childhood memory. Back then it had a graham cracker crust and canned blueberry pie filling. I loved it but this one is better.

PASTRY

    ¾ cup flour
    ¼ cup finely chopped walnuts
    ¼ teaspoon ground ginger
    5 tablespoons sugar
    8 tablespoons unsalted butter

CHEESE FILLING

    2 packages (8 ounces each) cream cheese
    ½ cup sugar
    2 eggs
    1 teaspoon vanilla extract

TOPPING

    1 pound fresh blueberries
    1 to 2 teaspooons peeled, grated fresh ginger
    ¼ cup sugar
    2 teaspoons cornstarch
    ½ cup water

To make the pastry, combine the flour, walnuts, ginger, and sugar in a mixing bowl. Cut in the butter to resemble fine crumbs. Distribute the crumbs evenly over the bottom and sides of a 9-inch pie plate and press in place to form a crust. (Do not extend the edges above the edge of the plate.) Press a piece of foil onto the crust and fill with pie weights or dried beans. Bake at 400° for 30 minutes and remove the blind carefully so as not to tear the crust, which is very fragile at this point. If the bottom is not completely set, cook for 5 minutes longer, protecting the edges with a ring of foil.

To make the cheese filling, whip the cream cheese and sugar in a processor or in a mixer until smooth. Blend in the eggs and vanilla. Put the cream cheese mixture into the cooled pie crust and bake at 350° for 30 minutes. Remove from the oven and let cool for 30 minutes.

To make the topping, combine the blueberries, grated ginger, sugar, and cornstarch, then drizzle the water on top and mix well. (If using frozen berries, omit the water.) Put the mixture into a saucepan and bring to a full simmer to activate the cornstarch. When the liquid turns glossy, remove from the heat.

Top the cheesecake evenly with the sauce, let it cool thoroughly, then refrigerate the dessert for at least 6 hours or overnight.

Tangy Lime Soufflé with Blackberry Lime Sauce

Serves 8.

A light, refreshing soufflé, imbued with the tangy zest of fresh lime. Served with a vibrant purée of ripe blackberries, this is the quintessential late-summer dessert.

> 2 cups Blackberry Lime Sauce (recipe follows)
> ¾ cup milk
> 1½ tablespoons cornstarch
> 3 tablespoons fresh lime juice
> 2 teaspoons lime zest
> 4 egg yolks
> 6 egg whites
> ⅛ teaspoon cream of tartar (optional)
> Pinch coarse salt
> ⅓ cup sugar

GARNISH
> 1 cup fresh, ripe blackberries

In a heavy saucepan, combine the milk and cornstarch thoroughly. Bring to a simmer and cook until thickened, stirring constantly. Remove from the heat and stir in the lime juice, zest, and egg yolks. Blend thoroughly with a whisk.

Beat the egg whites (preferably in a large copper bowl with a balloon whisk) until foamy. (If you are using a mixer, add the cream of tartar.) Add the salt and continue to whisk to the soft-peak stage. Add the sugar, a little at a time, and continue whisking until the egg whites form stiff peaks when lifted with the whisk.

Stir a scoop of the egg whites into the egg custard mixture to lighten it. Then gently and quickly fold in the remainder.

Lightly butter eight 1-cup soufflé dishes. Spoon the soufflé mixture into them, smoothing the tops. Bake at 350° for 20 minutes, until the soufflés have risen well above the rims of the dishes and are lightly browned.

Remove the soufflés from the oven, arrange them quickly on small dessert plates and pour ¼ cup of Blackberry and Lime Sauce over each. (The sauce will run down the sides of the soufflés and onto the plates.) Garnish each plate with a few fresh blackberries and serve immediately.

Blackberry Lime Sauce

Makes about 2 cups sauce.

   4 cups ripe blackberries
   ½ cup lime marmalade
   2 tablespoons blackberry liqueur or
       brandy
   ¾ cup sugar

Put the blackberries through a food mill, then put through a fine sieve. Heat the marmalade and liqueur in a saucepan just until the jelly melts. Add the sugar and stir to dissolve. Pour the marmalade mixture into the sieved berries and combine thoroughly. Chill.

Mint Soufflé with Huckleberry Sauce

Serves 6.

Soufflés do not deserve the fearful reputation they have garnered over the years. Contrary to popular opinion, they are not difficult to make and take a lot less effort than most other stellar desserts. Just be sure to have your guests ready with forks in hand about five minutes before you bring the soufflé to the table. It will begin to deflate almost immediately so you need to be quick about serving it before it collapses. Using large serving spoons, portion the soufflé by positioning the spoons back to back, then plunge them down into the soufflé and away from each other. Two movements like this, a few inches apart, will produce a tidy serving. Be sure to give each person a share of the crispy outside along with the saucelike interior—the variation in texture is sublime.

HUCKLEBERRY SAUCE
   4 cups huckleberries or blackberries
   ¾ cup sugar
   ½ cup red currant jelly
   2 tablespoons blackberry liqueur or
      brandy

SOUFFLÉ
   6 tablespoons unsalted butter
   6 tablespoons flour
   1 cup milk
   ½ cup cream
   ½ cup sugar
   5 eggs separated, plus 2 extra whites
   2 tablespoons peppermint schnapps
   Pinch cream of tartar (optional)

GARNISH
   Mint leaves
   Powdered sugar in a sieve

To make the Huckleberry Sauce, put the berries through a food mill, then put through a fine sieve. Heat the jelly and liqueur in a saucepan, just until the jelly melts. Add ¾ cup sugar and stir to dissolve. Pour the jelly mixture into the sieved berries and combine thoroughly. Chill.

To make the soufflé sauce base, melt the butter in a small heavy saucepan over medium heat until foamy. Stir in the flour and cook without browning for 2 minutes. Gradually whisk in the milk, the cream and ¼ cup of the sugar. Cook, stirring constantly, until thick and smooth.

Remove from the heat. Add the egg yolks, one at a time, whisking well after each addition. Stir in the peppermint schnapps.

Using a copper bowl and a balloon whisk, whisk the seven egg whites to soft peaks. Gradually add the remaining ¼ cup sugar and continue whisking to stiff peaks. (If using a mixer, add ¼ teaspoon cream of tartar to the egg whites to insure their stability.) Fold into the hot sauce base.

Butter and sugar an 8-cup soufflé dish fitted with a foil collar. Fill to within ½ inch of the top and then run your thumb around the edge to make a ½-inch-deep groove to produce a top-hat effect. Bake at 400° for 40 minutes on the lowest oven rack.

When the soufflé is done, remove it from the oven, sieve powdered sugar over the top, and serve immediately with the chilled Huckleberry Sauce. Garnish each serving with whole mint leaves.

Fall

SEPTEMBER • OCTOBER • NOVEMBER

Fall is a season of prolific abundance in the Pacific Northwest. In its early stages it offers a period of overlap when some of the fruits and vegetables of summer are still available together with a whole new spectrum of fall ingredients. It is without a doubt the most magnificent time to wander through Seattle's Pike Place Market, the culinary mecca of the region. Masses of dahlias, cosmos, and chrysanthemums shed their luminous glow over the new harvest: a procession of bell peppers, chili peppers, potatoes, apples, pears, leafy greens, apple cider, squash, wild mushrooms, and shellfish. For the creative cook, the culinary palette is rich with color, taste, and texture.

The foods of this season definitely need to be heartier than those of summer, though warm afternoons still call for a certain measure of lightness. Gratins, curries, and casseroles re-enter our cooking regimens now. Even desserts take on a homier, heartier, definitely comforting aspect. As the land nurtures its inhabitants with this final burst of frantic energy, those of us who cook take increasing pleasure in extending Nature's edible offerings to friends and family, who are ready once again for the pleasures of hearth and home.

I enjoy focusing on the season's newest offerings, both to increase my understanding of their potential and to increase my seasonal repertoire of tried-and-true dishes. So even though raspberries are still available during the early fall, intellectually and creatively, I am ready for apples. This chapter, then, contains those ingredients I consider of tantamount importance to this season. Basic information on apple cider, fresh pumpkin, sole and flounder, squid, clams, game birds, potatoes, wild mushrooms, peppers, leafy greens, cranberries and apples is included. Quick and easy concept recipes are supplied for pumpkin, potatoes, wild mushrooms, and leafy greens—four important comestibles that most cooks do not use to full advantage.

Within the context of cooking seasonally, it is interesting to note that foods of a particular season (not to mention a particular region) seem naturally to enhance one another. It is difficult to imagine, for instance, a combination of raspberries or strawberries with pumpkin. Yet cranberries are wonderful with pumpkin.

Apple Cider

Fresh cider is the natural, sweet liquid that is released by pressing finely chopped or ground apples. The liquid is fresh *cider* as long as it remains in its natural state and is not sweetened, preserved, pasteurized, clarified, or otherwise altered. If pasteurized or preserved with additives, the result should technically be called apple *juice*—a distinction not often made in the supermarket. Apple juice tastes absolutely pedestrian when compared to apple cider. All the life, subtlety, and nuance have been cooked out of it. Fresh cider is always sweet, full of apple flavor, and is not effervescent.

Fresh cider is alive and highly volatile and must be kept under refrigeration to slow or control the hardening process. Wild yeasts present on the skin of the apples inoculate the juice as it is being pressed and begin almost immediately to change the natural sugars in the juice to alcohol. As fermentation progresses and the solid particles slowly settle, the sweetness begins to subside and the cider appears clearer and lighter in color. The end result is called *hard cider* and is really the same thing as an apple wine.

Bottled cider is a clear and usually straw-colored liquid that is effervescent and often fruity in taste, with an alcohol content of between three and six percent. The style and taste vary greatly from maker to maker. Some ciders are left on the dry side; others are left with some residual sugar or given a dose of sugar just before being bottled. Different varieties of apples produce different flavors. It can be great fun to sample American, European, Canadian, and Australian ciders. Use the same types of tasting procedures and terminology that you would for wine. Fruitiness, balance, body, acidity, and sweetness are terms that all apply to cider. In some English bottled ciders, tannin is also present.

Season

Fresh cider is usually best in the fall when the apples are at their best. Some producers in the Northwest, such as Wax Orchards on Vashon Island, have the capacity to freeze the fresh crushed apple pomace and thus are able to make cider year-round from the best-tasting apples.

Selection

Fresh cider is generally a local commodity. In Washington there are several small commercial producers. Their ciders can be found at the Pike Place Market and in health food stores. Since each producer uses a different blend of apples and more or less quality control, each makes a different tasting cider. Be sure that what you are buying is very fresh. This said, I have never tasted a bad apple cider.

Storage

Fresh cider will remain in its sweet full-bodied condition for between ten and twenty-one days if stored at or below 38 degrees. In other words, refrigerated. (Cider may also be frozen.) The cool temperature slows but does not stop the natural fermentation process. Once this process begins, cider becomes, successively, a number of different beverages.

Hardening

Hardening, the process of turning sugar to alcohol, is best done with as little exposure to air as possible and in the lower temperature ranges. Cider will taste rough and strong when hardened at temperatures higher than 40 degrees. Successful fermentation is never guaranteed, but carefully made cider rarely goes bad if proper precautions are taken. (The cap on a bottle of cider should be slightly loose, enough to allow carbon dioxide to escape, but not so loose as to allow oxygen to enter the bottle.)

The first stage of natural fermentation is the semidry stage. At this point the cider is usually quite effervescent and noticeably drier than when first pressed. The alcohol content is usually no more than three percent. Semidry cider is fruity and still fairly sweet. Most bottled ciders fall into this category.

The second stage is called *dry-hard*. This stage will often take weeks at low temperature to achieve. Dry-hard cider is bone dry and has an alcohol content of between six and seven percent. Dry-hard cider is quite clear and, if stored for a number of weeks after fermentation is complete, will become completely clear as suspended particles sink to the bottom of the jug. Some fruitiness may be in evidence at this stage but most dry-hard ciders have virtually no apple flavor. Effervescence also disappears when cider is fully fermented.

To make apple cider vinegar, remove the cap from a bottle of cider and expose the still-fermenting contents to the air. The change from alcohol to acetic acid can take several weeks and for best flavor the bottle should be kept refrigerated below 40 degrees.

Cooking

Sweetness is a primary consideration when using cider in cooking. The natural sugar content of fresh sweet cider averages twelve percent; two tablespoons sugar per cup of liquid. If you prefer something less sweet, use semidry or dry-hard cider. Balance in the cider between sweetness and acidity is also important to the cook. Most well-made cider is high in acid. This acid can be desirable in many dishes. Fruitiness is also a consideration. The cook needs to determine whether a definite apple taste is desirable in a particular dish. If it is, use fresh sweet cider or semidry cider; if not, use dry-hard cider.

Apple Cider Recipe

Hazelnut-Fried Fresh Mozzarella with Apple Cider and Chives, *page 211*

Fresh Pumpkin

Fresh pumpkin, that bright harbinger of fall, is relegated primarily to the festivities surrounding Halloween. Even the pumpkin pies of Thanksgiving Day are made mostly with canned pumpkin. This is unfortunate because pumpkin is a most delicious squash and wonderfully versatile as well. The flesh is soft, moist, and sweet. As a bonus, it is inexpensive, easy to prepare, and because of its mild flavor, marries well with a variety of other foods.

Despite its being part of our national food heritage, it is difficult to find a good selection of recipes for pumpkin. There are the two Thanksgiving pies, custard and chiffon, an occasional quick bread, and French pumpkin soup. Of late, pumpkin ravioli have also entered the repertoire of trendy Italian and New American restaurants. But beyond that there is a great void, even though pumpkin originated on American soil (South American, that is). It is more frequently used in the cuisines of other countries, such as Mexico, Latin America, Spain, the Caribbean, southern France, India,

the Middle East, and Africa, than it is in our own. Cookbooks from those regions offer good starting points for an exploration into the uses of pumpkin. Aside from these, experimentation offers the widest avenue of possibilities. With a few guidelines in mind, pumpkin can be used as the exciting autumn vegetable that Nature intended it to be.

Selection

Select firm, clean, mature pumpkins with unblemished rinds. The size and shape do not affect the flavor noticeably, although the smaller pumpkins have more tender flesh and less waste.

Season

Pumpkins are harvested primarily in October, although it is possible to find them at a local farm or at Pike Place Market as early as mid-September and, if you are very lucky, as late as mid-December. They must be picked as they ripen because cold snaps and excessive rain will quickly ruin them. Most people buy pumpkins specifically for Halloween celebrations so growers and grocers alike see little sense in displaying them after October 31. If you plan to use recipes calling for fresh pumpkin in November and December, remember to buy several extra in October. They keep well.

Storage

Although they are available only for a short time, pumpkins will keep for up to three months in the refrigerator or in a cool, dry place. (I keep mine on a covered deck just off the kitchen.) Once cut, they will keep for three or four days if sealed in plastic wrap and refrigerated.

Preparation

Snap off the stem and cut the pumpkin into quarters, eighths, or even smaller pieces, depending on its size. Scrape out the fibrous material and the seeds with a spoon. With a sharp paring knife, peel the outer rind off the pumpkin pieces. Cut the pieces into manageable chunks and proceed as directed in the recipe. (Generally pumpkin is then cut into smaller pieces, chopped, or grated.)

Cooking

Fresh pumpkin has a very mild, sweet flavor, very different from that of commercially canned pumpkin purée. It blends well with other foods, but if you want the delicate pumpkin flavor to come through, do not combine it with overly assertive ingredients. Subtle curry blends, lime juice, garlic, cinnamon, nutmeg, cloves, ginger, green onions, chives, beef, pork, and poultry are all compatible with fresh pumpkin. You may or may not like desserts such as pumpkin pie or pumpkin mousse made with fresh pumpkin. They will not have the assertive flavor of canned pumpkin that most of us are accustomed to. Pumpkin is somewhat coarse and fibrous in texture and is easily reduced to a purée. Do not drown it in water or overcook it or it will fall apart.

To cook it, I usually cut the pumpkin into 1-inch pieces and steam them over boiling water in a covered pan. It will be quite tender in about twelve minutes. Pumpkin pieces may also be cooked in a very small quantity of water in a covered pan over low heat, until tender. They will release their own juices as they cook but be sure you do not cook them dry. You may also bake the vegetable, which is probably the easiest method of all. Simply cut the pumpkin in half, seed it, and bake in a 350° oven, on an oiled baking sheet, cut-side down, until the flesh is tender. This will take about an hour, depending on the size of the piece. To use, scrape the cooked pumpkin out of its rind.

For some recipes, you will want to thicken the pumpkin purée by continuing to cook it slowly (keep stirring) to evaporate excess liquid.

Pumpkin Recipes

Pumpkin Hazelnut Torte with Chocolate Glaze, *page 258*
Pumpkin and Rum Mousse, *page 260*
see also Recipe Notes, *below*

RECIPE NOTES

CAULIFLOWER AND PUMPKIN STRATA

Section a large cauliflower into small florets and steam until tender but still crunchy. Season with salt, pepper and 1 tablespoon butter. Put into a 6-cup baking dish. Sprinkle with 3 tablespoons Parmesan cheese. Put 2 cups thoroughly steamed pumpkin pieces through a food mill. Add 2 tablespoons butter, ¼ cup sour cream, and salt and pepper to taste. Spoon the purée evenly over the cauliflower. Sprinkle the top with ⅓ cup fresh, fine bread crumbs. Bake at 350° for 20 minutes to heat through. Wonderful as a side dish for the Thanksgiving buffet.

BAKED PURÉE OF PUMPKIN

Steam 3 cups diced pumpkin and 1 cup diced potato together until tender. Sauté half a chopped onion and 2 cloves minced garlic in 2 tablespoons butter until well softened but not browned. Put pumpkin, potatoes, onions, and garlic through a food mill. Beat 2 eggs lightly and combine with pumpkin mixture and ½ cup grated Gruyère cheese. Season to taste with salt, pepper, and nutmeg. Butter a 6- by 9-inch gratin dish and smooth the pumpkin purée into it. Sprinkle top with a mixture of ¼ cup grated Gruyère cheese and 1 tablespoon grated Parmesan cheese. Bake at 350° for 20 to 25 minutes to heat through and brown the cheese. This will serve as a light supper dish or as a vegetable dish with simple roasts and sautés. Try it with fried chicken.

GRATIN OF PUMPKIN, RICE, AND CHEESE

Sauté 1 minced onion in 2 tablespoons olive oil until nearly softened. Add 2 pounds diced pumpkin and continue stirring and cooking for about 10 minutes, until the pumpkin is almost tender. Combine 1 cup cooked rice, ½ cup grated Gruyère cheese, 1 beaten egg, ¼ teaspoon cinnamon, and a pinch nutmeg. Fold in the onions and pumpkin, season well with salt and pepper, and put into an oiled gratin dish. Sprinkle with ¼ cup grated Gruyère cheese mixed with ¼ cup fine bread crumbs and 1 tablespoon butter. Bake at 350° for 20 minutes or until heated through. A lovely luncheon or simple supper dish, it may also be served as an accompaniment to simple roasts and sautés.

PUMPKIN PURÉE

Season a thick purée of pumpkin with a pinch of allspice, mace, a little brown sugar, salt and pepper to taste, a dash of cream, and a final dollop of butter. Delicious as an accompaniment to roast pork or ham.

PUMPKIN FRITTERS

Dip ¼-inch-thick slices of uncooked pumpkin into your favorite fritter batter (well seasoned) and deep-fry. These make unusual and tasty appetizers.

WHEAT GERM-FRIED PUMPKIN

Dip ¼-inch-thick slices of uncooked pumpkin into flour and shake off the excess. Then dip into beaten egg and lastly into wheat germ. Put on a rack to dry for 30 minutes. Sauté in clarified butter or in a combination of butter and oil until golden brown on each side. Serve as a vegetable accompaniment to roasted or grilled meats.

POTATO AND PUMPKIN GRATIN

Using the Potato Gratin recipe on page 322, substitute sliced pumpkin for half of the potatoes, alternating the rows to produce a striped effect.

PUMPKIN AND APPLE CURRY

Sauté 1 chopped onion in 2 tablespoons butter until softened. Add 1 teaspoon best-quality Indian curry powder and 2 cloves minced garlic and continue cooking for 2 minutes without browning. Add 1 pound cubed pumpkin and ½ pound cubed, peeled tart green apple (such as Granny Smith). Cover and "sweat" over very low heat until the pumpkin and apple are tender but not falling apart. If the mixture tends to stick to the pan, add a dash of water or chicken stock. Combine gently and season to taste with salt and pepper. Use as a vegetable side dish.

INDIAN BRAISED PUMPKIN

Sauté 2 diced onions in 4 tablespoons butter until softened. Stir in 1 teaspoon best-quality Indian curry powder or your own *garam masala* (page 358) and continue cooking for 2 minutes. Add 1 teaspoon minced fresh ginger, 2 cloves minced garlic, 1 diced green pepper, 2 seeded, diced hot chili peppers, and 1½ pounds cubed pumpkin. Cover and "sweat" the mixture for about 10 minutes, until the pumpkin is tender but not falling apart. Add a dash of water or stock if necessary to prevent sticking. Gently combine the mixture and sprinkle with chopped cilantro just before serving.

PUMPKIN CRÈME BRULÉE

Whisk 8 egg yolks with ½ cup sugar just until smooth. Blend in 1½ cups pumpkin purée, 1½ teaspoons cinnamon, 1 teaspoon ginger, and ½ teaspoon allspice. Whisking constantly, add 2 cups hot, scalded half-and-half. Transfer the custard to a heavyweight saucepan and cook over medium heat, stirring slowly with a wooden spoon, until thickened, about 10 minutes. Do not cook beyond 180° or the

eggs will curdle. Portion the hot custard into 8 individual miniature soufflé dishes or custard cups. Chill, covered, for 2 hours or overnight. One hour before serving, sieve ¾ cup brown sugar, and cover the tops of the individual pumpkin custards evenly. Broil for less than a minute, just until the sugar melts and begins to brown. Chill for at least an hour and serve.

PUMPKIN AND GINGER ICE CREAM

Put a 2-inch portion of vanilla bean, split down the center, into a saucepan with 2 cups half-and-half. Bring just to a simmer and remove from the heat. Remove the vanilla bean. Whisk together 6 egg yolks, ⅔ cup sugar, 1 cup pumpkin purée, 1½ teaspoons ground ginger, and 2 tablespoons slivered candied ginger. Pour a little of the hot half-and-half into the egg mixture and blend. Pour this mixture back into the saucepan of half-and-half and blend. Stir slowly with a wooden spoon over medium heat until thickened. The custard will coat a spoon at around 175°. Do not go beyond 180° or you will curdle the egg yolks. Cool, cover, and refrigerate overnight. Using a Donvier ice cream machine (or a similar make that requires no salt or ice), churn the custard according to the manufacturer's directions. When the ice cream has reached the soft-set stage, add 1 cup of cream that has been whipped to a soft peak and continue to churn until set.

Sole and Flounder

No fish family lends itself more to such a variety of imaginative dishes as the flatfish. The texture and delicate flavor of these fish are ideally suited to the elaborate use of sauces, herbs, spices, fruits, and vegetables, as well as to contrasting seafoods. Cooking methods include most of the usual ones: poaching, steaming, baking, broiling, grilling, and frying. About the only methods incompatible with sole and flounder are braising and stewing as the lean, delicate flesh does not hold up to these treatments.

The term *sole* is definitely a misnomer on the West Coast. Fish marketed here as "Dover sole" and "English sole" are actually flounder. Authentic Dover sole, or any other type of true sole for that matter, is only obtainable in the United States as a frozen import from England or France. The term *flounder* refers to any one of three families of flatfish representing more than 200 species in the Atlantic and Pacific oceans. These encompass fish from the tiny sand dab to the giant Pacific halibut.

Season

The commercial fisheries for flounder use the entire length of coastline from southern Oregon to Northern Canada, thus making flounder available in some form during every month of the year. Generally the fish are filleted on

board and arrive at the market ready to cook. Whole, undressed flounder can be difficult to obtain, though Mutual Fish in Seattle sometimes has them.

Selection

With fillets, the best indicator of freshness is the smell. The fish should be clean and sweet smelling with no fishy aroma. The flesh should be glistening with moisture (though not floating in liquid), with no signs of drying out around the edges.

Storage

As with all fish, constant refrigeration is of utmost importance. If I am shopping more than thirty minutes from home, I will take along an ice chest to store the catch for the return voyage. Once home, I place a deep tray filled with ice in the refrigerator, wrap the fish well in plastic wrap, then in aluminum foil, and set it on top of the ice. If the fish is very fresh, it will keep thus for two or three days. Usually, however, it has already been out of the sea for too long and needs to be cooked as soon as possible to retain its flavor and texture.

Preparation

All fish should be gutted before being sold. Check to see that this has been done, then have the fish merchant scale the fish for you if you plan to cook it whole, or fillet it for you oth-

erwise. With ready-made fillets, there is no preparation necessary beyond a gentle dip in cold water to clear any surface bacteria. Do not subject fillets to the pressure of running water; this destroys enzymes within the cells that promote the quick cooking of the flesh.

Cooking

Most members of the flatfish family are very lean. Lack of fat means that the flesh can dry out easily during cooking. Cooking methods that supply extra moisture—poaching, steaming, and sautéing—are therefore the classic treatments for flounder and sole. However, as long as they are basted regularly, these lean fish may be baked, broiled, or even grilled.

THE NOMENCLATURE OF SOLE

Sole is the pivotal species around which European chefs of the past created their masterpieces. There are hundreds of classic sole preparations listed in the various tomes of French gastronomy. This type of fish, a lean, white flatfish, receives little attention from the current wave of American chefs. To judge from cookbooks produced by the more noted of these chefs during the past three years, salmon, trout, black cod, and halibut are much preferred, perhaps because grilling has become so important. Nevertheless what is called sole is still a fish with potential for the home cook. Following is a listing of the types most often

available in local markets and, as you will see, not all sole is created equal.

Dover Sole

In the United States, Dover sole is the common name of a large Pacific flounder, and is not to be confused with the true Dover sole of Europe. Found in deeper waters than most other flatfish are, few Dovers are taken in Puget Sound. The largest of the Northwest soles, reaching a weight of ten pounds, Dovers are mostly caught in the summer. Even at its best it is only a fair fish. Because of its slimy skin, Dover sole is always marketed as skinless, boneless fillets.

English Sole

English sole is a small Pacific flounder and the most common flatfish taken in Puget Sound. It averages fifteen inches in length and just under a pound in weight. Most of the catch comes in late winter and early spring, though the fish is available year round. Varying in quality from very fine to pretty good, it occasionally has an iodine aroma. It is priced midway between petrale and Dover sole.

Petrale Sole

Petrale sole is a large Pacific flounder and easily the tastiest, best-textured sole taken in Northwest waters. As it has the most value gastronomically speaking, it is also the most

expensive. Harvested along the coast, petrale is available throughout the year, though there is an especially active winter fishery. Petrale averages seventeen inches in length and 2½ pounds in weight.

Rex Sole

A small Pacific flounder, rex sole is extremely delicate with a fine texture. Being less numerous than other flatfish it is therefore usually more expensive. Too thin to fillet properly, rex sole are commonly cooked whole.

Rock Sole

Late winter is the main season for rock sole, a flounder of fair to good quality.

Sand Sole

A small Pacific flounder, sand sole is generally accepted as second to petrale in quality.

Yellowfin Sole

A small flounder, yellowfin sole comprises the largest sole fishery in the world. The main season is summer and the fish are reasonably priced, but only fair in quality.

THE NOMENCLATURE OF FLOUNDER

Alaska Plaice

Considered to be of comparable quality to the European plaice (an excellent flounder, though considered by most Europeans to be plebeian when compared to their sole and turbot), Alaska plaice can be expected to appear more on markets in the United States in the coming years.

Arrowtooth Flounder

Often marketed as turbot, arrowtooth flounder is not bad though its texture is soft. The reputation of this fish has been muddied because it is often frozen twice, first at sea and again after being filleted ashore. Its fragile flesh does not hold up well to such treatment.

Pacific Sanddab

A miniature but delectable flounder, the Pacific sanddab reaches a weight of two pounds but is more often seen at between eight and ten ounces in weight. A tasty panfish, it is best prepared whole after gutting and removing the fins. Very sweet and of a fine texture, dabs are no less venerated than are petrale and rex soles by many in the Northwest.

Starry Flounder

One of the most widely distributed of the Pacific flounders, the starry flounder is sometimes called the roughjacket. Their average market weight is two pounds, though these fish can reach a weight of fifteen pounds. Generally, this flounder is considered only fair at table when compared to many other Pacific flatfish.

Turbot

Turbot is a common name for several Pacific flounders, among them the diamond turbot, hornyhead turbot, and spotted turbot. This fish has nothing in common with the esteemed European turbot. These are fair flounders that are inaccurately marketed to increase their appeal.

Sole Recipes

Squid

Although squid has still not gained the popularity in America that it enjoys in other parts of the world—in particular Japan and Italy—it is definitely attracting the attention of seafood enthusiasts in the Northwest. It may be rather fantastic looking—a creamy mauve in color with long tentacles projecting from its head—but it is a highly economical, subtly delicious source of low-fat protein. Eighty percent of it is edible, which is unusually high compared to other finfish and crustaceans.

Puget Sound is home to large colonies of squid that range in length from one inch to 6 feet, but the bulk of the Northwest commercial catch comes from off the coast of Oregon. Because the smaller squid (generally the most desirable from a culinary point of view) travel in large schools, they are easily harvested. Commercial fishing boats find the schools during the day with a depth recorder, then anchor and wait for evening when the squid surface to feed. The squid are either netted or siphoned directly into the boats with a large hydraulic pump.

The Italians have always considered squid a great delicacy. Their name for it, infinitely more appealing than our own, is calamari. On Northwest restaurant menus, *calamari fritti* has long been a popular offering and probably the best way to initiate a would-be squid eater to the charms of this sweet and delicate seafood. Strips or rings of squid are lightly coated with a batter and deep-fried, sealing in all the tender juiciness. But as good as this dish is, it only hints at the gastronomic heights to which squid can ascend when properly prepared.

There are really only two ways to cook squid—quickly or slowly. Anything in between will produce the rubbery, tough texture that many people associate with squid. Cooks should think in terms of one or two minutes for sautéed, stir-fried, or deep-fried squid and an hour or longer for stewed preparations. If the squid is cooked in such a way that it loses all of its natural juices, such as in a sauce, it will have to be subjected to heat for much longer to make it fully tender once again. Although squid has a slightly chewy texture, it should always be tender enough to cut with a fork.

Season

Because so much of the catch is frozen, squid is available year-round.

Selection

Squid is one of the more perishable mollusks. Because of this, it is usually sold frozen, but on occasion you will also find it fresh. It is sold whole in its natural state, in entirely dressed "tubes," or as flat steaks. The latter are produced from larger specimens whose mantles have been dressed and opened out.

Storage

Just as with other seafoods, store squid on ice in the refrigerator and use as soon as possible.

Preparation

For dressed tubes or opened-out steaks, little preparation is necessary. Simply cut the tubes into rings and score both sides of the steaks lightly in a crosshatch pattern so that the cooking medium can penetrate. Check the following section, Cleaning Whole Squid, if you have purchased undressed squid.

Cooking

Squid is generally deep-fried, pan-fried, or stewed. Squid has a very mild flavor; if you want to taste it, keep the accompanying ingredients subtle. Or you can choose to use its succulent texture and interesting shape as a foil for very assertive sauces and let the flavor of the squid act as a background.

CLEANING WHOLE SQUID

Cleaning whole squid is a lot easier than it sounds and is very quick. Squid used to come only in their natural state at the market; now you can purchase them already cleaned if you like. Doing it yourself insures that you get the tentacles, which add drama to some dishes. The mantle, fins, and tentacles are edible, as is the ink. In smaller squid, the mantles are generally sliced into half-inch rings, while the tentacles are left whole. In larger specimens, the mantle may be slit, opened out flat, pounded or scored to tenderize it, then sliced into strips. Smaller squid mantles may be left whole and filled with any number of savory stuffings, some that include the chopped tentacles.

1. Begin by gently pulling the head, with tentacles attached, away from the main body cavity or "mantle." Most of the innards of the squid will come along too. Set aside the head sections for a moment.
2. With your fingers, feel inside the mantle, which now looks like a tube that is closed at one end, until you find the *pen,* a stiff, plastic-like structure. Pull it out and discard it.
3. With a small spoon or your fingers, remove any remaining viscera from the inside of the mantle. Flush the tube with running water.
4. Peel the thin skin of the mantle away from the white body and the triangular fin. Gently remove the fins from the mantle by carefully tearing them away.
5. Cut the tentacles from the rest of the head by slicing just below the eyes. The tentacles should remain attached to one another by a narrow rim of edible flesh. If you plan to cook the squid in its own ink, separate the silvery-gray ink sac from the viscera. Discard the head and viscera.

6. Lay out the tentacles opened like a flower and remove the small black "beak" in the center.

Squid Recipes

Braised Squid Mediterranean-Style, *page 226*
Linguini with Squid Marinara, *page 227*

Clams

More than two dozen varieties of clam inhabit the muddy, sandy tidelands of Oregon, Washington, and British Columbia: butter clams, Japanese littleneck clams, horse clams, sand clams, surf clams, razor clams, and geoduck clams to name only a few. Of these, it is the symmetrical, beautifully ribbed, small to medium-sized Japanese littleneck clam, also called the manila clam, that is most often brought to market by commercial clammers. The geoduck clam, also a favorite hereabouts, is harvested by sport clammers and commercial clammers alike. This very large, grotesque clam, with a shell of up to nine inches across and a protruding syphon as long as three feet, always fascinates visitors at Pike Place Market. "What are *those* horrible things?" people ask in astonishment. And even though I have been around geoduck all my life, I too can barely stand to look at them. Nevertheless, they make mighty fine eating.

Season

Clams stay firm while they are spawning and actually taste best during this period in the early summer. After spawning however, their meat is visibly darker, tough, and tasteless. Avoid them in late July and all of August. This is usually red-tide season, so you may have no choice. Clams improve in flavor by fall and are usually abundant all winter and spring as well.

Selection

Clam shells should be tightly closed or at least shut when you touch them, indicating that the clams are alive. Geoducks, which gape rather ludicrously, are an exception. Touch the protruding syphon; if it retracts, the clam is alive. Select all clams individually. Because their shells are heavy, I usually allow at least one pound of littleneck clams per person for a main course. For a substantial appetizer, allow one dozen small to medium-sized clams per person.

Storage

Clams live buried in the sand and feed by extending their syphons up into the water. If possible, store your clams for a few days in clean, very cold salt water, preferably hanging in a net bag in the ocean or sound. This will rid them of all sand and grit. Otherwise, store them on ice, loosely covered with a wet towel, in the refrigerator. (This is the only way to store geoduck clams.) Clams do not deplete the water of nutrients and oxygen the way mussels do, so it will do them no harm to be left immersed in very cold water. To be safe, store for no more than twenty-four hours, though if the clams are very fresh, they may live for up to seven days.

Preparation

Clams are often full of sand and should be purged before being used. Begin by scrubbing the bivalves thoroughly with a stiff brush under cold running water. Then soak them in cold salted water (using $\frac{1}{3}$ cup uniodized salt to a gallon of water), changing the water several times, for up to two hours. Some cooks insist on sprinkling the water with cornmeal which is supposed to induce the clams to open their shells to take a nibble. The clams never do this while *I'm* watching so I cannot verify whether this helps or not. In any case, clams will give up some of their flavorful juices into the water, but as these juices can be incredibly muddy, sandy, and salty, there is no choice but to sacrifice them.

To prepare geoduck clams, immerse them in boiling water for a few seconds, refresh under cold water, and then pull off the skin of the syphon along with the shell, using a paring knife to sever the muscle attachment on both sides of the shell. The syphon can then be cut off in one piece at its base and chopped, ground up, or sliced into steaks. The viscera surrounding the inner belly should be removed

neatly and in one piece with a paring knife. The belly meat, which is more tender than the syphon, is then edible as well. It is necessary to pound or score geoduck steaks to tenderize them.

Removing the Shells before Cooking

Small clams, mussels, scallops, and oysters can all be served raw on the half shell. Some recipes specify raw, shelled bivalves to begin with. Clams and oysters are both easier to open if they have been refrigerated for two or three hours or frozen for an hour. To open a clam, a clam knife with a straight blade and rounded tip is necessary, as is a thick mitt for your hand to avoid injuring yourself with a slip of the knife. Slide the blade of the knife between the shell halves at a point opposite the hinge. Twist the blade to force the halves apart. Slide the cutting edge of the blade along the inside of one half to sever the ends of the two muscles that hold it. Twist off the freed half shell. Run the blade under the clam to sever the other ends of the muscles holding it to the other half shell.

Cooking

Clams steamed in the same way as mussels take about 6 minutes to open. Unlike mussels, however, clams easily toughen with overcooking. Remove them as they open. If, after cooking, any clam refuses to open its shell, discard it; it was dead before you started.

The meat from the geoduck is generally chopped or ground and cooked in chowders. When the pieces are small enough, toughness is not a problem. Steaks should be cooked quickly, like squid, or rubber will be your reward.

Clam Recipes

> Baby Clam and Spinach Soup with Pepper Bacon, *page 38*
>
> Hot Sauced Clams with Fresh Thyme, *page 228*

Clams can be substituted in recipes calling for mussels. Just watch the cooking time closely, being careful not to overcook the clams.

Game Birds

The Northwest region has always attracted people who love the outdoors. There is so much beauty and so much space. Hunting, particularly bird hunting, is a big part of life here for many people. In eastern Washington and eastern Oregon and the more isolated parts of western Canada, great expanses of unpopulated terrain offer a treasure trove of feathered creatures, to the seasonal delight of bird dogs and their masters alike. Hunting season for game birds begins in September.

For those of us who do not hunt but love to eat, specialty poultry markets supply every exotic game bird imaginable. Though there is not yet a really large-scale producer of these birds, numerous small growers supply the various types and between them there is no end to the procurable variety.

The age of commercially raised game birds is monitored so that toughness is not as much of an issue as it is with wild birds. Even so, buyers should be aware that the flesh of a game bird has different characteristics from that of a chicken. Game birds are more sinewy at the bone, much leaner and more fibrous, and have much less fat than a chicken has. When cooked properly, the meat can be delectable; if abused, it will rebel and turn to leather.

Season

Game birds are available fresh year-round from specialty poultry markets, such as University Seafood and Poultry in Seattle's University District. The exception to this is goose, which is available fresh only during the holiday season. Otherwise it is on hand as frozen stock. At this particular market almost any kind of exotic bird is available if an order is placed a few days in advance.

Selection

As with all domesticated poultry, impeccable freshness is important. Texture suffers consid-

erably when poultry is frozen, so cooks should avoid frozen birds as much as possible. When buying poultry of any kind, check the package and make sure it is free of pink-tinged liquid, which indicates a lack of freshness or improper storage. The bird should appear plump and moist and not dried out around the edges.

Storage

If I am more than half an hour from home when marketing, I bring along a cooler filled with ice to store poultry (or seafood) purchases. If something unexpected comes up and you cannot cook your bird within two days of buying it, remove the neck, heart, liver, and gizzard, wrap the bird airtight with plastic wrap, seal in aluminum foil, then quick-freeze it and maintain the temperature at zero degrees for no more than six months. Longer than that, the texture and flavor will deteriorate. The giblets (neck, heart, liver, and gizzard) can be frozen separately if desired; their life span in the freezer is three months at most.

Preparation

There is very little to be done with a fresh bird other than to rinse it under cold water to remove any surface bacteria. Check the cavity to make sure it is clear of loose tissue or blood. If the bird is frozen, thaw it slowly in the refrigerator for best texture retention. You may wish to remove some of the fat under the skin of the back, thigh, and lower breast in a duckling.

Also, be sure to prick the skin evenly at half-inch intervals in those same areas to allow the fat underneath to render itself during the cooking process.

Cooking

Cooking any bird presents a special challenge in that the breast meat is more tender (and thus done to perfection in less time) than the active muscle tissue of the leg and thigh. So, the leg and thigh section is still somewhat tough when the breast is done; conversely, the breast is becoming tough by the time the thigh and leg section is done. Compromise is in order. Sometimes it is convenient to separate the breast meat and use it for one preparation, then cook the leg and thigh meat separately in another fashion. When this is not possible, the cook has to realize that one or the other of the bird's assets will be diminished slightly for the benefit of the other. One of the best examples of compromise I have encountered is that offered by Gerard Parratt, owner-chef of the Relais de Lyon restaurant in Seattle. He cuts a duckling in half, removes the bones and meat from the leg and thigh section, makes a mousse of the dark meat, stuffs it back into the opened half, ties the whole thing into a neat little bundle, and roasts it. The mousse and the tender breast meat then cook at the same rate, and the breast may then be served rare.

Domesticated game birds are more tender than their wild cousins are, both because they are brought to market when young and because

they have not had the room to roam that toughens the meat. Braising (a method for reducing tough tissue to at least some degree of palatability) then, is not necessarily indicated. The quick, dry-heat methods of roasting, grilling, and sautéing are generally fine for domesticated birds.

The question of internal temperature is disputed from one cuisine to another and even from one cook to another. American cookbooks sometimes cite temperatures as high as 190 degrees for doneness. The newest edition of *The Joy of Cooking* drops it to a more reasonable, and more palatable, 180 degrees to 185 degrees. French cookbooks often cite 175 degrees as the ideal. James Beard suggests a temperature as low as 160 degrees for a roast turkey, counting on the heat rising an additional 7 degrees in the resting period after roasting. I agree that poultry is often overcooked in American homes and restaurants alike. A temperature of somewhere between 170 degrees and 180 degrees, allowing for individual preference, protects the breast from losing all of its flavorful juices while allowing the leg and thigh meat to reach reasonable tenderness. There is no reason to overcook poultry; at these temperatures it is perfectly safe to eat. For dark-breasted poultry, such as duck, I usually aim for a much lower temperature, perhaps between 125 degrees and 130 degrees, because the meat is so good rare. When pricked with a knife at the thigh, the juices should run soft rosy pink.

VARIETIES OF NORTHWEST GAME BIRDS

In this discussion of a few of the more commonly available types of game birds, approximate prices are noted so that you will not plan an entire menu around any of these birds without first considering how much it will cost. Chicken is relatively inexpensive; game birds are not.

Quail (4 to 8 ounces)

The tiniest of the domesticated game birds, quail are a true delight. In Seattle two types are available: the smaller sparrow quail, weighing between four and five ounces and the larger bobwhite quail weighing between six and eight ounces. Currently they cost $3.00 and $4.00 each respectively. Since at least two birds per person are required, cost is a consideration.

Squab (12 to 16 ounces)

Squab is also sold as pigeon. The meat is all dark, fairly gamey, and has a distinct flavor. Priced at around $7.00 each, one bird per person is sufficient.

Poussin (14 to 16 ounces)

A French hybrid chicken, the *poussin* is somewhat like a Cornish game hen. They cost about $3.00 each. Purchase one bird per person.

Chukar (16 ounces)

A red-legged grouse, chukar is also sold as partridge. They cost about $8.00 each. Again, count on one bird per person.

Pheasant (1¾ to 3½ pounds)

In Seattle, two types of pheasant are available, range birds with their wilder taste and leaner texture and pen-raised birds that are somewhat fatter and milder in taste. Currently they are selling for about $6.00 a pound. A larger pheasant can satisfy two eaters.

Guinea Hen (2 to 2½ pounds)

Also called a prairie chicken, a guinea hen is dark-fleshed and gamey, somewhat like a pheasant in taste. They cost about $7.00 a pound. Count on one bird for every two eaters.

Duck (4 to 5 pounds)

Northwest duck is leaner than the commercially raised, frozen duck brought to our region from the East Coast. Ours is definitely the better bird because it is *fresh*. Duck sells for about $2.50 a pound. There is not as much meat on a duck as one might think; one duck will feed only two people.

Goose (6 to 14 pounds)

The largest of the so-called wild birds, goose has a reputation for being excessively fatty and having a fibrous texture but these traits are usually a sign of extreme age or improper cooking. The smaller the goose, the more likely it is to be tender. It is available fresh during the holiday season only or by special request the rest of the year. Geese cost about $3.00 a pound for fresh birds and a dollar less a pound for frozen.

Game Bird Recipes

Boned, Stuffed Duck with Prunes and Seckel Pears, *page 230*

Braised Duck with Apples, Prunes, and Walnuts, *page 236*

Breast of Duck with Honey-Glazed Garlic and Crystallized Orange Zest, *page 234*

Butterflied Roast Quail with Gingered Pear and Cranberry Sauce, *page 229*

Chinese Barbecued Duck, Peach, and Toasted Walnut Salad, *page 214*

Pheasant Terrine with Currants and Black Pepper, *page 232*

Potatoes

It used to be that only three varieties of potato were commercially available to cooks: the Russet Burbank, the Red Pontiac, and the White Rose. Now we can find Yukon Gold, Yellow Rose, Yellow Finn, Red Norland, German, Swedish, and Peruvian Purple, Kennebec, Katahdin, Nooksak, Fingerling, and Lady Finger potatoes as well as baby versions of the big three. And from all indications, more varieties are coming. Sometimes life is just too good.

Washington State has no rival as a producer of Russet Burbank potatoes. Idaho does not much like this claim but because Washington's Columbia River Basin has a potato growing season that is fifty-five days longer than Idaho's season, the potatoes are consistently high in solids, a description that means that the potatoes absorb less fat (which is important for frying), stay crisp longer, have a fluffier interior, and a longer shelf life when frozen. Aside from the large commercial growers working in the drier climate of central Washington, many small growers in the damper climate of western Washington are getting on the potato bandwagon as well, with everything *but* Russets.

It is important that the cook knows what type of potato is to hand and then to treat it accordingly. Starch content is the critical factor. Generally speaking, Russets have the most starch, White Rose potatoes have less, and Red Pontiac or "new" potatoes have the least. The more starch the potato has, the fluffier, drier,

and lighter it will be when baked or fried. Potatoes with less starch are said to be waxy and are best suited to boiling or steaming. Treated thus, their texture will be firm and dense and they will hold their shape when mixed with other ingredients, such as those of a potato salad.

Season

The thin-skinned "new" potato varieties begin arriving at Pike Place Market in August and continue through October. Norgold Russets arrive in July and continue on the market until December. Russet Burbanks are harvested in September but are not made available until the Norgold supplies have diminished in December.

Selection

Buy firm, heavy potatoes with smooth skins and no signs of discoloration or spotting. The depth of a potato's "eyes" is no indication of quality, though deeper eyes make the potato harder to peel. For baking or boiling, select potatoes of an equal size so they will cook in the same amount of time.

Storage

Store potatoes in a cool, dark, well-ventilated place. Storage potatoes (Russet Burbanks and Norgold Russets) kept in this manner will usu-

ally last for two or three months; "new" potatoes (dug before they reach maturity and
shipped immediately after being dug) last for
about two weeks. Potatoes kept at room temperature should be used within a week.

Do not refrigerate potatoes. Low temperatures convert the starch to sugar, giving potatoes an overly sweet taste. Should you have to
refrigerate them to keep potatoes from spoiling, remove and hold them at 70 degrees for a
week or so and the sugar will be converted
back to starch, making the potatoes edible
again. Do not freeze potatoes; they become watery when thawed.

Potatoes turn green when exposed to light.
Green areas contain solanin, a glycol alkaloid,
which, when eaten in quantity, is toxic. However, it does not affect the rest of the potato
because it is found only in the outer green layers.

Preparation

After peeling potatoes, keep them covered in
cold water to prevent them from darkening.
Change the water occasionally if it begins to
color. This process does leach out nutrients,
but if you want to peel the potatoes ahead,
there is no way to avoid this.

If you wish to remove some of the potato
starch, soak peeled potatoes in cold water for
an hour or more; drain, dry, and use as directed. The smaller the potatoes are cut, the
more starch will be removed by this process.

Cooking

The amount of potato starch governs how well
a particular potato will work in a particular
recipe. Potatoes, regardless of their initial
starch content, lose sugar and become starchier
as they age. Newly dug storage potatoes will
not be as high in starch as one might expect
from their type, while so-called new potatoes
that have been around for some time will be
higher in starch content than is normal for
their type. To test the starch level of any potato, cut it in half and rub the cut sides together for twenty seconds. The starches will
show up as a white froth. Press the surfaces
together and hold the potato up by one half.
The halves of a starchy potato will adhere to
each other tenaciously; the halves of a low-
starch potato will separate.

Starchy potatoes, such as the Russet Burbank, have a mealy texture when cooked. They
are usually described as baking potatoes.
Starchy potatoes are good when baked or
mashed because they are light and dry, and
when made into French fries because their low
moisture content produces an interior that remains fluffy while the surface becomes crisp.
Low-starch potatoes, such as Red Pontiacs,
have a firm, moist texture and are thus good
choices for boiling and steaming and for dishes
such as potato salads, sautés, or gratins in
which you want the potato to keep its shape.

Cook potatoes with their skins on whenever
possible as a good deal of the nutrition is found
on or just under the skin. Potatoes that are

being cooked in water should be started in cold water to allow the starches to swell slowly.

Potatoes vary in consistency and in their ability to absorb fats and liquids. It is therefore impossible to say exactly how much butter or liquid should be used with a particular batch of potatoes. When in doubt, use a smaller quantity to begin with and adjust as necessary.

Potatoes are decidedly acidic and tend to curdle milk or half-and-half. To minimize this effect, potato slices may be neutralized by blanching them for ten minutes in simmering milk. Another way to control this reaction is to regulate the oven heat and the cooking time so that the dish never boils. Or use cream, which can be boiled without curdling, even in the presence of potatoes.

Potato Recipes

Baby Red Potato, Snow Pea, and Prosciutto Salad, *page 34*

Baby Reds with Oregon Blue and Bacon, *page 106*

Cold-Smoked Salmon, Potato, and Green Bean Salad, *page 107*

Golden Fried Potato Cake, and variations, *page 324*

Layered Vegetable Purée with Yakima Valley Gouda, *page 325*

Potato Gratin, and variations, *page 322*

see also Recipe Notes, *which follow*

RECIPE NOTES

ONION-BRAISED BABY REDS

Braise 1 pound baby Red Pontiac potatoes, uncovered, in a combination of 1 cup water, 1 cup chicken stock, 4 tablespoons olive oil, 1 chopped onion, and a bay leaf. Simmer slowly until the potatoes are tender and all the liquid has evaporated. Continue cooking the potatoes in the residual oil just to brown them lightly. Season liberally with salt and pepper and serve with a sprinkling of Lemon Garlic Vinaigrette (page 359).

GARLIC POTATO MASH

Separate and peel the cloves of 2 whole heads of garlic. Slowly braise, uncovered, in ½ cup chicken stock and 4 tablespoons butter until very tender, about 20 minutes (there should be butter visibly remaining but little stock). Purée the garlic mixture in a processor and reserve. Peel, cut up, and boil 2 pounds Russet Burbank potatoes. Drain the potatoes, add the garlic purée, and put the mixture through a food mill. Add ¼ to ½ cup hot cream (sometimes the potatoes take more, sometimes less), an additional 2 tablespoons softened butter, and salt and pepper to taste, and mix well.

BABY REDS WITH
LEMON GARLIC VINAIGRETTE

Steam 1 pound baby Red Pontiac potatoes until barely tender. Remove from steamer and dry with paper towels. Make 4 or 5 ¼-inch slices into each potato, being careful not to cut all the way through. This will allow the vinaigrette to permeate more easily. Put the potatoes into a warm serving bowl and drizzle with a Lemon Garlic Vinaigrette (page 359) to which you have added the zest of a lemon and 2 teaspoons minced fresh oregano. Season to taste with salt and pepper.

ROASTED POTATO WEDGES
WITH HERBS

Peel and cut 4 large Russet Burbank potatoes into thick lengthwise wedges. Rinse and dry thoroughly with paper towels. Put the potatoes in a mixing bowl and toss with a combination of 3 tablespoons butter and 3 tablespoons olive oil. Sprinkle on salt, pepper and dried herbs (such as rosemary, oregano, basil, thyme, savory, cumin, and/or paprika) to taste. Arrange on a rimmed cookie sheet and bake at 450° for 20 to 30 minutes, until golden brown and tender at the center.

POTATO, SOUR CREAM, AND
CHEDDAR GRATIN

Bake 4 good-sized Russet Burbank potatoes until tender (350° for 1 hour). Split the potatoes and scoop out the interiors. Put through a food mill into a bowl. Add 1 cup room-temperature sour cream, 4 thinly sliced green onions, 1 cup grated Cheddar cheese, and salt and pepper to taste. Spoon into a buttered gratin dish and sprinkle with an additional ½ cup grated Cheddar cheese. Bake, uncovered, at 350° for about 30 minutes to heat through and melt the cheese.

INDIAN-STYLE MASHED POTATOES

Bake 4 large Russet Burbank potatoes until tender. Split and scoop out the interiors. Put through a food mill into a bowl. Blend in 4 tablespoons softened butter, ¼ cup hot cream, 2 seeded, minced hot green chili peppers, and salt and pepper to taste.

POTATO, ONION, HAM, AND
CHEDDAR GRATIN

Boil 4 good-sized Russet Burbank potatoes, cut into pieces, until tender (start in cold water). Meanwhile, melt 2 tablespoons butter in a sauté pan and add 1 chopped onion. Cook slowly until softened, then add 1 small, chopped red bell pepper. Cook for 2 minutes. Put the drained potatoes through a food mill, then add the onion and bell pepper mixture, 1 cup chopped honey-baked or Virginia ham, 2 additional tablespoons butter, ¼ cup hot cream, and ¾ cup grated Cheddar cheese. Combine thoroughly, salt and pepper to taste,

and put into a buttered gratin dish. Sprinkle additional ¼ cup grated Cheddar on top of the gratin and bake at 350° for 30 minutes to warm through and melt the cheese.

SPICY FRIED POTATOES

Steam 1 pound baby Red Pontiac potatoes until just barely tender. Cool and slice. Melt 2 tablespoons butter in a large frying pan and add the potatoes. While they are browning on both sides, sprinkle the potatoes with a mixture of 2 teaspoons coarse salt, ¼ teaspoon cayenne pepper, 1 teaspoon ground coriander, ½ teaspoon ground cumin, and ½ teaspoon best quality Indian curry powder. Fry until nicely browned on both sides, about 10 minutes.

BABY RED, ONION, AND GREEN PEPPER SAUTÉ

Boil 1 pound cubed, baby Red Pontiac potatoes (start in cold water) until just tender. Drain and dry with paper towels. Heat 1 tablespoon oil and 2 tablespoons butter in a nonstick skillet. Add 1 chopped onion, 1 chopped green pepper, the potatoes, and salt and pepper to taste. Sauté, turning occasionally, until the onion is starting to soften and the potatoes are browning. Add 1 clove minced garlic at the completion, toss to combine, and serve.

FRIED POTATO CAKES

Bake 4 good-sized Russet Burbank potatoes until tender, split them, and put through a food mill. Add 2 tablespoons butter, ¼ teaspoon turmeric, 1 clove minced garlic, 1 minced, hot green chili pepper, 4 tablespoons minced Italian parsley, 1 tablespoon lemon juice, and salt, pepper, and nutmeg to taste. When the mixture is cool enough to handle, butter your hands and shape the mashed potatoes into ½-inch-thick patties. Dust each side with flour. Heat a sauté pan, add 1 tablespoon butter and 1 tablespoon oil and fry the patties over low heat until they are golden brown on each side.

BABY REDS WITH CURRIED CREAM

Steam 1 pound baby red potatoes until just tender. Drain and cut into wedges. Salt and pepper to taste and arrange in a baking dish. Drizzle with a combination of ¾ cup reduced cream (reduced from 1 cup), ¾ teaspoon best-quality Indian curry powder, 2 finely sliced green onions, and salt and pepper to taste. Run under a broiler to glaze, sprinkle with 2 tablespoons minced parsley, and serve.

BROWN SUGAR-GLAZED POTATOES

Steam 1 pound baby Red Pontiac potatoes until just tender. Cool and cut into cubes. Melt 3 tablespoons butter in a nonstick skillet, add the potatoes, and toss to coat with butter. Sprinkle with 1 or 2 tablespoons brown sugar and continue cooking and turning until the sugar melts and the potatoes are nicely glazed.

Wild Mushrooms

Mushrooms are members of the fungi family. They obtain their sustenance from other living plants and sometimes animals or from decomposing matter. Many of the mushrooms that are popular in the Northwest grow in association with the roots of trees and woody plants. The mushrooms and the plant develop a partnership whereby the plant receives water and minerals from the fungi and the fungi receive nutrients from the plant. This partnership is what makes mushrooms so difficult to cultivate. Who among us has the wherewithal to plant a field of evergreens and then wait a generation or more for them to mature and become attractive to *Boletus* spores? Or the desire to burn down a forest, then root among the ashes the following spring for a potential crop of morels?

Thus most of us have become accepting and even appreciative of the one mushroom that it is possible to cultivate, *Agaricus bisporus*, which is, unfortunately, the least interesting mushroom of all. Since its succulent, aromatic wild cousins refuse to be tamed, those cooks of a more adventurous bent either take up foraging themselves or look to others to do it for them. Out of necessity mushroom hunting has become a Northwest pastime. The Puget Sound Mycological Society teaches would-be gatherers the basics, most particularly how to prevent poisoning one's self and one's dinner guests. Each fall the society holds a mushroom show for the public to showcase the many edible varieties that grow so abundantly in our region. This event is a great way for the novice gatherer to begin. And of course every would-be mushroom hunter should have at least one reliable handbook for reference. *The New Savory Wild Mushroom* by Margaret McKenny and Daniel Stuntz (published by the University of Washington Press in 1987) is particularly good and deals specifically with those mushrooms found growing in Washington, northern Oregon, northern Idaho, and southern British Columbia.

But if you do not care to tramp through field and forest for your supper, it is nice to know that at least some of these delectable morsels are available in season at Pike Place Market. Hardier souls are willing to do the gathering for you—at a price of course. Wild mushrooms are notoriously expensive. Fortunately they are so flavorful that huge quantities are not usually needed.

Caution: The descriptions of wild mushrooms in this book are not meant to be used as a guide to picking mushrooms in the field. Many poisonous mushrooms resemble edible ones, so be very careful, and purchase wild mushrooms from trusted markets only.

Season

Chanterelles, white oysters, matsutakes, king boletes, cauliflowers, and chicken of the woods appear in late summer and early fall. Early, heavy rains can damage all of these beyond salvaging. Morels are spring and summer mushrooms, usually appearing from April through June.

Selection

Like cultivated mushrooms, store-bought wild mushrooms should be firm, plump or fleshy, and free of blemishes. Avoid wet, slippery, slimy, spotted, broken, shriveled, or drying mushrooms. The caps on wild mushrooms are generally fully open when you purchase them. (Avoid cultivated mushrooms with open caps.) This sign of full maturity is acceptable (you will seldom have a choice) but do check the gills for small moving creatures. Occasionally, wild mushrooms are available with closed caps (and labeled number 1). These are preferable; get them if you can. Use your nose too; decaying mushrooms are unpleasantly odoriferous.

Storage

Mushrooms should not be damp when stored. Dry them off if necessary; do not wash them. Put them into a paper bag laid out in a single layer and close the bag tightly. Plastic bags seal in too much moisture and encourage the mushrooms to turn slimy before their time. Oyster mushrooms and boletes are very perishable; use them as soon as possible. The others, if fresh and in prime condition, can last for between two and six days in the refrigerator.

Preparation

Most mushrooms need a brief but thorough washing in cold water just before they are used. They should not be left to sit in water, as they will absorb it. Mushroom brushes are appropriate if you want to present the mushrooms raw and meticulously clean and if the mushrooms are firm enough to withstand the abrasiveness. A soft pastry brush is a gentle alternative. For cooked dishes, surface whiteness is not important. Usually I just hold a mushroom in one hand, wet the other hand in cold running tap water and use it to wipe off the surface and stem of the mushroom. In this way the mushrooms do not get overly damp. Wipe them dry with paper towels. Trim the tough base and slice as desired.

Cooking

To bring out the real taste of any of these mushrooms, just sauté them briefly, sliced, in a little unsalted butter, add a splash or two of stock, and finish by braising. (I learned this method the hard way on a particularly trying batch of oyster mushrooms. They wanted to absorb exorbitant quantities of butter before releasing their moisture to the pan; eventually I gave up and started giving them stock instead. This worked beautifully.) Too much butter or other fat will obscure the subtle mushroom taste as will other overpowering or complex ingredients. Keep wild mushroom preparations simple. *Shiitake* stems are often tough and should be chopped up and cooked separately in stock until tender.

Wild mushrooms have a natural affinity for cream, light meats such as veal, chicken, turkey, game hen, and rabbit, game birds, starches such as pasta, rice, and potato, and almost any grain.

VARIETIES OF NORTHWEST WILD MUSHROOMS

A few of the more commonly available types to be found in Northwest markets are the matsutakes (or Japanese pine mushrooms), white oysters, yellow chanterelles, white alpine chanterelles, black chanterelles, shiitakes, king boletes, false morels, golden morels, and black morels. Occasionally a gatherer will bring in cauliflower mushrooms, which are coral fungi, mushrooms with an erect, fleshy, branched body, or chicken of the woods mushrooms, which are polypores, stemless mushrooms (with tubes rather than gills) that grow in a shelflike pattern.

Matsutake

Found in the Northwest under Jack pine trees, the delectable *matsutake* mushroom costs about $40.00 a pound for number 2 and 3 grades. Premium number 1 grade can cost between $60 and $80 a pound. Matsutakes are strongly flavored; a little goes a long way. They are pungently sweet, aromatic, firm, and meaty. When fully open, matsutake caps are about five inches across, but the best specimens are no bigger than a strawberry.

White Oyster

White oyster mushrooms are mild and meaty and quite versatile to work with. Their texture benefits from a slow braise in flavorful stock. Cooked briefly in butter, they can be overly chewy. They are currently priced at around $7.00 a pound.

Chanterelle

Chanterelles are possibly the most popular and enthusiastically awaited mushrooms in our region. They are tender, succulent mushrooms that marry beautifully with a wide range of other foods. Of the three types, the yellow is the common chanterelle and the one that most cooks purchase. It sells for between $4.00 and $6.00 a pound. The white alpine chanterelle, which is gaining a reputation for superior flavor, is still unfamiliar to many buyers. It is a real bargain at $4.00 a pound. Black chanterelles (which are actually clustered blue chanterelles) are the most expensive as they are rarer and weigh less.

Cauliflower Mushroom

The cauliflower mushroom, a coral fungus, scientifically named *Sparassis crispa,* is a beautiful sight. A creamy white, ruffled ribbon, measuring between six inches and three feet in diameter, it looks nothing like the other mushrooms listed here. The texture is firm and the aroma delicate. It is available only occasionally.

Shiitake

Shiitakes are not natives of the Northwest but considerable efforts have been expended on their culture here. We have shiitake farms and greenhouses that provide a nearly year-round supply. Meaty, velvety, highly distinctive mushrooms, they cost about $10.00 a pound.

King Boletes

King boletes are silky, meaty mushrooms with a full, round flavor. Called *cèpes* in France and *porcini* in Italy, these mushrooms are dried in substantial quantities. Though they can grow to enormous sizes, the smaller, firmer ones are best for cooking. Select those that are no more

than six inches across. Boletes do not keep very well because they are soft. They cost about $11.00 a pound.

Chicken of the Woods

The scientific name for this polypore is *Laetiporus sulphureus*; it is also known as sulfur shelf. A beautiful crimson-orange on the surface with a white interior, the flesh has a soft, cheesy texture. You will recognize this mushroom when you come across it; it grows in a shelflike pattern, each layer a wavy ruffle. It is available only occasionally.

Morel

Every spring in the Northwest cries of, "The morels are in!" can be heard from one end of Seattle to the other. They do taste wonderful but the consumer should be aware that the delectable morel is not to everyone's gastrointestinal liking. Some people are very sensitive to these mushrooms, which do contain various toxins. The first morel to arrive at the market in spring is really no morel at all. *Verpa bohemica,* the early false morel, is the most likely of the three available types to make you ill. Eat it with caution in small quantities only until you know whether you are susceptible or not. In April, May, and sometimes into June comes the *Morchella esculenta,* the true golden morel. Later in the spring and on into summer comes

Morchella elata, the true black morel. These too can be upsetting to some individuals, so beware. Do not eat any morels raw in any case; cooking seems to eliminate much of the potential problem. Morels are currently priced at around $6.00 a pound.

RECIPE NOTES

The mushrooms specified in the following recipes are given as suggestions; many other wild or cultivated mushrooms may be substituted, with the possible exception of shiitakes, which are distinctively flavored and not suitable for every dish.

FRESH TOMATO AND SHIITAKE SAUCE

Make the Homemade Tomato Sauce on page 143 and add 4 ounces fresh, slivered shiitake mushrooms during the last 5 minutes of cooking.

CHANTERELLE PILAF

In a large saucepan, melt 4 tablespoons butter and cook ¼ cup minced onion until softened; add 2 tablespoons chicken stock and 1 cup sliced chanterelle mushrooms. Cook for a few minutes longer, adding a little more stock if necessary, until the mushrooms have released their liquid and are tender. Add 1 clove minced garlic and 1½ cups long-grain or converted rice. Stir to coat with butter and cook for about 2 minutes. All the mushroom liquid should by now be evaporated. Add 2½ cups chicken stock and ½ cup dry white wine, bring to a simmer, then cover and cook for about 20 minutes, until all the liquid is absorbed and rice is tender. Season to taste with salt and pepper and fluff with a fork.

SHIITAKE AND ONION OMELET

Melt 1 tablespoon butter in a sauté pan and add 2 ounces fresh, sliced shiitake mushrooms and 2 tablespoons chopped onion. (Use a little chicken stock if needed.) Cook until the onion is softened and mushrooms are tender. Make a 2- or 3-egg omelet, adding the shiitake and onion mixture to the unset top of the eggs. Continue to cook until just set, quickly finishing off the top of the omelet under a broiler. Season with salt and pepper, fold, and serve.

CREAM OF CHANTERELLE SOUP

Melt 2 tablespoons butter in a large saucepan and add 4 minced shallots. Cook slowly until softened, then add ½ pound chopped chanterelles, ½ teaspoon crumbled thyme, and a bay leaf. Continue cooking until the mushrooms release their liquid and most of it evaporates. Add 2 tablespoons flour and cook without browning for 2 minutes. Add 2 cups chicken stock and 2 cups cream; bring to a full simmer, whisking to smooth. Remove the bay leaf. Season to taste with salt, white pepper, and drops of lemon juice.

CHANTERELLES WITH CREAM AND MADEIRA

Melt 2 tablespoons butter in a sauté pan and add 1 pound sliced chanterelle mushrooms and 2 tablespoons chicken stock. Braise slowly until the mushrooms have released their liquid and are tender. Evaporate any remaining liquid, add 1 cup cream, and reduce it by one-third. Add 2 tablespoons good Madeira and continue cooking until the sauce lightly coats the mushrooms. Season to taste with salt, pepper, and nutmeg.

OYSTER MUSHROOMS WITH LINGUINI

Melt 6 tablespoons butter and sauté 4 chopped shallots until softened but not browned. Add 1½ pounds sliced oyster mushrooms and ¾ cup chicken stock and continue cooking slowly until the mushrooms have released their liquid and are tender. (You may need to give these mushrooms a little more stock. You should have about a cup of combined butter and stock in the pan after the mushrooms are tender.) Season boldly with salt, pepper, and hot red pepper flakes. Boil 1 pound linguini noodles until just *al dente*. Drain the pasta and toss it with the sauce and ½ cup grated Parmesan cheese. Serve immediately.

CHANTERELLE EGG SCRAMBLE

Melt 2 tablespoons butter in a nonstick skillet, add 2 tablespoons chicken stock, 1 clove minced garlic, and ½ pound sliced chanterelles. Braise slowly until mushrooms release their liquid and are tender. Evaporate all of the remaining liquid and add another tablespoon of butter to the pan if the mushrooms have absorbed the initial quantity. Add 4 lightly beaten eggs and 2 tablespoons minced parsley and stir very slowly over medium-low heat so that large, soft curds form. When the eggs are set, season to taste with salt and pepper. Serve immediately.

WILD MUSHROOM BUTTER

Braise wild mushrooms in a small quantity of butter and chicken stock until they have released their liquid and are tender. Evaporate the liquid and purée mushrooms in a processor. Let cool, then process with an equal quantity of cold butter until smooth. Roll into a log, wrap in plastic wrap, and freeze. To use: soften and add a tablespoon or so to veal, chicken, or fish just before serving; swirl into a cream soup; toss with steamed vegetables or pasta; or use as a sauté medium.

MARINATED SCALLOPS, SHRIMP, AND CHANTERELLES

In a saucepan, combine ½ cup chopped onion, 1 bay leaf, 1 teaspoon salt, and 4 cups water.

Bring to a boil and simmer for 5 minutes. Remove from the heat and add ½ pound scallops and ½ pound peeled shrimp. Cover and let stand for 5 minutes. Remove the shellfish with a slotted spoon. Mix the shellfish with ½ pound sliced, braised chanterelles and toss with the Lemon Garlic Vinaigrette (page 359). Refrigerate, covered, overnight. Toss well and sprinkle with minced parsley before serving as an appetizer.

MORELS IN RED BURGUNDY

Put ½ cup dry red burgundy, 1 clove minced garlic, 2 minced shallots, and ½ cup butter in a saucepan and simmer for 4 minutes. Add 1 pound small morels and continue simmering for 5 to 6 minutes until tender. Transfer to a chafing dish and serve as an appetizer.

OYSTER MUSHROOMS IN WHITE WINE

Melt 4 tablespoons butter and add 1 pound sliced oyster mushrooms and 4 minced garlic cloves, along with 1 cup reduced dry white wine (reduced from 2 cups of wine). Braise slowly until the mushrooms release their liquid and are tender. Season to taste with salt and pepper and sprinkle with minced parsley before serving.

WILD MUSHROOM SAUTÉ
WITH FRESH HERBS

Heat 4 tablespoons olive oil in a sauté pan and add 1 pound sliced wild mushrooms (not shi-itakes), 2 minced garlic cloves, and 2 tablespoons chicken stock. Cover and braise slowly until mushrooms release their liquid and are fully tender. Uncover, raise the heat, and evaporate most of the liquid. Sprinkle with 1 tablespoon fresh minced thyme and 2 tablespoons fresh minced parsley. Season to taste with salt, pepper, and a generous squeeze of lemon juice. (A mushroom ragout can also be produced using this formula: After adding the herbs, add 1 cup cream and continue cooking to reduce slightly. Season as above.)

Capsicum Peppers

Christopher Columbus set sail to find a trade route to the Orient with the expectation of procuring a profitable source for black pepper, then the most esteemed and costly spice in the world. Instead he touched land on the island now shared by Haiti and the Dominican Republic and discovered, not pepper but *axi* as the native Arawaks called it. Undaunted he renamed the hot flavoring *pepper* and the Arawaks *Indians,* assuming (wrongly) that he had found the trade route to the East Indies. It's a shame Columbus did not live long enough to

be adequately acknowledged for his discovery, for it took some time for the Old World to realize just how valuable these so-called peppers were. In popularity they have by now far outdistanced the various species of *Piper* of which black pepper, *Piper nigrum,* is one. The genus *Capsicum* today gives the world its most widely used flavoring.

Though everyone agrees that the flavors are divine, the name, *pepper,* continues to cause trouble. For the most part, capsicum peppers are called *peppers* except when they are noticeably hot. Then they are called *chili peppers* or sometimes just *chiles* if the Spanish spelling is preferred, as in, for example, *chile colorado.*

Color can cause confusion too. Red is not hotter than green in the same chili (note the anglicized spelling). Although chili peppers generally start out green or yellow, they mature into many shades of brown, purple, orange, and yellow before finally changing to red, brown-black or green-black at full maturity. Chili peppers are at their spiciest when they are fully formed but still green or yellow in color. After full form is reached, they continue to get a bit sweeter but no hotter as they go through subsequent color changes.

In Central Washington, roadside stands display a remarkable array of sweet and hot peppers in August and September. The hot, arid summers in the Yakima Valley produce hotter, spicier peppers than are possible from the cooler, wetter region west of the Cascades. Perhaps the most well-known pepper farm in the valley is Krueger's Pepper Gardens in Wapato.

Krueger's grows fifty different pepper varieties, from sweet to hot and everything in between. You can find a pepper of almost any shape here, from tiny peppers that look like clusters of daggers to fat, fleshy, single globes. The difference in taste, not just heat, from one pepper to the next is really remarkable. If you avoid the interior ribs, which contain eighty-nine percent of the pepper's heat (it is not the seeds as many people think), you can taste almost any pepper without subsequent discomfort. I wonder if Columbus knew that.

Season

Chili peppers are available fresh from August through October in western Washington, from the last week in July until frost in eastern Washington, and from cold storage for some time afterward.

Selection

Fresh peppers should appear very firm and feel slightly heavy for their size. Always avoid peppers that are uncharacteristically shriveled or wrinkled. Check also for spots of decay, especially around the stem.

Storage

Peppers should be kept in the refrigerator in a closed paper bag. Stored in this fashion, most varieties will keep for about a week.

Preparation

When handling chili peppers, always use disposable rubber gloves to protect your hands from the burn-producing oil, capsaicin. It is most heavily saturated in the interior ribs where the seeds are attached. Remove these ribs, along with the seeds, if you wish to tame the heat.

The skin is often removed (usually by charring) before cooking or adding the fresh peppers to a dish. This not only makes the pepper more digestible, it also adds a rich, smoky flavor. The easiest way to do this is to hold the pepper with long tongs and turn it slowly over the direct flame of a gas burner. Once the skin is evenly black and blistered, put the pepper in a paper bag, close tightly and let it "sweat" for fifteen minutes to separate the skin from the flesh. Remove, peel the skin away in strips, then pull out the core; open the pepper up and strip away the ribs and seeds. Doing this under cold running water sometimes helps. If you do not have a gas stove, put the pepper under a broiler and rotate it as the surface blackens. In either case, do not cook it for too long or the interior flesh will be overcooked (limp and mushy) or in thin-fleshed varieties may shrivel away to nothing.

It is not always necessary to peel peppers. Depending on how you cut them, on whether they are thick- or thin-fleshed, you may wish to leave well enough alone. For quick sautés and stir-fries I generally prefer to leave the skin on so that the pepper will keep its shape.

Cooking

Chili peppers vary in their heat-producing capacity from one specimen to another and, of course, from one variety to another. Always sample before using. It only takes a minute or two to cook a sliced or diced pepper. Peppers are good raw, so they can be left on the crisp side if desired. They also withstand long, slow cooking, becoming velvety in the process.

Special Remedies

Elizabeth Schneider, in her superlative book, *Uncommon Fruits and Vegetables—A Commonsense Guide,* suggests sugar or hard candy as a reliable antidote to chili-burn in the mouth. Milk products, bread, and rice help somewhat too. Whatever you do, do not gulp water; it makes the heat worse.

Jean Andrews, in her equally commendable book, *Peppers—The Domesticated Capsicums,* tells of her accidental discovery that a solution of 1 part bleach to 5 parts water effectively eradicates the burning effect of capsaicin on the skin if used soon after contact.

VARIETIES OF FRESH NORTHWEST CHILI PEPPERS

Anaheim (mild)

A generally mild, medium-fleshed pepper with a light to medium green color and long, narrow, slightly curved shape, Anaheims are

sometimes called *chile verde* or New Mexico green in their immature green pod state or *chile colorado* or New Mexico red when they are mature and red. To confuse things even more, this variety is often labeled Anaheim when mild and New Mexico when hot. Roasted, dried green pods are called *chile pasado.* Roasted red pods usually retain the name *chile colorado.* The classic chili for *chiles rellanos,* it is also used dried in chili powder and paprika.

Banana Peppers (no heat to hot)

A long, tapering, shiny yellow pepper with a heat level varying from sweet to hot, this pepper has two names: the sweet variety is called banana pepper, the hot variety is called the Hungarian wax pepper. The thin skin does not need peeling.

Cayenne (very hot)

Sometimes called finger peppers, cayenne peppers are named after the Cayenne River in South America. A long, narrow, sharp-tipped pepper with thin flesh and great pungency; red when ripe and four to twelve inches in length. It may be used fresh but is more often dried and ground.

Cherry Peppers (mild to hot)

As you might suspect, cherry peppers are round, like cherries. They may be green, orange, or deep red in color with heat levels from mild to hot. The flesh is medium-thick. You will find the two most common varieties labeled hot cherry peppers and sweet cherry peppers in the market. They are often pickled and used as a condiment.

Fresno (hot)

As hot as a jalapeño pepper with medium-thin flesh, the Fresno is tapered with a pointed tip and broad shoulders. Light green to red in color and 2½ inches in length, it is used for pickling and in sauces.

Green and Red Bell Peppers (no heat)

Bell peppers are mild, sweet, and thick-fleshed. They have a bright, clean, astringent taste that is welcome in numerous dishes. The red bell pepper because it is ripe is sweeter and mellower tasting than the more astringent, unripe green bell pepper.

Habanero (very hot)

A thin-fleshed, green to orange chili pepper with wrinkled skin, the *habanero* grows up to two inches in length. Jean Andrews says that "this is the chili pepper that separates the men from the boys." In other words, it is as hot as hell—reputedly a thousand times hotter than a jalapeño pepper. Highly aromatic with an unmistakable flavor, it currently costs $10.50 a pound in Seattle; most other peppers cost

$1.50 a pound. Obviously a small quantity will go a long way. *Habaneros* are usually eaten fresh.

Hot Portugal (very hot)

An extra-hot pepper, the hot Portugal has thin flesh, grows up to six inches in length, and is green to red in color with a pointed tip. It is used fresh or dried and ground.

Jalapeño (hot)

Probably the best-known pepper, the *jalapeño* originated in Mexico. Dark green in color with flesh of medium thickness, the pepper has smooth, shiny skin, broad shoulders, a blunt end, and a fiery bite. It is used fresh in sauces, salads, and main dishes, scattered over nachos and pizza, batter-fried or stuffed with various mixtures, or served cold as an appetizer. Jalapeño peppers are often preserved in oil, vinegar, and spices or canned in water. When fully ripened and smoked, the jalapeño becomes the *chile chipotle*. A cultivar used fresh, the TAM Jalapeño-1, is not quite so hot.

Pimiento (no heat)

The pimiento is a large, heart-shaped, sweet pepper with a distinctively aromatic flavor. It is used extensively in the canning industry. Pimientos are useful in casseroles and vegetable dishes, as a garnish.

Poblano (mild)

Sometimes called *mulato* or misnamed *pasilla,* the poblano is a glossy, black-green pepper that looks like a deflated bell pepper, only a little more heart-shaped. Very full flavored and aromatic, it needs to be roasted and peeled to bring out the flavor, which is usually mild, but may sometimes be pungent. Very thick fleshed, this pepper is often used fresh; when dried, the poblano is called *ancho.*

Serrano (hot to very hot)

A small, smooth, intensely hot, medium-green pepper, no more than two inches in length and about ½ inch in width, the *serrano* is usually eaten fresh, as part of guacamole or salsa, or to enliven any number of savory dishes. It is too small and thin-fleshed to peel. *Serranos* are usually sold green but are also available in the mature red form. They are sometimes called *japones* when dried.

Sweet Chocolate Bell Pepper (no heat)

A thick-fleshed, brown bell pepper with a mild, sweet taste. It may be used in the same ways as other bell peppers are used.

Thai (very hot)

A very hot, full-flavored chili pepper that was hybridized in Thailand, the Thai pepper is

small, very slender, and no more than two inches in length. Thai peppers are even hotter than serranos. They are usually sold green but occasionally they show up in the red form as well.

Yellow Wax (medium to hot)

The yellow wax is a small conical pepper, much like a Fresno in shape but usually marketed when yellow.

Pepper Recipes

Leafy Greens

One of the interesting features of the developing Northwest cuisine has been the rediscovery of the whole family of leafy greens. Asian immigrants, especially those in the locally sponsored IndoChinese Farm Project, are credited with much of this new interest as they continue to plant varieties from their various homelands and then introduce them at Pike Place Market and other forward-thinking retail outlets, such as Larry's in North Seattle. On any one day at Pike Place Market, the prospecting cook is likely to encounter savoy and napa cabbage; ornamental kale; spinach; red or white Swiss chard; hot, green, or purple mustard greens; collard greens; *yu choy;* beet greens; Chinese broccoli; broccoli rabe; baby bok choy; flowering bok choy hearts; Chinese broad-leaf mustard; Chinese leaf mustard; young turnip greens; and chrysanthemum leaves. Although many of these greens are members of the mustard family, I group them together in my own mind because of their fall and winter season and because they can all take the heat, unlike salad greens, which are better eaten raw.

Season

Generally, this category of cooking greens is available from local sources beginning in September and continuing into March, depending on the particular winter in question. Some of the greens, the kale, collards, and mustard greens, hit their peak a little later; November through January. Kale, in particular, intensifies in flavor after being subjected to the first hard frost. Swiss chard has a slightly different time table; it arrives in June and produces until November.

Selection

When choosing any greens, look for specimens that are on the small side with firm, crisp, unblemished leaves. Avoid woody stems and coarse veins; both indicate overly mature specimens. Color should be true to type and vivid to dark in hue. Avoid any greens with yellowing, wilted leaves. Also check for insects or evidence of them that shows up as little holes on the leaves. As a group, leafy greens are quite perishable; unpleasant flavors develop in older specimens, so look for just-picked produce whenever possible.

Storage

Most leafy greens do not keep long. Use right away or rinse very well, then dry thoroughly with paper towels. Store in an airtight plastic bag in the refrigerator for up to two days. Kale may develop a bitter taste if held too long. Cabbages are an exception. They will generally keep for a week or so if purchased in premium condition.

Preparation

Many greens harbor grit, sand, and aphids. Rinse very well under cold running water, feeling each leaf with your hands to be sure all soil and sand is gone. Sometimes is it easier to fill the sink with cold water and swish the leaves around in it to free the debris; change the water at least once if you use this method. For the specific preparation, see the entries for each type of green.

Cooking

Most greens can be cooked very simply; steam for four to eight minutes, boil for one to three minutes, or stir-fry or sauté for three to four minutes. If the stems are tougher than the leaves, they may need to be peeled and then braised in a little liquid for two to four minutes before the leaves are added. Leaves and tender stems can be added to soups without any precooking.

Braising in seasoned stock is one of my favorite ways with greens. To do this, use just the quantity of stock that will evaporate completely in the selected cooking time (add stock

in increments if you are not sure). Add one to two tablespoons of butter or oil at the onset and, as the liquid evaporates, the fat will glaze the greens beautifully.

If you plan to make a casserole, most of these greens will need to be cooked before being included in the dish. Do not use aluminum or unlined iron pans for cooking as some of the greens will discolor. I prefer to cook all members of the cabbage clan—green, red, napa, long napa, and savoy—as a simple, quick sauté in butter until just heated through. Cooked this way they are still crisp and delicate tasting. For embellishment, throw in some caraway or poppy seeds.

Many of the greens listed here are bold in flavor and take quite well to other assertive flavorings, such as garlic, black pepper, onions, hot peppers, ginger root, and curry spices.

VARIETIES OF LEAFY GREENS

Beet Greens

Beet greens are nothing more or less than the leaves growing from the tops of beets. They are usually sold with the beets attached, a two-for-one bargain. The leaves are generally dark green with red veins and stems and look like miniature versions of red Swiss chard. The flavor is mild and a little nutty. It is difficult, if not impossible, to find recipes for them. To prepare, cut the leaves and the tender upper section of the stem on the diagonal at ½-inch

intervals. Try substituting them for other greens. The thick stems usually have to be cooked a bit longer than the leaves.

Bok Choy

In *Bruce Cost's Asian Ingredients,* the author informs us that farmers in Hong Kong grow more than twenty kinds of *bok choy.* In Seattle we mostly see *Brassica chinensis,* the most common of the bok choys. The bulbous base consists of a cluster of very white stalks that give way to deep green leaves at the top. The stalks are mild in flavor; the leaves have just a touch more sharpness. Baby bok choy is the superb younger sibling of regular bok choy. The flavor is mild and somewhat sweeter. Bok choy sum, also called *choy sum* or bok choy hearts, is a smaller, thinner bok choy that has set yellow flowers. Separate the stems from the leaves of larger bok choy. Cut the stems and leaves diagonally at ½-inch intervals. Small bok choy hearts (*choy sum*) may be used whole. Remove the ribs from main stalk and separate the leaves of the larger hearts. Cut the stems and leaves diagonally at ½-inch intervals. Baby bok choy may be left whole or sliced in half lengthwise. The greens are cooked whole with the flowers when they are small enough not to be coarse or fibrous. The flavor is on the sweet side. All of the bok choys can be used interchangeably in recipes.

Broccoli Rabe

In the broccoli family, this distinctive green arranges for itself clusters of three or four well-rounded leaves that lead down to a connecting main stem. Each cluster has often set small buds and yellow flowers. The flavor is spicy-hot and intensely broccoli-like. Though some of the winter greens are good raw, broccoli rabe is not one of them. Trim the tough ends from stems; leave whole or slice at 2-inch intervals.

Chrysanthemum Leaves

As the name indicates, these greens come from a type of edible chrysanthemum, but not the garden variety. The leaves look very like those of ornamental chrysanthemums, each group of jagged leaves arising out of a single stem. They taste like their scent: spicy and flowery. The leaves are very tender and may be used raw as well as cooked. Remove the leaves from the stems and toss out the stems. Use the leaves whole or slice at ½-inch intervals.

Chinese Broad-Leaf Mustard

A popular, pungent mustard leaf (also called *dai gai choy*), this vegetable has only a little mustard bite after it is cooked. The broad stalks are used more often than the leaves are, so sometimes this green is sold with the leaves cut off. Cut the leaves from the stems and slice them crosswise at ¼-inch intervals. Cut the broad stems diagonally at ½-inch intervals. Leaves and stems are usually used separately in different dishes. The crisp texture adds an interesting note to stir-fry dishes.

Chinese Broccoli

This green, which is slightly dull in color, has slender leaves emanating from a central stem and often there are white flowers present as well. The flavor is assertive: slightly peppery with a touch of bitterness. Use Chinese broccoli just as you would regular broccoli. Trim the tough ends from the stems. Peel the tough outer layer from the stalk and use the vegetable whole or sliced diagonally at ½-inch intervals.

Chinese Leaf Mustard

Chinese leaf mustard is smaller in size than Chinese broad-leaf mustard. It has thin, ridged stems and serrated leaves that extend almost to the base of each stem. It has an assertive bite, much of which it loses when cooked. Trim the tough ends from the stems and cut stems and leaves diagonally at ½-inch intervals.

Collard Greens

Collard greens have long been associated with the American South. Traditionally these greens, which taste like cabbage and kale, with a touch of bitterness, are boiled to death with salt pork

so that the leaves take on a fleshy quality and substitute for meat in some regions. Trim the tough ends from the stems and cut the stems and leaves diagonally at ½-inch intervals.

Green and Red Cabbage

Green and red cabbage taste so similar that a choice is made more by color preference and price than anything else. I like to use red cabbage raw, when its color is an asset, but I generally choose green cabbage when I intend to give it some heat. Red cabbage turns an insipid pink if it is cooked to any degree at all. The flavor of both of these cabbages is mild and sweet, especially if they are not overcooked. Remove the outer layer of leaves from the cabbage if they look scruffy. Cut the cabbage in half through the core, then cut each half in half again. Trim out the core from each section. Slice the cabbage sections crosswise.

Kale

Kale, a leafy green that is close to my heart, is a frilly-edged beauty that comes in both variegated green and red and solid blue-green versions. The flavor is mild yet full, something like a cabbage. It can be bitter if it is old, but picked and eaten fresh, bitterness should not be a factor. The texture has a pleasing crunch when not overcooked and provides a nice contrast to other foods.

Flowering or ornamental kale or cabbage, sometimes called salad savoy, is becoming increasingly available. These plants look like the beauties we plant in our gardens in the late fall. As members of the cabbage family, they can be treated similarly, though they will lose their color if cooked and they do not taste nearly as good as regular cabbage does. The leaves are almost too gorgeous to cut up and cook anyway; they can be used raw in salads and as decorative bases for other foods.

Baby kale may be used stem and all. Remove the stem from larger leaves by folding each leaf lengthwise so that the insides touch. Then bend the stem back and pull it down. Many cooks prefer to blanch kale before using it. Blanching removes the slight crispness that remains when kale is steamed or sautéed. To blanch, bring a large pot of salted water (1½ teaspoons salt per quart water) to a boil. Add the washed and trimmed kale and boil for two or three minutes, or until barely tender. Kale wilts by a ratio of approximately 4 to 1. It may have to be blanched in batches.

Mustard Greens

Like collards, mustard greens have long been associated with the American South. Traditionally they are cooked with bacon or salt pork long enough to turn into a gloppy stew of sorts. I prefer to cook them quickly so as to retain the color and texture. Mustard greens are spicy-hot and assertive, with a combined flavor of watercress, horseradish, and mustard. Trim the tough ends from the stems. Cut the stems and leaves crosswise at ½-inch intervals.

Napa and Long Napa Cabbage

Also known as celery cabbage or Chinese cabbage, napa and long napa cabbage are even milder and sweeter than regular cabbage, with the long version being somewhat more intense. The texture is a real boon too, the thin leaves are crisp and juicy. People who do not like cabbage often enjoy napa cabbage. These cabbages are easily distinguishable from other members of the family because they are barrel-shaped rather than round. Long napa cabbage looks very similar to regular napa cabbage, except that it is longer and the leaves are narrower. To prepare napa cabbage, slice off an inch or so from the base, cut the cabbage in half or quarters lengthwise, and then cut the leaves crosswise at ¼- to ½-inch intervals. There is no need to section the head of long napa cabbage lengthwise as the leaves are narrow to begin with.

Savoy Cabbage

Savoy cabbage looks like regular cabbage except that the leaves are more ruffled; often it is sold with the outer, opened leaves intact. It has a mild, sweet flavor. Cut savoy cabbage in half through the core, then cut each half in half again; remove the core from each section. Slice each section crosswise.

Swiss Chard

A gorgeous green with dark ruffled leaves and striking red ribs and veins, Swiss chard has an earthy, full flavor, but is not strong or overly assertive. The flat stems are usually sliced and cooked separately from the leaves because they are fibrous. There is also a chard with deep green leaves and white stems. Cookbooks on the cuisine of southern France and the Mediterranean, where Swiss chard is used as extensively as we use spinach, will have useful recipes. Unless you have tiny baby chard, separate the stems from the leaves with kitchen shears. If the stems are fibrous, remove the strings as you would for celery. Trim the bases if they are at all wilted or ragged. Cut the stalks into two- to three-inch pieces. If the leaves are very large, cut them up.

Turnip Greens

Another of those winter greens used predominantly in the American South, turnip greens

are sold either without the turnips attached or complete with tiny, immature turnips. The leaves are long and oval-shaped with a sharp bite and a good degree of bitterness. Do not use them raw; they are too sharp and coarse. Trim the tough ends from the stems. Small leaves may be used whole; larger leaves and the tender part of the stems should be cut crosswise at ½-inch intervals.

Yu Choy

Also spelled *yow choy,* this Chinese green has narrow stems, oval leaves, and tiny yellow flowers. The flavor is bitter with the pungency of mustard. Trim the tough ends from the stems. Use small leaves whole or slice the stems and leaves at ½-inch intervals.

Leafy Green Recipes

Cabbage Gratin with Apples and Cougar Gold, *page 328*

Sauté of Pork Chops with Oregon Prunes and Cranberries, *page 240*

see also Recipe Notes, *which follow*

RECIPE NOTES

KALE AND HAZELNUT PILAF

Make a rice pilaf using 1 cup long-grain white rice, 2 cups chicken stock, and the zest of a lemon. Season to taste with salt and pepper. Heat 2 tablespoons butter and 1 tablespoon oil in a separate sauté pan and add 2 large handfuls sliced kale leaves. Sauté until just softened, turning the mass to cook evenly. Season to taste with salt, pepper, and cayenne and gently add to the prepared rice pilaf along with ½ cup finely chopped toasted hazelnuts.

LEAFY GREEN AND RICOTTA PIE

Sauté 1 chopped onion in 2 tablespoons butter until softened but not browned. Combine 1 pound ricotta cheese, 3 lightly beaten eggs, 1 cup grated Cheddar cheese, 2 tablespoons flour, and 1 cup chopped, cooked leafy greens of your choice. Spoon into a 9-inch partially baked, short-crust pastry shell and top with 1 cup sour cream. Bake at 375° for 40 minutes. The filling may also be baked in a gratin dish without the crust.

KALE AND RICE GRATIN

Sauté 1 chopped onion in 2 tablespoons butter until softened. Add 2 cloves minced garlic and stir to coat with butter. Add 1 pound shredded kale leaves and cook until the leaves are just

softened. Remove to a bowl and add 4 lightly beaten eggs, 1 cup milk, 1½ cups grated Cheddar cheese, 4 cups cooked long-grain white rice, ¼ cup minced parsley, and salt and pepper to taste. Spoon into a buttered gratin dish and bake, covered, at 350° for 35 minutes.

SWEET AND TANGY LEAFY GREEN SAUTÉ

Blanch 6 cups shredded leafy greens of your choice until just softened. Drain and squeeze dry. Sauté 1 chopped onion in 2 tablespoons light olive oil until softened. Mix 2 tablespoons red wine vinegar with 1 tablespoon brown sugar. Stir and add the greens. Season to taste with salt and pepper, toss, and serve.

SWISS CHARD GRATIN

Blanch 4 cups shredded Swiss chard leaves until just softened. Drain, squeeze dry, and chop. Make a *roux* with 2 tablespoons butter and 4 tablespoons flour. Cook for 2 minutes without browning, then add 1 cup milk and bring to a boil, whisking all the while. The sauce will be very thick. Remove from the heat and add 2 lightly beaten eggs. Blend with the cooked chard, season to taste with salt and pepper, and put into a buttered gratin dish. Bake in a *bain marie* (water bath) at 350° for 30 minutes.

ITALIAN FRITTATA WITH QUARK AND KALE

Blanch 1 cup kale leaves until just wilted. Drain, squeeze dry, and chop. Melt 2 tablespoons butter in a nonstick frittata pan (which is like an omelet pan but an inch or so larger in diameter). Add half an onion chopped and half a jalapeño pepper minced, and sauté until softened. Add the greens and stir to coat with butter. Over medium-low heat, pour in 4 or 5 lightly beaten eggs and stir quickly but gently to combine. Arrange ½ cup fresh Quark cheese (page 269) or cream cheese in dollops on top of the frittata while it is still loose. When set, season to taste with salt and pepper. Serve hot or at room temperature.

INDIAN-STYLE CREAMED LEAFY GREENS

Heat 4 tablespoons butter in a large sauté pan and add 2 teaspoons ground coriander, 1 teaspoon *garam masala,* ¼ teaspoon turmeric, ¼ teaspoon black pepper, and a pinch cayenne pepper. Cook slowly to mellow the spices—about 2 minutes. Add 2 large bunches roughly chopped or shredded leafy greens of your choice. Cover and "sweat" until softened. Remove cover, toss to distribute seasonings, and add ½ cup cream. Reduce the cream quickly until it thickens and coats the greens. Season to taste with salt and pepper and serve.

SAUTÉED LEAFY GREENS WITH CURRANTS AND TOASTED HAZELNUTS

Blanch 1 pound shredded or roughly chopped leafy greens of your choice until just softened. Drain and squeeze dry. Heat 4 tablespoons butter and add 1 tablespoon minced fresh ginger, 1 minced jalapeño pepper, and 1 teaspoon *garam masala* (page 358). Cook for 1 minute to release the flavors. Add ½ cup currants, ¼ cup chopped toasted hazelnuts, and the chopped greens. Toss, season with salt and pepper to taste, and serve.

SAVOY CABBAGE AND VEGETABLE PAUPIETTES

Blanch several large savoy cabbage leaves until they are quite pliable. Remove from water, drain, and pat dry. Melt 2 tablespoons butter in a sauté pan and add 1 chopped onion, 1 cup chopped white part of leek, 1 minced jalapeño pepper, and 2 cloves minced garlic. Cook until softened and add 1 cup chopped broccoli, 1 cup chopped apple, 1 cup chopped red bell pepper, 1 cup chopped cauliflower, and ½ cup chicken stock. Cover and cook until the vegetables are barely tender and are still crunchy. Remove from the heat, add 1 cup chopped ham, and season to taste with salt and pepper. Remove the central rib from each cabbage leaf.

Lay the leaf flat with the outside facing down and slightly overlap the cut edges. Portion out the drained vegetable mixture on to the leaves. Fold the edges of the leaf in over the filling and then roll up the leaf. Put the rolls into a baking dish and drizzle with an additional ½ cup stock. Cover and bake at 375° for 20 to 30 minutes, until heated through. Lift them one by one from the baking dish and serve 1 or 2 per person with either a drizzling of butter sauce (*beurre blanc*) or dollop of sour cream.

SAUSAGE AND KALE SCRAMBLE

Heat 2 tablespoons corn oil and sauté 1 pound bulk Italian sausage until cooked through. Drain off all but 1 tablespoon of fat. Add 2 chopped onions, ½ pound sliced mushrooms, ½ teaspoon crumbled oregano, and ½ teaspoon crumbled basil and cook until the mushrooms release their liquid and all of it evaporates. The onions should be softened by this time. Add 1 pound shredded or roughly chopped kale leaves and cook until softened. If any liquid is visible in the pan, evaporate it. Add 2 tablespoons butter to the pan along with 8 lightly beaten eggs. Move the eggs just enough to develop large, soft curds. When set, toss in 1 cup grated Cheddar or ½ cup grated Parmesan cheese. Salt and pepper to taste and serve.

LEAFY GREENS WITH
HOT VINAIGRETTE

Blanch the leaves of 2 pounds selected greens until softened. Drain, squeeze dry, and chop. Heat 2 tablespoons olive oil in a skillet along with 1 clove minced garlic. Add 1 tablespoon lemon juice and whisk to blend. Add the greens and ¼ cup chopped toasted hazelnuts. Toss to heat and coat. Season with salt and pepper to taste and serve.

Apples

Not too many years ago, in my newspaper column, "Seasonal Bounty—Northwest Style," I bemoaned the loss of the old-fashioned apple varieties. At the end of the nineteenth century, eight thousand growing varieties of apples were listed by the United States Department of Agriculture. In 1982 in Washington State, the largest single producer of apples in the nation, only two varieties of apple were grown in any quantity: Red Delicious and Golden Delicious and they were grown exclusively in eastern Washington. Only occasionally would one see local Gravensteins, Jonathans, Winesaps, Rome Beauties, or Newtown Pippins. Granny Smiths were at that time imported from Australia. By 1988, the scene had changed considerably. Commercial growers now produce Granny Smith apples and small

forward-thinking growers in western Washington are producing an increasing number of varieties that most of us have never heard of. Today it is estimated that over two hundred varieties of apples are grown in western Washington. So it is now possible to find Akane, McIntosh, Prima, Jonagold, Chehalis, Mutsu, Tydeman, Spartan, Criterion, and Gala apples in local markets and roadside stands. In six short years public demand has resurrected a nearly extinct industry, the production of specialty apples. And just in the nick of time. People were beginning to think they did not like apples anymore. And who could blame them? A Red Delicious apple has a fabulous texture, but not much taste. The Golden Delicious tastes a little better, but the texture is more fragile and is frequently ruined in the warm temperature of the grocery store.

Years ago I learned how important the variety of an apple is to something as simple as an apple pie. While I was visiting my Dad on his farm in Cathlamet, Washington, an elderly neighbor came over with a just-baked apple pie, still warm from the oven. It was the most magnificent thing I have ever tasted. For years I tried to duplicate this gracious woman's prize apple pie. More cinnamon I thought; maybe a little cardamom; perhaps a squeeze of lemon juice? Why did her apple pie taste so much better than mine? Much later, on another visit, I came home with a bag of nameless, mottled apples from one of the old trees dotting that lovely rural countryside. I almost threw them away, they looked so scruffy. I am sure you have guessed by now that the resulting apple pie had just that elusive taste I had been trying to achieve with various spices and tricks. There really is no substitute for an apple with full, perfumed taste and a nice balance of acidity. You cannot bake a sublime apple pie without it. In western Washington the apples almost always look mottled because of the rain, but I never pass by an abandoned roadside tree now without tasting one of its offerings. The old saying, "You can't judge a book by its cover," goes for apples as well.

Season

Full-scale harvesting begins in mid-September. Though some varieties are ready to pick as early as mid-July, it can take until mid-October to fill the pipeline. Red Delicious, Golden Delicious, Granny Smith, and Rome Beauty apples keep well in controlled atmosphere (CA) storage and are thus available in good condition longer than are other apple varieties. Red and Golden Delicious apples are now year-around staples; Granny Smith and Rome Beauty apples are available through June.

Selection

Controlled atmosphere storage notwithstanding, apples are still at their premium when purchased and eaten in season. Apples should feel very firm to the touch and be free of surface blemishes and bruises. The prettiest apples are, however, not always the tastiest. In our Northwest climate, russeting is common on apples and does not affect their quality in any way. Look for unique apple varieties at roadside stands, at the Pike Place Market in Seattle, and at Remlinger Farms in Carnation. They are worth searching out.

Storage

Apples ripen ten times as fast at 70 degrees and five times as fast at 40 degrees as they do at 32 degrees; therefore refrigeration is absolutely necessary to maintain quality. Apples should be enclosed in a plastic bag to prevent them from picking up other flavors.

With good keepers such as the Red Delicious, I have had remarkable results by wrapping each apple individually in paper, boxing them, and storing them in a cold garage. They often keep in perfect eating condition until spring. Golden Delicious—and most other apples—are not as durable and should be consumed soon after they have been purchased.

Preparation

Apples will turn brown when cut and exposed to the air for any length of time. To prevent this from happening they must be immersed, immediately after cutting, in acidulated water (¼ cup lemon juice to 1 cup water). Or each slice of apple may be dipped in lemon juice or any other acidic juice, such as orange, lime, or pineapple.

Cooking

It is true that Golden Delicious apples hold their shape well during cooking, but I can think of no other reason to recommend them. Granny Smith, Melrose, and Jonagold apples hold their shape and have superlative flavor as well. A crisp, acidic, highly flavored apple is what is needed for cooking. Some apples break down too rapidly or too thoroughly to be used for anything other than applesauce—though they may have a marvelous taste. Check the following listing for individual attributes.

When you want to caramelize the surface of apple slices without overcooking the interior, remember to use clarified butter (so that it does not burn), high heat, and a heavy pan that is big enough for all of the apples to fit in one layer. Do not turn and move the apples too much or they will steam rather than brown. Do not attempt this with slices less than ½-inch thick or you will have a mush rather than crispy, browned apples.

VARIETIES OF NORTHWEST APPLES

Criterion

The Criterion apple is new on the markets here. It is light green with a rosy blush, medium-sized, and slightly elongated. The flavor is worth writing home about: very aromatic with a sensational flowery aftertaste—something like a good German Riesling; very crisp, juicy, and slightly tart.

Golden Delicious

A crisp, firm, sweet-tart apple, Golden Delicious has a fairly mild flavor. Although this apple is fine for eating out-of-hand and a very dependable all-purpose cooking apple, it is perhaps the least interesting choice for both. Harvested from late September through early October, though available year-round due to controlled atmosphere storage, it does not in fact store particularly well, regardless of all the heroic attempts to the contrary. It loses much of its fresh appeal as the season progresses.

Granny Smith

A medium-sized, very round, lime-green apple with a tart, pleasant flavor and juicy flesh, the Granny Smith is an all-purpose apple, equally suited to being eaten fresh, general cooking, and baking. It makes excellent applesauce and keeps well too. Until 1982, most of our

Granny Smith apples were imported from Australia. Since then Washington state has been increasing local production. A late-harvest apple, the local crop is available from November through June.

Gravenstein

A medium to large apple, the Gravenstein is roundish with an irregular shape. The skin is red-striped over light green. Gravensteins have a fine texture, are crisp in season, firm, and juicy. Admirers of this apple claim its excellent flavor as its chief asset. It makes an outstanding applesauce. Harvest time is from late July through late August.

Jonathan

A small to medium apple, uniformly round to oblong in shape, the Jonathan has a skin that is red-striped over yellow. The flesh is firm, crisp, and juicy. Jonathans are tart with a characteristic spicy flavor. They make excellent eating apples and are fine to cook with too. They are harvested during the latter part of September.

McIntosh

A medium-sized apple with a very round shape, the McIntosh has a color that leans to golden with a bright crimson blush. These apples are sweet, moderately soft, and juicy. Many consider them to be a fine dessert apple, although they disintegrate quickly when cooked. Harvested in late September.

Melrose

A medium to large-sized apple, the Melrose has a yellow undertone blushed with bright red. Firm, juicy, crisp, and nicely acidic with a good flavor balance, it also stores well. The Melrose is a cross between a Red Delicious and a Jonathan. An excellent dessert and cooking apple, it arrives at the market in mid-October.

Newtown Pippin

A rather round, pale green to greenish-yellow apple with a very firm texture, the Newtown Pippin has an extremely full flavor and is a good all-purpose apple, equally suitable for eating fresh and cooking. A good cider apple, Newtowns also keep well and are available from October through May.

Red Delicious

An elegantly shaped, elongated apple, the Red Delicious is the perfect gift for teacher. In prime condition this bright red, mildly sweet, juicy, and crisp apple makes a good snack. Although its looks are its strongest suit, a Red Delicious just plucked from the tree can be a fine taste experience. It does not contain enough flavor or acidity to hold its own in cooking.

Rome Beauty

A spherically shaped apple with a brilliant, almost solid red color, the Rome Beauty has juicy, crisp, very firm, and aromatic flesh. Its subtle flavor is enhanced in cooking. It is available from late October through June.

Tydeman

Tydeman is a new apple on the Northwest commercial apple scene. Looking like a McIntosh with bright red skin, it is fine textured, moderately firm, good for eating and cooking. Tydemans are harvested between mid-August and early September.

Winesap

The best snack apple according to many apple aficionados, the Winesap is a round apple with a dark red color. Its texture is firm and crisp; its flavor is tart. It is good for baking and cooking too and is available from October through August.

Apple Recipes

Baked Onions and Apples with Rosemary, Crème Fraîche, and Tillamook Cheddar, *page 246*

Braised Duck with Apples, Prunes, and Walnuts, *page 236*

Caramelized Apple Tart with Grand Marnier, *page 254*

Cinnamon Applejack Soufflé with Honey-Glazed Jonathan Apples, *page 255*

Petrale Sole with Walla Walla Sweets and Granny Smith Apples, *page 221*

Sauté of Chicken with Caramelized Apples and Toasted Hazelnuts, *page 237*

Sweet and Spicy Apple Cake, *page 253*

Cranberries

The inestimable cranberry (specifically *Vaccinium macrocarpon*) enjoys the distinction of being one of only three native American fruits, the others being the Concord grape and the blueberry. With its high vitamin C content the fruit not only saved early settlers from scurvy, but also added considerable interest to their otherwise meager diets. Cranberries are commercially cultivated in only five regions today: southeastern Massachusetts, central and northern Wisconsin, southern New Jersey, southwestern British Columbia, and coastal Washington and Oregon. Washington and Oregon rank fourth and fifth respectively in commercial production levels.

The soil requirements for growing cranberries are specific: sandy, acidic soil with plenty of fresh water. Peat is also desirable because of its capacity to retain water. So coastline bogs are usually where cranberries, with their impenetrable thatch of ground-hugging vines,

are seen, though it is possible to grow them further inland given the right soil and plenty of water.

Times have been so good for cranberry growers of late that the crop has been nick-named "red gold" to indicate its profit-making potential. The industry has not always been so lucrative. It takes between five and seven years to realize a full-sized crop of berries from newly planted acreage. Land usually has to be drained of water, leveled, and covered with a few inches of sand before being planted. There was also the problem of springtime killer frosts in the early days of commercial production. A severe frost could wipe out an entire crop just as the blossoms were setting buds. Then in the mid-1920s, a Washington grower by the name of Jim Crowley developed an automatic sprinkler system that is activated as temperatures drop to freezing levels. A sheath of ice on the vines protects the buds from damage. (Interestingly enough, water radiates heat in the process of freezing.) This system is now used nationwide.

A cranberry harvest is a fascinating sight. Most cranberry acreage is wet-picked; the bogs are first flooded with water, then special machinery is used to break the berries from the plant so that they will float to the top of the water where they can be corraled and scooped out. A bog under harvest is a crimson sea of bobbing berries. Because much of the crop harvested this way is slightly bruised, wet-picked berries are destined for the processed market. Only ten percent of the cranberry crop

is gathered by the more expensive dry-pick method. Jules Furford, a grower in the Northwest, is credited with the development of the innovative Furford Picker that mechanically dry-picks the berries and prunes the bushes in one operation. These carefully handled—and of course more expensive—berries account for all those sold to the fresh market.

About eighty-five percent of the nation's cranberry growers belong to a grower-owned cooperative, Ocean Spray Cranberries. Growers deliver their berries to Ocean Spray processing facilities in return for research, marketing, processing, and distribution services. Thus cranberry lovers from coast to coast know the Ocean Spray name very well.

Season

The harvest generally begins during the first week of October and continues through the first half of November. Because of their waxy skins, fresh cranberries keep remarkably well and are usually available in the market from October through December. To have them available longer, buy extra packages and freeze them.

Selection

Fresh Cranberries are always prepackaged in clear plastic bags and are usually kept chilled along with the vegetables in the supermarket. Berries should look firm and plump without any discolored or mushy specimens. One

pound packages contain four cups of berries; twelve-ounce packages contain three cups of berries.

Storage

Cranberries will keep in the refrigerator for about a month. Frozen they will keep for about a year. Leave them in their original plastic bag.

Preparation

Pick over your berries carefully and discard dark, soft, or mashed specimens. Rinse them under cold running water and drain.

Cooking

If using frozen cranberries, there is no need to thaw them before cooking.

Cooking cranberries in sugar tends to set the skins, toughening them somewhat. Though many recipes specify that the cranberries be cooked in sugar and liquid, you can sometimes rearrange the method and cook the cranberries in water alone before adding the sugar. It usually takes about four minutes to cook cranberries until just tender. Cooked longer they will turn into a thicker, more homogeneous mixture. Cranberries are rich in pectin which is why they jell when cooked with sugar or honey.

The vivid color of cranberries can bleed into or muddy the color of other ingredients, par-

ticularly batters. To minimize this effect in muffins, quickbreads and pancakes, add frozen berries to the batter rather than fresh.

The extreme tartness of cranberries demands sugar. Grape growers measure sugar content of grapes in degrees Brix. A ripe grape has a sugar level of 22 degrees Brix; an unripe grape a sugar level of 15 degrees Brix. Really ripe cranberries have a sugar level of 2 degrees Brix. This astringency, when tempered with added sweetener, can really do magic with rich meats such as turkey, ham, pork, and game birds. Cranberries are equally delicious with other fruit such as apples and pears. They also lend themselves to flavorings of orange, lemon, lime, fresh ginger, anise, cinnamon, nutmeg, and cloves, not to mention raisins, toasted walnuts, toasted hazelnuts, cider vinegar, curry spices, mustard, port, cornmeal, oatmeal, sweet potatoes, yams, onions, sausage, spareribs, chicken, maple syrup, rosemary, black pepper, and almost anything else you can think of—except chocolate.

Cranberry Recipes

STARTERS

Walnut-Fried Polenta with Crème Fraîche and Green Onions

Makes about 22 pieces.

Here we have Italian polenta with a hot, buttery coating of walnuts and a dollop of crème fraîche. This simple treatment works well as a first course with something flavorful and saucy to follow or as a side dish for straightforward preparations of meat, poultry, or fish with companion sauces. Be sure to make the crème fraîche at least a day ahead.

> 6 cups homemade chicken stock (page 345)
> 2 cups medium-grind cornmeal
> 4 tablespoons unsalted butter
>   Coarse kosher salt
> ½ cup finely grated Parmesan cheese
> 1½ cups walnuts
> 4 tablespoons plus ½ cup flour
> 1½ cups fresh whole-wheat bread crumbs
> 2 eggs, beaten
> 4 tablespoons unsalted butter
> 6 tablespoons corn oil
> 4 green onions, slivered
>   Crème Fraîche (page 357)

To make the *polenta,* put the chicken stock in a deep pot and slowly sprinkle in the cornmeal, stirring constantly with a long-handled wooden spoon. Bring to a simmer. Add the butter and salt to taste. Cook slowly for 15 to 20 minutes, stirring steadily. When done, *polenta* will be thick, smooth, and soft, and should tear away from the sides of the pot as you stir. Do not make it too stiff or the finished cakes will taste dry. Finish by folding in the Parmesan.

Pour the *polenta* into an oiled jelly-roll pan, spreading to an even depth of ½ inch and let cool. When cool, cut into 2- by 3-inch oblique diamonds.

Process the walnuts with 4 tablespoons of the flour until they are finely minced; do not go so far as to bring out the oil in the nuts. Add the bread crumbs and whirl just to combine.

Dip the *polenta* slices into the remaining ½ cup flour, shaking off the excess, then dip them into beaten egg and finally into the mixture of bread crumbs and walnuts. Lay on a mesh cooling rack to air-dry. Cover them loosely with plastic wrap and refrigerate.

In batches, fry the polenta in butter and oil until golden on each side. (Use only half the butter and oil to begin with and wipe the pan clean between batches.) Arrange two for each serving and top with a spoonful of crème fraîche and a sprinkling of green onions. Serve right away.

Chilled Mussels with Basil Mint Vinaigrette

Serves 4.

In the fall when Northwest mussels are beginning to taste their best again and fresh herbs are overflowing the garden, this dish provides a vehicle for enjoying them both. Because the preparation is so straightforward, it is particularly important to select the finest, smallest mussels available. If only the marginally alive, oversized mussels that are sometimes shipped in from out of the area are available, do not bother. Small clams are also tasty when treated in this manner. Crostini (sliced French bread brushed with olive oil and fresh minced garlic, then toasted on both sides) are particularly good with these.

> 3 pounds Washington blue mussels,
> cleaned and debearded

BASIL MINT VINAIGRETTE
> ¼ cup rice wine vinegar
> Coarse kosher salt
> Freshly ground black pepper
> ¼ cup cold-pressed olive oil
> ¼ cup corn oil
> 1 tablespoon minced fresh basil
> 1 tablespoon minced fresh mint

GARNISH
> Fresh sprigs of basil and mint

Put the mussels into a kettle with ½ cup water, cover, bring to a simmer, and steam for about 4 minutes, or until they have opened. Remove from the heat right away and uncover. Once they are cool enough to handle, remove the mussels from the kettle and arrange them, still in their shells, on a large platter. (The broth makes a wonderful addition to a seafood soup or stew. Freeze it for later use if you like.)

Make the vinaigrette by combining the vinegar with salt and pepper to taste. When the salt has dissolved, whisk in the olive oil, corn oil, and herbs.

Drizzle the vinaigrette carefully over each mussel to coat it lightly. Garnish the platter with fresh sprigs of basil and mint.

Hazelnut-Fried Fresh Mozzarella with Apple Cider and Chives

Serves 6.

This is a wonderfully subtle, savory first course. It depends critically on fresh mozzarella cheese; the supermarket variety is little more than rubber. If fresh mozzarella is unobtainable, use a good quality Monterey Jack cheese for its melting quality and mild taste. The vinaigrette that accompanies the mozzarella here is sweet and tangy, and can be hot or not depending on how much cayenne you elect to use. Fresh apple cider is apple juice that has not been pasteurized and thus has a livelier taste than the supermarket variety (see page 159). You may be able to find it in the refrigerated juice section of a good grocery store or, more reliably, from a local apple purveyor on a farm, roadside stand, or public market. Bottled sweet sparkling cider (not hard, that is, alcoholic, cider) may be substituted here if necessary.

½ cup toasted, skinned hazelnuts
2 tablespoons flour
1 pound 3 ounces fresh mozzarella, approximately (small balls if possible)
   Flour for dredging
1 egg
2 tablespoons unsalted butter
2 tablespoons corn oil

GARNISH
   Whole chives

Put the hazelnuts and flour into a processor and pulse-chop very finely without going so far as to bring out the oil in the nuts.

Shave the ends off the balls of mozzarella, then slice them crosswise into six ¾-inch slabs. (If you have small balls, you may get more slices.) Dip the cheese into flour and slap-pat the excess off thoroughly. Dip into beaten egg, then into the combination of minced hazelnuts and flour. Set on a wire rack in the refrigerator to dry for 30 minutes. (Cover lightly with plastic wrap if stored for longer.)

Make the Cider Vinaigrette (recipe follows) and set it aside.

Melt the butter and oil and when hot sauté the mozzarella, in batches if necessary, over medium-high heat to brown both sides nicely. Do this as quickly as possible, so as just to soften the cheese without causing it to ooze out of its breading. Arrange on plates and drizzle with vinaigrette. Garnish each serving with 2 slender chives, crossed to one side of the mozzarella.

GARNISH VARIATION

Diced Granny Smith apples sautéed over high heat in unsalted butter with a sprinkling of sugar to speed the caramelization, make an interesting and tasty garnish. They need to be

done at the last minute and should be left a little on the crisp side to contrast with the melting softness of the cheese.

Cider Vinaigrette

½ cup fresh apple cider
2 tablespoons cider vinegar
1 clove garlic, minced
½ teaspoon dry mustard

Coarse kosher salt
Cayenne pepper
4 tablespoons cold-pressed olive oil
2 tablespoons minced chives

Put the fresh cider in a saucepan and reduce to a light syrup. Remove from the heat, cool slightly, and add the cider vinegar, garlic, mustard, salt, and cayenne to taste and whisk to dissolve the salt. Whisk in the olive oil, then add the chives. Reserve.

Autumn Vegetable, Black Bean, and Rice Salad

Serves 6 to 8.

This recipe makes a pretty, creamy salad, well-fla-vored with curry paste and peach chutney—great for the final picnics and grills of fall. If you would like a heartier main course salad, just add one and a half boned, skinned chicken breasts, cooked and shredded.

Curry paste is available in Indian grocery stores. Its main advantage over raw curry powder is that is has been cooked in oil and can be used right from the jar. Curry powder tastes much sweeter, mellower, and less acrid if it is cooked in butter or oil for a minute or so to release its volatile flavor before being used. (The same holds true for dried herbs of all kinds. Cook them first in a little fat, then proceed with the recipe.) If you have only curry powder, cook it briefly and use it, to taste, instead of the paste. The amount will vary considerably from one powder to another and in any case will be different from the paste.

  1 cup raw black beans (2¼ cup cooked black beans)

  2 cups homemade chicken stock (page 345)

  1 cup long-grain white rice (3¼ cup cooked rice)

  ½ cup diced carrots

  ½ cup green beans, trimmed and cut into ½-inch slices

  ½ cup diced celery

  ½ cup diced green pepper

  ½ cup chopped Walla Walla sweet onion (or other mild, sweet onion)

  1 cup mayonnaise

  ½ cup cream, whipped

  1 to 2 tablespoons curry paste, to taste

  2 to 4 tablespoons lemon juice, to taste

  2 tablespoons peach or apricot chutney

  4 tablespoons minced cilantro

  Coarse kosher salt

  Freshly ground black pepper

Soak the black beans overnight in cold water to cover. Drain, cover with fresh water, and simmer for about 90 minutes, until tender but not at all mushy.

Bring the chicken stock to a simmer in a medium saucepan and stir in the rice. Cover and simmer slowly for 20 minutes, until the rice is tender and the liquid absorbed. Remove from the heat and let cool.

Blanch the carrots and green beans in a pot of boiling water for 1 to 2 minutes, until just barely cooked but definitely still vivid in color and crunchy. Drain and refresh under cold running water. Dry lightly with paper towels.

Combine the carrots and green beans with the celery, green pepper, onion, black beans, and cooled rice.

Whisk together the mayonnaise, whipped cream, curry paste, lemon juice, chutney, and

2 tablespoons of the cilantro. Toss with the salad. Refrigerate for several hours; sprinkle on the remaining 2 tablespoons cilantro, and season to taste with salt and pepper.

Chinese Barbecued Duck, Peach, and Toasted Walnut Salad

Serves 4.

There is an excellent Chinese barbecue joint, called the Kau Kau, in Seattle's Chinatown. The window is strung with all sorts of barbecued goodies, including chicken, duck, and pork. They will prepare Peking duck too if you order ahead and, best of all, the prices are reasonable. The everyday barbecued duck is succulent, flavorful, and meltingly tender. It is perfect for this first-course salad in which the flavor must assert itself among several other dominant tastes. (To make a main-course salad, add one more duck.)

> 1 Chinese-style barbecued duck (2 cups boneless, skinless duck meat)
> Coarse kosher salt
> 1 cup fresh walnuts
> 2 tablespoons unsalted butter
> 1½ teaspoons sugar

> 8 cups salad greens: arugula, dandelion greens, butter lettuce, watercress (⅔ mild and ⅓ bitter)
> 3 tablespoons balsamic vinegar
> 1 teaspoon Dijon mustard
> 3 tablespoons peach chutney
> Coarse kosher salt
> 8 tablespoons olive oil
> 2 ripe peaches
> Fresh lemon juice (optional)

GARNISH
> Peach chutney
> Freshly ground black pepper

Remove the meat from the duck carcass, remove all the fat and tendons, then slice the meat into julienne strips. Season to taste with salt. Scrape the fat from the underside of the skin, place the skin on a cookie sheet, and bake it at 375° for 15 to 20 minutes or until crisp. Remove the cracklings to paper towels to drain. When cool, crumble or chop them and reserve.

Check your walnuts: if they taste bitter, blanch them first for 2 minutes, then drain and let them dry. Melt 2 tablespoons unsalted butter, add the walnut halves, sprinkle with sugar, and sauté to toast lightly, tossing frequently.

Clean and tear the greens into manageable pieces.

To make the vinaigrette, combine the vinegar, mustard, peach chutney, and salt to taste.

Whisk to dissolve the salt. Whisk in the olive oil.

Bring a saucepan of water to a boil, drop the peaches in, rotating to heat all sides, and blanch for 15 to 30 seconds only. Remove and peel the skin off with your fingers or a small paring knife. It should slip off easily if the peach is ripe. Cut the peaches in half, remove the pits, and slice each half lengthwise, leaving the slices attached slightly on one end. (If you must hold them, brush the peaches well with lemon juice.)

Toss the greens lightly with some of the dressing, then mix in the walnuts. Mound equally on 4 salad plates, arranging half a peach to one side of each mound, spreading the slices slightly. Divide the duck meat into 4 equal portions and put it in the center of the greens with the breast portions on top. Drizzle the remaining dressing on the duck. Put a small dollop of chutney on top of the peach slices and sprinkle cracklings on each serving. Grate black pepper liberally on top and serve.

Tomato Mint Salad with Creamy Herb Dressing

Serves 4.

The only trick to this simple salad is to get ripe, full-flavored tomatoes. When a more elaborate pre-sentation is needed, layer the tomatoes with fresh mozzarella slices or try an arranged composition of diced tomatoes, diced fresh mozzarella, and calamata olives. The dressing is also good as a dip for crudités.

- ½ teaspoon cumin seeds
- ½ cup unflavored yogurt
- 1½ teaspoons white wine vinegar
- 1 clove garlic, minced
- 2 tablespoons minced spearmint
- 1 green onion, minced
- 2 tablespoons olive oil
- 4 ripe tomatoes
  Handful fresh spearmint
  Coarse kosher salt
  Freshly ground black pepper

GARNISH
  Fresh mint leaves

Toast the cumin seeds in a small, dry sauté pan until fragrant, then grind them in a spice mill (or with a mortar and pestle). (The extra flavor that is released by using this simple toasting method is more than worth the effort. Try it with other dried herbs and spices as well.) Combine with the yogurt, vinegar, garlic, mint, and green onions. Add the oil in a stream, whisking.

Slice the tomatoes and arrange them, alternating with leaves of mint, on 4 salad plates. Season with salt and pepper. Drizzle the dressing over each salad.

Country Autumn Herb Soup

Serves 4 to 6.

Fresh herbs are available in Northwest gardens and at local markets until the first serious frost, often well into November (more on herbs on page 82). From August on, I am frantically trying to use my own overgrown crop and this creamy soup provides the perfect vehicle. Dried herbs should not be used in this recipe, so if something is unavailable, just leave it out or substitute another fresh herb. I have yet to find a combination of fresh herbs that is not pleasing, so allow yourself free rein.

    1 pound fresh spinach
    4 tablespoons unsalted butter
    2 cloves garlic, minced
    4 tablespoons flour
    ½ cup firmly packed fresh basil,
        chopped
    ¼ cup firmly packed Italian parsley,
        chopped
    ¼ cup firmly packed fresh chives,
        chopped
    2 tablespoons fresh mint, chopped
    3 cups homemade chicken stock (page
        345)
    1½ cups cream or half-and-half
        Coarse kosher salt
        Freshly ground white pepper

GARNISH
Fresh spearmint leaves

Cook the spinach in a large skillet with just the water remaining on its leaves from rinsing until it has wilted. Turn with tongs or two wooden spoons to wilt it evenly.

Melt the butter in a large saucepan and sauté the garlic for 1 or 2 minutes without browning. Add the flour and cook for an additional 2 minutes while whisking. Do not brown.

Add the basil, parsley, chives, mint, and chicken stock. Stir to smooth the soup and continue cooking over low heat for 5 to 10 minutes. The color should still be a vivid green. (Too much cooking destroys the flavor of delicate herbs and of course ruins the color.) Purée the soup in a processor and return it to a clean pan. Add the cream and heat through. (If you are using half-and-half, do not boil the soup after this point—and even when using cream there is no reason to boil the soup.) Season with salt and white pepper to taste.

Serve hot, garnished with mint leaves.

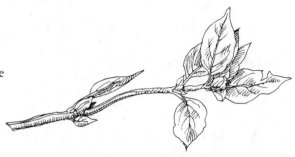

Fresh Pumpkin Soup with Green Onion and Parsley

Serves 6 to 8.

Pumpkin is a native American vegetable but it took the French to come up with this delectable and colorful soup. Unfortunately, few of us use fresh pumpkin much, which accounts for the relatively short season in the local markets. Once Halloween is over, most merchants discard their remaining pumpkins. In order to assure my own supply through Christmas, I purchase a dozen or so small pumpkins at the end of October and store them on a table on a covered deck. If you have enough space, pumpkin may be refrigerated. Served in its own shell, this soup provides an elegant beginning to a festive meal. This particular version was inspired by Gerard Parratt, the chef of the Relais de Lyon restaurant in Seattle. It is a classic.

2 whole small pumpkins
¼ cup unsalted butter
2 large onions, chopped
1 stalk celery, chopped
2 leeks, white and light green parts only, chopped
3 large carrots, chopped
3 large potatoes, peeled and cut into 1-inch chunks (about 1½ pounds)
6 cups homemade chicken stock (page 345)

1½ cups cream
¼ cup parsley, minced
¼ cup green onion, minced
Coarse kosher salt
Freshly ground black pepper
¼ cup unsalted butter for finishing

Cut the top off the nicest looking pumpkin and reserve it for a lid. Scrape out the fibrous material and seeds to make a container for the soup. Quarter and seed the second pumpkin, and cut the quarters into 1-inch chunks. Peel each chunk with a sharp paring knife. You should have about 1½ pounds.

Melt the butter in a soup pot and add the onions and celery. Cook gently until tender but not browned. Add the leeks, carrots, potatoes, and pumpkin chunks. Pour in the chicken stock and continue to cook, gently, until the vegetables are very tender, about 30 minutes.

Separate the solid chunks from the soup and purée them in a processor or pass them through a food mill. Add a little of the liquid if necessary to accomplish this, then gradually add all of the remaining liquid to the purée.

Add the cream, parsley, and green onions. Thin with a little more stock if necessary. Heat but do not boil. Season to taste with salt and pepper. Just before serving, whisk in the remaining butter.

Just before serving the soup, warm the pumpkin shell in a 350° oven for about 15 minutes. Pour the soup into it and serve.

Garlic Soup with Sage Leaves and Herb Profiteroles

Serves 4.

A soup made of these key ingredients was listed on the menu at San Francisco's Stars restaurant in 1985. I did not taste it while I was at the restaurant, but was so intrigued with the concept that I developed this recipe anyway. My version is just as dependent on sweetly sautéed onions as it is on garlic. The profiteroles are optional but they do add a pleasing crunch to the otherwise rich and creamy soup. Do not be afraid of the large quantity of garlic; it mellows dramatically with cooking.

> Herb Profiteroles (page 356), about
>   20 small puffs (optional)
> 2 tablespoons unsalted butter
> ¼ cup garlic cloves, thinly sliced
> 2 large onions, cut from root to tip
>   into eight equal wedges, each
>   thinly sliced widthwise
> 1 tablespoon flour
> 4 cups homemade chicken stock (page
>   345)
> 2 egg yolks
> 1 tablespoon lemon juice
> 8 good-sized fresh sage leaves, shredded
>   lengthwise

If you are going to include the herb profiteroles, make them first.

To make the soup, melt the butter and add the garlic and onions over moderate heat. Cook until softened and golden but do not brown in the least. Sprinkle on the flour and continue cooking and stirring for an additional 2 to 3 minutes. Do not let the flour brown.

Slowly pour in the stock, stirring to eliminate any lumps. Simmer slowly for about 30 minutes.

Just before serving, beat the egg yolks lightly. Take 1 cup of the hot soup and slowly mix it into the yolks to raise their temperature gradually. This precaution usually prevents the eggs from curdling. Then slowly stir the egg yolk mixture back into the soup, which should not be simmering at all. Continue stirring; at between 165° and 180°, the soup should thicken slightly. If you make the soup any hotter, the eggs will probably curdle. I say probably because the flour in this recipe might hinder the curdling process. I would not risk it myself.

Just before serving, stir in the shredded sage leaves, ladle the soup into bowls, and top or accompany each serving with several Herb Profiteroles.

Hazelnut Gazpacho

Serves 4.

*In Spain there is a white gazpacho made with al-
monds that is very tasty. This variation on the theme
uses hazelnuts and a more modest amount of both
garlic and vinegar than is traditional. It is very
important to the smoothness of the soup that the hazelnuts be puréed to a butter before going on with the
recipe. Because the soup is pale, it looks best in colored or earthenware bowls.*

1 cup lightly toasted, skinned
hazelnuts
¼ cup olive oil
1 or 2 cloves pressed garlic, to taste
1 tablespoon white wine vinegar
½ cup white, crustless bread, soaked
with 2 tablespoons chicken
stock

3 cups homemade chicken stock
(page 345)
Coarse kosher salt
Freshly ground white pepper

GARNISH
½ cup toasted, skinned, chopped
hazelnuts
Crostini (page 103)

Purée the hazelnuts to a butter, using 2 tablespoons of the oil. When smooth (after about 3
minutes), add the rest of the oil, blend well,
and add the garlic and vinegar to taste, the
soaked bread, and finally enough stock to produce the desired consistency. Season to taste
with salt and pepper and refrigerate.

Serve in chilled soup bowls with a sprinkling of chopped nuts on top and crostini on
the side.

Petrale Sole and Mussels with Saffron Cream

Serves 6.

The term coulis *originally referred to a liquid purée of chicken, game, or fish that was sometimes served as a soup. Today the word has evolved considerably and is usually used to denote a thick, nearly melted, vegetable compote. In this dish, sole fillets rest on a coulis of onions and shallots. Other variations worth considering are combinations of diced red bell pepper and onion, diced tomato and onion, or chopped leek and onion. The important thing to remember with any of these combinations is that they must be cooked down to a thick, but not mushy, consistency to produce the right effect.*

    2 pounds Washington blue mussels, cleaned and debearded
    1½ cups dry white wine
    ½ cup water

COULIS
    3 tablespoons unsalted butter
    2 onions, chopped
    ¼ cup chopped shallots
    1 clove garlic, minced
    Coarse kosher salt
    Freshly ground white pepper

    ¾ cup flour
    1 teaspoon coarse kosher salt

    ½ teaspoon freshly grated black pepper
    ¼ teaspoon cayenne pepper
    6 fillets petrale sole (about 1½ pounds)
    2 tablespoons unsalted butter
    2 tablespoons corn oil
    ¼ teaspoon saffron threads, crumbled
    1 cup cream
    1 teaspoon lemon juice
    ¾ cup grated Gruyère cheese

Put the mussels into a pot with the wine and water. Cover, bring to a boil, and cook for 4 minutes, until the shells have opened. Remove from the heat. Strain the liquid into a small saucepan and reduce it to a syrupy essence (about 3 tablespoons). Remove the mussels from their shells. If any have not opened, put them back to cook for a minute or two; if they still do not open, discard them.

To make the coulis, melt the butter and sauté the onions and shallots slowly until softened but not browned. Add the garlic and cook slowly for another minute or two without browning. Season to taste with salt and white pepper. Butter a 9- by 12-inch baking dish or 6 individual baking dishes that are long enough to hold the petrale fillets and spread the onion mixture on the bottom.

Mix the flour with salt, pepper, and cayenne. Season the fillets with salt and pepper and then coat both sides with seasoned flour, shaking and patting off the excess.

Heat the butter and oil and sauté the fillets

quickly, turning to brown both sides. Do not cook all the way through. Lay the fillets on top of the coulis. Scatter the mussels on top.

In a small saucepan reduce the cream with the crumbled saffron to ½ cup. Whisk in the mussel essence. Season to taste with salt, pepper, and lemon juice.

Drizzle the sauce over the gratin, sprinkle with the cheese, and broil to heat through and glaze the surface. (If you wish to make this ahead, complete the assembly up to broiling, and refrigerate. Heat slowly at 325° for 15 minutes or so, then broil.) Serve right away.

Petrale Sole with Walla Walla Sweets and Granny Smith Apples

Serves 6.

Walla Walla sweets are incomparable Washington State onions with the mild, decidedly sweet taste (page 81). They are particularly good here, though other brown-skinned onions will also work. Be sure that the fish is extremely fresh. Use your nose on fillets, as there is no other way to ascertain their age.

½ cup + 1 tablespoon unsalted butter
3 medium-sized Walla Walla sweet onions (or other brown-skinned onions), peeled, halved, and sliced
Coarse kosher salt
Freshly ground white pepper
3 Granny Smith apples, peeled, cored, cut into quarters, and sliced lengthwise
6 to 8 fillets petrale sole (about 1½ pounds)
1½ cups bone dry white wine (preferably muscadet, sauvignon blanc, chardonnay, or, if all else fails, dry Vermouth)
3 tablespoons flour
1 cup cream
2 egg yolks
Lemon juice
Tabasco sauce
Salt and pepper to taste
¾ cup grated Gruyère cheese

Melt 3 tablespoons butter and sauté the onions until golden and well softened but not brown, about 20 minutes. Season to taste with salt and pepper. Reserve.

In another sauté pan, melt an additional 3 tablespoons butter and sauté the apple slices over brisk heat to slightly caramelize the surface. Turn only once and leave on the crisp side. Reserve.

First butter then line the bottom of a 12-inch baking dish with the onions. Place the fillets on top, overlapping slightly. Season with salt and pepper. Arrange the apples around the outside edges.

Bring the wine to a boil in a small saucepan and immediately pour on top. Cover the casserole with buttered parchment paper and poach in a 350° oven for 10 minutes per inch of fillet thickness. (This cooking time assumes that sufficient heat is present. For poaching, the liquid should register between 180° and 190° on an instant-read thermometer. If the fish is cold (and it should be), the temperature of the boiling wine may be lowered to the point that the dish takes longer to cook.)

When the fish is just beginning to flake, remove it from the oven and, carefully tilting the casserole, pour the liquid into a saucepan. Cover and keep the fish warm.

Reduce the cooking liquid down to 1 cup by boiling it rapidly. Taste to be sure that the alcohol has dissipated; if not, continue cooking until it does. Meanwhile, in another saucepan, melt the remaining 3 tablespoons butter and

stir in the flour. Cook for at least 2 minutes without coloring. When the liquid is properly reduced, add it to the butter and flour *roux,* whisking to smooth. Add ¾ cup of the cream, whisk, and simmer for 5 minutes. Remove from the heat.

Combine the egg yolks and remaining ¼ cup cream and whisk a bit of the hot sauce into them to warm them gradually. Whisk in a little more sauce and then whisk the egg yolks back into the sauce, being sure the sauce is no longer simmering and is off the heat. Put the pan back over moderate heat and cook briefly, just to thicken the egg yolks; do not exceed 175°.

Carefully tip and drain the casserole again. Use the liquid to thin the sauce further if necessary. Season the sauce with lemon juice, Tabasco, and salt and pepper to taste, and pour over the fish, leaving the apples exposed. Sprinkle Gruyère evenly on top of the fish and sauce. Dot the apples with the remaining 1 tablespoon butter. Glaze under a hot broiler for 1 to 2 minutes and serve.

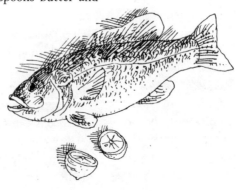

Dungeness Crab-Stuffed Petrale Sole

Serves 6.

This dish is only as good as the quality of the fish and the crab. If petrale fillets are unavailable or unsavory looking, do not hesitate to buy a different lean, mild fish, such as rockfish, flounder or true cod fillets. Shrimp may be substituted for crab. These golden bundles with the sauce and garnish on the inside are particularly pleasing when nestled in a bed of butter-sautéed kale or spinach, which provides a contrast of color and flavor.

3½ tablespoons unsalted butter
1½ tablespoons flour
½ cup milk
2 tablespoons grated Gruyère cheese
  Coarse kosher salt
  Freshly ground white pepper
  Lemon juice
1 cup flaked Dungeness crabmeat (or cooked shrimp meat)
6 small petrale sole fillets (nicely shaped rectangular fillets)
½ cup fine dry bread crumbs
  Coarse kosher salt
  Freshly ground black pepper
½ cup flour
1 egg, lightly beaten
2 tablespoons corn oil
  Chive Butter (page 85) (optional)

In a small saucepan, melt 1½ tablespoons of the butter and stir in the flour. Cook the mixture, stirring constantly for 2 minutes. Add the milk and whisk to smooth out the sauce. Bring to a simmer, whisking, then remove from the heat. Stir in the Gruyère and season to taste with salt, pepper, and drops of lemon juice. Place a sheet of plastic wrap directly on the surface to prevent its crusting and allow to cool.

Combine just enough of the cooled sauce with the crab to bind it. Season each fillet with salt and pepper, place about 2 tablespoons of the crab mixture on each fillet and roll up lengthwise. (If the fillets are thicker than ⅜ inch, flatten them slightly between sheets of plastic wrap.)

Season the bread crumbs with salt and pepper to taste. Dip each roll into flour, shake, and pat-slap off the excess. Brush evenly with beaten egg, then coat with the seasoned bread crumbs. Place on a wire rack and refrigerate until ready to sauté. These should be allowed to set up for at least 30 minutes.

Heat the oil and the remaining 2 tablespoons butter in a sauté pan and add the rolls. Turn carefully to brown all sides. The rolls will cook through in about 10 to 15 minutes. If desired you may brown the rolls ahead and finish the cooking by placing them in a 350° oven, uncovered, for 10 minutes.

Serve as they are or with a drizzling of Chive Butter.

Dungeness Crab in Black Bean Sauce

Serves 4 to 6.

This recipe was developed to challenge the idea that the only way to eat fresh crab is simply boiled with hot butter. Certainly that is one of the best ways. The many friends and students who have tried this recipe have become easy converts. Although somewhat messy to eat, this Cantonese specialty serves as an excellent first course or, in larger quantities, as a main course accompanied by steamed rice to absorb any extra sauce. The eating procedure is necessarily informal—the only way to get the crabmeat out of the shell is to use your hands, mouth, and whatever you can think of. You might begin by snapping off one of the claws to use as a tool. Be sure to provide a finger bowl garnished with a thin slice of lemon at each place setting, along with plenty of napkins. And be sure to read this recipe ahead and have all ingredients including the sauce mixture and the thickening mixture entirely prepared before beginning.

SAUCE MIXTURE

3 tablespoons pale, dry sherry
4 tablespoons soy sauce
½ cup chicken stock
2 teaspoons sugar
2 tablespoons corn oil
1 tablespoon finely minced garlic
2 teaspoons finely minced fresh ginger
2 tablespoons salted black beans, mashed
1 onion, cut into ½-inch pieces
1 green pepper, cut into ½-inch pieces
2 or 3 medium-sized Dungeness crabs, cleaned, boiled, and legs separated and cracked in several places (page 76)

THICKENING

1 tablespoon cornstarch
1 tablespoon water

GARNISH

2 tablespoons finely sliced green onion

Prepare the sauce mixture by combining the sherry, soy sauce, chicken stock, and sugar. Stir to dissolve the sugar and set aside.

Prepare the thickening by stirring together the cornstarch and water. Set aside.

Heat the oil in a large wok or heavyweight skillet over medium-high heat. Add the garlic, ginger, and black beans. Stir-fry for 15 seconds. Do not brown the garlic.

Add the onion and green pepper. Stir-fry for 15 seconds. Stir the sauce mixture, add it to the wok, and stir to combine with the other ingredients.

Add the cracked crab legs and cover the wok. Heat for 5 minutes or so. The sauce should be bubbling and the crab heated through. Tip the wok toward you to collect all of the sauce on one side. Stir the thickening mixture to dissolve the cornstarch again and add it to the sauce. Whisk to smooth the sauce. Continue cooking until the sauce has boiled, thickened, and taken on a shiny appearance.

With tongs, remove the crab legs to a heated serving platter and pour the sauce with the vegetables evenly over the top. Sprinkle with green onion. Serve hot.

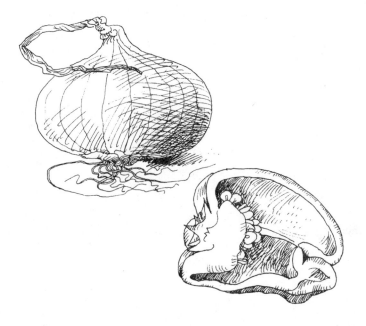

Braised Squid Mediterranean-Style

Serves 4 to 6.

The trick in cooking squid is not to overdo it. One to two minutes is the maximum before the very lean meat toughens beyond redemption. This is a beautiful dish with the white squid rings, black olives, and brilliant tomato sauce. It makes an excellent first course but may also be served over pasta for a heartier entrée. I like it spicy-hot but have left the cayenne measurement to your discretion. This sauce is so good that you may want to use it with other shellfish and fish as well.

SAUCE

 3 tablespoons unsalted butter
 1 onion, chopped
 2 cloves garlic, minced
 2 cups peeled, seeded, diced tomatoes
 1 teaspoon tomato paste
18 calamata olives, pitted and quartered
  lengthwise
 2 tablespoons currants
  Zest of 1 large orange
 1 cup bone dry white wine
  Coarse kosher salt
  Freshly ground black pepper
  Cayenne pepper

2 pounds whole squid, cleaned, skinned, and cut into ½-inch slices (1 pound cleaned, skinned slices)

24 thin slices French bread, buttered and toasted on both sides (crostini)

Melt the butter and sauté the onions until softened but not browned. Add the garlic and cook a minute longer without browning. Add the tomatoes, tomato paste, olives, currants, orange zest, and wine and simmer until lightly thickened. Season to taste with salt, pepper, and cayenne.

With the sauce simmering gently, add the squid, cover, and cook for 1 or 2 minutes just to heat through.

Arrange crostini around the edges of serving bowls and mound the squid with its sauce in the center.

Linguini with Squid Marinara

Serves 4 to 6.

I cannot think of anything that cooks more quickly than squid. If you have the sauce made ahead, this simple supper dish can be on the table in a matter of minutes. Serve with lots of crusty French bread and put the pepper grinder on the table.

MARINARA SAUCE
- 2 tablespoons olive oil
- 1 medium-sized onion, peeled and chopped
- 2 cloves garlic, finely minced
- ½ teaspoon fennel seeds
- 2 pounds peeled, chopped, juicy ripe tomatoes with their juice
- 1 teaspoon sugar (optional)
- Coarse kosher salt
- Freshly grated black pepper
- 1 pound fresh linguini
- 4 tablespoons unsalted butter, melted
- 2 pounds whole squid, dressed, skinned and cut into ½-inch slices (1 pound dressed, skinned, sliced rings)

To make the sauce, heat the olive oil and add the onion. Cook slowly until the onions begin to soften, about 15 minutes. Add the garlic and fennel seed and cook for 5 minutes longer.

Add the tomatoes with all of their juice and simmer slowly, uncovered, for 30 to 45 minutes until the sauce is fairly thick. Taste and adjust the flavor with sugar (to offset the acidity), salt, and pepper.

Bring a large pot of generously salted water to a boil. Add the linguini and boil for 2 to 3 minutes, until just tender. Drain. Toss with 4 tablespoons melted butter.

Add the squid rings to the sauce just as the pasta is finishing and simmer for 1 to 2 minutes—no longer. Toss the hot, drained, butter-coated pasta with the sauce and serve immediately.

Hot Sauced Clams with Fresh Thyme

Serves 6 as a first course.

This dish is splendidly messy to eat. The clams are left in their shells for effect and the sauce is drizzled over them, shells and all. The flavors are wonderful and the informality sparks conversation, so I do not worry about it. Be sure to provide plenty of hot, crusty French bread and napkins.

3 tablespoons minced shallots
1¼ cups bone dry white wine
     (preferably muscadet)
4 pounds small clams
2 sprigs parsley
1 bay leaf
1 small celery stalk, cut into chunks
3 tablespoons unsalted butter
2 tablespoons flour
¾ cup cream
2 large garlic cloves, minced
1½ tablespoons minced fresh thyme
2 tablespoons minced green onions,
    green part only
2 tablespoons minced parsley
   Coarse kosher salt
   Freshly ground white pepper
   Lemon juice

In a small saucepan, combine the shallots with ¼ cup of the wine and cook over high heat to reduce the wine to 1 tablespoon. Remove from the heat and reserve.

Clean the clams well in several changes of cold water, scrubbing the shells if they are especially grubby. Put the clams in a large pot with the remaining 1 cup wine, and the parsley, bay leaf, and celery. Cover and bring to a simmer. Steam over medium heat until the clams are open, about 5 minutes. Remove the clams from the pot as they open and strain the broth through a fine sieve lined with professional quality cheesecloth. Reserve 1½ cups of this broth and use the remainder for another purpose.

Mound the clams with their shells on a large heated serving platter. Cover and keep warm in a 200° oven.

In another medium-sized saucepan, melt the butter, add the flour and cook without browning for 3 to 4 minutes. Add the wine and shallot reduction and 1½ cups clam broth and whisk swiftly while bringing to a simmer. Add the cream and simmer gently for 5 minutes. Stir in the garlic, thyme, green onions, and parsley. Season to taste with salt and pepper, and drops of lemon juice.

Drizzle the sauce over the clams and serve immediately.

Butterflied Roast Quail with Gingered Pear and Cranberry Sauce

Serves 4.

In spite of its elegant appearance, this dinner-party dish is very easy to prepare, especially if the Gingered Pear and Cranberry Sauce is made ahead. The contrast between hot bird and cold sauce is particularly interesting.

Gingered Pear and Cranberry Sauce
  (recipe follows on page 230)
8 quail

GARLIC LEMON BUTTER
  4 tablespoons unsalted butter
  4 cloves garlic
  2 tablespoons lemon juice
  Coarse salt
  Freshly ground black pepper

BUTTER SAUCE
  1 tablespoon minced shallots
  ½ cup dry white wine
  ½ cup unsalted chicken stock
  1 cup unsalted butter, cut into 16
    squares
  Coarse salt
  Freshly ground black pepper
  Lemon juice to taste

Prepare the Gingered Pear and Cranberry Sauce. This may be done days ahead.

With a pair of poultry shears or a French knife, cut each quail open along the center back. Open the birds out and give the center breast sections a sharp whack with the heel of your hand to break the breastbone. The birds should lie flat. Lift the skin over the breasts and insert your fingers between the skin and the flesh to pry it loose over as much of the bird as possible while still leaving it attached at the back, wings, and leg ends.

To make the Garlic Lemon Butter, process the butter with the garlic and lemon juice until smooth. Season to taste with salt and pepper. Divide the butter into 8 portions and spread most of the butter under the skin, directly on the flesh, of each of the birds. Smear the remaining butter over the surface of each bird. Sprinkle the underside of each bird with additional salt and pepper.

Scatter the minced shallots on the bottom of a buttered glass baking dish large enough to hold the flattened birds and lay the birds on top. Pour the combined wine and chicken stock around them. Roast at 450° for about 15 minutes, until just done. Remove the birds from the baking dish and keep them warm.

To make the butter sauce, strain the juices from the baking dish into a small saucepan and reduce them to a syrup. Lower the heat so that the reduction is no longer simmering (or remove from the heat for a moment) and add the butter all at once. Stir slowly with a wooden

spoon, letting the butter slowly emulsify into the reduction. Use a little more heat if the butter does not melt completely but do not bring the sauce near a boil. When the butter is completely incorporated, season to taste with salt, pepper, and drops of lemon juice.

Serve 2 birds per person with a pool of Butter Sauce underneath and the Gingered Pear and Cranberry Sauce alongside.

Gingered Pear and Cranberry Sauce

Makes about 2 cups.

> 1 cup water
> ¾ cup sugar
> 2 teaspoons slivered candied ginger
> 1 medium-sized Anjou or Bartlett pear, peeled, cored, and diced
> 2 cups whole cranberries
> Juice and zest of 1 lemon
> ¼ cup ginger-flavored liqueur

Combine the water, sugar, and candied ginger in a saucepan and stir over medium heat until the sugar dissolves and the liquid clears. Boil for 5 minutes, washing down the sides of the pan occasionally with a pastry brush dipped in cold water to prevent crystals from forming. Add the diced pear, reduce the heat, and simmer for 3 minutes. Add the cranberries, lemon juice, and zest and continue simmering without stirring until the berries pop and the sauce

thickens. Remove from the heat and cool. Stir in the ginger-flavored liqueur. Serve chilled or at room temperature.

Boned, Stuffed Duck with Prunes and Seckel Pears

Serves 2.

This is a sensational dish for a special dinner. It is time consuming to bone the duck, but your guests will appreciate the extra effort. In the market look for duck that is labeled First Pack—meaning that it is of premium quality with no deformities or flaws. This dish can also be made with a large pheasant or guinea hen.

> 1 duck, preferably fresh
> ½ cup very cold cream
> Coarse kosher salt and freshly ground black pepper
> 1 tablespoon corn or peanut oil
> 1 onion, minced
> 1 carrot, minced
> 1 stalk celery, minced
> 1 pound ripe tomatoes, diced
> 2 parsley sprigs
> Half a bay leaf
> Pinch thyme
> 1 cup full-bodied dry red wine

3 large Oregon prunes, pitted and
    slivered
1 tablespoon cornstarch
1 tablespoon water
4 tiny Seckel pears
½ cup sugar
¼ cup water

Bone the duck, starting with a lengthwise cut along the center back and continuing around each side, severing the connection between the thigh bones and the main body section and the shoulder bones and the main body section. Divide the duck into two halves with a lengthwise cut down the center of the breast. Remove the wing tips by cutting through the second joints. Slicing along the thigh bones, being careful not to puncture the skin, remove the bones and the tough cartilage at each bone end. Using a cleaver, hack the ends off each of the drumsticks. Then, working from the inside again, pull or slice the meat away from the remaining bones. The only bones now remaining in the bird should be the upper wing bones. Carefully remove all the leg meat from the carcass and set aside. With your fingers, gently pry the breast sections away from the skin almost entirely, leaving the widest end still attached so that, when the meat is repositioned it can be encased in the surrounding skin. Remove any obvious tendons from the leg meat.

Chop the leg meat in a processor until it is finely minced. With the processor running, gradually add the very cold cream. Season with a generous ¼ teaspoon salt and several grindings of black pepper. This mixture is now a duck mousse and should be quite smooth.

Season the breast sections with salt and black pepper and mound half of the mousse alongside each section. Fold the 4 sides of the skin in around the breast meat and mousse. Sew with heavy-duty carpet thread and a large-eyed needle to keep the packet in shape. Truss each one with kitchen string, but not too tightly; the bird will expand in the oven.

Place the duck halves in a deep, ovenproof casserole, being sure to prick the skin in several places on each half. Bake at 400° for 15 minutes, then reduce the heat to 350° and continue baking until the packets are a rich dark brown, about 30 minutes. The internal temperature of the duck should read 175° when done.

Once the duck has been boned and stuffed, the following procedures may all be done well ahead of time and the stuffed duck may rest in the refrigerator until 1 hour or so before being served. To make the sauce, heat the oil and add all the duck bones and the neck and gizzard, chopped into 2-inch pieces in a stockpot. Brown the bones as well as possible and add the onion, carrot, and celery. Continue cooking and stirring to soften and brown the vegetables. When everything is well browned, add the tomatoes, parsley, bay leaf, and thyme. Stir to combine and add the red wine and enough water to barely cover. Simmer for 45 minutes or longer, skimming as necessary. Strain the resulting stock through a very fine-

meshed strainer and reduce it to about 1 cup, or until the stock has a very full flavor. While the stock is still boiling, mix the cornstarch and water and add it, a little at a time while whisking, until the sauce is just barely thickened. Add the slivered prunes. Season to taste with salt and black pepper. Reserve until the duck is cooked and ready to serve.

Peel and poach the pears in simmering water or in the simmering stock for 20–30 minutes. They should be tender when tested with the tip of a sharp knife. Keep warm. Just before serving, heat the sugar and water in a small skillet and stir constantly until the sugar is lightly caramelized. Immediately pour the caramel over each of the hot, poached pears.

To serve, remove the thread from each of the duck halves. Pour a pool of sauce on each dinner plate, position the duck on top and place two of the bite-sized pears alongside.

Pheasant Terrine with Currants and Black Pepper

Makes one 9- by 5-inch loaf.

This is a lovely terrine with a pheasant breast in the center and a visible speckling of crushed black
pepper throughout. Serve in half-inch thick slices accompanied by a dollop of mayonnaise, tiny dill pickles, Niçoise olives, and perhaps pickled cherries or green beans. A little leafy salad with an acidic dressing is a perfect foil for the richness of the terrine. Do not forget the French bread. Duck may be substituted for the pheasant.

Reduce the pork fatback to half a pound if you do not plan to line the mold with it.

1 whole pheasant (or duck) breast, separated into halves and cut into lengthwise strips
½ pound fat- and tendon-free pheasant meat, cubed
½ pound pork, cubed
½ pound veal, cubed
Finely shredded zest of 2 oranges
1 teaspoon Spice Blend (page 358)
1½ teaspoons coarsely cracked black pepper
½ cup orange juice
½ cup dry Madeira
1 pound pork fatback, half of it cubed, the rest thinly sliced
3 eggs, lightly beaten
1 tablespoon coarse salt
2 tablespoons unsalted butter
2 shallots, minced
1 small onion, minced
½ cup currants
12 cloves of garlic, simmered in water until tender, then peeled

Lay the strips of pheasant breast in a glass baking dish and surround them with the cubed pheasant, pork, and veal. Sprinkle on the orange zest, Spice Blend, and pepper. Then add the orange juice and Madeira and marinate overnight in the refrigerator, covered with plastic wrap.

The next day, melt the butter and sauté the shallots and onion to soften slightly. Drain the marinade from the meat into the sauté pan, add the currants, and reduce the liquid by half.

Using a processor, process 4 ounces each of the cubed pheasant, pork, and veal and 4 ounces of the cubed pork fatback to a smooth purée. Thoroughly blend in half of the beaten eggs. Do not let the mixture get even close to room temperature; *it must stay very cold.* Remove to a mixing bowl.

With the processor, pulse-chop the remaining 4 ounces each of cubed pheasant, pork, and veal and an additional 4 ounces cubed pork fatback to a coarse but even texture. Add the salt and the remaining eggs and blend well. Add to the mixing bowl.

Add the shallot, onion, and currant mixture and the poached garlic cloves and mix well. Sauté a small ball of the ground meat mixture in hot oil until done and taste for seasoning, overcompensating somewhat because the terrine will be served cold. Adjust the seasoning if necessary.

Line a 9- by 5-inch (7-cup capacity) loaf pan with slightly overlapping sheets of fatback (you may not need the entire half pound), leaving several inches of overhang to smooth over the top of the terrine. (If you are not lining the mold, butter it well.)

Layer half of the ground meat mixture into the mold, then position the breast strips lengthwise on top, and cover with the remaining ground meat, slightly rounding the top. Bring the ends of the fatback up to cover the surface smoothly. Cover tightly with heavy-duty foil. Prick the foil once or twice to allow steam to escape.

Bake in a *bain-marie* (the water should reach at least halfway up the sides of the mold) at between 350° and 375° for about 1½ hours or until the terrine reads 160° when tested with an instant-read thermometer. The water in the water bath should not exceed 180° during the cooking time.

Remove the terrine from the oven; let it rest in the water bath for 30 minutes, then remove, set in a larger baking dish (to catch the juices), cover with a board (or another pan) that fits just inside the baking pan and weight it down with 2 pounds weight, distributed evenly across the terrine until entirely cool.

When the terrine is cool, remove it from its pan and wipe it clean of all coagulated meat juices. Wash and dry the pan and return the terrine to it. Cover with foil and refrigerate for 2 days before eating for best flavor. A terrine will keep for up to 10 days.

Breast of Duck with Honey-Glazed Garlic and Crystallized Orange Zest

Serves 4.

The gamey succulence of rare duck breast paired with an intense cream sauce, burnished nuggets of succulent garlic, and glistening orange shreds provides just the ticket when a grand meal is what you have in mind. The duck breast is treated to an eight-hour dry marinade that firms, flavors, and tenderizes the flesh. As beautiful as this dish looks, it is not difficult to make. You will have plenty of energy left to make a gratin of new potatoes (with stock only— no cream—but with perhaps just a hint of Parmesan) and a medley of lightly steamed vegetables to provide a necessary counterpoint.

DRY MARINADE

2 teaspoons black peppercorns
1 teaspoon juniper berries
1 teaspoon allspice berries
1 teaspoon dried thyme
1 teaspoon dried marjoram
1 tablespoon coarse kosher salt

2 whole duck breasts, halved and boned, with skin intact
2 very fresh, whole heads garlic, separated into cloves and skin removed

CRYSTALLIZED ORANGE ZEST

1 cup water
½ cup sugar
Zest of 1 large orange

1 cup bone-dry white wine
Juice of 1 orange
3 cups homemade chicken stock (page 345) reduced to 1 cup
½ cup cream
Coarse kosher salt
Freshly ground white pepper
1 tablespoon rendered duck fat
1 teaspoon honey

A day ahead, finely grind the black peppercorns, juniper berries, allspice berries, thyme, and marjoram together in a spice grinder or with a mortar and pestle. Mix with the salt.

Trim the excess fat from each breast section and sprinkle the meat side liberally with the spice, herb, and salt mixture. Place in a glass baking dish, cover tightly with plastic wrap and refrigerate overnight, or for at least 8 hours.

The next day, cook the garlic cloves in boiling water for 30 minutes, or until tender.

To make the crystallized orange zest, combine the water and sugar in a small saucepan. Heat gradually over low to medium heat until the syrup is transparent. There must be no visible sugar crystals present. (To keep the syrup from crystallizing, occasionally brush down the sides of the pan with cold water.) Add the

orange zest and simmer until the shreds are shiny and transparent. Remove the zest from the liquid, separate into strands, and set to dry on a plate.

Wipe the breast sections dry, brushing away excess salt from the meat. Let them come to room temperature for 30 minutes.

Dry the breasts once again with paper towels, prick the skin evenly with a sharp fork, and make 5 or 6 evenly spaced diagonal cuts just through the skin on each. Place skin-side down in a heavy skillet and sauté over brisk heat until the skin is crisp and well browned and the fat visibly rendered, about 3 minutes. Remove to a baking sheet lightly greased with duck fat and finish in a 350° oven for 10 minutes, or until the meat is pink and just firm to the touch. An instant-read thermometer should register 125°; duck breast should be served rare. Drain and reserve the remaining duck fat.

After all fat is removed from the skillet, add the white wine and orange juice, scrape the bottom of the pan to loosen all browned bits, and reduce to a syrupy glaze. Add the reduced chicken stock and reduce again by half. Pour the reduction into a small saucepan, bring to a vigorous simmer, and add the cream. Without stirring, simmer at a lively pace for 5 minutes. The sauce should thicken nicely in this time; if it does not, give it another minute or two. Season to taste with salt and white pepper. Strain and keep warm for a moment.

While the sauce is reducing, heat 1 tablespoon duck fat and sauté the garlic to brown it nicely on all sides. About halfway through the browning process, drizzle with honey and toss and turn to coat. Keep warm.

Remove the breast sections from the oven, let them rest for 1 or 2 minutes, then diagonally slice all the way through the cuts that you made earlier on the skin. Arrange, slightly overlapping, on 4 individual plates and pour the sauce around each. Divide the garlic cloves among the 4 plates and garnish each with a few shreds of crystallized orange zest.

. ≼.≼.≼.≼.≼.≼.≼.≼.≼.≼.≼.≼.≼.

Braised Duck with Apples, Prunes, and Walnuts

Serves 4.

When developing recipes and menus that use North-west foods, I often turn for inspiration to cookbooks focusing on southern France, a region that has many of our own natural food resources. One such book is Roger Vergé's Cuisine of the South of France, *from whence this adaptation comes. The duck breasts are not used here; they are much better off treated to a quick sauté.*

2 ducks (5 pounds each)
1 carrot, chopped
1 onion, chopped
1 stalk celery, chopped
1 teaspoon black peppercorns
6 crushed juniper berries
1 clove
½ teaspoon dried thyme
1 teaspoon finely grated orange zest
2 bay leaves
Several parsley sprigs
1 bottle fruity, dry red wine, such as a Northwest pinot noir
2 tablespoons corn oil
1 tablespoon flour
½ cup dried Oregon prunes, pitted and sliced lengthwise (9 large prunes)
¼ cup walnut halves
Coarse kosher salt
Freshly ground black pepper
1 tablespoon unsalted butter
1 large tart, green apple, such as a Granny Smith, peeled, cored, and diced

Section the duck into drumsticks and thighs, or keep the leg section in 1 piece for a more elegant presentation. Reserve the breasts for another use. Reserve the back. Combine the duck, carrots, onion, and celery. Tie up in a piece of cheesecloth the peppercorns, juniper, clove, thyme, orange zest, bay leaves, and parsley. Add this to the bowl. Add enough water to the wine to make up 4 cups liquid and pour this over the duck, vegetables, and seasonings. Cover and refrigerate, turning the duck pieces in the marinade two or three times, for at least 8 hours or overnight.

Remove the duck pieces from the marinade and dry well with paper towels. Drain the marinade from the vegetables, strain, and re-serve. Dry the vegetables with paper towels and hold.

Heat the oil in a large cast-iron casserole. Season the duck with salt and pepper and prick the skin evenly all over, being careful not to penetrate the meat. Sauté the duck very slowly in the hot oil in order to release the fat. Turn and brown all surfaces. Remove and hold.

Remove all but 2 tablespoons of the fat from the skillet and add the marinated vegetables.

Cook, stirring, over brisk heat to brown the surfaces lightly. Sprinkle the vegetables with flour and cook for another 2 to 3 minutes, being careful not to burn the flour. Stir in the wine marinade and the seasoning bundle. Add the duck back to the casserole, cover and simmer slowly for about 1 hour. The duck is done when the leg is easily pierced with a fork. Arrange the duck pieces on a heated platter, cover, and keep warm.

Strain the sauce into a bottom-pouring degreaser, then pour it, without the fat, into a small saucepan. Add the prunes and walnuts and simmer, reducing the sauce to about 1 cup or until it tastes good and lightly coats a spoon. Adjust the seasonings, adding salt and pepper to taste.

Melt the butter and quickly brown the diced apple on all sides Scatter apples over the platter of duck. Nap with the sauce and reheat the dish in a 350° oven for about 10 minutes before serving.

Sauté of Chicken with Caramelized Apples and Toasted Hazelnuts

Serves 4.

As is often the case with foods found growing together in the same region, apples and hazelnuts have a happy affinity for each other. To make the chicken easy to brown and easy to eat, cut it into ten pieces: two thighs, two drumsticks, two breast halves, and four wing sections (save the wing tips for the stockpot).

1 Washington or Oregon fryer (about 3
    pounds), cut into 10 serving pieces
   Coarse kosher salt
   Freshly ground black pepper
2 tablespoons unsalted butter
2 tablespoons corn oil
1 medium-sized onion, chopped
¼ cup aged apple jack (or calvados)
1 cup unsalted, homemade chicken
    stock (page 345)
2 tart, firm apples, peeled, cored, and
    sliced into ½-inch thick wedges
2 tablespoons sugar
2 tablespoons unsalted butter
½ cup cream
¼ cup hazelnuts, lightly toasted,
    skinned, and coarsely chopped

Season the chicken with salt and pepper. Heat the butter and oil in a large sauté pan. When hot, add the chicken pieces, skin-side down, making sure not to overcrowd them. Brown the pieces well on all sides and remove to a platter.

Add the onions to the pan and cook until softened and beginning to brown, about 15 minutes. Continue to sauté the onions, deepening the color to a rich brown while warming the apple jack.

Warm the apple jack in a small saucepan, stand back, and ignite it with a long-handled match. When the flames have subsided, pour the liquid over the onions. Add the chicken stock and the chicken pieces, cover, and simmer gently for 10 to 15 minutes. At this point the breasts are done and should be removed from the pan and kept warm. Continue cooking the rest of the chicken, covered, for another 15 minutes or so, until the juices of the thigh run clear when deeply pierced with a paring knife.

When the chicken is close to done, sprinkle the sugar over the apples. Melt the remaining butter in a sauté pan large enough to contain them in a single layer, add the apples, and sauté, turning once or twice, until they are all nicely browned and caramelized.

When the chicken is done, remove it to a warm serving platter and place the apples between and on top of the pieces. Keep warm.

Reduce the stock remaining in the sauté pan to a syrupy consistency. Add the cream, stir, reduce slightly, and season with salt and black pepper to taste. Nap the chicken and apples with the sauce. Sprinkle the hazelnuts over the top.

Chicken Fricassee with Apples, Onions, and Herb Dumplings

Serves 4.

There is a great deal of confusion in culinary literature about the precise definition of the word fricassee. *Some say that a fricassee is little more than a braised dish to which cream and egg yolks are added at the finish. Others use the word to define a dish in which the main ingredient—chicken for instance—is stewed without benefit of initial browning. Perhaps it is safe to say that a fricassee almost always involves more liquid than does a braise (more than two cups) and that the liquid is frequently finished with a fillip of cream. Hence a fricassee is usually distinguished by a generous amount of creamy sauce. This is an updated version of a very old-fashioned and wonderfully comforting dish, chicken and dumplings.*

Rendered chicken fat—reserved when making stock—contains 9 percent cholesterol; butter contains 22 percent. The flavor of this dish is much enhanced by the chicken fat.

1 broiler-fryer chicken (3½ pounds)
3 tablespoons rendered chicken fat or
    unsalted butter
Coarse kosher salt
Freshly ground black pepper
1 teaspoon thyme, crumbled
Tiny pinch cloves
Tiny pinch nutmeg
1 bay leaf
2 cups homemade chicken stock (page
    345)
2 cups dry white wine, reduced from
    3 cups
12 small boiling onions (about 1
    pound)
2 medium-sized, tart, firm apples,
    peeled, cored, and sliced into 8
    wedges
4 cloves garlic, minced
4 tablespoons flour
1 cup cream

HERB DUMPLINGS
1½ cups flour
2 teaspoons baking powder
½ teaspoon coarse kosher salt
½ teaspoon freshly ground black
    pepper

1 tablespoon parsley, minced
1 tablespoon fresh chives or green
    onion tops, minced
3 tablespoons cold shortening
¾ cup cold milk

Cut the chicken into 10 serving pieces and dry them thoroughly. Reserve the back, neck, and innards for the stockpot. Heat the fat in a large sauté pan and brown the chicken pieces lightly on all sides, seasoning them with salt, pepper, thyme, cloves, and nutmeg as you go. Remove the chicken, except the breasts, to a stovetop casserole equipped with a cover and add the bay leaf, chicken stock, and wine. Bring the liquid to a bare simmer, cover, and simmer gently for 15 minutes.

In 4 tablespoons of fat remaining in the sauté pan (drain off the rest), brown the onions lightly all over and remove them from the pan. Very briefly sauté the apple slices, adding a little more fat if necessary. Remove the apples. Add the garlic, sauté for only a moment, then add the flour. Cook the flour with the remaining fat, adding a bit more fat if necessary, for two minutes, coloring it only lightly. Remove from the heat and reserve. Do not wash the pan.

When the chicken has been simmering for 15 minutes, add the onions to the casserole, cover, and continue cooking for 5 minutes or so.

To make the dumplings, combine the flour, baking powder, salt, pepper to taste, parsley, and chives. Cut in the shortening with a pastry cutter or with the tips of your fingers until the mixture resembles a fine meal. Add the milk all at once and blend it in quickly and lightly with a rubber spatula. If the dough is over-mixed, the baking powder will not puff the dumpling properly. The dough does not have to be quite smooth.

Quickly deglaze the sauté pan with a little of the liquid in the casserole. Add it all back to the casserole along with the cream and sim-mer with the lid off if necessary, to reduce the liquid to the desired flavor and body. The liq-uid may need to be thickened slightly with the addition of a *beurre manié* (equal parts of flour and butter rubbed together until smooth with the fingertips) added in small pieces.

Add the apples and the chicken breasts to the casserole, pushing them down into the liq-uid, then heap mounds of dumpling dough on top in an appealing pattern. Cover the casse-role, maintain a gentle simmer, and cook for 20 minutes without lifting the lid.

If the casserole is attractive, serve the fricas-see straight from it. Otherwise, lift out the dumplings one by one and arrange them around the outside of a deep platter. Mound the chicken pieces in the middle and pour the sauce, apples, and onions over the top.

Sauté of Pork Chops with Oregon Prunes and Cranberries

Serves 8.

This dish, with its ebony prunes, russet cranberries, and glistening green kale, glorifies the deep bur-nished colors of autumn. A beautiful party dish, it is not too elaborate for a family supper either; chil-dren especially love the combination of sweet and tart flavors.

2 cups dry red wine
¼ teaspoon cinnamon
⅛ teaspoon cloves
1 cup Oregon prunes, pitted and
    quartered lengthwise
8 pork loin chops (1-inch thick),
    trimmed of excess fat
4 tablespoons olive oil
2 tablespoons corn oil
1 medium onion, chopped
3 cloves garlic, minced
1 cup finely diced tomatoes with their
    juice (unless the tomatoes are vine-
    ripened, use a good brand of
    canned tomato, such as S&W
    Diced Tomatoes in Juice)
1 teaspoon tomato paste
    Coarse kosher salt
    Freshly ground pepper

½ cup orange juice
 Zest of 1 orange
1 cup fresh cranberries
2 tablespoons fragrant honey
1 teaspoon cornstarch mixed with 1
 teaspoon cold water
1 large bunch kale, center ribs removed
 and leaves coarsely chopped (pieces
 should be roughly 2 inches square)

GARNISH
 2 thin slices of orange

Mix the wine with the cinnamon and cloves
and pour it over the prunes. Marinate overnight if possible (but even an hour will produce good results).

Dry off the pork chops. Heat a sauté pan,
add the 2 tablespoons of the olive oil and the
corn oil and swirl to coat the pan. Brown the
chops very quickly on both sides; do not cook
them through. Remove from the pan and arrange in an ovenproof gratin dish.

Drain all but 2 tablespoons of the oil from
the sauté pan and add the onion. Scrape up the
bits from the bottom of the pan and cook the
onion until well softened but not browned.
Add two-thirds of the garlic and cook for a
minute longer without browning. Add the tomatoes, tomato paste, and wine drained from
the prunes. Simmer, uncovered, until thickened. Season to taste with salt and pepper and
pour over the pork chops. Cover and bake at
450° for 12 to 15 minutes, or until the chops

are just cooked through. Do not overcook or
the pork will be tough.

Combine the orange juice, zest, cranberries,
and honey. Bring to a simmer and cook until
the cranberries begin to pop open, from 2 to 4
minutes. Reserve.

When the pork is tender, remove the chops
from the casserole, arrange in the center of an
oval serving platter, cover, and keep warm.
Pour the sauce into a saucepan and reduce it to
thicken slightly and intensify the flavors.
Whisk in the combination of cornstarch and
water a bit at a time (you may not need it all)
and bring the sauce to a simmer to activate the
cornstarch properly. Add the cranberry mixture and the prunes. Season to taste with salt
and pepper. Keep warm.

Heat the remaining 2 tablespoons olive oil
in a sauté pan over brisk heat and add the kale.
Just as it warms through, scatter on the remaining minced garlic and salt and pepper to
taste. Arrange the kale around the outside edge
of the serving platter. Pour the sauce over and
around the chops, making sure that lots of
cranberries and prunes are in evidence. Garnish
the platter with a slice of orange on either end
and serve.

Pork and Veal Terrine with Caramelized Apples, Toasted Walnuts, and Cranberries

Makes one 9- by 5-inch loaf.

There is probably nothing easier to make in the French culinary repertoire than a terrine (or a pâté—the words are interchangeable in common usage), yet mystery and awe surround its preparation. It is going a bit far perhaps to say that a terrine is nothing more than a glorified meat loaf but it actually does not take much more skill to produce.

Do not worry too much about the large amount of fat specified here. It lends needed moisture to the rest of the meat while cooking and much of it melts out of the pâté by the time it is finished and is then discarded.

A word about lining the mold with fat. The practice is traditional and by now we are used to seeing pâtés and terrines in delicatessen cases in snow-white wrappings. However, you can omit it if you prefer. This terrine stays sufficiently moist without a surrounding layer of fat. Buy only half a pound of pork fatback if you are not going to line the pan with it.

 2 medium-sized apples, peeled, cored, and diced
 2 tablespoons unsalted butter
 1 onion, chopped

 ¼ cup Madeira
 ½ cup cranberries, halved
 ½ cup parsley, minced
 ½ cup walnuts, lightly toasted
 ½ cup ham, diced
 ¾ pound ground pork
 ¾ pound ground veal
 1 pound thinly sliced, pure white, pork fatback (ask a specialty butcher for it)
 3 eggs, lightly beaten
 1 tablespoon coarse salt
 2 teaspoons black peppercorns, very coarsely cracked
 2 teaspoons Spice Blend (page 358)

Sauté the diced apple in the butter to caramelize it lightly. When the apples are nicely browned, add the onions and continue to cook for 1 or 2 minutes. Add the Madeira and reduce by half. Remove from the heat and stir in the cranberries, parsley, walnuts, and ham. Cool.

Using a processor, process half of the ground pork and half of the veal and 4 ounces pork fatback (cut into pieces) to a smooth purée. Thoroughly blend in half of the beaten eggs. Do not let the mixture get even close to room temperature; *it must stay very cold.* Remove to a mixing bowl.

With the processor, pulse-chop the remaining pork and veal and an additional 4 ounces pork fatback (cut into pieces) to a coarse but even texture. Add the remaining eggs and blend well. Add to the mixing bowl.

Thoroughly stir in the salt, pepper, and Spice Blend. Add the cooled apple, cranberry, and walnut mixture. Mix well with your hands or a large rubber spatula to be sure everything is thoroughly combined.

Sauté a small ball of the ground meat mixture in hot oil until done and taste it for seasoning, overcompensating somewhat because the terrine will be served cold. Adjust the seasoning if necessary.

Line a 9- by 5-inch (7-cup capacity) loaf pan with slightly overlapping sheets of fatback, leaving several inches of overhang to smooth over the top of the terrine. (If you are not lining the mold, butter it well.) Pack the ground meat mixture into the lined pan, slightly rounding the top, and bring the ends of the fatback up to cover the surface smoothly. Cover tightly with heavy-duty foil. Prick one or two holes in the foil to allow steam to escape.

Bake in a *bain-marie* (the water should reach at least halfway up the sides of the mold) at between 350° and 375° for about 1½ hours or until the terrine reads 160° when tested with an instant-read thermometer. The water in the water bath should not exceed 180° during the cooking time.

Remove the terrine from the oven; let it rest in the water bath for 30 minutes, then remove, set in a larger baking dish (to catch the juices), cover with a board (or another pan) that fits just inside the baking pan and weight it down with 2 pounds weight distributed evenly across the terrine until entirely cool.

When the terrine is cool, remove it from its pan and wipe it clean of all coagulated meat juices. Wash and dry the pan and return the terrine to it. Cover with foil and refrigerate for 2 days before eating for best flavor. A terrine will keep for up to 10 days.

Deep-Fried Cauliflower with Garlic and Vinegar Sauce

Serves 8.

I do not understand why it is, but these cauliflower fritters end up tasting surprisingly like crab. Guests have a hard time guessing what they are but finish the platter off just the same. They are a favorite of mine.

> 1 to 1½ pounds cauliflower, trimmed and separated into florets
> Coarse kosher salt
> Freshly ground white pepper
> ½ cup flour
> 2 eggs, lightly beaten
> ¾ cup fresh white bread crumbs, seasoned with salt and pepper
> Vegetable oil for deep frying

GARLIC AND VINEGAR SAUCE
> 6 tablespoons olive oil
> 2 cloves garlic, put through a press
> 2 tablespoons dry white wine vinegar
> Pinch crushed, dried red pepper

Blanch the florets in plenty of boiling water until just barely tender. Drain them, pat dry, and season with salt and pepper.

Dip each floret into the flour and shake off the excess. Then dip it into the egg and finally into the seasoned bread crumbs. Arrange the florets on a wax paper-covered cookie sheet and refrigerate until ready to fry.

Heat the oil, which should measure 3 to 4 inches in a deep saucepan, to 350°. Fry the cauliflower, a few pieces at a time, turning once or twice, until golden. Remove with a slotted spoon and drain on paper towels. Arrange on a heated platter and keep warm.

To make the sauce, heat the olive oil over low heat. Add the garlic and cook for 2 minutes without coloring. Add the white wine vinegar and cook for an additional minute. Season to taste with crushed red pepper, salt, and pepper.

Either pour the sauce directly over the cauliflower, turning the pieces to coat them evenly, or serve the sauce alongside as a dip. The latter method is better for stand-up cocktail service.

Fried Spinach with Garlic, Currants, and Prosciutto

Serves 4.

There is a trick to cooking spinach. Do it very quickly over high heat or an immense quantity of water will be released, resulting in a soupy mess. In other words, just warm it through and do not wait until it is uniformly wilted.

> 2 tablespoons currants
> 2 tablespoons Madeira
> 2 large bunches spinach
> ¼ cup olive oil (not cold-pressed olive oil, which will burn too easily)
> ¼ cup shredded prosciutto (3 paper-thin slices)
> 1 clove garlic, minced
> Coarse kosher salt
> Freshly ground black pepper

Soak the currants in the Madeira for 30 minutes, drain them, and squeeze them lightly.

Clean the spinach of all dirt and sand and spin it dry in a salad spinner. If a spinner is not available, shake each leaf over the sink and pat it dry with paper towels.

Heat a large skillet until quite hot, then add the oil and swirl to coat the bottom and the sides. Toss in the prosciutto and garlic, cook for only a few seconds, then add the spinach and currants. Over high heat, rotate the spinach leaves from the bottom of the pan to the top as they begin to wilt. Season quickly with salt and pepper and serve immediately. (The spinach should not be entirely wilted so that it ends up as a wet heap.)

Baked Onions and Apples with Rosemary, Crème Fraîche, and Tillamook Cheddar

Serves 4.

This recipe results in a tasty side dish for any number of simple roasts, grills, or sautés.

> 1 cup crème fraîche (page 357); not too thick, seasoned with salt
> 1 teaspoon unsalted butter
> 2 tart green apples, peeled, cored, and sliced (1 pound)
> 2 onions, cut in half and thinly sliced (1 pound)
> 1 tablespoon fresh minced rosemary (or 1 teaspoon dried)
> Coarse kosher salt
> Freshly ground black pepper
> ½ cup grated sharp Tillamook Cheddar (or other good quality Cheddar) cheese

Make the crème fraîche at least a day ahead.

Butter a 9- by 13-inch gratin dish with 1 teaspoon butter and alternate in it layers of apples and onions, sprinkling each layer with rosemary, salt, pepper, and half of the Cheddar. Drizzle with crème fraîche, top with the remaining Cheddar and bake, covered, at 350°

for 30 minutes, then uncovered for an additional 30 minutes, until the top is nicely browned and the apples and onions are tender.

Carrot, Orange, and Fresh Chèvre Gratin

Serves 6.

Carrots do not often get the opportunity to star in a recipe, but this gratin shows them off. With the addition of ham this makes a good supper dish; without, it offers a distinctly different side dish for simple roasts, sautéed chops, or grills. Rosalyn Rourke, a member of the test team, worked this version out as a variation on a traditional French tian that I teach at the Northwest Culinary Academy. You might like to experiment with it, using other vegetables, cheeses, and smoked or cured meats as whim dictates; it is an incredibly versatile concept.

The goat cheese specified here—Fagottino di capra—is a fresh, very soft, Italian cheese available in Seattle at Delaurenti's; I highly recommend it.

Many of the local Okanogan Highland or Quilla-sascut fresh goat cheeses will work beautifully here. In this recipe Parmesan cheese may be substituted. The authentic Italian variety of provolone is far more pungent than our domestic version; if you prefer a milder cheese, choose the latter.

½ cup long-grain white rice (Uncle Ben's converted rice is suitable)
4 medium-sized carrots, cut into ¼-inch slices (should equal 1¾ cups)
4 tablespoons unsalted butter
1 medium onion, chopped
2 cloves garlic, minced
2 tablespoons flour
¾ cup homemade chicken stock (page 345)
¾ cup milk
Juice of 1 orange (about ¼ cup)
¼ pound Black Forest or other good-quality ham cut into ¾-inch dice (omit if serving as a side dish)
6 ounces provolone cut into ¾-inch dice (1 cup)
¼ cup chopped green onion
¼ cup chopped parsley
Zest of 1 orange
Coarse kosher salt
Freshly ground black pepper
6 tablespoons fresh goat cheese (Italian *Fagottino di capra* is wonderful) or 2 tablespoons grated Parmesan

Blanch the rice in 2 cups boiling water for exactly 5 minutes and drain. Hold.

Blanch the carrots for 4 to 5 minutes, drain, and refresh under cold running water. Drain again and pat dry. The carrots should be almost tender with a bit of crunch left. Hold.

Melt the butter and "sweat" the onions until they are tender but not browned. Add the garlic and stir to coat with butter. Stir in the flour. Cook for at least 2 minutes, stirring, without browning.

Slowly pour in the combined chicken stock, milk, and orange juice, whisking all the time. Bring to a simmer to thicken the sauce, continuing the whisking all the while. Remove from the heat.

Combine the sauce with the onions, carrots, rice, ham, provolone, green onion, parsley, orange zest, and salt and pepper to taste. Fold in the goat cheese. (If you are using Parmesan instead, just sprinkle it on top of the assembled gratin.) Butter a 4-cup gratin dish or round baking dish and pour in the rice mixture.

Bake at 425° for about 20 minutes, until the gratin is bubbling, the top has browned, and the rice is tender. There should be a light coating of sauce; the gratin should not be too dry.

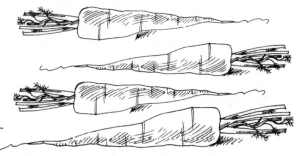

Spoonbread with Italian Sausage and Sweet Peppers

Serves 6 to 8.

An American innovation, originating in colonial times, spoonbread has the consistency of a heavy souf-flé or a very moist bread pudding. Normally it is plain, thus serving well as a side dish instead of potatoes or rice. But here it provides a simple, homey meal in itself. Fresh apple cider is so much better than the bottled, pasteurized varieties sold in the supermarket; do make an effort to get it. Check health food stores, farmers' markets, roadside stands, and the like. (See page 159 for more on apple cider.) It is also worth the effort of finding good Italian sausage. In the Northwest, I find that the Isernio brand sausage is excellent.

½ pound Italian-style sausages
1 cup fresh apple cider
7 tablespoons unsalted butter
1 medium-sized onion, chopped
1 red bell pepper, cored, seeded, and
  cut into 1-inch dice
2 cloves garlic, minced or pressed
1 tablespoon minced parsley
1 tablespoon minced fresh oregano (or
  1 teaspoon dried)
3 cups milk
1 cup coarse stone-ground yellow
  cornmeal

1½ teaspoons coarse salt, or to taste
½ teaspoon freshly ground white
  pepper, or to taste
4 eggs, separated and at room
  temperature
Pinch salt
Pinch cream of tartar (optional)
1 cup grated sharp Tillamook Cheddar
  cheese
Hot Tomato Vinaigrette (page 360)

Prick the sausages very lightly and put them in a sauté pan with the cider. Cook over medium heat, turning occasionally until the cider evaporates and the sausages have released enough oil to fry in, about 15 minutes. Cook for an additional 15 minutes, rolling the sausages to brown and glaze them evenly. Remove from the pan, slice into disks, and reserve.

In another skillet, melt 2 tablespoons of the butter and add the onion. "Sweat" until tender, about 20 minutes. Add the diced red pepper and the garlic. Sauté for 2 minutes, tossing to heat the vegetables evenly. Remove from the heat, add the parsley and oregano, and reserve.

Butter a 9- by 13-inch baking dish with 1 tablespoon of the butter.

Put the milk in a deep, heavyweight saucepan. Sprinkle in the cornmeal slowly, whisking constantly. Slowly bring to a simmer and continue stirring with a wooden spoon for 2 minutes, or until thick. Add the remaining 4 tablespoons butter and salt and pepper to taste.

Mix well and cook for 2 minutes longer. Remove from the heat and add the lightly beaten egg yolks. Mix to incorporate all the ingredients.

Beat the egg whites (preferably in a copper bowl with a balloon whisk, otherwise add a pinch of cream of tartar) with pinch of salt until stiff but not dry, and quickly fold into cornmeal mixture. Add the sausages, the red pepper mixture, and the cheese.

Pour the mixture into the buttered baking dish, spreading it evenly and smoothing the top with a spatula. Bake at 375°, uncovered, for 30 to 40 minutes, until puffed and browned. (The internal temperature will read 180° if you care to test it.) Serve at once with Hot Tomato Vinaigrette.

The Perfect Muffin

Makes 6 giant muffins or 12 regular-sized muffins.

Everyone has a different idea of what perfect *means when it comes to muffins. For me, this recipe produces muffins that come the closest to what I have been searching for all these years: a high, light muffin with an open, tender texture and no perceptible taste of chemical leavener. There are so many contradictory formulas around that it took long and diligent testing to pinpoint the problems and isolate the solution.*

It turns out that the easiest preparation method is also the most reliable. Thus I am using a standard muffin mixing procedure: all the dry ingredients are combined in a bowl, then all the liquid ingredients are poured over and gently folded in. There is no need to cream butter and sugar together or to fold in whipped egg white to get a wonderful texture.

This particular recipe works so well because of the proportions of the ingredients. A level tablespoon of baking powder is used for every two cups of flour. This is enough to insure a proper rise but not so much as to be discernible in the cooked muffin. There is a high proportion of fat that adds needed lubrication and keeps the muffins from drying out and becoming stale as quickly as muffins usually do. If stored airtight, all of these muffins are almost as good on the second day with just a thirty-second refresher in the microwave oven. You will note that the batter is rather stiff because a relatively small quantity of liquid is used in proportion to the flour. It is this stiffness, I believe, that keeps the muffins up so well during baking; they do not ooze out at the top like those made with wetter batters.

An oversized, separated-cup, six-unit pop-over pan yields gigantic muffins with tall, narrow bases and a high-hat effect at the crown. Because air circulates evenly around each cup, the muffins develop a thin, crisp crust from bottom to top that provides a nice contrast to the tender interior.

Gluten flour (available in health food stores) is used in batters made with grains that lack gluten. The extra rising power keeps the muffins light. Regular white flour can be used in place of gluten flour but the finished muffin will be somewhat dense.

Basic Recipe

2 cups all-purpose flour
6 to 8 tablespoons sugar
1 tablespoon baking powder
½ teaspoon coarse kosher salt
1 egg
8 tablespoons butter, melted and cooled
¾ cup cold milk

In a large mixing bowl, combine the flour, sugar, baking powder, and salt. Mix well.

In a small bowl, whisk the egg briefly, then stir in the melted, cooled butter and the milk.

Pour the liquid ingredients over the dry and stir quickly and gently with a wooden spoon just to moisten evenly. The batter should still be lumpy.

Lightly spray an oversized 6-unit popover pan or a traditional 12-unit muffin pan with vegetable spray. Divide the batter among the cups, letting the batter mound naturally. (The batter should almost reach the top of the cups.)

Bake at 400° for 30 minutes if using a popover pan or 20 minutes if using a muffin tin.

VARIATIONS

Cranberry Cornmeal Muffins
Use 1¼ cups all-purpose flour, ¼ cup gluten flour, and ½ cup yellow cornmeal in place of the flour measurement. Use 8 tablespoons sugar to compensate for the tartness of the berries. Add 1 cup roughly chopped cranberries to the liquid ingredients before folding them into the dry.

Cheddar and Bacon Muffins
Fry 12 slices of bacon until crisp, drain them well on paper towels, and crumble. Use only 1 tablespoon sugar. For the fat measurement, use 2 tablespoons of bacon fat and 6 tablespoons of butter. Add the bacon, along with 1 cup grated sharp Cheddar cheese to the liquid ingredients before folding them into the dry. Increase the milk by 2 tablespoons and the salt by ½ teaspoon.

Dried Oregon Cherry Muffins
Add 2 cups of chopped, dried Oregon cherries and the minced zest of 1 lemon to the liquid ingredients before folding them into the dry.

Hazelnut Butter Muffins

Blend ½ cup hazelnut butter and ½ cup honey (to replace the basic sugar measurement) together to obtain a smooth paste. Gradually add 4 tablespoons butter (to replace the basic butter measurement) and the milk to the nut butter and honey blend and whisk until smooth. Add the egg and then pour this mixture over the dry ingredients.

Spicy Lemon Cardamom Muffins

Use 1¼ cups all-purpose flour, ¼ cup gluten flour, and ½ cup wheat germ in place of the basic flour measurement. To these dry ingredients, add ½ teaspoon ground cardamom, ½ teaspoon white pepper, a pinch of cloves, and the minced zest of 2 lemons. Proceed with the basic recipe.

Oat Bran and Apple Muffins

Use 1¼ cups all-purpose flour, ¼ cup gluten flour, and ½ cup oat bran or oatmeal in place of the basic flour measurement. Add ½ teaspoon cinnamon and a pinch of nutmeg to the dry ingredients. Fold ½ cup peeled, diced tart apples into the dry ingredients along with the liquid.

Brown Rice and Onion Pilaf with Cream and Gruyère

Serves 4 to 6.

A substantial, toothsome side dish that is more interesting than plain rice.

> 2 tablespoons unsalted butter
> 1 large onion, chopped·
> 4 large shallots, minced
> 1 cup long-grain brown rice
> 2 cloves garlic, minced or pressed
> 2 cups homemade chicken stock (page 345), seasoned highly with salt
> ½ cup cream
>   Freshly ground black pepper
> ½ cup grated Gruyère cheese

Melt the butter in a large saucepan. "Sweat" the onion and shallots in the butter over low heat until tender, about 15 minutes. Add the rice and stir to coat with the butter; cook for 2 minutes. Stir in the garlic.

Butter a gratin dish and pour the rice and onion mixture into it. Add the chicken stock and cream, cover tightly with heavy-duty foil, and bake at 350° (a bare simmer) for about 45 minutes, or until tender. The liquid should be completely absorbed.

Remove the foil, grate pepper over the casserole, sprinkle with cheese, and broil for a minute until the cheese melts and starts to color.

Pumpkin Cornbread with Maple Butter

Makes sixteen 2¼-inch squares.

Cornbread with a difference.

½ cup unbleached white flour
½ cup gluten flour
1 cup yellow cornmeal
1 tablespoon baking powder
½ teaspoon coarse kosher salt
2 eggs
1 cup milk
¼ cup pure maple syrup
4 tablespoons unsalted butter, melted
1 cup finely grated pumpkin (or
  butternut squash)

MAPLE BUTTER
8 tablespoons unsalted butter
1 tablespoon maple syrup

Combine the white flour, gluten flour, cornmeal, baking powder, and salt. Whisk the eggs briefly, then add the milk and the maple syrup; combine. Pour the egg mixture, melted butter, and grated pumpkin over the dry ingredients and fold quickly and gently.

Butter a 9-inch square baking dish and pour in the batter. Bake at 400° for about 30 minutes.

Whip the remaining 8 tablespoons butter until light and smooth. Whip in the maple syrup. Keep at cool room temperature until ready to serve with the cornbread.

Sweet and Spicy Apple Cake

Serves 6 to 8.

An earthy dish of caramelized apples and currants arranged comfortably on a tender bed of batter cake, this is everyday fare at its best, easy to make and comforting to eat. Though no accompaniment is listed here, lightly sweetened crème fraîche or heavy cream would always be welcome.

> 5 large, tart, firm apples, peeled, cored, and sliced into ¼-inch thick wedges
> 1½ cups sugar
> ½ cup + 2 tablespoons unsalted butter
> ½ teaspoon cinnamon
> ¼ teaspoon freshly grated nutmeg
> ¼ cup aged applejack, rum, or brandy
> ¼ cup currants
> 1 cup flour
> 1½ teaspoons baking powder
> ¾ cup milk

Dry the apples well and sprinkle them with ½ cup of the sugar. Melt the butter in a small saucepan. Put 2 tablespoons into a large skillet and set the rest aside to cool. Sauté the apples briefly over high heat until the sugar begins to caramelize and turn an appetizing golden brown. Sprinkle on the spices and toss to combine. Add the applejack and currants and continue to cook over high heat until the liquid is reduced by half. Set aside to cool for a moment.

Coat the bottom and sides of a large 9- by 12-inch gratin dish with the rest of the melted butter.

Sift together the flour, remaining 1 cup sugar, and the baking powder. With a wooden spoon, beat in the milk to produce a smooth batter. Pour the batter into the buttered gratin dish. Scatter the apples and their remaining liquid evenly over the batter, leaving a 1-inch margin all the way around the cake.

Bake at 375° for 40 minutes, or until golden brown.

Caramelized Apple Tart with Grand Marnier

Serves 6 to 8.

An elegant cousin to American apple pie, this tart, presented open-faced and glistening with orange marmalade, is decidedly sophisticated. Having grown up on the heady cinnamon-infused American standard, I found that the flavor of this French classic never seemed to measure up—until I came upon the idea of caramelizing some of the apples first and using them as a base for the concentrically arranged raw apples on top. There is nothing lacking in taste now. Because this tart is best freshly made, I usually put it into the oven as guests are seated for dinner to insure that it will still be warm when we are ready for dessert. It may be assembled several hours ahead, covered lightly with plastic wrap.

> A 9- or 10-inch, partially prebaked,
> Rich Short-Crust Pastry shell
> (page 353)
>
> 4 tablespoons unsalted butter
> 3½ pounds tart green apples (about 9),
>   peeled, cored, quartered
>   lengthwise, and sliced
> 1-inch piece vanilla bean
> 2 tablespoons powdered sugar
> ½ cup best quality orange marmalade
> 1 tablespoon Grand Marnier liqueur
> 2 tablespoons hazelnuts, toasted,
>   skinned and chopped (or almonds
>   slivered)

Be sure to have the Rich Short-Crust Pastry prepared and partially baked.

Heat the butter in a large, heavy sauté pan and add half of the apples. Add the vanilla bean and cook slowly for about 30 minutes, stirring, until the apples are dry and golden brown.

Spread the apple mixture into the pastry shell and even it out. Arrange the remaining apple slices, slightly overlapping, in concentric circles on top of the caramelized apples. You will probably have a couple of layers; be sure that the top one is arranged with care.

Sieve the powdered sugar over the top of the tart and bake in a 400° oven for about 1 hour. Halfway through the baking, cover the edges of the pastry with foil, leaving the center of the tart exposed, to prevent the pastry from burning.

Combine the marmalade and liqueur in a small saucepan and melt them together. Stir to dissolve any lumps.

Remove the tart from the oven and set it on a wire rack. Using a pastry brush, glaze the top of the tart with the still-hot marmalade. Sprinkle evenly with hazelnuts. Serve warm.

Cinnamon Applejack Soufflé with Honey-Glazed Jonathan Apples

Serves 8.

Dessert soufflés are the height of glamor and they need not be impossible for the busy host to prepare. The pastry cream can be made ahead and rewarmed before the egg whites are folded in, the apples can be sautéed ahead, and the sauce can be completed and rewarmed just before serving. The sauce is also good cold; the play of cold against hot is quite nice. If you are willing to sacrifice just a little of the volume, you may also freeze the uncooked soufflés. Bring them right from the freezer to the oven and add about 15 minutes to the cooking time. Yes, it really works.

PASTRY CREAM BASE

Two 3-inch cinnamon sticks, crushed slightly
1½ cups milk
6 tablespoons unsalted butter
6 tablespoons flour
¼ cup sugar
5 egg yolks
2 tablespoons applejack

GLAZED APPLES

3 tablespoons unsalted butter
3 Jonathan apples, peeled, cored, and diced
2 tablespoons honey

EGG WHITES

7 egg whites
4 tablespoons sugar
¼ teaspoon cream of tartar (optional)

CUSTARD SAUCE

3 egg yolks
¼ cup sugar
1 cup milk
1 teaspoon vanilla extract
2 tablespoons applejack or calvados

GARNISH

Powdered sugar in a sieve
Cinnamon

To make the pastry cream base combine the crushed cinnamon sticks with the milk and bring to a simmer. Immediately remove from the heat and let set for 30 minutes. Strain. Melt the butter in a saucepan, add the flour, and cook together for 2 minutes without browning. Slowly whisk in the strained milk and keep whisking to smooth out any lumps. Bring to a simmer, then remove from the heat and whisk in the sugar, egg yolks, and applejack. Keep warm.

To glaze the apples, melt the butter in a sauté pan and sauté the apples over high heat for a few minutes to caramelize the surfaces. Turn only once or twice to encourage browning. Drizzle the honey over about halfway through. Remove from the heat and hold.

Prepare the egg whites by whisking them in a copper bowl with a balloon whisk to soft peaks, gradually add the sugar and continue whisking to stiff peaks. (If using a mixer, add ¼ teaspoon cream of tartar to the egg whites to insure their stability.) Fold into the hot pastry cream base, lightening the base first with a large scoop of egg white.

Butter and sugar eight ¾-cup soufflé dishes and divide the apples among them. Fill to the brims with the soufflé mixture, being sure to level the tops. Bake at 375° for 20 minutes.

To make the Custard Sauce, lightly whisk the egg yolks with the sugar, then add the milk. Stirring with a wooden spoon, heat until thickened; do not bring near a simmer. Remove from the heat. Add the vanilla and the applejack. (If you do not want the alcoholic element of the applejack, add it to the egg yolks with the milk and most of the alcohol will have evaporated by the time the sauce is cooked.)

To serve, sieve powdered sugar over each soufflé and follow with a dusting of cinnamon. Serve the Custard Sauce alongside or cut into the center of each soufflé and pour some of the sauce inside. Serve immediately.

Cranberry Ginger Mousse

Serves 8 to 10.

A tangy, crimson mousse that is useful when entertaining around the holidays.

> 2½ cups (10 ounces) whole cranberries
> 1¼ cups + 2 tablespoons sugar
> 4 tablespoons slivered candied ginger
> ¼ cup lemon juice
> 1 teaspoon lemon zest
> 4 egg yolks
> 1 teaspoon cornstarch
> 1½ cups milk, warmed
> 2 tablespoons ginger-flavored liqueur or brandy
> 2 teaspoons unflavored gelatin, softened in a little water
> 2 cups cream

GARNISH
> Sugared cranberries

Combine the cranberries, ¾ cup of sugar, 2 tablespoons of the candied ginger, lemon juice, and zest in a large saucepan. Cook over medium-low heat, stirring occasionally, until the mixture is thick. Put through a food mill and set aside.

Combine egg yolks, cornstarch and the remaining sugar in a heavyweight saucepan and whisk just to blend. Stir in the warm milk, whisk just until smooth, then using a wooden spoon continue to stir slowly over medium heat, until the custard coats the spoon, about 10 minutes. (Do not go beyond 180° or the custard will curdle.)

Remove the custard from the heat, add the liqueur, the softened gelatin, and the remaining slivered candied ginger and continue stirring until the gelatin is dissolved, 1 to 2 minutes. Transfer the custard to a bowl and refrigerate *just until the custard begins to set.*

Meanwhile, whip 1 cup of the cream until just stiff. When the custard begins to set, fold in the cooled cranberry purée and the whipped cream. Spoon into a 6-cup clear-glass soufflé dish. Cover and chill until set, at least 4 hours or overnight.

Just before serving, whip the remaining 1 cup of cream until stiff. Put the cream into a pastry bag fitted with a fluted tip and pipe rosettes of whipped cream around the edges of the mousse. Garnish with a few sugared cranberries if desired. (To sugar cranberries, dip them one by one in egg white and then roll them in sugar.)

Pumpkin Cheesecake with Hazelnut Praline

Serves 10 to 12.

This luscious fall dessert was developed after I sampled something similar at McCormick's, one of the better fish houses in Seattle. Fresh pumpkin is called for here, but be sure to cook it down to the consistency of canned pumpkin; in other words, very thick. Otherwise it will not have the intensity of flavor needed. You can substitute canned pumpkin if you wish, though its flavor is nowhere near as subtle as that of fresh and it often tastes metallic. To keep a supply of fresh pumpkins on hand through the Thanksgiving and Christmas holidays, buy several during October. They keep very well in a cold, dry place.

CRUST
    1 tablespoon unsalted butter
    ⅓ .cup fine dry cookie crumbs

FILLING
    2 packages (8 ounces each) cream
        cheese, at room temperature
    ¾ cup firmly packed brown sugar
    ¾ cup fresh, thick pumpkin purée
    3 eggs
    1 teaspoon cinnamon
    ½ teaspoon ginger
    ¼ teaspoon cloves

TOPPING

>   2 cups sour cream
> ½ cup granulated sugar
>   1 teaspoon vanilla extract
>   1 tablespoon Hazelnut Praline (page
>   342)

Melt the butter and stir in the cookie crumbs until they are all evenly coated. Butter the sides and bottom of a 10-inch springform pan and sprinkle the buttered crumbs evenly on the bottom.

Cream the cream cheese, add the brown sugar, and continue beating until the mixture is smooth. Add the pumpkin purée, eggs, and spices. Blend well. Pour this mixture on top of the cookie crumbs. Bake at 350° for 20 to 25 minutes. The top will not be fully set.

Mix the sour cream with the granulated sugar and vanilla and stir until the sugar dissolves. Pour this mixture carefully over the cheesecake and return to the oven for 10 minutes more. Remove and cool to room temperature. Refrigerate overnight.

Just before serving, sprinkle the Hazelnut Praline evenly over the top.

Pumpkin Hazelnut Torte with Chocolate Glaze

Serves 12.

This is one of those accommodating cakes that tastes better the day after it is made. Something like an elegant version of carrot cake, it is neither too rich nor too sweet. It has a texture that is chewy and light at the same time. Perfect as a take-along dessert, it travels well. Note that the glaze is not meant to be refrigerated. It will lose its gloss. Just store the cake, covered, at room temperature.

>   Parchment paper
>   Unsalted butter
>   Flour
> 6 eggs, separated
> ¾ cup brown sugar
> ¾ teaspoon cinnamon
> ½ teaspoon nutmeg
>   Pinch cloves
> ½ cup fine dry bread crumbs (not
>   toasted)
> 1 cup hazelnuts, toasted, skinned, and
>   coarsely chopped
> 1 cup peeled and very finely grated
>   fresh pumpkin or other winter
>   squash
> ¼ cup granulated sugar
> 1 ounce best quality semisweet
>   chocolate, coarsely chopped

CHOCOLATE GLAZE
¾ cup unsalted butter
8 ounces semisweet chocolate
4 ounces unsweetened chocolate

Butter a 10-inch removable-bottom cake pan (or a 10-inch springform pan). Cut out a circle of parchment paper to fit the bottom and strips of parchment to line the sides of the pan. Butter the paper and line the bottom and sides of the pan. Sprinkle with a bit of flour and rotate and pat the pan to coat evenly. Tip the pan and pat out the excess flour.

With a mixer, beat the egg yolks with the brown sugar, cinnamon, nutmeg, and cloves until thick. Stir in the crumbs and hazelnuts. Fold in the pumpkin.

In a large, preferably copper, bowl, beat the egg whites slowly with a balloon whisk until a foam appears on the top. Continue more rapidly, adding the granulated sugar gradually after the eggs reach a soft peak, and continue beating to a stiff peak. Do not beat the whites until they are clumpy.

Fold half of the egg whites into the pumpkin mixture, then fold in the chopped chocolate and the remaining egg whites quickly and lightly. Pour the batter into the prepared pan and bake for 45 minutes at 350°. When done, a skewer inserted into the center will come out clean and the internal temperature will read 195°. Remove from the oven, place on a wire rack, and cool completely.

To make the Chocolate Glaze, put the butter, then both types of chocolate in a heavy saucepan over very low heat. Stir as the mixture melts, being careful not to overheat or scorch the chocolate. (This can be done in a double boiler.) Remove from the heat as soon as the chocolate has melted.

Remove the cooked cake from the pan. Then, with the cake on a wire rack set in a jelly-roll pan, pour the glaze onto the center of the cake and use a metal spatula to spread the glaze evenly over the top, allowing the excess to drip down the sides. If an even smoother finish is desired, let the glaze set for 30 minutes, carefully remelt the unused glaze, and give the cake a second coat. The glaze that runs down onto the jelly-roll pan may be scraped up and reused. (Leftover glaze will keep in the refrigerator in an airtight container for about 2 weeks. Reheat it over warm water.)

Pumpkin and Rum Mousse

Serves 6.

A rich, delicate mousse, this is just right for fall entertaining. To vary the recipe somewhat, try adding slivers of candied ginger or layers of pulverized praline. A few crisp cookies served alongside provide a satisfying contrast of texture. And if you have easy and inexpensive access to miniature pumpkins, which are about four inches in diameter, hollow them out and use them to hold the mousse. Frozen squash can be substituted for fresh pumpkin.

1 tablespoon gelatin
6 tablespoons dark rum
6 eggs, separated and at room
    temperature
½ cup sugar
1½ cup fresh pumpkin purée (page 163)
1½ teaspoons cinnamon
½ teaspoon allspice
½ teaspoon nutmeg
    Pinch cream of tartar (optional)
1½ cups cream

GARNISH
1 cup cream, whipped and flavored
    with 1 tablespoon sugar and
    1½ teaspoons dark rum

Sprinkle the gelatin over the rum in small bowl and let stand until softened. Place the bowl over simmering water and stir until the gelatin is completely dissolved (or microwave the mixture for a few seconds).

Beat the yolks with ¼ cup of the sugar until they are very thick and pale. Fold in the pumpkin purée and the spices. Stir in the gelatin and rum mixture.

Beat the egg whites (preferably in a copper bowl with a balloon whisk, otherwise add a pinch of cream of tartar) until soft peaks form, then gradually add the remaining ¼ cup sugar and beat until peaks are capable of standing on their own when lifted with a spatula.

Whip the cream until soft peaks form and gently fold it into the pumpkin mixture along with the beaten egg whites.

Spoon into 6 individual parfait glasses and chill thoroughly.

Garnish with the flavored whipped cream shortly before serving.

*W*inter

Ah the bleak, cold, dreary face of winter. Unfortunately this is how all too many Northwest inhabitants feel about this time of year. My recommendation to them is to take up skiing. You can always recognize the skiers in this region by their manic exuberance once the mountain ranges receive the first requisite layer of snow. Or take up cooking. The other group of native dwellers that maintains nearly as cheery an attitude throughout the winter season is made up of cooks. What better time to stay indoors and fill the house with irresistible aromas? Just *because* so many of the otherwise impelling outdoor activities are curtailed at this time of year, the winter season can be a time of paramount creativity for the kitchenbound.

The seasonal cook's palette is not as limited during December, January, and February as one might imagine. Mussels and oysters are at their peak. Dried legumes, particularly lentils, are plentiful, as are grains of all types. Winter pears supply plenty of sweetness, hazelnuts and walnuts plenty of richness, for a wide range of desserts. Smoked fish and nicely aged cheeses are at their best. To make things even better, temperatures are often so mild in this coldest of our Northwest seasons (at least on the west side of the Cascades) that many an herb garden continues to send up copious quantities of mint, rosemary, sorrel, and other hardy herbs throughout the season. What more could a reasonable cook ask for? Many of the key ingredients of fall are still available in good supply: leafy greens of all types, storage potatoes, controlled-atmosphere apples, fresh fish, fresh crab, and all the various meats.

This chapter features a number of hearty rib-warming dishes. Most of the soups are meals-in-a-bowl, each providing the nourishing warmth so welcome on a bone-chilling day. Meats are emphasized more now too, both because they are virtually seasonless, thus in plentiful supply, and because they offer the extra measure of heartiness that is essential when the weather turns cold. And there is probably no season of the year in which desserts are more appreciated than in winter.

During this season, I make an exercise of pretending that all transportation from outside the region has been curtailed. Then I try to come up with wonderfully tasty dishes using what is available from cold storage or the frost-bitten earth. I do not claim to be a purist in this of course. I am not about to give up lemons, limes, oranges, or grapefruit and certainly not olives or olive oil either; nor any of the tropical spices. These are never the focal point of the dish, however. The objective is really to let Northwest ingredients star. And even in winter there is abundance.

Northwest Cheese

In the past few years there has been an explosion in the variety of good artisan-made cheeses produced in the Northwest. Production levels correspond directly to keen, expressed interest from the cheese-eating public, many of whom have traveled through the French countryside where so many great country cheeses are made. Frequently, small producers here have waiting lists for their cheeses and cheese shops are known to call customers to alert them of an impending delivery from one of the special makers. It seems that the Northwest has become, in just a few short years, a national center of excellence and innovation in cheesemaking. The goat's milk cheeses, among which are some of the world's most exquisite, most expensive cheeses, are particularly good. The distinctive, sour, hot pepper taste of goat's milk is not for everyone and, like all cheeses, the younger, the milder. For fledgling turophiles, it is best to start with the youngest goat cheese obtainable and work up the pungency ladder, step by step. Mature goat cheeses are very piquant and usually disagreeable to the uninitiated. There is such a wide variety of local goat cheeses available now that selection should not pose a difficulty.

Season

Seasonability should be a major factor in purchasing cheese but since most cheeses are mass produced year-round, it is not something most of us consider. Local farm cheeses produced from local milk do have their best seasons though and sometimes these are the only seasons in which they are sold. Fresh farm cheeses (without any aging) are best in the late spring and early summer when the grasses that the milk-producing animals feed on are at their best. The animal's food source plays a critical role in the final taste of the cheese. Local farm cheeses that are aged somewhat are usually better in the fall and winter months because these too are made with the milk from late spring and early summer. Soft-ripening cheeses are seldom at their best during the summer.

Selection

Since selection guidelines vary so much from one cheese to another, they are covered separately. Check out the section on Purchasing Cheese, page 265.

Storage

All cheese is highly perishable and must be kept in the refrigerator at between 45 degrees and 50 degrees, preferably in the warmest, moistest part. The vegetable cooler is the best place. Heat, air, and excessive moisture are all harmful to cheese. Always keep cheese securely wrapped in a tight covering of plastic. Each time you use a cheese, rewrap it in a new piece of plastic wrap to ensure a tight, bacteria-free seal.

Cheeses vary considerably in the length of time they can be stored before losing quality or becoming moldy. Soft, fresh cheeses such as cottage cheese and cream cheese have short shelf lives. Fully ripened soft-ripening cheeses such as Brie should be eaten immediately as they become sharp and ammoniated with age. Cheddars and other firm types will keep for months if stored properly, and dry grating cheeses such as Parmesan will keep even longer. Remember that all real cheeses (not processed types) will continue to age while in storage and develop a noticeably sharper taste. This can be very beneficial for many cheeses but may make some types too sharp.

Ideally, cheese, once it has been brought to room temperature, should not be refrigerated again. Therefore cut and serve only as much as you are planning to eat. A series of temperature changes causes cheese to sweat, sag, toughen, and dry out. If absolutely necessary though, most cheeses can be refrigerated again. Brie- and Camembert-types, however, should simply be wrapped and left out, preferably at a cool room temperature, for consumption at the next meal.

Most cheeses should not be frozen. You can do it though if you are willing to sacrifice a lot of the texture; the cheese will usually be crumbly. Thaw frozen cheese slowly in the refrigerator.

Any mold that develops on cheese should simply be cut off. Sometimes the mold bacteria will have worked its way through the entire piece of cheese; you will be able to taste it but it is not always visible. Such pieces must be discarded.

Preparation

Most cheeses are ready to use as they are. The soft-ripening cheeses may need further ripening. The rind should be removed from most cheeses before the cheese is eaten or cooked. If it is to be melted, cheese should be grated as finely as possible. The hard grating cheeses, such as Parmesan, will not melt at all if the particles are left too large.

Cooking

All cheese should be cooked at low temperatures, for short periods of time, otherwise it becomes stringy and granular. When cooking semifirm to firm cheese choose those that are well aged because the younger cheeses tend to curdle or turn to string when heated. When cooking Cheddars, for instance, look for pieces that have been aged for at least six months. Cheese curdles above 150° unless some starch, such as flour, has been used as a stabilizer. Even with a stabilizer, do not ever bring cheese to a boil unless you are using one of the hard grating cheeses such as Parmesan or Asiago. Grated very finely, they melt evenly and quickly and do not turn to string or curdle even at relatively high temperatures.

Eating

A word about eating cheeses with rinds. Very few cheeses have edible rinds. Those that do are the extremely thin-skinned, washed-rind cheeses such as American Muenster, some bloomy-rind types such as Boursault, and some blue cheeses. Many people find the rind of soft-ripening cheeses and even of some goat cheeses edible; most cheese connoisseurs do not. I find nothing pleasant in the rind of a Brie, for instance. Ask yourself if you really *like* the taste of the rind? If so, eat it; if not, cut it off.

PURCHASING CHEESE

It is always preferable to buy cheese at a specialty shop where the staff really understands proper storage principles, age deadlines, and in general how cheese should be treated during its stay at the shop. Most supermarkets can be relied on only for the most basic and nonperishable of the cheeses and even then you should know how to evaluate what you are purchasing so that you do not end up with a bad piece. In addition to paying attention to the overall quality of the cheese and offering the opportunity to sample whatever looks interesting, a specialty shop can provide you with choice that is available nowhere else. The cook should not live by Cheddar alone, not when there are so many wonderful cheeses just waiting to be discovered. Regardless of where you buy your cheese, the following standards should be met.

The Shop

Frequent a shop with a high turnover; cheese is highly perishable. Buy only at stores that replenish their supply regularly. The shop should be impeccably neat, clean, and odor-free. All cheeses should be wrapped in plastic wrap and most of them should be under refrigeration. Only those that are intended for sale and consumption the same day may plausibly be left out on the counter. The cheeses should look good. There should be nothing odd, shrunken, or out of character about them. Pungent cheeses should be positioned well away from the milder types and, of course, no cheese should be stored next to salami, pepperoni, and the like. The shop should be willing to accept a return if the cheese should turn out to be bad.

The Cheese

On all types of cheese the rind should be intact and look fresh. The cheese should not look crumbly when it should be firm, or wet when it should be dry. The cheese should not appear mealy, mottled, spotted, or moldy. It should not feel greasy, pasty or be exuding moisture. The texture of the cheese should be true to type. There should not be a smell of mold when it is not characteristic of the cheese. Cheese should never smell ammoniated, stale, yeasty, excessively unpleasant, or foreign to its particular smell. It should not taste acidic, bitter, sulfuric, flat, or rancid.

Specific Cheeses

Soft cheeses should have clean wrappings; be evenly dusted and uniformly colored; smell good; yield uniformly from edge to center with finger pressure; be even, plump, and uniform in shape; show no evidence of a blue mold on the crust; be ripe enough and yet not over the hill; not be shrunken underneath their wrappings or overly bulging either.

Semisoft cheeses should have the proper gloss; be attractive with no evidence of sweating; have clean surfaces; be plump; not look soggy or mealy.

Hard cheeses should have even rinds without cracks; be free of off-color spots; appear regular, even, and hard.

Blue cheeses should have a mold that is clearly defined; be clean and pleasant looking, especially near the rind; be moist looking; have an even covering that is thoroughly clean.

Fresh cheeses should smell like sweet milk; be white with no yellowing; be well drained with no leakage; be free from mold; be dated.

Goat cheeses should be characteristic in color; be pleasant tasting and not overripe; be free from mold.

Waxed cheeses should have intact paraffin wrappings that are not apparently too tight for the cheese.

SERVING CHEESE

Presenting cheese so that it can be enjoyed at its best demands a little more planning than simply taking it from the refrigerator. The following guidelines are useful.

- Always serve cheese at room temperature to permit its full flavor to come out. A medium to firm cheese may well require two to three hours at room temperature to be at its peak of flavor. A soft-ripening cheese should be ready to eat in only an hour.
- Cheese should be simply arranged with a minimum of fussy garnishes. Wood, marble, and straw or wicker trays are suitable containers and grape leaves may be placed underneath the cheeses.
- Be sure to leave enough room around the cheeses to allow guests to cut pieces from the wedges easily.
- Provide a separate cheese knife for each cheese. A small cheese server—something that looks like a miniature pie server—is a useful tool for the cheese tray. Guests should be given plates, small knives, and napkins.
- Identify cheeses with small cocktail flags (or something similar) so that people know what they are eating.

- Do not place mild and strong cheeses next to each other; arrange separate groupings.
- Delicate cheeses should be accompanied by neutral breads or crackers.
- Leave on the rind of soft-ripening cheese but remove at least one side of the rind on a cheese that has a hard or waxed rind.
- Cut the first piece from a whole cheese; your guests will feel reluctant to do it themselves.
- Pie-shaped flat cheeses should be cut into wedges; Edams and Goudas are cut into wedges as one would cut an apple; blocks and logs are cut into slices; pyramids are cut into wedges from the top. Stilton is sliced through the top parallel to the surface and about one and a half inches below. Then that slice is cut into wedges. When the first layer is finished, slice the cheese horizontally again, and cut the next layer into wedges. Roquefort should be cut with a wire cutter to keep it from crumbling.
- Do not preslice cheeses or cut them into numerous wedges before serving, since small portions dry out quickly.
- A good rule of thumb for serving cheese is to provide four ounces per guest. For an appetizer before dinner, three ounces are sufficient; for a cheese-tasting, four ounces are usually adequate; and for a cocktail party, six ounces per person will likely be required.

VARIETIES OF NORTHWEST CHEESES

The following list of cheeses represents some of those more commonly available in the Northwest. Check good grocery stores, delicatessens, and cheese shops for current lists of those they carry. New cheeses join the ranks yearly.

Cedar Creek Butter Cheese

Produced in Kalama, Washington, in the traditional German manner, Cedar Creek Butter Cheese is extremely mild, buttery, and semisoft, with an interior the color of butter. A superb cow's milk table cheese, it is unfortunately only sporadically available in Seattle.

Cougar Gold

Created and produced by Washington State University's creamery, Cougar Gold is aged in a can for at least a year before being released. Eighteen months to three years is considered the ideal age for this cheese. An absolutely superb cheese reminiscent of a combination of two parts Cheddar to one part Swiss (some say Gouda rather than Swiss) but with an individuality and complexity all its own, it is a sweetly mellow cow's milk cheese with a pleasing tang. It is firm, smooth, and creamy with a lovely, lingering aftertaste. It is the color of unsalted butter. Next to Tillamook Cheddar,

Cougar Gold is Washington's most famous cheese. It is expensive and makes an ideal gift from the Northwest.

Marblemount Cheeses

Excellent quality goat's milk Cheddar and goat's milk feta are produced in Marblemount, Washington (on the North Cascades Highway) by Michael and Carmen Estes.

Mazza's Seal Brand Cheeses

Provolone, mozzarella and a Greek-style feta have been produced by the Mazza family in Orting, Washington, for the past sixty years or more. The feta is considered the most exciting of the three. It is a chalky, crumbly cow's milk cheese that becomes creamy and rich with age and will keep in its brine for three years or more.

Mount Capra Cheeses

Distinctive, superlative, firm goat's milk cheeses are produced in Chehalis, Washington, by Frank and Ann Stout. Chehalis Natural has a medium sharpness and a texture that becomes crumbly with age. Chehalis Caraway is the Natural with caraway added. Chehalis Herb is the Natural with rosemary, thyme, sage, basil, and garlic added. Cascadian, a goat's milk Cheddar that is complex and mild at the same time, is reputed to be one of the best goat's milk Cheddars in the country.

Okanogan Highland Cheeses

On their farmstead near the border between Washington and British Columbia, Sally and Roger Jackson produce exemplary cheeses as they are made in the French countryside. The Jacksons' cheeses continue to increase in variety. Most of those I have enjoyed are goat's milk cheeses, including Fresh Chèvre in Grape Leaves, Fresh Chèvre in Rosemary, Aged Chèvre with Sweet Peppers and Chives, Fresh Chèvre in Paprika, and Aged Smoked-Applewood Chèvre. There are also sheep's milk cheeses, most notably a firm, softly veined Sheep's Milk Blue that is most distinctive and pleasant.

Oregon Blue

Oregon Blue is a cow's milk cheese that is one of the most praised cheeses of the Northwest. Produced in the Rogue River Valley amidst a lush profusion of pear orchards, Oregon Blue at its best is very complex, rich and creamy, with a delightful tanginess. It has a lovely coloration—creamy white with dark blue-green veining.

Pleasant Valley Cheeses

Pleasant Valley Gouda is a superlative, completely natural farm cheese produced from premium whole cow's milk in Ferndale, Washington, by George and Delores Train. The flavor is mellow and nutty, the texture is creamy,

something like Dutch Gouda, but also distinctively Northwest. The cheese is aged for at least sixty days in a controlled environment where both humidity and temperature are closely monitored. The best cheeses are made in May and June and then again in September when the meadow grasses that the cows feed on are at their finest. Pleasant Valley cheeses are dated. The dairy's true raw cow's milk farmstead cheese is also produced from the cheesemaker's own cows and has a bit more tang than Gouda.

Quark

From Appel Farm in Ferndale, Washington, Quark is a very enjoyable fresh cow's milk cheese. Available in whole-milk, skim-milk and low-fat versions, it is perhaps best described as being a cross between cream cheese and ricotta in texture and sour cream and crème fraîche in taste. You might detect a cottage cheese taste in there somewhere too, except there are no visible curds. Some people use it as a substitute for yogurt. This dairy also makes crème fraîche.

Quillasascut Cheeses

Produced near Quillasascut Creek outside Rice, Washington, by Lora Lee and Rick Misterly, Quillasascut cheeses are very fine indeed. They are quite distinctive goat's milk cheeses with such names as Selkirk with Garlic and Black Pepper, Selkirk with Tashkent Spices,

Fresh Goat Cheese with Peppercorns and Thyme in Olive Oil, Goat Cheese with Dried Cherries and Oregano, and Lavender and Fennel Goat Cheese.

Rogue River Gold Cheddar

This Cheddar is a bright orange cheese made in the soft, creamy Northwest Cheddar style, but has been just a touch drier and more crumbly when I have sampled it. (It gets more so with age.) Rich, full tasting and nicely balanced, it is produced in Central Point, Oregon, by the Rogue River Valley Creamery, which also makes Oregon Blue, Jack, and Colby cheeses.

Rolling Stone Chèvre

Produced in Parma, Idaho, the Rolling Stone goat cheeses are among the best—perhaps *the* best—I have ever tasted. Their Chèvre with Jalapeño is snow white with a wax rind and creamy-soft with a pronounced, absolutely brilliant taste; a four-star cheese. The Chèvre with Pecans is unusual as well; sweet and exotic—best served for dessert.

Tillamook Cheddar

Our most famous Northwest cheese, that has been produced by the Tillamook County Creamery Association for almost 100 years now in Tillamook, Washington, Tillamook Cheddar is the forerunner of the Northwest Cheddar

style, which is soft and smooth rather than being dry and crumbly as is traditional Cheddar. Made with raw milk, the better Tillamook Cheddar is aged for at least nine months and marketed as "sharp" (which it is not). The best "extra-sharp special reserve" is aged for at least eighteen months. Tillamook County Creamery also makes an excellent Jack cheese.

WSU Smoky Cheddar

A good full-smoked Cheddar is made by Washington State University's Creamery in the creamy Cheddar style. It is a full tasting, balanced cheese with good body.

Yakima Valley Gouda

Produced by the Yakima Valley Dairy Cooperative in eastern Washington, Yakima Gouda is produced in the Dutch manner with milk from Dutch-bred Holstein cows and a cheese culture imported from the Netherlands. The cheese is distinctive, smooth, and nutty tasting.

Cheese Recipes

Washington Blue Mussels

Penn Cove is a tranquil little borough nestled on the eastern shore of beautiful Whidbey Island, about forty-five miles north of Seattle. It is home to a number of mussel cultivation enterprises, or sea farms as aquaculturists like to call them. Some of the best tasting shellfish in the world comes from this tiny area and the Department of Natural Resources has desig-

nated Penn Cove as one of the most ecologically perfect areas in the nation for mussel cultivation.

It is tempting to be blasé about our regional mussels in the late eighties now that they are so readily available. A few years ago, however, not many people had even tasted a mussel. The sea farms in Washington were fledgling enterprises, struggling with the unknowns of mussel cultivation as well as with a reluctant public. Fortunately for all of us, adventurous chefs and culinary educators in the region took to Washington blue mussels with a passion, serving them in simple and ingenious ways and harping on their glories with a nearly religious fervor, until consumers began to take notice. Once that happened, the local blue mussel began replacing the larger, much inferior, Eastern mussel in our retail markets. A shellfish star was born.

No one forgets tasting perfectly fresh, perfectly prepared Washington blue mussels for the first time. There is absolutely nothing like them. The meat is plump, delicate, and incredibly tender. Attached to fourteen-foot-long polypropylene lines supported by buoys or thirty-foot-square rafts, cultivated mussels are always in the water. This allows them to feed continually and grow to maturity in only one-third the time required by a typical beach mussel. And because they are suspended far above the floor of Puget Sound, cultivated mussels are almost entirely free of barnacles and extraneous debris. The glossy black-blue shells are easy to clean and the byssus (the

threadlike beard protruding from the shell) is pulled off with relative ease.

Season

Mussels are at their best from November through April, with January being the height of the season. Avoid them in May and June when they are spawning and of little culinary value. You may find mussels difficult to obtain during the summer months due to the onset of red tide, a life form eaten by the mussels that is extremely toxic to humans. The mussel beds in Washington are monitored carefully to prevent this potentially harmful organism from entering the retail market. Mussels available at the retail level can be assumed to be safe to eat.

Selection

When selecting fresh mussels—the only kind to buy—look for those with tightly closed shells. If a shell is open or slides when you press on it, the mussel should be discarded. Always choose your mussels individually to ensure that each one is alive and edible; reach down into the bed of ice and select the mussels that have been well protected from warmth and air. Look for Penn Cove or Washington mussels. I prefer the smallest mussels I can find, though many cooks prefer larger specimens, especially for stuffing and displaying on the half shell.

I generally allow three-quarters of a pound of Washington blue mussels per person if the dish is intended as a main course. A batch of particularly small mussels will yield about six dozen to the pound; three or four dozen is more usual. East Coast mussels have bigger, thicker, and thus heavier shells than do the cultivated mussels from our waters. Remember this when you purchase them because you will be getting less mussel meat per pound than you might expect.

Storage

Once home, the mussels should be stored in the refrigerator on a thick bed of ice, covered lightly with a damp towel. Do not seal them in a plastic bag or the mussels will suffocate. Nor should you allow the mussels to soak in water for any length of time. Mussels quickly deplete the water of oxygen and nutrients and then drown. (If you travel quite a distance from home to purchase mussels, be sure to bring along a cooler filled with ice. Put the mussels on top of the ice for the journey back. They will like it a lot better.) Cultivated mussels generally have a seven-day shelf life from the time they are removed from the water—*if properly stored*. Do not hesitate to ask your merchant when the mussels were delivered to him so that you will have some indication of their life-expectancy.

Preparation

Sand is not a common problem with Northwest mussels, contrary to what some food writ-

ers will tell you. In any case, do not cover the mussels with water for any reason. Clean the shells under very cold running water as well as you can. Remove any barnacles by rubbing two mussels together to scrape them loose, or scrub with a very stiff toothbrush. There will usually be a fibrous mass extending from each mussel. This is called the byssus or beard; its function is to hold the mussel to a piling or long line. It must be removed before cooking. To remove the beard, grasp it firmly and pull downward and *away* from the hinge with a sharp jerking motion. If the beard will not budge, cut it off with a small pair of scissors close to the shell; but then you must remember that part of it is still inside the mussel and should be removed after cooking. Once the beards have been removed, the mussels should be cooked within an hour or so as the debearding process weakens them considerably.

Cooking

Mussels could not be simpler to cook. Although most recipes specify an herb and onion infused cooking liquid (sometimes of wine, sometimes of water), I can fathom no reason to bother with this procedure unless you intend to use the resulting nectar in some other part of the recipe or later in a seafood soup. Simply steam the cleaned mussels in a large covered kettle with half to a whole cup plain water for about four minutes, or just until they have opened. If you overcook them slightly it does not matter. Mussels do not get tough and rub-

bery as easily as clams do, thus they give the cook a greater margin for error. They even reheat well.

Since the shells are so lovely, I leave them on whenever possible. Sometimes this requires thinning the accompanying sauce somewhat so that it will evenly coat the batch.

Mussel Recipes

Cream of Mussel Nectar Soup, *page 301*
Mussel and Saffron Bisque, *page 304*
Mussel Bouillabaisse, *page 304*
Mussel Bourride, *page 302*
Mussels in Lemon Butter Sauce, *page 307*
Steamed Mussels with Fennel Beurre Blanc, *page 306*

Oysters

Lovers of shellfish are divided on the issue of whether oysters are better cooked or raw. In my classes on shellfish, I present a challenge to those students who have never consumed a raw oyster (a good percentage of the class usually), offering for their first attempt the tiny Olympia oyster or perhaps a small, sweet Kumamoto. Pleasant surprise is the unanimous response. "Why, this isn't gross at all," they say. No, of course not. I remember my own first time with a raw oyster though and have to admit that I was definitely unnerved by the pros-

pect. Everyone around me was guzzling them with gusto. Steeling myself against a mounting feeling of revulsion, I swallowed a particularly large specimen, whole. The next one I actually chewed a little bit and like my students I was surprised by the clean, sweet, and light briny taste. The essence of a fresh sea breeze. And the texture was also a surprise. It was crisp and succulent at the same time. So if you have not yet eaten an oyster raw, you might like to try one of the smaller oysters available.

More than ninety percent of all West Coast oysters are grown in Washington State and more than half of those come from Willapa Bay. Though there are over a hundred species of oysters, only three are harvested in the Northwest: the Pacific oyster—originally from Japan, the native Olympia oyster, and the European flat oyster, sometimes called the Belon. The quality, appearance, and taste of all types of oyster vary considerably from one area to another. Aficionados develop preferences for certain localities.

Season

Although oysters are generally available year-round, avoid buying them in the summer months when they are spawning, because they are watery, milky in color, and much too sweet. The flavor is much better during the fall, winter, and early spring.

Selection

In the Northwest you will see oysters called Shoalwater Bay, Willapa Bay, Tillamook Bay, Yaquina Bay, Westcott Bay, Hamma-hamma, Lasqueti, Malpeque, Penn Cove Select, Portuguese, Quilcene, and Rock Point. These are all Pacific oysters that have adapted themselves to their specific environments and have taken on interesting characteristics from the water, its nutrients, and changes in salinity. So each tastes different. The tiny and delicious Olympia oyster is now plentiful too, although just a few short years ago it was nearly extinct. We have resourceful, tenacious sea farmers to thank for its recovery. There are also the wonderful Westcott European flat oysters and the small, deep-cupped Kumamotos, which are a Pacific hybrid.

When buying live oysters in the shell, tap the oyster gently to make sure its shell closes. If it does not, the oyster is probably dead and should be bypassed. Fresh shucked oysters should be plump and have a natural creamy color; the liquid should be clear. Oysters vary in size and are marketed with this distinction. Shucked Pacific oysters are available in large, medium, small, and extra small sizes; the smaller the oyster, the more it usually costs.

Three to six oysters are sufficient for an appetizer serving; a dozen oysters per person is considered a main-course serving; and a quart of oysters extended with other ingredients will usually serve eight.

Storage

Live oysters in the shell should be kept out of the sunlight, at a temperature between 35 degrees and 40 degrees, with the deep-cupped shell down to keep the oysters immersed in their natural juices. Proper handling will keep an oyster alive for between seven and ten days. Shucked oysters stored in their container at a temperature between 35 degrees and 40 degrees should keep for up to seven days.

Preparation

Scrub the shells with a vegetable brush under cold running water if desired.

Shucking

Die-hard oyster lovers insist that the bivalves are at their best raw, eaten off the half shell with all their briny juices intact. Shucking oysters in expectation of this kind of feast takes practice. First of all, protect the hand that will hold the shell with a thick mitt. Arm the other hand with an oyster knife—a special knife with a short strong blade, a pointed tip, and a heavy hand guard at the base of the handle. The tip will pierce the oyster's thick hinge and the rigid blade and hand guard serve as protection while the oyster is being opened, a process that often requires considerable force. To begin, hold the oyster in the mitted hand, flatter shell up. Insert the tip of the knife into the hinge and twist it to open the shell. Slide the knife

along the inside of the upper shell to cut the muscle that attaches it to the flesh. Pull off and discard the upper shell. Slide the knife under the oyster to free it from the lower shell. Remove any bits of broken shell with the point of the knife. Be careful not to spill any of the juices contained in the bottom shell. Eat with a squeeze of lemon juice and freshly ground black pepper.

Cooking

Oysters taste awful and their texture is ruined when they are overcooked. Heat just until the mantle around the oyster starts to curl. Once cooked, oysters must be served immediately.

Oyster Recipes

> Oyster and Spinach Soup with Pepper Bacon,
>   *page 39*
> *see also* Recipe Notes, *which follow*

RECIPE NOTES

CORNMEAL-FRIED OYSTERS

Combine 1 cup cornmeal with salt, pepper, and cayenne pepper to taste. Coat about a pint of freshly shucked oysters with the cornmeal and deep fry at 375° for about 2 minutes, until crisp and golden brown. Blot on paper towels and keep warm in the oven until the entire batch is done. Serve immediately.

WHEAT GERM-FRIED OYSTERS

Combine 1 cup raw wheat germ with salt and pepper to taste. Dip freshly shucked oysters in flour, pat off the excess, dip in beaten egg, and then into wheat germ. Set on a wire rack to dry for 15 to 30 minutes. Fry in a combination of 2 tablespoons corn oil and 2 tablespoons butter, turning once so that both sides are crisp and brown. Oysters will cook in just under 2 minutes; you will need high heat to brown the coating in this time.

RYE-FRIED OYSTERS

Proceed as for Wheat Germ-Fried Oysters but substitute fine, dry rye bread crumbs for the wheat germ and spark them with a dash of cayenne.

OH-SO-EASY OYSTER SOUP

Melt 4 tablespoons butter in a large saucepan and add 4 cups half-and-half. Heat to just beneath a simmer, then add 2 cups freshly shucked, chopped oysters with their liquor and cook for just a minute or so. Season to taste with salt and white pepper and stir in 2 tablespoons minced parsley. Do not continue to heat or the oysters will toughen.

OYSTER FRITTERS

Combine 1 cup flour, 1 teaspoon baking powder, and salt and plenty of black pepper to taste in a bowl. Mix well. Pour on a combination of 1 cup milk, 1 beaten egg, and 1 teaspoon lemon juice. Blend gently with a wooden spoon until smooth. Add 1 cup chopped, freshly shucked oysters to the batter and stir. Scoop the batter out with a large spoon and deep-fry at 375° until well browned on all sides, about 4 to 5 minutes. Blot with paper towels and keep warm in the oven while completing the batch. Then serve immediately.

BACON-WRAPPED OYSTER BITES

Shuck a couple of dozen fresh oysters and pat them dry with paper towels. Wrap each oyster with a half slice of partially fried bacon (the bacon should still be flexible) and secure with a toothpick. Broil on a wire rack for about 2 minutes per side, until the bacon is crisp and the oysters are just cooked.

HERB-STUFFED OYSTERS

Combine 1 cup fine dry bread crumbs, 1 teaspoon crumbled tarragon, 1 teaspoon crumbled oregano, ¼ cup minced Italian parsley, 4 cloves garlic minced, 2 green onions minced, a pinch of cayenne pepper, and salt and pepper to taste. Drizzle with a combination of 5 tablespoons melted butter and 5 tablespoons olive oil. Toss to distribute the butter and oil evenly. Shuck 2 dozen fresh oysters. Scrub and reserve the bottom, cupped shells. Drain the oysters and cut each into a few pieces. Place them back into the shells and top with a portion of the stuffing. Bake at 450° for about 10 minutes, until the topping is browned and the oysters are just cooked.

CURRIED OYSTERS

Melt 2 tablespoons butter and cook 4 minced shallots and 2 cloves minced garlic, along with a large pinch of crumbled saffron and ½ teaspoon Madras curry powder until softened but not browned. Shuck a dozen or so fresh oysters, being careful to save the liquor. Scrub and reserve the bottom cupped shells. Add the liquor to the butter mixture. Reduce the liquor by half and add ½ cup cream. Continue cooking until the cream is reduced and the sauce lightly thickened. Season to taste with salt, pepper and drops of lemon juice. Put the oysters, chopped if you like, back into the shells and top

with a portion of the hot sauce. Heat and glaze under the broiler for a minute or two and serve.

OYSTERS WITH HERB BUTTER

Process 1 cup butter until smooth. Add 1 cup cooked, minced spinach squeezed of all moisture, ¼ cup minced parsley, 1 minced green onion, 2 cloves minced garlic, ½ teaspoon thyme, ½ teaspoon basil, ½ teaspoon cayenne pepper, and salt and pepper to taste. Purée until smooth and blend in 2 tablespoons Pernod, an anise-flavored apéritif. Spoon the butter lengthwise onto a sheet of plastic wrap and roll up into a sausage shape. Refrigerate to harden. Shuck a couple of dozen large oysters. Scrub and reserve the bottom, cupped shells. Put the oysters back into the shells. Slice the butter into 2-teaspoon-sized pieces and put one piece on top of each oyster. Nestle the oyster shells in a baking pan filled with rock salt to hold them upright and bake at 450° until the butter is melted and hot and the oysters just done, 3 to 5 minutes.

HOT SAUCED OYSTERS

Make a cream sauce using 2 tablespoons butter, 2 tablespoons flour, and 1 cup cream. Season well with salt, white pepper, cayenne pepper, and drops of lemon juice. Shuck a dozen

or so large oysters and scrub and reserve the bottom, cupped shells. Cut each oyster into a few pieces. Spoon 2 tablespoons of the cream sauce into each of the reserved shells. Top with cut oysters, then with a portion of 6 fried, drained and crumbled slices of bacon and a portion of 1½ cups grated Cheddar cheese. Place under a hot broiler until the cheese melts and the oysters are just cooked, about 4 minutes.

CREAMED OYSTERS AND HAM

Make a *roux* with 2 tablespoons butter and 2 tablespoons flour. Add ½ cup cream and ½ cup oyster liquor and bring to a boil, whisking, to produce a creamy *velouté* sauce. Season boldly with salt, pepper, cayenne pepper, and drops of lemon juice. Add 1 cup fresh shucked oysters, halved if they are large, and ½ cup chopped ham. Heat through just long enough to cook the oysters, about 2 minutes. Spoon onto toasted rye points to serve.

OYSTER AND BACON OMELET

Fry ¼ pound bacon slices until crisp. Blot on paper towels and crumble. Dip 6 small oysters in flour, patting off the excess, then dip them in beaten egg, and lastly into fine cracker crumbs. Sauté in butter, turning to brown and crisp both sides, for about 2 minutes. Begin to cook a 2- or 3-egg omelet using 1 tablespoon butter in the omelet pan. Place the oysters evenly over the unset top of the omelet and sprinkle with the crumbled bacon. Cook until just barely set, running the top of the omelet under a broiler for a few seconds only to finish off the top. Sprinkle with salt and pepper, fold, and serve.

Smoked Fish

The smoking of fish, especially salmon, over alderwood is a Northwest tradition begun eons ago by native Indian tribes. Today there are specialty smoking houses that infuse all manner of sealife with the delicate aroma and flavor of hardwoods. People in the industry claim that the market for smoked seafood is just beginning. This optimistic projection seems credible. In Washington the variety of smoked products available has expanded dramatically in the past few years. Smoked salmon is plentiful as it has always been, but smoked trout, black cod, sturgeon, mussels, scallops, and oysters are also being produced. There is, as one might expect, varying quality among these smoked seafoods and it pays to know enough about the different processes to be able to ask educated questions of the supplier.

To begin with, good quality smoked fish comes from good quality fish. Reputable smokers use the best—the freshest, the fattest—fish they can get their hands on. They do not count on the smoking process to disguise an inferior product. There is just no way,

for instance, in which a dark, over-the-hill, chum salmon going bad before it was frozen, can then be thawed, smoked, and somehow magically turned into anything you would want to eat. Though inferior stuff is out there, good quality smoked fish abounds. Port Chatham's Portlock brand is one of the best. At Port Chatham, the freshest, highest quality fish is selected then treated to carefully monitored procedures that enhance the original taste, texture, and look of the natural fish. When buying smoked fish, it pays to ask about the specific type and where it comes from. You may not know one from another, but the merchant's reply will tell you if pride is involved in the product.

Process

The various styles of smoked fish can usually be divided into one of two categories: cold-smoked or hot-smoked. Both processes begin with brining. The fish is soaked in a water and salt solution of a specific strength to discourage bacterial growth. But because salt levels have lessened substantially in recent years (the Food and Drug Administration no longer requires a minimum of 5 percent salt in the water content of the fish), consumers should not think that brining will make the fish keep forever. It will not.

After the fish has been brined for about twenty-four hours, it is rinsed in fresh water, allowed to dry, then introduced to smoke. The internal temperature of cold-smoked fish never rises above 85 degrees. The fish is technically raw. The internal temperature of hot-smoked fish progresses up to 140° or more. The product is definitely cooked. Differences in finished style arise (aside from the type and quality of the fish) from variations in the brining solution, the amount of time the fish is in contact with the smoke, the type of wood, chips, or sawdust used to produce the smoke, and even the smoker itself and whether or not it can be regulated.

Nomenclature

Unfortunately the terms used to describe smoked fish in the markets are not crystalline. Take the word *lox* for instance. In New York the word is applied only to a fish (specifically salmon) that has undergone a simple salt and water brining period and cold water rinse. No cooking. No smoking. On the West Coast, the word more commonly refers to a fish that has been salt and water brined and cold-smoked.

Then there is the word *nova*. In the early part of this century it was used as an abbreviation for the Nova Scotia salmon that arrived in New York for curing. It has since lost its original meaning because much of the salmon that is smoked today comes from our own Pacific waters. On the East Coast, nova refers to a salt and water brined fish that is also cold-smoked. On the West Coast nova refers, usually, to a fish that has been salt, water, and sugar brined, then cold-smoked.

Or you might run into the word *kippered.*

Some Northwest smokers will not use the term at all because so much inferior smoked fish has borne the name in the past. Technically it just refers to a hot-smoked product and can be good or bad depending on the producer. Most grocery-store kippered salmon, for instance, is awful—salty, dry, and off-tasting.

Whichever smoked product you choose, expect the price to be high. Sometimes the difference between an inferior smoked product and an excellent one is only a matter of pennies per pound though. A little goes a long way. There is nothing more spectacular at a party than a whole side of cold-smoked salmon surrounded with sliced French and pumpernickel breads, a crock of sweet butter, capers, lemon or lime wedges and a large pepper grater, but a fraction of that fish incorporated into a sumptuous spread, encased in tender ravioli, or embellishing a risotto, can also create a luxurious effect.

Season

Since most of the fish used for smoking are frozen first, availability is constant. Enjoy smoked seafoods year-round, but especially in the winter when the harvest of fresh fish slacks off.

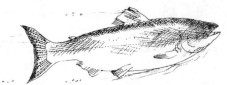

Available Forms

Currently you should be able to find hot- and cold-smoked king, sockeye, chum and pink salmon; cold-smoked black cod; cold-smoked sturgeon; hot- and cold-smoked trout; and hot-smoked mussels, oysters, and scallops. Also hard-smoked salmon called salmon jerky or squaw candy are available; these forms are heavily salted, low in moisture and generally smoked—cold usually—for a much longer time than usual.

Storage

All smoked seafood, except that packed in special retortable pouches, must be held at 38 degrees or lower—in other words, refrigerated. Vacuum packing is no guarantee against bacterial contamination. Treat smoked seafood the same way as you would fresh seafood. You have a little more time to consume your supply but it does deteriorate with time.

Cooking

The textural difference between hot- and cold-smoked fish is dramatic. The first is drier, firmer, and flakier; the second is very moist and silky. When cooking it is important to remember that hot-smoked fish may be chunked, flaked, or puréed coarsely. Cold-smoked fish cannot be chunked or flaked but it can be draped, wrapped, layered in one piece, thinly sliced, chopped, or puréed smoothly. Depend-

ing on the dish you intend to make, it may be that either will work. The big exception to this is when you are making a mousse that relies on the unset protein of the fish so that it will set and have a silky texture. Cold-smoked (uncooked) fish should be used for this.

Smoked Fish Recipes

Cold-Smoked Salmon, Potato, and Green Bean Salad, *page 107*

Smoked Black Cod Ravioli with Baby Leeks and Chive Cream, *page 60*

Wild Rice and Cornmeal Waffles with Smoked Salmon Mousse, *page 30*

see also Recipe Notes, *which follow*

RECIPE NOTES

Though most of the following recipes specify smoked salmon, other types of smoked fish can be used as well.

SMOKED SALMON AND POTATO GRATIN

Using 6 thinly sliced potatoes, ¼ to ½ pound flaked or chopped hot- or cold-smoked salmon, and 1 thinly sliced onion, arrange alternating layers in a buttered gratin dish. Season the potato layers with salt and pepper and dot the top of the gratin with 1 tablespoon butter. Combine 2 cups half-and-half and 1 egg and pour over the gratin. Bake at 350° for just under an hour, until the potatoes are done.

TIAN OF SMOKED SALMON, MUSHROOMS, AND CHEDDAR

Combine 2 cups cooked rice, 1 egg, 1 cup milk or half-and-half, ¼ to ½ pound hot- or cold-smoked salmon, 1 chopped onion, ½ cup grated Cheddar cheese, ¼ pound sliced, sautéed mushrooms, 1 minced green onion, and salt and pepper to taste. Put into a buttered baking dish and bake at 350° for 45 minutes until hot and bubbly.

SPINACH AND PEAR SALAD WITH SMOKED SALMON AND TROUT

Make a vinaigrette by combining 6 tablespoons corn oil, 2 tablespoons red wine vinegar, 1 tablespoon lemon juice, 2 teaspoons capers, and salt and pepper to taste. Just before serving, toss 1 bunch cleaned and shredded spinach with the vinaigrette, reserving 2 tablespoons of the vinaigrette. Arrange the spinach on 6 individual salad plates and place a few slices of ripe pear around the edges of each. Drizzle the pear with the remaining vinaigrette, then alternate thin slices of cold-smoked salmon and cold-smoked trout (about ½ pound each) in a slightly ruffled manner around each salad. Add a lemon wedge to each. Accompany with thinly sliced pumpernickel, sweet butter, and a pepper grinder.

SMOKED SALMON QUICHE

Combine 1 cup cream, 2 lightly beaten eggs, ½ teaspoon tarragon, 2 tablespoons minced fresh parsley, and ¼ pound flaked or chopped hot- or cold-smoked salmon. Season to taste with salt and pepper. Pour this mixture into a partially baked, shallow, 9- or 10-inch pastry shell. Bake at 350° for about 30 minutes, until just slightly puffed around the edges and still somewhat loose in the center. Let cool for 30 minutes before cutting.

SMOKED SALMON, ZITI, AND GREEN BEAN SALAD

Combine 2 cups cooked ziti pasta, 2 teaspoons olive oil, 2 tablespoons lemon juice, 2 thinly sliced green onions, 2 tablespoons minced parsley, 1 teaspoon dried dillweed, ½ cup mayonnaise, ½ pound flaked or chopped hot- or cold-smoked salmon, and 1 cup diagonally sliced, barely cooked green beans. Chill. Season to taste with salt and pepper and arrange on a platter. Surround with sprigs of parsley and lemon wedges. Great for picnics or buffets.

SMOKED SALMON PILAF

In a large saucepan, melt 3 tablespoons butter and cook ¼ cup minced onion until softened. Add 1½ cups long-grain or converted rice. Stir to coat with butter and cook for about 2 minutes. Add 2½ cups chicken stock and ½ cup dry white wine, bring to a simmer, then cover and cook for about 20 minutes, until all the liquid is absorbed and rice is tender. Add ¼ pound flaked or chopped hot- or cold-smoked salmon, ½ cup grated Parmesan cheese, and salt and pepper to taste. Fluff gently with a fork and serve.

SMOKED SALMON WITH GREEN PEPPERCORN AND LIME MARINADE

Arrange 1 pound of thinly sliced cold-smoked salmon or trout, or a combination of the two, on a serving platter. Combine ¼ cup minced onion, 2 teaspoons drained green peppercorns, ½ cup lime juice, 2 teaspoons minced fresh dill, a pinch of sugar, and salt and pepper to taste. Pour over the smoked fish and marinate, covered, for an hour or so. Serve with toasted French or pumpernickel bread and a crock of sweet butter.

SMOKED SALMON PÂTÉ

Sauté 1 small minced onion in 4 tablespoons butter until softened. Add 1 pound cooked, flaked fresh salmon, ½ pound flaked or chopped, hot- or cold-smoked salmon, and 2 chopped anchovies and purée in a processor. Add ¾ cup melted butter slowly to the processor while continuing to purée. Season the pâté with salt, pepper, and drops of lemon

juice to taste. Mound into a decorative serving crock, cover and refrigerate overnight. Serve with crostini or crackers.

SMOKED SALMON-STUFFED EGGS

Hard boil 6 eggs, peel, and halve lengthwise. Remove the yolks and purée them with ¼ pound hot- or cold-smoked salmon, ¼ cup minced onion, 2 tablespoons lemon juice, 1 tablespoon capers, 2 to 4 tablespoons mayonnaise, a dash cayenne pepper, and salt and pepper to taste. Fill the egg whites with the salmon purée, mounding the mixture slightly. Arrange the eggs on a serving platter, garnishing each with a few capers. Surround with parsley and lemon wedges.

SPAGHETTINI WITH SMOKED SALMON, PARMESAN, AND CREAM

Combine 2 cups cream with 2 tablespoons butter in a saucepan. Bring to a simmer and reduce by about one-third. Season to taste with salt, fresh nutmeg, and white pepper. Boil 1 pound spaghettini until just *al dente*. Drain and toss with 2 tablespoons softened butter. Add 2 tablespoons Parmesan cheese, ½ pound flaked or chopped hot- or cold-smoked salmon, 2 tablespoons chopped fresh dill, and the reduced cream. Toss and serve.

OMELETS WITH CREAMED SMOKED SALMON

Reduce ¾ cup cream to ¼ cup. Let cool. Add 4 thin slices of chopped, cold-smoked salmon, 1 teaspoon minced fresh dill and white pepper to taste. Prepare 2 omelets and fill each with a portion of the creamed salmon. Fold and serve. Garnish each with a sprig of fresh dill if desired.

SMOKED SALMON AND LEEK CUSTARD

Poach 6 cleaned, trimmed leeks (or asparagus) in water to cover until tender, about 10 minutes for leeks or 4 minutes for asparagus. Drain. Wrap a thin slice of cold-smoked salmon around each leek and arrange in a buttered gratin dish. Combine 1 cup cream with 2 eggs and 1 teaspoon Dijon mustard. Season to taste with salt and white pepper. Add ½ cup grated Gruyère cheese to the custard and pour over the leeks. Top with 2 tablespoons grated Parmesan cheese. Bake at 350° for 30 minutes, until the custard is lightly set, slightly puffed, and golden.

Lentils

Although many of us take beans for granted, barely giving them a thought when planning our grand and even our everyday menus, could we really do without these manifold members of the legume family? String beans, sugar snap peas, snow peas, yard-long beans (eaten pods and all), fresh shelled green peas, fava beans, lima beans, and a plethora of dried varieties—kidney beans, navy beans, cranberry beans, Great Northerns, pink beans, garbanzos, black beans, pinto beans, green and yellow split peas, and the tiny, toothsome lentil.

It is perhaps the destiny of the delicate, earthy lentil to raise the consciousness of legumes to new levels in America. The Washington/Idaho Dry Pea and Lentil Commission certainly thinks so. It is touting the lentil as "a New World classic—a food that's just now coming of age in America." Along with the gorgeous and tasty black bean of South America, lentils, originally from Southwestern Asia, are becoming increasingly popular. They are showing up frequently in New American cookbooks and in innovative restaurants up and down the West Coast. One of the reasons for their increased popularity, I believe, is their ease of preparation. Most dried beans need to be presoaked; lentils do not. Lentils go from the package to the table in as little as twenty minutes, depending on the variety used. For ease and speed they match rice and pasta.

And they are nutritionally impressive, containing 112 grams of protein per pound; T-bone steak has 59 grams per pound. In 1971 Frances Moore Lappé published a book, *Diet for a Small Planet,* in which she espoused a complicated formula for combining the various proteins contained within the plant kingdom to achieve "protein complementarity" so that all eight essential amino acids are available in one meal. (Actually there are twenty-three essential amino acids, but the human body produces fifteen of them on its own.) The theory states that, in order to get complete protein in a vegetarian diet, one is supposed to eat beans at the same time as either cereals or grains, nuts or seeds, rice, or dairy products—in certain important proportions. The theory may be technically correct, but it generated enormous concern in people's minds about whether they were getting enough protein. Protein deficiency is *extremely* rare in this country; an excess is more likely. Recently scientists have claimed that the body has a reservoir of amino acids in the bloodstream; these can be used to produce complementarity at any time. A varied diet will maintain adequate protein levels easily.

On a national scale, Washington State ranks first in the production of lentils and dry edible peas; Idaho ranks second. Together they produce the Chilean green lentil (which is brown) and the smaller Red Chief lentil which is bright orange in the dried state and vivid gold when cooked. They also produce enormous quantities of green split peas and a lesser quan-

tity of yellow split peas. All of this production takes place along a fifty-mile-wide strip that runs for 200 miles north to south from Spokane in Washington to Grangeville in Idaho. This area is known as the Palouse region. The dry climate makes it possible to dry the crops in the field before harvesting.

Season

Sown in April and harvested in August, lentils are dried before being sold, so they are a year-round staple. Because fresh beans are so abundant during the summer months, the dried legumes, which lend themselves to heartier dishes, are generally reserved for the colder months.

Selection

Green lentils are available in every supermarket. Red lentils are more likely to be found in a health food store or specialty food market. Ask for local Red Chief lentils; the imported Persian red lentils are not as tender as Red Chiefs and take twice as long to cook. Red Chiefs are sold whole and are quite a bit larger than Persian red lentils, which are usually sold split. Lentils should appear dry and free of extraneous debris.

Storage

Store in a cool, dry place in an airtight container.

Preparation

Lentils do not need presoaking. Just rinse them, check for foreign debris, and cook.

Cooking

The mild, earthy, almost nutty taste of lentils complements many other foods. Use them with onions, tomatoes, cream, yogurt, cheese, Italian or Polish sausage, fresh pumpkin, toasted walnuts, garlic, pasta, rice, oregano, basil, bay leaf, cumin, cinnamon, chili powder and chili peppers.

Green lentils are more assertive in taste than are red lentils and hold their shape well when cooked. Red lentils usually have disintegrated at the surface by the time they are completely tender at the center. They are preferably used in purées. To cook 1 pound of green lentils, combine them with 5 cups of water and bring to a simmer. Cover and cook for 30 minutes. Cook for 45 minutes if you want a purée. Season and use as desired. Reduce the water to 4 cups for red lentils and cook them for 10 minutes if you want to retain some shape; 20 minutes if you want a purée. Do not salt the water when you cook lentils; it toughens the outer coating.

Pears

By the time the glory of fall comes to a close in the Northwest and the reality of winter begins to settle disconsolately upon all of us, there are only two seasonal fruits left for the cook—apples and pears. Apples come to the market from controlled-atmosphere storage fully ripened and are variable in quality by the time they are purchased, but pears, picked long before they ripen, are usually in good form and have the decided advantage of not turning immediately to mush as apples do when subjected to room temperature.

Only two types of pears are grown in the Northwest: summer pears, ripening during the first half of August, and winter pears, ripening toward the end of August and into September. Bartlett pears, both golden and crimson, fall into the first category. Everything else, Anjou, Bosc, Comice, Winter Nelis, Forelle, and Seckel included, lands in the second.

Although California leads the nation in the production of Bartlett pears, harvesting more than three hundred thousand tons annually, only one-fifth of that amount is sold to the fresh market; Washington and Oregon therefore supply the nation with more than two hundred thousand tons of fresh Bartletts each season. Washington State produces more than one hundred fifty thousand tons of winter pears annually. Oregon produces about half as much. Together the two states account for nearly ninety percent of the nation's winter pear crop.

An oddity in the fruit world, pears benefit from being harvested unripe. Both flavor and texture are improved by a brief to lengthy storage period off the branch. When Bartletts are picked early and ripened off the branch the fruit escapes a tendency to mealiness. Winter pears need a longer storage time to develop their full flavor and texture. Today growers use two methods: simple cold storage, which slows the ripening process sufficiently to allow the beneficial characteristics to emerge, and the recently developed controlled-atmosphere storage (CA), which virtually stops the aging process altogether. In controlled-atmosphere storage facilities the oxygen levels in the sealed cold storage vaults are substantially reduced, so the pears are surrounded with the carbon dioxide they themselves produce. Together, cold storage and controlled-atmosphere storage make it possible to enjoy fresh pears well into early spring, securing their position as a most important winter fruit.

Season

Summer pears, Bartlett and Red Bartlett, are available from August to December. Winter pears, Comice, Anjou, Bosc, Seckel, Winter Nelis, and Forelle, are available from October through May.

Selection

When choosing pears it is important to remember that they may not be sufficiently ripe when you buy them. Summer pears lighten in color as they ripen. Green Bartletts turn golden; Red Bartletts become an even deeper shade of crimson. Winter pears seldom change color at all. To tell if they are ripe, press them with your thumb at the stem end. If the flesh yields to gentle pressure, the pear is ready to eat. If the stem gives way under pressure, the pear will probably be mushy at the core. If you have a few days to ripen the pears at home, buy them unripened. For some preparations, poached pears for instance, unripened pears are desirable.

Storage

Pears will usually ripen perfectly if allowed to sit at room temperature for between three and five days. Once a pear has ripened, it must be refrigerated. Ripe pears will keep in the refrigerator, sealed in a plastic bag to prevent them from absorbing the odors from other foods, for about five days.

Preparation

If the skin of a pear is thin and smooth, such as that of a Bartlett, it may be left on. The skin of many of the winter pears is too coarse to be edible. Simply remove it with a vegetable peeler. Pears darken (though not as quickly or as extensively as apples) when their flesh is exposed to air. Brush cut surfaces with lemon juice to prevent discoloration. Pears can be left whole with the stem on for many preparations. Just as frequently they are cut into quarters lengthwise, the core sliced from each section with a small paring knife, and the stem removed.

Cooking

When they are to be cooked, all pears, regardless of type, should be slightly underripe. The heating process will soften the texture sufficiently. Pears that are thoroughly ripe to begin with may well disintegrate during cooking. Jane Grigson, in her fine cookbook, *Jane Grigson's Fruit Book,* is of the opinion that cooked pears, because of their delicate flavor, always need help from another fruit, if only fresh lemon juice or zest. I agree with this, except when the pears are caramelized, which in itself adds a great deal of flavor. Pears should not be overwhelmed with too assertive a secondary ingredient if you want the delicate pear flavor to come through. I am of the opinion that chocolate and pears should never meet on the same plate. Not because the combination is unpleas-

ant but because you just cannot taste the nuances of the pear when chocolate is present. So much for the classic French dessert, *Poires Hélène*.

Flavors that are particularly harmonious with the delicate, sweet acidity of pears are anise, black pepper, cardamom, vanilla, cloves, cinnamon, allspice, mint, lemon, orange, toasted hazelnuts, raisins, blue cheese, butter, cream, caramel, fresh and preserved ginger, watercress and other peppery greens, and in moderation, apricots, peaches, and raspberries.

One of the most dramatic ways to alter and add dimension to the basic flavor of the pear is to poach it in either a simple syrup flavored with spices or in sweetened white or red wine. Heightened in this way, pears can stand up to more assertive accompaniments and flavorings.

VARIETIES OF NORTHWEST PEARS

A few of the more commonly available types include:

Bartlett

The Bartlett is a bell-shaped summer pear that ripens in late July and continues to be available throughout December. Bartletts turn from green to yellow (sometimes with a crimson blush) as they ripen. This is due to the disappearance of chlorophyll during the ripening process. The flesh is white, smooth, and juicy, with excellent flavor. Bartletts are prized as canning pears and are excellent all-purpose pears. They are good for eating fresh and for cooking.

Red Bartlett

The Red Bartlett has the same general characteristics as the regular Bartlett pear, with a gorgeous dark red skin that turns to crimson as it ripens. The supply is somewhat limited. They are generally available from August to October only.

Anjou

A winter pear, available from October through May, the Anjou or D'Anjou as it is often called, may be light green or yellow-green and still be in any stage of maturity from hard to ripe and ready to eat. This pear is almost egg-shaped with little neck or shoulder definition; it has a short stem. It is thin-skinned, with smooth-textured white flesh. When ripe, its flavor is sweet and spicy and its flesh is very juicy. The Anjou is the most abundant of all fresh pear varieties and is excellent for eating fresh and for cooking.

Bosc

This winter pear, available from September through May, is easy to recognize with its long tapering neck and slim stem. A ripe Bosc has golden brown skin with a network of russeting

over golden yellow. The flesh is tender, buttery, and aromatic. An excellent pear for baking, broiling, and poaching, it is also a great eating pear. It is best peeled as the skin tends to be tough.

Comice

A winter pear, available from October through March, the Comice will sometimes turn from green to greenish yellow and exhibit a crimson blush on its cheek as it ripens, though the pressure test is a more reliable method for determining ripeness. The Comice has a chubby shape with a short, defined neck and a short stem. These pears are very sweet and juicy and are best for eating fresh as they disintegrate too easily with cooking.

Winter Nelis

The Winter Nelis is available from October through April. It is a medium to small pear with light brown russeting over a light green skin that becomes more golden when ripe. Its shape is fairly rounded with almost no neck definition. The creamy, sweet flesh is good for cooking and canning.

Forelle

The Forelle is a small winter pear, available from October through February, that is somewhat larger than the Seckel. In shape it is more elongated, often with a fairly definite shoulder, and an overall bell-like appearance. It is a very attractive, highly colored pear. As it ripens, the Forelle turns a golden yellow with brilliant red contrasting blush and pronounced freckles on its tender skin. The flesh is sweet and juicy.

Seckel

A winter pear, available from August to January, the Seckel is the smallest of all the pears. Often bite-sized, it may be green with a substantial dark red blush or nearly all red. In the ripening process the red becomes brighter and the green takes on a yellow hue. The flesh is a warm light ivory. Excellent for eating fresh, this pear is also fine for cooking.

Pear Recipes

Caramelized Pear and Anise Tart, *page 336*
Pear and Ginger Tart, *page 338*
Poached Pears and Sabayon with Toasted Walnuts, *page 335*
Boned, Stuffed Duck with Prunes and Seckel Pears, *page 230*
Butterflied Roast Quail with Gingered Pear and Cranberry Sauce, *page 228*
Noisettes of Pork with Pears and Crème Fraîche, *page 319*

Hazelnuts

According to ancient Chinese legend, hazelnuts were among the five sacred foods bestowed upon mankind by God. Anyone tasting a freshly toasted hazelnut will attest to the wisdom of the ancient Chinese (and God, for that matter). Hazelnuts are truly incomparable in flavor. There is no substitute for them. And I am not alone in my admiration. Some eighteen hundred years ago, Dioscorides was proclaiming their virtues, albeit medicinal. Through the ages, many others have attributed magical healing powers to this lovely nut. For instance, if baldness is a problem, you might try mashing burnt hazelnut shells with suet and rubbing the combination on your head. Or, if you get a cold, you can eat ground hazelnuts with honey or toasted hazelnuts with black pepper. Actually there may well be some truth in these ancient bits of folklore. The modest little hazelnut is very nutritious. A two-ounce serving (about fifty nuts) contributes significantly to the body's daily food requirements, yielding about thirteen percent protein, nineteen percent thiamin, eleven percent iron, seven percent niacin, and seven percent riboflavin, along with appreciable amounts of vitamin C and calcium. Not bad for a handful of nuts. But watch out if you are dieting. That same handful will set you back nearly four hundred calories. A momentary lapse while munching and you have just eaten an entire day's calorie allotment.

The mild weather and the rich soil of the Northwest combine to produce perfect growing conditions for hazelnuts. Washington and Oregon together produce nearly all of the nation's commercial crop. Oregon's Willamette Valley accounts for ninety-eight percent with Washington making up the other 2 percent. The annual crop is somewhere in the neighborhood of twenty thousand tons, nearly half of which is sold in the shell. Compared to world production, this seemingly enormous amount is paltry. Turkey, Italy, and Spain (in that order) lead the world in the production of hazelnuts. The United States comes in fourth with only 3 percent of the world crop. But considering that the first American hazelnut tree was not planted until 1858, we are doing surprisingly well. We now have more trees (the rest of the world grows hazelnuts on bushes, the only difference being in the way the tree or bush is pruned) than ever before and more plantings are planned for the future.

Nomenclature

Hazelnuts and filberts are the same nut, the filbert being a somewhat improved variety of the Old World hazelnut. The Oregon Filbert commission is leaning toward the adoption of the word *hazelnut* because the rest of the world uses it and because it produces a lot of confusion in the mind of the consumer when the two names are used interchangeably.

Season

Fresh in-the-shell hazelnuts arrive in October, but they are available shelled year-round.

Selection

Hazelnuts should be uniformly clean, but other than that it is difficult to tell what is in the shell without cracking it and tasting. Usually, the quality is high. Know your source and purchase fresh crop nuts whenever possible.

Storage

Hazelnuts will keep for two years if packaged in sealed plastic containers (or burlap bags if a relative humidity of between sixty and sixty-five percent is maintained) and stored at between 32 degrees and 35 degrees Fahrenheit. They should be stored away from odor-producing materials. Heeding the same precautions, at temperatures not exceeding 70 degrees, the nuts will keep for up to fourteen months. If frozen in plastic containers, they can be stored satisfactorily for two years. Allow the nuts to warm in closed plastic bags or in a well ventilated area if plastic bags are not used, to prevent their turning moldy and rancid.

Preparation

Most commercially processed hazelnuts are already dried. Those purchased at roadside stands and small farms may need to be hung in a mesh bag near a heat source to dry properly. Open a few each day to see how they taste. When they are creamy all the way through and somewhat crisp, remove them from the warm area and store. Improperly dried nuts turn rancid and moldy rapidly.

To toast hazelnuts, shell them and arrange them on a shallow pan without overcrowding. Bake in a 275° oven for 20 to 30 minutes, until the skins crack. To remove the skin, rub nuts together with your hands while still warm or rub them against a rough cloth. The tough part of the skins will easily come off. Do not worry about what remains; there is always some skin left on the nuts.

Cooking

Any recipe specifying any nut whatsoever will probably benefit from the substitution of hazelnuts. (You know by now that I am prejudiced.) Remember when using hazelnuts that they have an assertive, distinctive flavor that can overwhelm other ingredients. Be judicious. Frangelico, a hazelnut liqueur, is lovely used with this nut.

Raw hazelnuts and toasted hazelnuts are two different ingredients. Use the first when a mild, unprepossessing flavor is called for; the latter when you want the dish to have a pronounced flavor.

Hazelnuts have a natural affinity for so many other good things, including goat cheese, mild and bitter greens, apples, pears, poultry, caramel, and chocolate.

Hazelnut Recipes

Mahogany Chicken Wings

Serves 6 to 8.

This easy appetizer is always a success. The sectioned wings come out with a glossy glaze of rich mahogany. The flavor is so addictive that I seldom make just one batch. There is enough marinade for a double quantity of wings if you do some turning and coating while marinating.

    20 chicken wings
     1 cup orange juice
     1 cup soy sauce
     1 cup water
     1 cup brown sugar
       Zest of 2 oranges, minced
     4 cloves garlic, minced
     1 quarter-sized piece fresh ginger,
         minced (to equal about 1 teaspoon
         minced)

GARNISH
     2 orange slices
     1 green onion

Cut each chicken wing into three pieces at the flexible joints. Reserve the wing tips for the stockpot.

Combine the orange juice, soy sauce, water, brown sugar, orange zest, garlic, and ginger in a large bowl. Stir to dissolve the sugar. Add the 40 wing pieces and stir to coat them with marinade. Cover with plastic wrap and refrigerate overnight, turning the wings once or twice to make sure that the marinade coating is even.

Remove the wings from the marinade and arrange them on well-oiled baking sheets. (The marinade may be reserved in the refrigerator or freezer for use again.) Bake at 375° for 45 to 60 minutes, turning the wings half way through the cooking time, until they are glossy and look a little sticky. If there is still liquid on the baking pan, keep baking a bit to evaporate it.

Mound the wings on a serving platter and garnish with a slice or two of orange, and a green onion. Provide plenty of napkins. This is good hot or at room temperature.

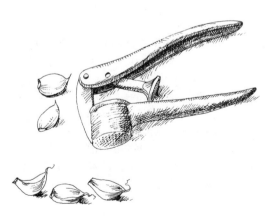

Spicy Fried Shrimp with Herbed Cucumber and Yogurt Sauce

Serves 4 to 6.

This Indian-style appetizer with its creamy dipping sauce is a far cry from the usual batter-fried shrimp with cocktail sauce. I discovered wheat germ as a coating some years ago and continue to appreciate its crunchy nuttiness on all kinds of sautéed and deep-fried foods. The two jalapeño chili peppers make a fairly spicy marinade. You can reduce the quantity if you like, although the dip adds enough of a cooling element for most palates.

1½ pounds medium-sized shrimp, shelled, deveined, and with the tails left on
4 cloves garlic, minced
2 quarter-sized pieces fresh ginger
1 medium onion, peeled, cored, and roughly chopped
2 jalapeño peppers, halved lengthwise and seeded (leave ribs in for heat)
4 tablespoons cilantro
4 tablespoons lemon juice
1 teaspoon *garam masala* (page 358)
2 teaspoons coarse salt
1 cup flour
3 eggs, beaten
2 cups raw wheat germ, salted to taste
Oil for deep-frying

CUCUMBER AND YOGURT SAUCE
2 cups good quality yogurt
1 medium cucumber, peeled, seeded, coarsely shredded, and squeezed dry
1 clove garlic, minced
4 teaspoons lemon juice
2 tablespoons minced cilantro
2 tablespoons minced fresh mint
1 teaspoon coarse salt

After deveining the shrimp down their backs, increase the depth of the incision, cutting to within ¼ inch of the inner curved edge. Spread the shrimp out butterfly fashion and flatten them slightly with the back of a heavy French knife.

In a processor, process the garlic, ginger, onion, peppers, cilantro, lemon juice, *garam masala,* and salt together to a purée. Spread the purée on both sides of the shrimp, put them into a glass baking dish, cover, and refrigerate for at least 4 hours and preferably overnight.

To make the Cucumber and Yogurt Sauce, cut a square of professional-quality (tightly woven) cheesecloth large enough to line and slightly overlap a sieve. Rinse it, wring dry, and smooth it into the sieve. Spoon the yogurt into the cheesecloth and leave it to drain for about 1 hour. Put the drained yogurt into a mixing bowl and add the shredded cucumber, garlic, lemon juice, cilantro, mint, and salt to taste. Set aside.

Pat the shrimp dry with paper towels but do not remove any of the purée. Salt both sides

of the shrimp lightly. Dust them evenly with a light coating of flour, dip into the beaten egg, then coat evenly with wheat germ. Put the shrimp on a wire rack to dry the coating; this will take about 1 hour. (May be made ahead to this point.)

When you are ready to eat, heat the oil in a deep saucepan or deep-fat fryer to 375°. Cook the shrimp, a few at a time, being careful not to decrease (or increase) the oil temperature. As they brown, remove them and drain on paper towels. Keep warm while frying the remainder.

Center a bowl of sauce on a large round platter and surround with shrimp. Serve immediately.

Cold-Smoked Fish with Lime and Caper Vinaigrette

Serves 6.

You might want to check the Smoked Fish primer (page 278) before running out to buy your fish. It is important for this recipe to get cold-smoked or nova-style fish with their meltingly tender texture rather than the drier textured hot-smoked fish. It is quite a treat to have all three of these delicacies together on one plate, but the recipe may be made with only one of the types.

6 thin slices cold-smoked salmon
6 thin slices cold-smoked black cod
6 thin slices cold-smoked sturgeon

LIME AND CAPER VINAIGRETTE
  2 teaspoons small capers
  ¼ cup fresh lime juice
  2 teaspoons fresh minced dill
    Pinch sugar
    Coarse salt
  ¼ cup cold-pressed olive oil

GARNISH
    Freshly ground black pepper
    Small rounds of toasted pumpernickel bread
    Individual crocks of unsalted butter

Lay the slices of smoked fish out in a single layer in 1 or 2 glass baking dishes.

Make the vinaigrette by combining the capers, lime juice, dill, sugar, and salt to taste in a small bowl. Whisk to dissolve both the sugar and salt, then whisk in the olive oil to emulsify.

Drizzle the fish with the vinaigrette and marinate, covered, for an hour or so at room temperature. When ready to serve, ruffle 1 slice of each of the 3 fish onto 6 individual serving plates. Arrange a crock of butter off-center and group several pieces of toast alongside. Grate black pepper over the fish.

Tillamook Cheddar and Creole Spice Profiteroles

Makes 15 to 20 small puffs.

These small puffs are a zippy, spicy tidbit that can be used as an adjunct to soup or salad, or served as a simple appetizer on their own.

> 4 tablespoons butter
> 2 cloves garlic, minced
> 2 tablespoons minced green onion
> ⅛ teaspoon cayenne pepper
> ⅛ teaspoon white pepper
> ⅛ teaspoon black pepper
> ¼ teaspoon thyme
> ¼ teaspoon oregano
> ½ cup water
> ½ cup flour, sifted
> 3 eggs
> ½ cup grated Tillamook sharp
>   Cheddar (or other good quality
>   Cheddar) cheese, finely
>   shredded

In a small saucepan, melt the butter and slowly cook the garlic, green onion, cayenne, white, and black pepper, thyme, and oregano together for 1 minute without browning. Add the water, stir, bring to a boil, and dump in the flour all at once.

Beat vigorously with a wooden spoon over moderate heat until the mixture is smooth and pulls away from the sides of the pan to form a ball. Continue beating over low heat for 1 to 2 minutes to dry the paste a bit. It should form a cohesive mass and begin to film the bottom and sides of the pan. (If you take this too far, the butter will surface on the paste and the puff will not rise properly. Be careful.) Remove from the heat.

Cool the paste until it reaches a temperature of about 150°. Beat the first two eggs, one at a time, into the paste, thoroughly incorporating each one before adding the next. Beat the remaining egg in a small bowl, then begin adding it to the paste, in increments, until the paste has the right consistency: it should be light enough to drop from a spoon with a little push, yet able to hold a rounded shape. You probably will not need all of the third egg.

Stir in the shredded cheese.

Fill a pastry bag, fitted with a ½-inch round tip, with the *pâté à chou* mixture and pipe the paste onto buttered baking sheets, making small mounds about 1 inch in diameter and ½ inch high. Space the mounds 2 inches apart. Dip a small pastry brush into the remaining beaten egg and flatten each puff very slightly with the side of the brush while glazing it with egg. Be careful not to drip the egg down onto the baking sheet as this will keep the puff from rising properly.

Bake in a 425° oven for 20 minutes. The puffs should double in size, turn golden

brown, and be firm and crusty to the touch. Remove from the oven and slit each puff with the point of a paring knife. Set in the turned-off oven, leaving the door ajar, for 10 minutes to dry out. Serve warm or put on a wire rack to cool. (The cooked puffs may be done ahead, cooled, then frozen. Take them straight from the freezer and warm in a 425° oven for 3 or 4 minutes.)

Julienne of Carrot and Daikon Radish with Lemon Garlic Vinaigrette

Serves 6.

This salad is addictive. Sometimes I make it only with carrots and keep a jar in the refrigerator to snack on. Without the lettuce it holds up well. When you want a more formal salad, the daikon radish adds a nice zip. Jicama can replace the daikon.

8 young sweet carrots, peeled and cut
    into 1½-inch julienne
1 daikon radish, peeled and cut into
    1½-inch julienne
Half a head butter lettuce
Lemon Garlic Vinaigrette (page 359)

Blanch the carrots in boiling water to cover for 1 minute. Drain and refresh them under cold running water. Dry carefully with paper towels.

Combine the carrots and radish together with the vinaigrette and marinate in the refrigerator for at least 2 hours and preferably overnight. Bring to room temperature, arrange on butter lettuce, and drizzle the remaining vinaigrette over.

Mussels in Mustard Mayonnaise with Julienne of Celery Root

Serves 4.

In this interesting two-part salad, mussels are first steamed and combined with a tangy mustard mayonnaise, then celery root (also called celeriac) is julienned and marinated in a vinaigrette. The combination offers a very nice contrast of tastes and textures.

2 pounds Penn Cove mussels,
    cleaned and debearded
1 pound celery root, peeled and
    julienned
1 tablespoon lemon juice

VINAIGRETTE
2 tablespoons wine vinegar
    Coarse Salt
    Freshly ground white pepper
3 tablespoons cold-pressed olive oil
3 tablespoons corn oil

½ cup mayonnaise, preferably
    homemade (page 347), well-
    flavored with Dijon mustard
2 to 3 tablespoons parsley, finely
    chopped

Put the mussels with ½ cup water into a large pot, cover, and steam for 4 minutes, until they have opened. Remove them from the pot and discard the shells. Strain and reserve the broth in a small saucepan.

Toss the celery root, immediately upon cutting it, with the lemon juice.

To make the vinaigrette, combine the vinegar with salt and pepper to taste and whisk in the olive and corn oils. Drain the celery root, pat it dry, and toss with the vinaigrette. Arrange it in a circle on a round serving platter.

Set the reserved mussel broth over high heat and cook until very much reduced and slightly syrupy. Thin the mayonnaise with a little of the reduced broth. Fold enough mayonnaise into the mussels to coat them lightly and arrange them in the center of the circle of celery root. (You may have a little extra mayonnaise.) Sprinkle with chopped parsley and serve.

Cream of Cougar Gold

Serves 4 to 6.

The taste of this soup, with its last-minute fillip of wine, reminds me of liquid fondue. A well-aged cheese is important here because younger cheeses often become stringy or grainy when subjected to this much heat. In any case, once cheese, well-aged or not, has been added never let any dish come to a boil. Cougar Gold is a remarkable cheese produced by Washington State University in eastern Washington. It is flavorful and supremely mellow at the same time. To get its full taste in this soup, we need to use twice as much of it as we would any other well-aged Cheddar.

> 4 cups homemade chicken stock (page 345)
> 1 leek, white and light green part only, minced
> 2 medium stalks celery, minced
> 1 medium onion, minced
> 2 tablespoons cornstarch
> 2 cups shredded Cougar Gold cheese (4 ounces) or 1 cup other well-aged sharp Cheddar cheese
> 1 egg yolk
> ½ cup cream
> 2 tablespoons very dry white wine
> Coarse salt
> Freshly grated black pepper

In a large saucepan bring the stock to a simmer. Add the chopped leek, celery, and onion and simmer gently for 30 minutes. Remove from the heat and strain. Discard the vegetables. Put the stock back into a clean saucepan.

Combine the cornstarch with 2 tablespoons cold water, whisk to smooth, and stir into the soup. Bring to a full boil and cook briefly until thickened. Remove the soup from the heat and stir in the cheese.

Whisk the egg yolk together with the cream. Stir in ½ cup of the hot soup to warm the egg yolks, then transfer them back to the soup pot, whisking briefly. Cook gently for about 2 minutes. Do not let the soup go above 180° and nowhere near a boil. Season to taste with salt. Just before serving, stir in the wine. Grate black pepper on top of each serving.

Cream of Mussel Nectar Soup

Serves 8.

This creamy mussel soup had its origins in Paris, but it could not be more suited to our own Pacific Northwest bivalves. It makes a sublime first course.

> 1 cup chopped onions
> 4 tablespoons chopped shallots
> 4 tablespoons unsalted butter
> 1½ cups dry white wine
> 4 sprigs parsley
> 4 pounds mussels, cleaned
> 2 egg yolks
> 2 cups cream
> 1 teaspoon coarse salt
> Freshly ground black pepper
> 1 tablespoon minced parsley

In a large nonaluminum stockpot, combine the onions, shallots, butter, wine, and sprigs of parsley. Lay the mussels on top, cover tightly, bring to a boil, and steam for about 4 minutes, until the mussels have opened. Discard any that do not open after giving them a few more minutes of cooking time.

Remove the mussels from the shells and discard the shells. Strain the liquid through several layers of cheesecloth, pressing down on the vegetables to extract their flavor. Reserve the liquid in a large saucepan and discard the vegetables.

Bring the mussel liquid to a boil, then remove from the heat. In a small bowl, beat the egg yolks with the cream, stir in a few tablespoons of the hot broth, then blend the egg mixture back into the broth, stirring constantly. Return the soup to the heat and continue stirring until it has thickened slightly, but do not let it rise above 180° or the egg yolks will curdle. Season to taste with salt and pepper.

Remove from the heat, add a couple handfuls of mussels and ladle the soup into bowls. (The remaining mussels can be reserved for another recipe.) Sprinkle with parsley and serve hot with a loaf of crusty French or Italian bread.

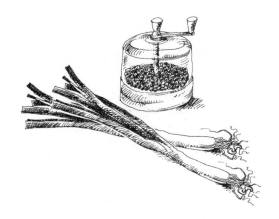

Lentil Soup with Ancho Chili Peppers and Cilantro

Serves 8 to 10.

Dried chili peppers are fun to work with and lend a subtleness of flavor that no chili powder can produce. Dried ancho chilies are easy enough to find nowadays but pure chili powder may also be used. Just be sure to get unadulterated powdered chile ancho, *not the American blends of chili powder because they contain cumin and other spices.*

> 2 dried ancho chili peppers (or 1 tablespoon *chile ancho* powder)
> 4 tablespoons unsalted butter
> 1 large onion, chopped
> 4 cloves garlic, minced
> 1 quarter-sized piece fresh ginger, peeled and minced (1 teaspoon minced)
> 1 tablespoon *garam masala* (page 358)
> 1 pound lentils
> 7 to 8 cups homemade chicken stock (page 345)
> Coarse salt
> 2 tablespoons fresh lemon juice (½ lemon)
> ¼ cup minced cilantro

GARNISH
> Sour cream or crème fraîche (optional)

Prepare the dried chili peppers by boiling them in water to cover for 10 minutes. Remove from the heat, cover, and let them sit for 45 minutes. When softened, scrape the pulp from the skin. Discard the skin and the soaking liquid, both of which may be bitter.

In a soup pot, melt the butter and cook the onion until softened but not browned. Add the garlic, ginger, *garam masala* (and chili powder if using) and cook gently for another minute or two.

Add the lentils, ancho chili paste and stock; stir and partially cover. Simmer slowly for about 35 minutes, stirring occasionally until the lentils are tender but not falling apart.

Season to taste with salt and lemon juice. Just before serving, stir in the cilantro and swirl in the optional sour cream or crème fraîche.

Mussel Bourride

Serves 4.

Bourride *is a Mediterranean fish stew similar to* bouillabaisse. *The difference is that bourride is thickened with aioli before serving and bouillabaisse is left as it is, with a* rouille *(a garlicky red bell*

*pepper and chili pepper mayonnaise) passed along-
side. Both are made with a large, contrasting variety of fish and a hearty broth, and are usually
flavored with fennel, saffron, and orange peel. Because of the expense and time involved, I seldom prepare a true, albeit Northwest, bourride or bouillabaisse. It is a simple matter, though, to use mussels
or clams alone with the classic broth and seasonings.
Here then is a bourride made of mussels and their
liquor served with aioli, and a variation that is a
bouillabaisse served with rouille. The bouillabaisse
is light enough to serve as a first course, the bourride
is really quite rich and is best as a main dish. With
both, serve plenty of toasted French bread that has
been brushed with olive oil in which a clove of garlic
has been pressed.*

    4 tablespoons olive oil
    1 large onion, diced (about 1½ cups)
    4 cloves garlic, crushed and minced
    1 large pinch saffron, crushed
    6 cups fish fumet (page 346), or 4 cups
        clam nectar or juice and 2 cups dry
        white wine
    4 large, ripe tomatoes, peeled and
        seeded, with their juice, or 1 can
        (16 ounces) diced tomatoes with
        juice
    2 tablespoons parsley, finely minced
    1 tablespoon orange zest, finely minced
        (1 whole orange)
    1 tablespoon anise-flavored liqueur
        (Pernod or Anisette)

    4 pounds Penn Cove mussels, cleaned
        and debearded
    Aioli (page 52)
    4 egg yolks

GARNISH
    Parsley, finely minced

Heat the olive oil in a large casserole, preferably of enameled cast-iron, and add the onion,
garlic, and saffron. Cover and cook slowly,
stirring occasionally, until the onion is tender.

Add the fish fumet, tomatoes, parsley, orange zest, and anise-flavored liqueur. Put the
mussels on top, cover, and bring to a simmer.
Cook for 4 minutes and check to see if the
mussels have opened. Remove those that have
with a slotted spoon and keep them warm. If
any mussels remain unopened, replace the
cover and simmer for an additional 1 or 2 minutes. (Those that have not opened by this time
were dead to begin with and should be discarded.) Remove the last of the mussels and
keep them warm with the rest.

Simmer the broth, uncovered, for 15 minutes or so to intensify the flavors and evaporate
the alcohol in the wine.

Just before serving, divide the aioli in half.
Add the egg yolks to 1 portion of the aioli,
then gradually add some of the hot broth, stirring constantly. Pour this mixture back into
the soup pot and heat slowly until thickened
slightly. (Do not bring the broth to a simmer

or the egg yolks will curdle, leaving an unpleasant gritty texture.) Season to taste with salt and pepper.

Fill individual bowls with the mussels (still in their shells) and ladle the hot broth over them. Garnish with a sprinkling of parsley and serve hot with the remaining aioli on the side.

VARIATION

Mussel Bouillabaisse
Proceed exactly as prescribed above but do not thicken the broth with aioli. Ladle the hot broth over the mussels and serve with Rouille (page 349) on the side.

Mussel and Saffron Bisque

Serves 4 to 6.

Saffron has a wonderful affinity for mussels. This creamy bisque makes an elegant first course.

  4 tablespoons unsalted butter
  1 large onion, minced
  2 large shallots, minced
  1 large carrot, minced
  4 cloves garlic, minced
  ½ teaspoon thyme

  ½ teaspoon saffron
  2½ pounds Penn Cove mussels, cleaned and debearded
  1 cup dry white wine
  2 pounds tomatoes, peeled, seeded, and chopped (with their juice)
  ½ cup cream
    Coarse salt
    Freshly ground black pepper
    Fresh lemon juice

In a stockpot, melt the butter and add the onion, shallots, carrot, garlic, thyme, and saffron. "Sweat" over low heat until the vegetables are softened, about 20 minutes.

Add the mussels and white wine, cover, and steam for about 4 minutes, until most of the mussel shells have opened. Discard those that will not open even after a minute or two of extra cooking time. Remove the mussels from the pot and separate them from their shells, being sure to return any liquid to the pot. Reserve the mussels.

Add the tomatoes to the stockpot and cook for 20 minutes or so, until the flavors have melded and the vegetables are tender. Taste the broth for strength and reduce it further if necessary.

Add the cream and mussels and season to taste with salt and pepper and drops of lemon juice. Heat through and serve.

Curried Red Lentil and Tomato Soup

Serves 8 to 10.

Red lentils are wonderful legumes. They look as good as they taste, which is something of a feat for a member of the legume family. This is a fine supper soup. From start to finish it takes just over an hour to prepare—and for most of that time it simmers quietly on its own. For extra protein, top each serving with a dollop of yogurt or sour cream.

2 tablespoons unsalted butter
2 large onions, chopped
4 cloves garlic, minced
1½ teaspoons *garam masala* or more, to taste (page 358)
1 teaspoon ground coriander
3 jalapeño chili peppers, halved, cored, seeded, and minced
1 pound red lentils, rinsed and checked for extraneous material
1 can (28 ounces) diced tomatoes with juice (or the equivalent of peeled fresh tomatoes in season)
8 cups homemade chicken stock (page 345)
6 tablespoons lemon juice
Coarse salt
Freshly ground black pepper

GARNISH
Yogurt or sour cream (optional)

In a soup pot, melt the butter and cook the onions until softened but not browned. Add the garlic, *garam masala,* coriander, and chili peppers and cook gently for another minute or two.

Add the lentils, tomatoes, and stock. Stir and bring to a simmer. Simmer slowly, partially covered, for about 30 minutes, stirring occasionally, until the lentils are tender but not falling apart.

Add the lemon juice and season to taste with salt and pepper.

Steamed Mussels with Fennel Beurre Blanc

Serves 8 as a first course or 4 as a main dish.

Fennel seeds with their taste of anise are a subtle and surprising complement to the deep, briny flavor of mussels. Designed as a first course, this dish may also be served in somewhat larger portions as a main dish.

3 pounds Washington blue mussels,
    cleaned and debearded
1 small onion, minced
2 shallots, minced
1 garlic clove, minced
1 pinch fennel seeds (about 12),
    crushed in a mortar and pestle
1½ cups dry white wine

BEURRE BLANC
3 tablespoons brandy or cognac
1 cup unsalted butter, cut into 16
    pieces
Coarse salt
Freshly ground black pepper

Put the mussels in a large stockpot with the onion, shallots, garlic, and fennel seeds. Add the wine, cover the pot and bring to a simmer. Cook for about 4 minutes, or just until the mussels have opened. Remove the mussels from the pan, cover, and keep warm. Strain the broth through a layer of tightly woven professional-quality cheesecloth into a clean saucepan and reduce over medium-high heat until only 4 tablespoons remain.

Arrange the mussels, still in their shells, on a large serving platter or on individual serving dishes. Cover with foil and keep warm in a 200° oven.

To make the *Beurre Blanc*, heat the brandy in a small pan and ignite with a long-handled match. Once the flames have subsided pour into the reduced stock. Reduce the stock by another tablespoon or so. Lower the heat or remove from the heat altogether. Add the pieces of butter all at once to the stock, stirring slowly with a wooden spoon. Do not let the sauce come anywhere near a boil. Too much heat will separate the emulsion. Season to taste with salt and pepper.

The sauce may be kept, in a warmed Thermos, for five hours or so without separating. The mussels, of course, cannot be kept warm that long, but you might choose to make an additional batch in the morning to get the necessary stock and then chill these for use another day with a tangy vinaigrette. Mussels can also be gently reheated with steam for a minute or two.

Mussels in Lemon Butter Sauce

Serves 4.

The sauce that accompanies these mussels is a modified beurre blanc. *There is a lot more liquid in the initial reduction than would be used in a standard* beurre blanc *and a lot less butter is added at the end. The result is a lightly thickened sauce with considerably fewer calories. This sauce, like its parent, lends itself to numerous variations.*

3 pounds Washington blue mussels,
    cleaned and debearded
1 onion, chopped
1 clove garlic, minced
2 shallots, chopped
½ cup minced parsley
    Freshly ground black pepper
10 tablespoons unsalted butter
1½ cups dry white wine
3 tablespoons fresh lemon juice
    Coarse salt
    Freshly grated black pepper

Put the mussels into a large stockpot with the onion, garlic, shallots, parsley, pepper, and 7 tablespoons of the butter. Add the wine, cover the pot, and steam for about 4 minutes, until most of the mussels have opened. Remove those that have opened and steam the rest for a few minutes longer. Discard any that do not open after this additional time. Transfer the mussels to a serving bowl, cover with foil, and keep them warm.

Strain the liquid into a small saucepan. Over high heat, reduce the liquid to one-third its original volume. Off the heat, whisk in the remaining 3 tablespoons butter, in chunks, and keep whisking until the butter disappears into the sauce. Whisk in the lemon juice, season to taste with salt and pepper, and pour the sauce over the mussels.

VARIATIONS

Basil
Add ½ cup shredded basil to the sauce with the lemon juice.

Cilantro
Add ¼ cup chopped cilantro leaves to the sauce and use lime juice rather than lemon juice.

Mint
Add ½ cup shredded mint leaves to the sauce along with the lemon juice.

Riesling
Use a Northwest riesling for the wine.

Apple Cider

Use a dry (alcoholic) apple cider in place of the wine.

Pernod

Add a splash of Pernod to the sauce as it is reducing.

Orange

Add the zest of 1 orange to the stock pot when cooking the mussels and substitute ½ cup orange juice for ½ cup of the wine.

Fillet of Rockfish Niçoise

Serves 4.

The sauce for this dish is bright and forthright. Other fish may also be used. Try fresh flounder or sole, halibut, or even swordfish. Everything may be done ahead and arranged in a casserole so this is an easy dish for entertaining. Bake it just before serving.

> 4 tablespoons olive oil
> 2 onions, chopped
> 2 cloves garlic, minced
> 1 teaspoon dried thyme
> 1 14½ ounce can diced tomatoes in juice
> ¼ cup dry white wine
> 1 tablespoon tomato paste
> Salt and pepper
> 4 rockfish fillets, ½ inch thick
> ¼ cup calamata olives, pitted and quartered

Heat 2 tablespoons of the olive oil and sauté the onions until well-softened but not browned, about 20 minutes. Arrange the onions on the bottom of a 9- by 12-inch oval baking dish.

To make the sauce, heat the remaining 2 tablespoons olive oil, and gently sauté the garlic and thyme for a minute or so without browning. Add the tomatoes, wine, and tomato paste and simmer until nicely thickened. Season to taste with salt and pepper.

Season the fillets with salt and pepper on both sides and lay them on top of the bed of onions. Spoon the sauce over the top, sprinkle with the olives, and bake at 375° for about 15 to 20 minutes, until the fish just barely flakes with a fork. (If the fish is thinner than ½ an inch, the cooking time must, of course, be shortened accordingly.)

Stir-Fried Chicken on Exploded Rice Noodles

Serves 4 as a main dish.

The preparation here takes some time, but once every-thing has been cut, marinaded, and assembled, the cooking is easy. Make sure that all the cutting, mincing, and other preparation that is indicated with each ingredient is completed before you begin to cook. Gather all the ingredients together, and have at hand a large sauté pan, a skimmer spoon, a fine strainer, paper towels, pot holders, a large serving platter, a long-handled curved spatula, cooking chopsticks, and several small bowls. Once you begin to stir-fry, there is no stopping to look for some miss-ing item.

The velveting process may be new to you; it is what makes the meat so succulent and tender in the best Chinese restaurants. Without it the chicken strips would contract and toughen as soon as they hit the skillet.

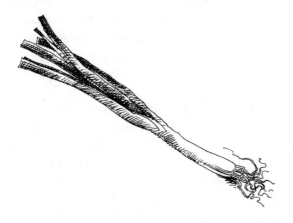

Woks were never engineered to work properly on American stove tops. A large, heavy sauté pan is better for stir-frying. Your wok will be very useful for deep-frying the noodle nest and blanching the chicken. Be sure to stabilize it by using the bottom ring.

This dish is hot in the Szechuan style; the red pepper can be moderated if desired.

1 pound boneless, skinned chicken breast, cut against the grain into ¼-inch slices, then cut into ¼-inch matchsticks.

VELVETING MARINADE

2 quarter-sized pieces of fresh ginger, flattened with the broad side of a French knife
1 egg white, lightly beaten
1 tablespoon rice wine or dry sherry
2 teaspoons cornstarch
1 teaspoon coarse salt
4 dried Chinese black mushrooms

SAUCE

½ cup chicken stock
2 tablespoons soy sauce
2 tablespoons rice wine or dry sherry
2 teaspoons sugar
1½ teaspoons coarse salt
2 teaspoons sesame oil
2 teaspoons cornstarch
1 tablespoon cold chicken stock
1 ounce rice sticks
4 cups corn or peanut oil

AROMATICS

    2 cloves garlic, peeled and minced
    6 paper-thin slices peeled fresh
        ginger, finely julienned
    1 teaspoon crushed red pepper
    1 green onion, cut on the long, thin
        diagonal into 2-inch lengths

    3 tablespoons good quality ham or
        prosciutto, julienned into 2-inch
        lengths
    2 large carrots, julienned into 2-inch
        lengths
    1 small green pepper, cored and cut
        into ¼- by 2-inch julienne
    1 cup blanched slivered almonds,
        toasted

To make the marinade, combine the ingredients and toss them well with the shredded chicken. Let rest for at least 30 minutes at room temperature or longer under refrigeration.

Soak the dried mushrooms in hot water to cover for 15 minutes, or until they are soft and spongy. Drain, remove and discard the stems, and cut the caps into ¼-inch shreds. Set aside.

Combine ingredients for the sauce and set aside.

Mix together the cornstarch and chicken stock in a small bowl. Leave a spoon in the bowl.

To make a noodle nest, place the bundle of rice sticks in a large paper bag, cut it in half through the looped ends of the skein, and pull apart the strands. Set aside on a plate. Heat 4 cups corn oil in a wok to precisely 375° and add the noodles. Fry them, turning once, for just a few seconds, or until they are puffed. Push them gently down into the oil if you can see noodles that have not expanded. Remove from the oil with two skimmer spoons and set on paper towels to drain. Once drained, arrange on an attractive serving platter.

To oil-blanch the chicken, reduce the heat under the wok and the oil temperature to 275° precisely. Remove and discard the ginger slices from the velveting marinade, stir the chicken shreds to separate them and add them to the hot oil. Stir slowly with chopsticks to keep the shreds separated. Cook for only 40 seconds, until the pieces turn white but are not cooked all the way through. Pour the oil and chicken into a fine strainer set over a metal bowl. Set the velveted chicken on a plate and reserve the oil for the stir-fry. (What oil you do not use here may be strained, decanted, and saved for another use.) Wipe the wok clean with paper towels.

To assemble the dish, heat a large sauté pan until very hot, then add 2 to 3 tablespoons of the reserved oil to it, swirling to coat the lower sides. Heat until the oil will evaporate a bead of water on contact, then turn the heat down slightly so that the oil will not burn the aromatics. Add the aromatics, that is, the garlic, ginger, crushed red pepper, and green onion to the pan and stir-fry for 15 seconds, until fragrant.

Add the mushrooms and ham and stir-fry for 30 seconds. Then add the carrots and green

pepper and stir-fry for 5 seconds more, just to coat the vegetables with oil.

Add the combined sauce ingredients and the chicken, cover the wok and steam for 1 minute longer, until the sauce comes to a simmer.

Stir the cornstarch mixture again, tip the sauce to one side of the pan, and add the cornstarch mixture. Stir and make sure that the sauce boils to activate the cornstarch. Add the almonds. Toss the contents of the pan with the sauce to coat each piece and turn out on top of the noodle nest.

Honey-Glazed Sausages with Lentils and Orange-Cilantro Butter

Serves 8.

This is real food, the kind you yearn for after eating too much haute cuisine. *There is absolutely nothing prissy about it; the taste is substantial and satisfying. I like to arrange the lentils and sausages in individual gratin dishes, place these on dinner plates, and serve salads of radicchio and butter lettuce with a tangy vinaigrette alongside. Cranberry Cornmeal Muffins (page 250) are perfect accompaniments, as is a hearty California zinfandel.*

Do not be tempted, as I have on occasion, to use red lentils here. They do not hold their shape well enough.

1 pound brown lentils, well rinsed
1 medium-sized onion, skinned and halved
2 bay leaves
½ teaspoon thyme
4 cups homemade chicken stock (page 345)
½ cup water
1 tablespoon unsalted butter
1 tablespoon corn oil
2 medium-sized onions, finely diced
1 teaspoon dried thyme
1 teaspoon dried oregano
1 pound diced canned tomatoes with juice (or fresh tomatoes if they are ripe and flavorful)
4 large cloves garlic, peeled and pressed or minced
½ cup cream
Coarse salt
Freshly ground black pepper
2 tablespoons corn oil
16 Italian sausages, mild or hot
1 cup fruity dry red wine (such as California zinfandel)
1 teaspoon fragrant honey (in the Northwest, snoberry or pear blossom honey are good)

ORANGE-CILANTRO SAUCE
Grated zest of 1 orange
2 sprigs cilantro, or to taste
2 cloves garlic, peeled
½ cup unsalted butter
A few drops Tabasco sauce
Coarse salt

GARNISH
Cilantro sprigs

Put the lentils, onion halves, bay leaf, thyme, chicken stock, and water in a large saucepan and bring to a simmer. Cook gently, covered, for about 15 minutes, until the lentils are half tender.

Melt the butter and oil, add the diced onions, thyme, and oregano and "sweat" over medium-low heat until tender, stirring occasionally. Add the tomatoes with their juice and the garlic. Simmer, uncovered, until most of the liquid has evaporated.

Remove the onion and bay leaves from the lentils and drain any liquid that remains. Add the lentils to the onion and tomato mixture, along with the cream, and stir gently to combine. Simmer, covered, for about 20 minutes, until the lentils are completely tender but not mushy. If the mixture seems too wet, cook it uncovered for part or all of the time. Be careful about scorching the bottom though. Adjust the seasoning with salt and pepper. Keep warm while preparing the sausages.

Heat the oil in a large skillet and add the sausages. (After some experimentation, I no longer prick the sausages. They are not usually overly fatty to begin with and keeping them tightly closed keeps in the juices. Pricked, they have a tendency to become tough.) Roll to coat with the oil, then cook over medium heat, turning occasionally until well browned on all sides, about 10 minutes. Pour off the oil and accumulated fat and add the wine and honey to the skillet. Stir, cover, and cook for 10 minutes more. Uncover and turn up the heat to reduce the liquid to a syrup. It should coat the sausages nicely.

While the sausages are cooking, mince the orange zest, cilantro, and garlic in a processor. Add the butter, blend well, then season to taste with Tabasco and salt. Remove from the processor, shape into a log, and refrigerate unless you are going to be using it within 2 hours. If refrigerated, bring to room temperature before using.

Portion the lentils into 8 individual-sized gratin dishes and place 2 or 3 sausages on top of each. Top each serving of sausages with 1 tablespoon of softened Orange-Cilantro Butter. Garnish each dish with a small sprig of cilantro.

Chicken Thighs Sautéed with Savory Herbs and Garlic

Serves 4 to 6.

This recipe illustrates the ease and richness possible from a simple reduction sauce enriched with just an egg yolk and cream. For a change of flavor, tarragon may be substituted for the thyme, basil, and fennel combination.

> 4 tablespoons clarified unsalted butter (or 2 tablespoons unsalted butter and 2 tablespoons corn oil)
> 8 to 12 chicken thighs
> 1½ teaspoons dried thyme
> ½ teaspoon dried basil
> ¼ teaspoon ground fennel
> Coarse salt
> Freshly ground white pepper
> 4 cloves garlic, peeled and minced
> ½ cup dry white wine
> 1 egg yolk
> ¼ cup cream
> 1 tablespoon lemon juice
> 2 tablespoons butter
> 1 tablespoon fresh parsley, finely minced

Dry the chicken pieces off carefully. Heat the butter in a skillet until it foams, then add the chicken pieces making sure not to overcrowd them. There should still be space visible between each piece. Crush the herbs by rubbing them through your hands and sprinkle on the chicken. Season liberally with salt and pepper.

Turn the chicken thighs as they brown to color them evenly. This should take about 10 minutes. When the chicken is nice and brown, add the minced garlic, cover the skillet, lower the heat, and cook slowly for another 20 minutes, or until the juices of the meat run clear when tested with a knife tip.

Remove the chicken to a heated serving platter and keep warm. Raise the heat under the skillet, add the wine, and reduce by half.

Combine the egg yolk and cream and whisk them together until thick. Beat in a little of the liquid from the skillet, drop by drop, to raise the temperature of the egg yolk, then whisk the mixture back into the skillet juices, making sure that the skillet is not too hot and that the sauce does not come back to a simmer. Season with salt, pepper, and drops of lemon juice. Finish by swirling in the remaining butter.

Nap the chicken with the sauce, sprinkle on the parsley, and serve.

Walnut-Breaded Chicken Suprêmes with Mustard Sauce

Serves 4 to 8.

Chicken suprêmes (individual halves of a whole breast section) are the quintessential fast food. They cook in less than 7 minutes and take to a wide variety of sauces and accompaniments. This rendition is also good served at room temperature with a mustard-flavored mayonnaise—great picnic food.

MUSTARD SAUCE
  ½ cup dry white wine
  ½ cup chicken stock
  1 cup cream
  3 tablespoons Dijon mustard
    Coarse salt
    Freshly ground black pepper
    Lemon juice

  8 chicken breast suprêmes (4 whole
    chicken breasts, boned, skinned,
    and separated)
    Coarse salt
    Freshly ground black pepper
    Flour for dredging
  1 cup fine dry bread crumbs
  1 cup minced walnuts
  2 eggs, beaten
  2 tablespoons unsalted butter
  2 tablespoons corn oil

The sauce may be made ahead. Combine the wine and chicken stock in a small saucepan and reduce to a syrup, about 2 tablespoons. Add the cream and simmer briefly until it is thick enough to coat a spoon lightly. Whisk in the mustard, not letting the sauce boil again after this point, and season to taste with salt, pepper, and lemon juice. Keep warm while cooking the suprêmes.

Remove the white tendon from each suprême. Flatten the suprêmes slightly between sheets of wax paper to even out the thickness. Season both sides with salt and pepper, then dredge in flour, shaking and slapping off the excess.

Combine the bread crumbs and walnuts. Dip each suprême into the beaten egg, then dredge the suprêmes evenly with the walnut mixture. Let them dry on a wire rack for at least 30 minutes to set the coating. (Refrigeration is fine for longer periods of time.)

Heat the butter and oil in a large sauté pan and arrange the suprêmes without overcrowding them. Sauté at moderate heat for about 3 minutes per side. The heat should be lively enough to brown each side nicely in this amount of time.

Arrange 1 or 2 suprêmes per serving and nap with sauce.

Braised Chicken with Hazelnuts and Prunes

Serves 4.

This dish is a hybrid inspired by the cuisine of the Caribbean Islands and is an amalgam of Spanish, African, Indian, and aboriginal influences with a Northwest interpretation. The ground nuts in the sauce give it body and an irresistible flavor.

3 tablespoons olive oil
1 broiler-fryer chicken (3½ pounds)
    Coarse salt and freshly ground black
    pepper
1 onion, minced
3 cloves garlic, minced
1 small green bell pepper, cored,
    seeded, and diced
1 small red bell pepper, cored, seeded,
    and diced
1 can (16 ounces) Italian plum
    tomatoes, chopped
½ cup dry white wine
¼ teaspoon ground cumin
½ teaspoon oregano
2 tablespoons hazelnuts, lightly
    toasted, skinned, and chopped
¼ cup Oregon prunes, pitted, halved,
    and cut into slivers
¼ cup green olives, pitted, halved, and
    cut into slivers
2 tablespoons capers, drained
1 cup chicken stock

GARNISH
1 tablespoon chopped hazelnuts

Cut the chicken into 8 or 10 serving pieces (the neck, wingtips, back, and innards may be reserved for the stockpot) and dry the pieces thoroughly. Heat the oil and add the chicken pieces. Sprinkle with salt and pepper and continue to cook until well browned on the first side. Turn the pieces with tongs, season the browned side with salt and pepper, and cook for about 5 or 6 minutes longer to color the second side nicely. Pieces such as the drumstick will need to be rotated a quarter turn at a time to brown the entire surface area. Transfer the chicken to a plate.

Drain off all but 3 tablespoons of oil, and in it sauté the onion and garlic until softened but not browned. Add half of the red and green bell peppers and cook for a minute longer. Add the tomatoes and simmer, stirring, until most of the liquid has evaporated.

Add the wine, cumin, and oregano and simmer for an additional few minutes.

Add the chicken back to the pan. In a spice grinder, finely grind 1 tablespoon of the hazelnuts and add them to the chicken along with the chopped hazelnuts, prunes, olives, and capers. Add the chicken stock, stir, coating the chicken well with the sauce, cover, and

simmer gently for 20 to 25 minutes. Remove the chicken breast sections after 10 minutes to prevent them from overcooking, then add them back again during the last 5 minutes to heat through. Also add the remaining red and green bell peppers for the last 5 minutes.

Arrange the chicken on a heated serving platter and keep it warm while checking the sauce for seasoning and consistency. If the sauce is too thin, boil it rapidly to reduce; if too thick, thin with a little more chicken stock. Pour the sauce over the chicken, sprinkle with a few chopped toasted hazelnuts, and serve.

Marinated, Grilled Flank Steak with Red and Green Bell Peppers

(FAJITAS)

Serves 8.

There is probably no Mexican dish that I enjoy more than this straightforward grill with its mixture of sweet and hot peppers and liberal dousing of fresh lime juice. I like to put it on a warm flour tortilla, top it with chunky hot salsa, chopped raw onion, chopped fresh tomato, and a creamy guacamole, then roll it all up to eat. A Margarita is always a good accompaniment. Also, this makes great picnic or

barbecue fare for a large gathering of friends. The guests put together their own Mexican sandwich hot off the grill. All you do is slice the meat. For tips on grilling, see page 363. If grilling is not feasible, the steak may be broiled.

MARINADE

    4 cloves garlic, minced
    3 serrano chili peppers, stemmed, halved, seeded, and deribbed (wear gloves)
   ¾ cup fresh lime juice
    1 tablespoon Worcestershire sauce
   ¼ cup corn oil
      Freshly ground black pepper

    1 flank steak (about 2 pounds), trimmed of fat
1½ tablespoons unsalted butter
1½ tablespoons corn oil
    1 large onion, sliced into narrow wedges
    2 red bell peppers, sliced into ¼- by 3-inch strips
    2 green bell peppers, sliced into ¼- by 3-inch strips
     Coarse salt
  16 or more flour tortillas, warmed

Purée the garlic and serrano peppers together in a processor, then add the lime juice, Worcestershire sauce, oil and pepper to taste. Blend everything together well.

Arrange the steak in a shallow baking dish and pour the marinade over. Marinate for 2

hours at room temperature or up to 8 hours in the refrigerator. Turn the steak over halfway through the allotted time. When ready to cook, remove the steak from the marinade. Strain the marinade and reserve.

Prepare the grill, using mesquite charcoal if possible. Pat the steak dry, brush it on both sides with a light coating of corn oil and grill, close to the coals, for about 2 minutes on each side; the outside should be appetizingly charred but the interior should still be rare or medium-rare at the most. (Flank steak cooked beyond this point will be tough no matter how you slice it.)

Heat a heavy cast-iron skillet or griddle and add the butter and oil. Lift the skillet to coat the bottom evenly, then add the onion wedges. Sauté over fairly high heat to brown the onions for a few minutes. Add the red and green peppers. Keep the heat lively enough to char the vegetables without cooking them all the way through. They should still be crisp. Keep warm for a minute while slicing the steak.

Take the steak from the grill, lay it on a cutting board and cut it precisely against the grain into thin (¼-inch) sheets. (Do not cut on the diagonal. This would negate the effect of tenderness to be gained by cutting directly against the grain.)

Raise the heat on the griddle to very hot, toss the steak sheets with the peppers, and pour on 4 to 6 tablespoons of the remaining strained marinade. If the griddle is hot enough it will sizzle dramatically and the marinade should evaporate upon contact. Do not add so much marinade that there is a puddle of liquid left in the pan. Serve at once with warm tortillas and whatever topping condiments you wish.

Marinated, Grilled Flank Steak with Ancho Chili Butter

Serves 8.

This recipe is slightly different from the recipe for Mexican fajitas. The basic marinated, grilled flank steak is presented in a straightforward manner with a toasted chili pepper butter on top. The result is a little more elegant than fajitas yet just as satisfying.

MARINADE

    4 cloves garlic, minced

    3 serrano peppers, stemmed, halved, and seeded (wear gloves)

    ½ cup fresh lime juice

    1 tablespoon Worcestershire sauce

    ¼ cup corn oil

      Freshly ground black pepper

    1 flank steak (about 2 pounds), trimmed of fat

ANCHO CHILI BUTTER

> 3 cloves garlic, unpeeled
> 1 large ancho chili pepper
> 2 or 3 small sprigs fresh cilantro, or to taste
> ½ cup unsalted butter
> Coarse salt

GARNISH

> 8 small red chili peppers (optional)
> Fresh cilantro sprigs (optional)

To make the marinade, purée the garlic and peppers together in a processor, then add the lime juice, Worcestershire sauce, oil, and pepper to taste. Blend everything together well.

Arrange the steak in a shallow baking dish and pour the marinade over it. Marinate for 2 hours at room temperature or up to 8 hours in the refrigerator. Turn the steak over halfway through the allotted time. When ready to cook, remove the steak from the marinade.

To prepare the Ancho Chili Butter, heat a dry sauté pan and add the unpeeled garlic. Toast over moderately high heat for a few minutes until the skin is brown, tossing the cloves in the air to turn them over occasionally. Remove and peel. Add the chili pepper to the hot pan and cook over medium heat until the flesh swells and it gives off a rich aroma. Remove the chili pepper, split it, and take out the seeds and veins (use gloves to do this). Put the pepper in a bowl with enough boiling water to cover for 30 minutes. Remove and pat dry. Purée the chili pepper, garlic, and cilantro in a processor, then add the butter and salt to taste. Blend until a smooth consistency is obtained. Arrange the butter on a sheet of plastic wrap and shape into a log. Refrigerate or place in a zip-lock bag and freeze.

Prepare the grill (page 363), using mesquite charcoal if possible. Pat the steak dry, brush it on both sides with a light coating of corn oil and grill, close to the coals, for about 2 minutes on each side; the outside should be appetizingly charred but the interior should still be rare or medium-rare at the most. (Flank steak cooked beyond this point will be tough no matter how you slice it.)

Take the steak from the grill, let it rest for a few minutes, then cut it precisely against the grain into thin (¼-inch) sheets. (Do not cut on the diagonal. This would negate the effect of tenderness to be gained by cutting directly against the grain.)

Arrange 5 slices of the steak on each plate, top with a ¼-inch slice of softened Ancho Chili Butter, and garnish with a red chili flower (directions below) and a good-sized sprig of cilantro if desired.

Red Chili Flower Garnish

Cut 8 small, narrow chili peppers from the tip to within ½ an inch of their stems in 4 or 5 straight lines; be sure to leave the stems intact. Carefully remove the seeds and veins (wear gloves to do this). Drop the peppers into ice water for 1 hour. The sections will curl outward like a flower. Use as a garnish.

Noisettes of Pork with Pears and Crème Fraîche

Serves 4 to 6.

Another of those dishes that is easy enough for a family supper yet elegant enough for a dinner party, this one offers an unusual accompaniment in the caramelized pears. Contrary to its reputation, pork is quickly cooked. In this, pork tenderloin is very like chicken breast and the meats may almost be used interchangeably. Certainly they have an affinity for the same types of sauces.

The Paul Thomas Winery in Washington makes an excellent Bartlett pear wine.

¾ cup Crème Fraîche (page 357)
1 medium onion, minced
1 cup dry pear wine
1 cup chicken stock
2 whole strips of pork tenderloin, each
    about 9 ounces in weight and 8
    inches long
  Coarse kosher salt
  Freshly ground black pepper
  Flour for dredging
4 tablespoons unsalted butter
2 tablespoons corn oil
3 large, firm Bartlett pears, peeled,
    cored, cut into 8 wedges each and
    tossed with 1 tablespoon lemon
    juice
1 tablespoon honey
  Lemon juice

Remember to prepare the crème fraîche a day or so ahead. Heavy cream may be used instead.

Combine the onions, pear wine, and stock in a small saucepan and reduce the liquid slowly to ½ cup. Strain, pressing the solids with the back of a spoon. Discard the onions and reserve the liquid.

Slice the tenderloin on a slight diagonal into noisettes ½ inch thick. Season both sides of each slice with salt and pepper and dredge in flour, shaking well to remove the excess.

Heat 2 tablespoons of the butter and oil in a large, heavy sauté pan and sauté the *noisettes*, turning so that each side browns nicely. Cooking should not take longer than 10 minutes— by the time both sides are browned the pork is done. This may need to be done in batches. (Remember pork only needs to reach a temperature of 137° to kill *trichinae* larvae. Do not dry out the meat.) Overlap in two rows on a heated platter and keep warm. Set the pan aside, unwashed.

In another sauté pan, melt the remaining 2 tablespoons butter. Dry the pears well with paper towels and arrange them in the pan. Turn occasionally to brown all sides. After about 5 minutes, drizzle on the honey, toss gently to coat the pears, and continue cooking until they are tender-crisp and slightly caramelized.

While the pears are cooking, add the pear wine and stock reduction to the pork sauté pan, scraping up the bits clinging to the bottom. Reduce to 4 tablespoons. Whisk in the crème fraîche and simmer briefly until the sauce just coats a spoon. Season to taste with salt, pepper, and drops of lemon juice.

Arrange the sautéed pears on one long side of the overlapped noisettes and pour the sauce on the bottom of the platter. These can also be served on individual plates, in which case allow for one-third to one-half a tenderloin per person.

Spinach Torta with Hazelnuts and Oregon Prunes

Serves 8.

A hearty, earthy vegetarian main dish or interesting side dish with a cabbage "crust"; this torta always elicits praise from students. The curry flavoring is subtle; feel free to double the quantity. Although the word torta *generally refers to a round shape, this entrée works as well in an oval gratin dish or in individual gratin dishes.*

> 1 small head cabbage, scruffy outer leaves removed
> 2 large bunches fresh spinach, washed and stemmed
> 1 cup ricotta cheese
> ½ cup finely shredded Parmesan cheese
> 2 eggs, lightly beaten
> 3 tablespoons toasted, skinned, and coarsely chopped hazelnuts
> 4 tablespoons slivered Oregon prunes
> 2 teaspoons best-quality Indian curry powder
> 1 teaspoon coarse salt
> Freshly ground black pepper
> 2 tablespoons unsalted butter

Blanch the whole cabbage in boiling water to cover for about 20 minutes. Do not cover the pan. Remove, drain, and cut out the core in a conical wedge. Separate the leaves carefully so as not to tear them. Cut a V-shaped notch in each leaf to remove the coarse stem. Dry thoroughly with paper towels.

Put the spinach into a large skillet and heat, turning occasionally, until the leaves wilt; this will just take a minute or two. Remove from the pan and, when cool enough to handle, squeeze out as much liquid as possible. Chop the spinach, squeeze it dry again, and combine with the ricotta, Parmesan, eggs, hazelnuts, prunes, curry, and salt and pepper to taste.

Butter a 9-inch, deep-dish pie plate and arrange the cabbage leaves, slightly overlapping, to cover the bottom and sides completely, being sure to leave an inch overhang on the edges. Repeat to use all of the leaves; you will have several layers. (Use the best looking leaves on the sides and the others on the bottom.)

Scoop the filling into the cabbage shell and smooth. Pat the overhanging cabbage leaves inward on top of the filling, producing a nice edge all the way around.

Dot the butter generously over the top, being certain to distribute it evenly, and bake at 350° for about 20 to 25 minutes, until the eggs have just set. Remove from the oven and drain any liquid from the bottom of the torta. Let the dish sit for 10 minutes, then cut into wedges to serve.

Potato Gratin and Variations

Serves 4 to 6.

Is there anything finer in the world of vegetable cookery than a properly made Potato Gratin? In French cooking there are three basic types: One is made with heavy cream, gratin jurassien; *one with half-and-half or milk,* gratin dauphinois; *and one with chicken or beef stock,* gratin savoyard. *Although the method for all three is simple, there is a complicating factor that needs consideration. Potatoes are surprisingly acidic and have a definite tendency to curdle milk, half-and-half, and even, but to a lesser degree, heavy cream. To minimize this possibility, the potato can be neutralized with a preliminary blanching for ten minutes in simmering milk. Because the potatoes are then partially cooked, the quantity of liquid required for the gratin decreases by about one-third. The liquid is also less likely to curdle if the oven heat is regulated so that the gratin is never actually boiling and the length of time that the dish is in the oven is monitored so that it is not overcooked. Yet another trick to discourage the curdling is to use 1 teaspoon flour with the liquid. I prefer to use heavy cream, which is more stable than either half-and-half or milk, and chicken stock for a gratin that is both wonderfully creamy and flavorful, but has fewer calories than a gratin made entirely of cream.*

By baking potatoes in this recipe I mean the common brown-skinned potatoes called Russet Burbank. They cook to a homogeneous mass with some separation remaining between slices. If you prefer separate slices of potato in the gratin, use boiling potatoes, such as Red Pontiac "new" potatoes or White Rose potatoes. They will taste a little sweeter than do the Russet Burbanks.

1 tablespoon unsalted butter
2 pounds baking potatoes, peeled, sliced ¼-inch thick, and put into cold water to cover
Coarse salt
Freshly ground white pepper
1 or 2 cloves garlic, finely minced (optional)
1 cup grated Gruyère, Emmenthaler, Jarlsberg, or other Swiss-type cheese
¾ cup heavy cream
¾ cup chicken stock
2 to 3 tablespoons unsalted butter (optional)

Butter an oval 6-cup gratin dish. Carefully dry the potato slices with a clean kitchen towel and begin layering them into the dish. Season each layer well with salt and pepper and sprinkle with the garlic if desired and some of the grated cheese. End with a topping of cheese. Then pour on the cream and chicken stock

combined. (The amount of liquid a given batch of potatoes will absorb is always variable. The liquid should reach a little more than halfway up to the top of the potato layers. Check the gratin periodically and add more liquid if needed. Remember, though, that you want only a light binding of sauce present when the potatoes are completely tender. Too much liquid makes the gratin soupy.)

Bake, uncovered, in the upper third of the oven at 425° for 45 to 50 minutes if cream or stock is being used; otherwise, bake at 325° for about 75 to 90 minutes, or until the potatoes are tender and the top is nicely browned. (If you have blanched the potatoes, the cooking time at the higher temperature will be approximately 30 minutes, at the lower temperature, 45 minutes.)

This dish can wait, loosely covered, for half an hour or so. To hold it any longer, stop the cooking process just before the last bit of liquid has been absorbed and heat gently just before serving.

VARIATIONS

Potato and Onion Gratin

Peel and thinly slice 1 medium-sized onion and layer it with the potatoes. The natural sweetness of the onion will be enhanced with the addition of cinnamon, nutmeg, and cloves—just a tiny pinch of each added to the liquid ingredient.

Potato and Wild Mushroom Gratin

Saute ½ pound boletes, chanterelle, morel, or other edible wild mushrooms, sliced, in 1 tablespoon unsalted butter until they release their juices. Add the juices to a combination of heavy cream and chicken stock to make up 1½ cups. Layer the mushrooms with potatoes. Finely minced fresh or dried rosemary is very nice with this combination.

Potato Gratin with Fresh Herbs

Up to 2 tablespoons fresh herbs—parsley, tarragon, rosemary, oregano, thyme, or chives—can be used singly or in combination with one another for this gratin. Layer them, finely minced, with the potatoes.

Potato and Carrot Gratin

Alternate sliced potatoes with sliced carrots, seasoning with a bit of dillweed, and proceed as in the master recipe.

Smoked Salmon and Potato Gratin

Layer ¼ to ½ pound cold-smoked salmon, chopped, with the parboiled potatoes. Add an egg to 1½ cups half-and-half, mix well, and pour over the gratin. Regulate the heat so that the gratin never reaches a simmer. This gratin is slightly different in that it has a light custard sauce.

Potato Gratin with Ham, Sausage, or Bacon

Layer ¼ to ½ pound fully cooked, sliced or diced ham, sausage, or bacon with the potatoes. Aged Cheddar works particularly well with these meats.

Potato, Onion, Apple, and Sausage Gratin

This gratin takes the concept to its limit, creating a complete meal in the process. Layer with the potatoes: 1 medium-sized onion, peeled and sliced, 2 tart green apples, peeled, cored, and sliced, and ¼ to ½ pound fully cooked bulk breakfast or Italian-style sausage. For the liquid use half chicken stock and half cream, increasing the total amount to 1¾ cups. A pinch of fresh or dried thyme is good here.

Golden Fried Potato Cake

Serves 4.

Notice here that I specify baking potatoes. It stands to reason that if you want the cake to hold together, there must be adequate starch. Generally speaking, baking potatoes (Russet Burbanks, sometimes called Idaho Russet Burbanks) have quite a bit more starch than do boiling potatoes (Red Pontiac "new" potatoes). Russet Burbanks cook to a tender mass in hot fat but get really mushy with any hint of water. Therefore it is important to control the heat so as to

cook the potatoes all the way through without using a lid which would add unnecessary moisture by keeping the steam in.

> 1½ to 2 pounds baking potatoes, peeled
> 4 to 6 tablespoons unsalted clarified butter
> Coarse salt
> Freshly ground black pepper

Grate the potatoes coarsely. Put them into a bowl of cold water as they are grated but do not leave them there for very long or they will discolor and you will lose too much of the starch. Drain and dry the grated potatoes thoroughly with a clean kitchen towel or with paper towels to remove as much of the excess moisture as possible. This is important. Too much moisture will ruin the potato cake. Season the loosely strewn potatoes well with salt and pepper.

Heat 4 tablespoons butter in a heavyweight, nonstick 10-inch diameter pan. Add the potatoes. (The potato cake should be about an inch thick.) Flatten the cake with a spatula. Regulate the heat so that the underside of the cake is nicely browned in 10 or 12 minutes. To make sure that the potato cake is not sticking, shake the pan back and forth. The cake should hold together and move in one piece. (Small pieces of butter can be added around the top sides of the cake to keep the mass of potatoes from sticking.)

Make sure that the potato cake is not sticking, position a flat plate over the skillet, and invert it. Add a little more butter to the pan and carefully slide the potato cake back into it. (Or you might like to try flipping the cake with a strong forward and upward jerking motion to save yourself the trouble of using a plate. This is really not difficult, especially when you are using a nonstick pan.) Continue cooking until the second side is golden brown, about 10 to 12 minutes. Slide the cake out of the pan and serve, cut into wedges.

VARIATIONS

Shredded Potato Cake with Celeriac and Chives

Combine 1 pound peeled, grated potatoes with ½ pound peeled, grated celeriac (also called celery root), and 2 tablespoons finely minced fresh chives or green onions. Continue as in the master recipe.

Shredded Potato Cake with Fresh Herbs and Garlic

Finely chop 2 tablespoons parsley and 1 tablespoon fresh chives or green onions. Put 2 cloves garlic through a garlic press. Mix these all together with the potatoes and proceed as outlined.

Layered Vegetable Purée with Yakima Valley Gouda

Serves 6 to 8.

This quintessential buffet vegetable dish is easily transported, may be reheated, tastes good, and looks intriguing. Layers of puréed spinach, potatoes, carrots, and cauliflower, separated by copious quantities of cheese make a dish that tastes like more than a composite of its parts. Be forewarned though, it is time consuming to prepare, blanche, and purée all these vegetables. Do not volunteer to make anything else.

  1 bunch (1 pound) fresh spinach, cleaned and stemmed
  ½ pound potatoes, peeled and quartered
  ½ pound trimmed carrots, peeled and sliced
  ½ pound trimmed cauliflower, cut into small pieces
  3 tablespoons unsalted butter
  3 tablespoons flour
  1 cup milk
  1 egg, lightly beaten
  ½ pound Yakima Valley Gouda cheese
    Coarse salt
    Freshly ground black pepper
    Freshly ground nutmeg
  1 teaspoon unsalted butter, melted
  2 tablespoons dry bread crumbs

Put the spinach, with just the water that is clinging to its leaves, into a large sauté pan and cook to wilt. Turn the entire mass over once or twice so that all the leaves wilt evenly. When cool enough to handle, squeeze as dry as possible with your hands and purée in a processor. Put into a small bowl. Reserve.

In a large saucepan, cover the potatoes with cold water, bring to a boil and simmer until tender, about 20 minutes. Drain well and press through a sieve. Put into a small bowl. Reserve.

In a large pot of boiling water, cook the carrots until completely tender, about 5 minutes. Remove with a slotted spoon, purée in a processor, and put into a small bowl. Reserve.

Add the cauliflower to the boiling water and cook until completely tender, about 5 minutes. Remove with a slotted spoon, purée in a processor, and put into a small bowl. Reserve.

To make the sauce, melt the butter in a small saucepan, add the flour and cook for at least 2 minutes without browning. Whisk in the milk, bring to a full boil, reduce the heat,

and simmer for another 3 minutes, whisking all the time to prevent scorching. Remove from the heat. Stir a little of the hot sauce into the egg to warm it gradually, then pour all of this mixture back into the sauce and whisk to combine. Season to taste with salt and pepper.

Divide the sauce evenly among the 4 vegetable purées, mixing to combine well. Season each purée carefully to taste with salt and pepper, adding nutmeg to the carrot and spinach purées. (The potato and cauliflower purées will take more salt than the other two will.)

In a buttered 2-quart soufflé dish (of clear glass preferably), layer first the potato, then the spinach, then the carrot, then the cauliflower, covering each layer with one fourth of the grated cheese.

Toss the remaining butter with the bread crumbs and sprinkle them over the top of the layered purées.

Bake at 350° for 30 minutes, until heated through (150° in the center). Using the broiler, brown the top lightly if necessary.

Spicy Onion Tian with Currants and Gruyère

Serves 6.

This is an unusual and wonderfully tasty side dish or simple main course. The onions are sautéed to a melting sweetness with just a hint of cinnamon and saffron and the currants add a welcome contrast as would other dried fruits such as diced dried Oregon cherries or dried apricots. Use a mellow Gruyère or a Swiss-type cheese that is not too sharp. Feel free to vary the cheese. Leave in the Parmesan for seasoning but use a mellow Cheddar or a creamy fontina in place of the Gruyère if you like.

  8 tablespoons unsalted butter
  4 cups diced onion
  ¼ teaspoon cinnamon
  ⅛ teaspoon white pepper
  2 cups long-grain white rice
  ¼ cup currants
  3 tablespoons flour
  ⅛ teaspoon saffron
  1 cup chicken stock
  1 cup milk
  ½ cup shredded Parmesan cheese
  1 cup grated Gruyère cheese
    Coarse salt
    Freshly grated white pepper

Melt 4 tablespoons of the butter in a large sauté pan and cook the onion over low heat until completely soft but not browned, about 20 minutes. Stir in the cinnamon and pepper. Continue with the rest of the recipe while the onions are cooking.

Blanch the rice in 2 cups boiling water for exactly 5 minutes, then drain in a colander.

Pour boiling water over the currants and leave them to plump for 5 minutes. Drain.

In a small saucepan, heat 3 tablespoons of the butter, add the flour and cook together for at least 2 minutes without browning. Crumble the saffron into a tablespoon of the chicken stock and stir to combine. Add this mixture to the rest of the stock, then add the milk. Pour the liquids into the flour and butter *roux,* bring to a boil, and cook slowly for 2 to 3 minutes, whisking continuously to smooth.

Combine the onion mixture, rice, currants, sauce, Parmesan, and Gruyère cheeses in a large bowl. Fold well to make sure everything is evenly distributed. Season to taste with salt and pepper.

Butter a 6-cup baking or soufflé dish. Turn the mixture into the dish and dot the top with the last tablespoon of butter.

Bake at 425° for about 20 minutes, until the *tian* is bubbling. Brown the top briefly under the broiler. The rice should have absorbed all of the liquid and be completely tender.

Cabbage Gratin with Apples and Cougar Gold

Serves 8 to 10.

This dish works especially well with Cougar Gold cheese (page 267) but you can substitute another smooth, mellow Cheddar if desired. New York, Vermont, or Canadian Cheddars can be very good. If you must use a more aggressive cheese here, reduce the amount by half so as not to overpower the delicate sweetness of the cabbage.

1 head cabbage, core removed
3 tablespoons unsalted butter
1 large onion, diced
1 teaspoon ground caraway seed
2 large tart, green apples, peeled,
    cored, and cut into ½-inch dice
1 tablespoon flour
2 cloves garlic, minced
1 cup cream
½ cup minced parsley
   Coarse salt
   Freshly ground black pepper
1 cup grated Cougar Gold or other
    smooth, mellow Cheddar cheese

Bring a large pot of water to a boil, add the cabbage, cover, and simmer for 20 minutes. The cabbage will float to the top of the water. Remove, drain, and separate the leaves. Dry each leaf thoroughly with paper towels. Cut out the tough center rib of each leaf. Chop into ½-inch pieces and reserve.

Melt 2 tablespoons of the butter in a sauté pan, add the onion and caraway and cook until well softened but not browned, about 20 minutes.

After 15 minutes, add the apples and combine gently. When the onions are softened (the apples should be only partially cooked), add the flour and cook for 2 minutes without browning. Add the garlic and cook briefly to meld. Add the cream, bring to a full simmer, then remove from the heat, and add the parsley.

Combine the chopped, cooked cabbage and the onion mixture in a mixing bowl. Season well with salt and pepper.

Butter a 9- by 12-inch baking dish with the remaining tablespoon of butter and spoon in the cabbage mixture. Sprinkle the cheese evenly over the casserole. Bake at 350° for 30 minutes.

Sunchoke Pancakes with Two Sauces

Serves 4 to 6; makes 8 to 12 pancakes.

These light and delightfully flavored pancakes provide an interesting beginning for fall and winter meals. Choose one or the other of the sauces depending on what is to follow. These pancakes also make a welcome luncheon dish and are fine for breakfast, accompanied by applesauce and sour cream.

    1 pound sunchokes (also called
        Jerusalem artichokes)
    2 tablespoons lemon juice
    4 eggs
    2 cloves garlic, minced
    2 green onions, finely sliced
        Coarse salt
        Freshly ground white pepper
    2 tablespoons unsalted butter
    2 tablespoons corn oil

With a sharp paring knife, peel the sunchokes, working around their knobby exteriors as you go. Acidulate 1 quart of water with the lemon juice and drop the chokes in as they are peeled.

Mix the eggs, garlic, green onions, and salt and pepper to taste.

Dry the chokes with paper towels, grate them directly into the egg mixture, and combine well.

Heat a large skillet or griddle and add half of the butter and oil to begin with. Drop the pancake batter, about ¼ cup at a time, onto the hot skillet and spread the pancake out as thinly as possible. Repeat with more batter until the skillet is full. Turn the pancakes with a metal spatula as they become nicely browned on the bottom; brown the other side. Each side will take about 5 minutes.

Arrange the cooked pancakes on a heated serving platter and keep them warm while finishing the rest of the batter, using the remaining butter and oil.

Serve hot, with or without a dipping sauce.

Herbed Cream Cheese

Makes about 1 cup.

    6 ounces cream cheese
    1 clove garlic, minced
    1 large sprig parsley, minced
    ½ cup cream

GARNISH
    4 green onions, green ends sliced
        lengthwise 2 or 3 times to create a
        feathered effect

With a mixer, whip the cream cheese with the garlic and parsley until it is entirely free of lumps. With the machine running, slowly add the cream and beat until the cream has whipped. The sauce should be light and fluffy. Serve slightly chilled with the hot pancakes, garnishing each serving with a green onion off to one side.

Oriental Dipping Sauce

Makes about ¼ cup.

2 tablespoons soy sauce
1 tablespoon cider vinegar
½ teaspoon sesame oil
⅛ teaspoon sugar

Combine all ingredients and serve at room temperature, drizzled over the pancakes.

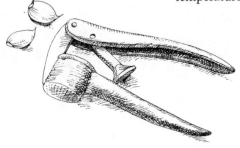

Polenta with Mushroom Sauce, Monterey Jack, and Cream

Serves 12.

Polenta *prepared this way has a soft, almost puddinglike texture. It is wonderful beyond words. Simple, homey fare, this is perfect for blustery winter evenings. Though I generally serve this dish as a main course, it can also be a first course. For the latter, serve small quantities, preferably in individual gratin dishes. Dried bolete mushrooms are called for here but small dried Chinese mushrooms or dried chanterelles may be substituted.*

1½ ounces dried bolete mushrooms

MUSHROOM SAUCE

2 tablespoons unsalted butter
1 teaspoon dried basil
1 teaspoon dried oregano
¼ teaspoon cinnamon
1 medium onion, diced
1 pound fresh mushrooms, sliced
2 cups skinned, diced tomatoes with their juice
1 tablespoon tomato paste
1 cup dry white wine

POLENTA

6 cups homemade chicken stock (page 345)
¾ cup coarse cornmeal
¾ cup fine (regular) cornmeal
Coarse salt
Freshly ground black pepper
1 tablespoon unsalted butter
½ cup grated Parmesan cheese
½ cup cream
¼ pound shredded Monterey Jack cheese

Soak the dried mushrooms for at least 30 minutes (occasionally they take as long as 2 hours to hydrate fully) in a small bowl with 2 cups warm water. After soaking, lift them out of the water, rinse to get rid of any remaining grit, and chop into large pieces. Strain the soaking water through a fine-meshed sieve and reserve.

To make the sauce, melt the butter in a large sauté pan and add the basil, oregano, cinnamon, and onion. Sauté until the onion is softened. Add the fresh mushrooms and cook until they begin to lose their liquid. Add the tomatoes, tomato paste, wine, hydrated bolete mushrooms, and their liquid. Simmer slowly until the liquid is reduced and the sauce well thickened.

While the sauce is simmering, prepare the *polenta*. Put the stock into a deep pot and slowly sprinkle in all the cornmeal, stirring constantly with a long-handled wooden spoon.

Bring to a simmer and cook slowly for 20 to 30 minutes, stirring steadily with the spoon. (The deep pot and the long-handled spoon are needed to keep your hand and arm away from the bubbling brew. It is quite thick and tends to spurt up at you. Be careful.) When done the *polenta* should be smooth, soft, and fairly thick, but not as thick as *polenta* that is meant to be sliced. Season to taste with salt and pepper.

Butter a 2-quart baking dish with 1 tablespoon butter. Spread half the *polenta* evenly over the bottom of the dish. Sprinkle with ¼ cup Parmesan. Spread all the sauce mixture over the *polenta*. Sprinkle with the remaining ¼ cup Parmesan. Top with the remaining *polenta*, smoothing with the back of a large spoon, and drizzle with the cream. Sprinkle the Monterey Jack over the top. (The dish may be made ahead to this point.)

Bake at 350° until golden and hot, about 30 minutes. The *polenta* will absorb the cream. Serve right away.

Bradley's Own Yakima Valley Granola

Makes 6 to 8 quarts.

I have been making this granola for my husband James since our college days together in eastern

Washington. *It usually requires a trip to the health food store, but the smell of all these goodies toasting in the oven is more than worth the effort. And it is so nutritious that you could probably live on it if you had to. I would certainly want a large supply of it on my desert island.*

The only ingredients really essential to the success of the batch are the oatmeal, honey, butter, and oil. Feel free to substitute one seed, nut, or grain for another but be sure to keep everything in proportion; if dried fruit is not readily available, raisins, both dark and golden, can be substituted.

8 cups rolled oats (old-fashioned oatmeal)

4 cups wheat flakes

1 cup raw wheat germ

1 cup sunflower seeds

1 cup sesame seeds

1 cup pumpkin seeds

1 cup unsweetened coconut shreds

1 cup chopped walnuts

1 cup chopped hazelnuts

2 cups snoberry honey (or other fragrant honey)

¼ cup molasses

1 cup unsalted butter, melted

½ cup corn oil

¼ cup vanilla extract

¼ cup grated orange zest

1 cup chopped dried apricots

1 cup chopped dried Oregon cherries

1 cup chopped dried pears

1 cup chopped dried peaches

Mix the rolled oats, wheat flakes, wheat germ, sunflower, sesame, and pumpkin seeds, coconut, and nuts together in a large bowl. Add the honey, molasses, butter, corn oil, vanilla, and orange zest, cover with plastic wrap, and leave overnight to mellow the flavors.

The next day, spread the granola onto rimmed cookie sheets, about ½-inch deep and toast in a 325° oven for 30 minutes, turning with a spatula 2 or 3 times during the process to keep the color even. You will probably need to do this in 4 batches.

After all the batches of granola are nicely toasted, combine them in a very large mixing bowl and add the apricots, cherries, pears, and peaches. Let the mixture cool thoroughly, then store in an airtight container. (If you plan to have the granola on hand for more than 2 weeks, refrigerate it to keep the grains and nuts from becoming rancid.)

Basmati Rice Pilaf with Onions and Yogurt

Serves 6.

Basmati *rice is wonderful stuff. Grown in India, it is classified as an aromatic rice. When you smell it cooking you will understand why. It exudes a warm nutty fragrance and taste that is both subtle and compelling. In America the species has been hy-*bridized *and transplanted to produce strains called Texmati, Calmati, and Pecan Rice. Unfortunately these are not nearly as fragrant or tasty as the original and I heartily recommend a trip to the nearest Indian grocery for a supply of the authentic mother strain. The longer the* basmati *has aged, the more wonderful it will be.*

2 cups *basmati* rice
2 tablespoons unsalted butter
1 to 2 teaspoons *garam masala* (page 358)
2 large onions, chopped
1 tablespoon minced garlic
1 tablespoon minced fresh ginger
1 cup unflavored yogurt
Zest of 1 lemon
2 tablespoons lemon juice
2¼ cups homemade chicken stock (page 345)

To clean the rice thoroughly, put it into a bowl, cover with cold water, wait a few seconds, then tip the bowl and drain off the now cloudy water. Repeat the process several times until the water runs clear. Sift through the rice to remove any foreign particles. Now cover the rice with 2 or 3 inches of cold water and let it soak for 30 minutes. Drain. (Soaking will help to keep the rice from cracking while it is cooking.) The long slender grains are now very fragile, so be careful when you handle them.

Melt the butter in a large saucepan and cook the *garam masala* for 1 minute without burn-

ing it. Add the onions and cook until softened and just beginning to brown. Add the garlic and ginger and cook for 2 minutes.

Over rather brisk heat, add the yogurt, 2 tablespoons at a time, to the onion mixture, letting the liquid evaporate before each new addition.

When all the yogurt has been assimilated, add the lemon zest, lemon juice, chicken stock, and soaked rice. Cover the pan very tightly, using aluminum foil and a lid if necessary, and cook over low heat for 20 minutes. Remove from the heat and let the *pilaf* rest for 5 minutes before serving. Do not open the pan and do not stir the rice. Just before serving, fluff the pilaf with a fork.

Poached Pears and Sabayon with Toasted Walnuts

Serves 6.

There are many variations on the classic egg yolk and wine custard sauce known as sabayon. A few are given here to illustrate the versatility of this particular sauce. It is delectable on all types of fruit, both fresh and poached, and may be flavored a little differently for each type. It may be served hot or cold, and in the latter case, with or without the final addition of whipped cream specified here.

6 pears, Bartlett, Anjou, or Bosc
2 quarts cold water acidulated with
 the juice of half a lemon
6 cups water
1½ cups sugar
 3-inch piece vanilla bean
 3-inch cinnamon stick

SABAYON
 4 egg yolks
 ½ cup sugar
 ¾ cup white wine, champagne,
  sauternes, Madeira, or *Marsala*
 ½ teaspoon dissolved gelatin (optional)
 ½ teaspoon cinnamon (optional)
 ⅛ teaspoon freshly grated nutmeg
  (optional)

 Grated zest of 1 orange or 1 lemon
  (optional)
 ½ cup cream, whipped (optional)

GARNISH
 ½ cup walnuts, toasted and coarsely
  chopped

Peel the pears, leaving the stems on, and drop them immediately into the acidulated water to prevent them from turning brown.

In a large saucepan or stovetop casserole, combine 6 cups water, 1½ cups sugar, the vanilla bean, and the cinnamon stick. Bring to a boil, add the pears, reduce the heat, and simmer for 20 to 25 minutes, or until the pears are tender when tested with the tip of a sharp knife. When all the pears are done, transfer them to a bowl. Pour the poaching liquid over them and let them cool.

To make the sauce, combine the egg yolks and sugar in a heavyweight saucepan and whisk until the mixture is pale yellow and thick. Add the wine. Place the pan over simmering water or low direct heat and whisk the sauce until it is thick and light. It will coat a spoon heavily. Do not overcook or the sauce will curdle. (Since the sauce is going to be chilled, some cooks suggest the addition of ½ teaspoon dissolved gelatin at this point to stabilize it. I have not found that this sauce separates in the refrigerator, but the addition of gelatin is a precaution that you may wish to take.)

Transfer the sauce to a bowl and add whatever flavoring you prefer: ½ teaspoon cinnamon and ⅛ teaspoon nutmeg or the lemon or orange zest. Chill for 30 minutes. Fold the whipped cream into the sauce and chill again.

To serve, arrange the pears on individual dessert plates, spoon some of the sauce over each pear, and sprinkle with walnuts. Serve well chilled.

Caramelized Pear and Anise Tart

Serves 6 to 8.

A luscious upside-down tart, this is covered with a rich glaze of caramel. The success of this dish depends a great deal on the proper pan. Ideally, you should use a heavy, shallow, sloping-sided skillet measuring about eight inches in diameter, such as a Teflon-coated heavy-duty aluminum omelet pan. A well-seasoned Calphalon omelet pan will also work. The pan should be dark in color to facilitate the browning of the caramel and have a handle that can take a thirty-five-minute stay in a hot oven. If you have doubts about the handle, wrap it with damp paper towels and enclose tightly with foil. Because of its delicate, not-too-sweet taste, this dessert is best on its own with afternoon tea or following a meal that does not include a flamboyant level of herbs, spices, or hot peppers.

PASTRY
    1 cup flour
    1 tablespoon sugar
    Pinch coarse kosher salt
    ¼ teaspoon freshly ground anise seed
        (use a mortar and pestle)
    2 teaspoons grated lemon peel
    4 tablespoons unsalted butter, frozen
    1½ tablespoons shortening, cold
    3 tablespoons ice water,
        approximately

FILLING
    4 tablespoons unsalted butter
    6 tablespoons sugar
    6 firm, almost ripe pears, peeled,
        cored, and quartered
    2 tablespoons cornstarch
    ½ teaspoon freshly ground anise seed
        (use a mortar and pestle)
    1 teaspoon grated lemon peel
    1 cup cream, whipped and sweetened

To make the pastry, combine the flour, sugar, salt, anise, and lemon peel in the bowl of a processor and pulse to blend, or combine lightly in a bowl by hand. Add the frozen butter, cut into 1-inch pieces, and the cold shortening, also in pieces, to the work bowl and

process until the dough looks like a coarse meal. (When making the pastry by hand, use cold butter rather than frozen and a pastry cutter to blend it in.) Sprinkle the water over the top of the flour mixture and process or mix by hand until the dough just begins to mass together. (A little more water may sometimes be necessary on occasion but do not make the dough too damp or it will be tough.) This takes only a few seconds. The dough should not form a ball. Gather the dough together with your hands and flatten it into a disk. Wrap in plastic wrap and refrigerate for at least an hour, longer if possible. Dust a pastry cloth and a cloth-covered rolling pin with flour and roll out the dough to a 9- or 10-inch circle (remember, the skillet is larger at the top). Cut with an appropriately fluted quiche pan rim. Refrigerate, sealed in plastic wrap, until ready to use.

To make the tart, melt the butter in your chosen skillet, and mix in 5 tablespoons of the sugar over low heat. Toss the sliced pears with the cornstarch, anise, and lemon peel. Arrange the pears evenly around the pan, starting from the middle and working outward. The narrower ends should be pointed toward the center and the pieces should be placed curved-side down. (Do not worry too much about how the pears look at this point.)

Cook the pears over medium heat until the sugar just begins to caramelize. The carameli-zation process will continue in the oven. Shake the pan occasionally to prevent the pears from sticking and burning.

Sprinkle the remaining 1 tablespoon sugar over the pears and carefully set the prepared pastry dough on top. Puncture the dough in several places to allow the steam to escape.

Bake at 375° for 35 to 40 minutes, or until the crust is nicely browned. Remove the skillet from the oven and swirl and shake it over high heat for a minute to loosen the caramel. Place a serving platter lined with a paper doily directly on top of the skillet and carefully invert. Serve the tart warm with whipped cream.

Pear and Ginger Tart

Serves 8.

Pears poached in a flavored syrup have a haunting perfumed quality; the flavorings become an inseparable component of the pears, heightening and expanding their flavor. The cream cheese base here is lightened with whipped cream and flavored with succulent, spicy stem ginger. (Stem ginger is bottled in syrup and is generally available in oriental markets.)

 A 9- to 10-inch fully baked Short-
   Crust Pastry shell, made with
   hazelnuts (page 352)
 2 quarts cold water
   Juice of half a lemon (about 2
     tablespoons)
 1 cup sugar
   3-inch vanilla bean
   3-inch cinnamon stick
 6 Bartlett or Anjou pears, peeled,
     cored and halved
 8 ounces cream cheese
 4 tablespoons powdered sugar
 ½ cup cream
 1 tablespoon lemon juice
 1 tablespoon finely slivered preserved
     stem ginger
 ½ cup fine-shred ginger marmalade

Be sure to have the hazelnut Short-Crust Pastry done ahead.

In a large, nonreactive casserole, combine the water, lemon juice, sugar, vanilla bean, and cinnamon stick. Bring to a boil and add the pears. Reduce the heat and simmer gently for about 20 minutes, or until the pears are tender when tested with the tip of a sharp knife. Remove them from the heat and let them cool in the poaching liquid. These will be even better if left to soak overnight in the refrigerator.

No more than two hours before serving, remove the pears from the syrup and dry them thoroughly with paper towels. Slice lengthwise into ¼-inch thick slices. Pat dry again with paper towels.

With a mixer (not a processor), beat the cream cheese and powdered sugar together until completely smooth and light. Add the cream and continue beating just until the cream is whipped. Mix in the lemon juice and the preserved ginger.

Spread the cream cheese mixture on the bottom of the fully baked, cooled tart shell. Tightly overlap the slices of pears in concentric rings on top of the cream cheese, completely covering the tart.

Bring the marmalade to a simmer and whisk to smooth. Simmer for one minute, remove from the heat, cool for 1 minute, then brush the pears evenly with the glaze. Refrigerate for at least 1 hour before serving; but for no more than 2 hours or the pastry will become soggy.

Hazelnut Toffee Tart

Serves 12 to 14.

This recipe originally entered my files as an unusual Scandinavian Christmas cookie. Later I met a native Italian cook who claimed a slightly different version as part of her culinary heritage. In January of 1982, Sunset magazine printed yet another variation, labeling it a dessert tart, and in the process Americanized the concept of nuts and caramel in a pastry crust. This particular recipe is just different enough from the others I have seen and eaten to make it my own favorite. It does indeed make a lovely dessert tart. Serve in small wedges as it is quite rich.

A 10- to 11-inch partially prebaked
   Short-Crust Pastry shell (page
   350)
1½ cups sugar
½ cup honey
½ cup cream
½ cup unsalted butter
2 cups hazelnuts or walnuts (6
   ounces), lightly toasted, skinned,
   and coarsely chopped
½ teaspoon hazelnut extract (or vanilla
   or walnut extract)
1 teaspoon grated lemon peel

In a large saucepan, combine the sugar, honey, cream, and butter. Over moderately low heat, bring the mixture very slowly to a boil. Wash down the sides of the saucepan occasionally with a pastry brush dipped in cold water to discourage the sugar from crystallizing. Stir constantly and make sure that the sugar dissolves before the mixture is allowed to boil or the caramel may become granular. Then boil the mixture, without stirring, until a candy thermometer registers 240°. It will be a very light brown. Do not allow it to become too dark or the caramel will overcook and harden too much in the oven.

Add the nuts, flavoring extract, and lemon peel, and stir. Remove the caramel from the heat and let it cool for a few minutes before pouring it into the partially baked pastry shell. (There is nothing hotter or more dangerous than hot sugar syrup; be very careful.)

Bake the tart in a 375° oven for 20 to 25 minutes. The tart will be bubbling and a beautiful caramel color. (Again, if you allow it to become too dark, the cooled caramel will be much too stiff, but if the caramel is not dark enough, the tart will be runny.) Remove from the oven and let the tart cool on a wire rack.

Remove the outer ring of the tart pan and serve the tart on an attractive round platter. Cut into thin wedges with a very sharp knife. The tart should be served at room temperature and may be made a day ahead if desired.

Hazelnut Ginger Flan

Serves 8.

In this recipe a lush combination of cream cheese and succulent stem ginger is encased in a hazelnut cookie-crust. This is best served a little warm but may also be left at room temperature for a number of hours with no ill effect, making it perfect for the buffet table. Stem ginger consists of young knobs of fresh ginger put up in simple syrup. It is wonderfully sweet, spicy, and succulent and preferable in most cases to the stiffer, dried candied ginger.

> A 9-inch, fully baked Short-Crust
>   Pastry shell, made with hazelnuts
>   (page 352)
> 8 ounces cream cheese
> 6 tablespoons sugar
> 4 eggs
> ½ cup cream
> 1 tablespoon finely slivered preserved
>   stem ginger
> 1 tablespoon lemon juice
> 2 tablespoons powdered sugar
> 2 tablespoons hazelnuts, toasted,
>   skinned, and finely chopped

Beat the cream cheese and sugar together until smooth. Add the eggs and blend just until creamy. Incorporate the cream, stem ginger, and lemon juice.

Pour the filling into the prebaked pastry shell. Bake at 350° for 10 minutes. Slide the oven rack out partially and sieve the powdered sugar on top of the flan. Sprinkle with the hazelnuts. Continue baking for 10 minutes. *Do not overbake.* The flan will not appear to be fully set when you remove it from the oven. (If the edges of the pastry begin to burn, cover them with foil, leaving the center of the flan exposed to the heat.)

Cool the flan on a wire rack for 10 minutes before cutting it into wedges to serve.

VARIATIONS

Hazelnut Cheese Flan
Omit the stem ginger and flavor the filling with the zest of 1 lemon and ¼ cup lemon juice instead.

Walnut Cheese Flan
Vary the Hazelnut Cheese Flan version by substituting toasted walnuts for the hazelnuts.

Hazelnut Praline Mousse

Serves 8.

This dessert is definitely three-star and worthy of your most favored guests. Best served in clear parfait or wine glasses in which the subtle layering can be seen, it has the rich, deep flavor of caramelized hazelnuts.

> 2 teaspoons gelatin
> 2 tablespoons Frangelico hazelnut
>   liqueur
> 8 egg yolks
> 6 tablespoons sugar
> 2 cups cream
> 1 teaspoon vanilla extract
> 1½ cups Hazelnut Praline (page 342)
> 6 egg whites
>   Pinch of cream of tartar (optional)
> 4 tablespoons sugar
> 1 cup cream, whipped

In a small bowl, sprinkle the gelatin over the liqueur to soften for 10 minutes.

In a heavyweight saucepan, whisk the egg yolks and sugar just to combine and gently stir in the cream without letting foam develop on the top of the sauce. Stir slowly with a wooden spoon over moderate heat until thickened. Do not let the custard boil. Remove the pan from the heat, stir in the gelatin mixture and the vanilla, and stir the custard until the gelatin is completely dissolved. If the custard has lumps in it (it's not *your* fault, the devil did it) strain through a fine sieve. Add ½ cup of the Hazelnut Praline and stir to combine.

Set the bowl of custard over a larger bowl of cracked ice mixed with a cup or two of water and let it cool, stirring occasionally, until it just begins to thicken.

In another bowl, preferably copper, beat the egg whites and salt with a large balloon whisk until they hold soft peaks. (Add the cream of tartar if you are not using a copper bowl.) Gradually beat in the 4 tablespoons sugar until stiff peaks are formed. (This may also be done in a mixer with a whisk attachment.)

Lighten the custard a little by incorporating a large scoop of the beaten egg whites to begin with. Fold in the remaining egg whites gently and quickly into the lightened custard.

Divide one-third of the mousse among eight ¾-cup ramekins or parfait glasses. Sprinkle on half of the remaining praline, dividing it equally among the 8 glasses. Repeat with 2 more layers of mousse and 1 of praline, ending with the mousse. (Save about 2 tablespoons praline for garnish.) Chill for at least 1 hour.

Garnish each mousse with a rosette of whipped cream and a sprinkling of praline.

Hazelnut Praline

Makes 2 cups.

Praline is a delicious caramel and nut powder that is often used in desserts. Although this amount is

more than you will probably need for any one recipe, it is nice to have on hand. Store the powder in an airtight container.

2 cup fresh, shelled hazelnuts
2 cups sugar
¾ cup water

Put the shelled hazelnuts on a cookie sheet and bake them at 325° for about 15 minutes, or until lightly toasted. Lay the hot nuts on a clean kitchen towel, fold the towel over, and rub the nuts between the layers of cloth to remove much of the skins. Do not worry about the skin that does not come off.

Mix the sugar and water and clear the liquid over low heat. Raise the heat only after the sugar is completely dissolved and you can clearly see the bottom of the pan. Bring to a simmer, stop stirring, and cook to a golden brown. Add the nuts and pour the mixture onto a buttered baking sheet; let cool to a nut brittle. Break the brittle up into pieces and pulverize in a processor. The mixture should be very fine.

VARIATION

Walnut Praline
Use walnuts instead of hazelnuts. Do not bother to skin them.

Pinot Noir-Glazed Oregon Prunes with Lemon Crème Fraîche

Serves 8 to 10.

This dessert is old-fashioned and new-wave at the same time. Certainly it is a painless, even pleasurable, way to eat prunes. Oregon prunes—plump and sweet with a fine texture—are available at the Pike Place Market. They are nothing like the sticky, gooey prunes packaged for the grocery store trade. Though this recipe indicates lemon shred marmalade, which has fine shreds of lemon peel rather than chunks, I have also made it with lime shred and it is just as wonderful. I imagine ginger shred would be equally delectable if you can find it. This is a cozy, comforting, not-too-sweet dessert; add a toasty fire, a blustery night, and savor it slowly. This dessert also makes a wonderful sauce for a very rich vanilla ice cream. The crème fraîche must be made at least one day ahead.

2 pounds dried Oregon prunes, pitted
but left whole (1 pound 8 ounces
when pitted)
1 bottle Oregon pinot noir (or other
dry fruity red wine)
⅓ cup sugar
1 tablespoon lemon juice
Zest of 1 lemon
3-inch cinnamon stick
10 peppercorns, lightly crushed
¾ teaspoon anise seed, ground in a
mortar and pestle
2 cups Crème Fraîche (page 357)
½ cup lemon shred marmalade

GARNISH
Lemon zest
Cinnamon sticks

Combine the prunes with pinot noir, sugar, lemon juice, lemon zest, cinnamon stick, peppercorns, and anise seed. Simmer gently for about 35 minutes, until the prunes have softened but are not at all mushy. Remove the prunes and reduce the syrup by half. Quarter the prunes lengthwise to make them easier to eat or leave them whole, which is prettier. Add the prunes back to the glaze and cool to room temperature.

Flavor the crème fraîche by stirring the lemon marmalade into it.

Serve the glazed prunes at room temperature or slightly warmer with an abundance of lemon-flavored crème fraîche. Garnish each serving with a cinnamon stick and a sprinkling

of lemon zest. A few crisp cookies would be a nice addition here.

Daddy Mike's White Chocolate Cheesecake

Serves 8 to 12.

This is my stepfather Mike's own personal cheesecake. He sampled a similar dessert in a Northwest restaurant and liked it so much that he asked me to "figure it out" for him. After playing around with the quantities of white chocolate a bit, I perfected it to his satisfaction. He says this is the best cheesecake in the known world. It is really rich. Mike can eat the whole thing but most people prefer a slender slice.

¼ cup fine, dry, chocolate cookie
crumbs (French butter cookies may
be used)
6 ounces white chocolate
2 packages (8 ounces each) cream
cheese
6 tablespoons sugar
2 eggs
2 cups sour cream
½ cup sugar
1 teaspoon vanilla extract

GARNISH
2 ounces white chocolate

Sprinkle the cookie crumbs on the bottom of a 10-inch springform pan or removable-bottom cake pan.

Over very low heat in a heavy saucepan or in a double boiler set over hot, not simmering, water, carefully melt the white chocolate. (White chocolate cannot tolerate the same degree of heat that dark chocolate can. If it is even slightly overheated it will turn granular.)

In a processor (or use a mixer) blend the cream cheese with the sugar until completely smooth. Add the eggs and the melted white chocolate and combine well.

Pour the filling into the prepared pan and bake at 350° for 20 minutes. Remove from the oven and let the cheesecake rest for 5 minutes. The cake will not appear set; that is as it should be.

While the cheesecake is baking, whisk the sour cream with the sugar and vanilla and let it set until the sugar is completely dissolved.

Slowly, so as not to disturb the cream cheese layer, pour the sour cream mixture over the top of the cheesecake. Return to the oven for 10 minutes, remove, and let it cool to room temperature on a wire rack. Chill for at least 6 hours and preferably overnight.

Grate the remaining white chocolate and sprinkle it evenly over the top.

Homemade Chicken Stock

Makes 2 to 3 quarts.

This all-purpose stock has plenty of body, a rich golden hue, and a full though neutral flavor that blends easily with a host of other ingredients. Often the cook wants a stock that is absolutely neutral, in which case the optional seasonings, with the possible exception of parsley, are best omitted. In any case, never salt a stock before you use it. If you intend to use it for a reduction sauce, the salt level will rise as the liquid evaporates.

> 6 pounds poultry necks, backs, wings, giblets, and fat (no liver)
> Cold water to cover
> 2 carrots, roughly chopped
> 2 onions, halved and the skin left on
> 2 stalks celery, roughly chopped, leaves and all

OPTIONAL SEASONINGS
> Small handful of parsley, stems and all
> 2 unpeeled cloves garlic
> 1 bay leaf
> 2 whole cloves
> 1 sprig fresh thyme (or ¼ teaspoon dried)

Rinse the chicken parts and put into a large 12- to 16-quart stockpot. Add cold water to cover the chicken by 1½ inches. Heat slowly. This encourages the release of albuminous particles. When the liquid comes to a bare simmer, regulate the heat to maintain the simmer. Begin skimming off the rising scum and continue until the scum ceases to accumulate. Never stir the contents of the stockpot. If you do, the clouding particles will become part of the liquid and mar its appearance.

After the skimming process is completed (usually in 15 minutes), add the vegetables and whatever seasonings you are using. Maintain a bare simmer and continue to cook for 3 hours or more, until your taste convinces you that all the flavor from the solid ingredients has been rendered into the water. Pour the stock through a very fine strainer. Discard the solid ingredients; they have no flavor or nutrition left.

When the hot stock has settled for 5 to 10 minutes, the fat may be removed. Either skim the surface with a spoon, draw a "grease-catcher" brush across the surface, or use a "bottom-pouring degreaser" (available at most kitchenware stores) to decant the stock. If time allows, the stock can be refrigerated, *uncovered,* until the fat hardens on the surface and can be removed easily.

When the stock has been thoroughly degreased, check it for strength. If the taste is not intense enough, simply boil the stock down to heighten the flavor. When the desired intensity is reached, salt may be added; or the stock may be left unsalted, the final adjustment to be made in the particular dish the stock eventually goes into. (This last is my preference.)

Refrigerate, remembering to boil the stock for 5 to 10 minutes every few days to keep it from spoiling, or freeze in 2- to 4-cup batches.

CHICKEN STOCK WITH VEAL

For a neutral stock that is even more gelatinous than the one above, replace one-third to one-half of the chicken parts with meaty veal neck bones.

Fish Fumet

Fish heads are the key to good fish fumet *as they supply gelatin which gives the stock body. It is important to use lean, mild, white fish trimmings; fish like salmon and trout are too distinctive tasting for an all-purpose* fumet.

        2 pounds fish heads and bones; rock
             cod, flounder, ling cod, halibut, or
             any other lean, mild, white fish
        1 onion, skin and all, chopped
        1 carrot, sliced
        1 rib celery, sliced
        1 bay leaf
          Several parsley sprigs, coarsely
             chopped
        1 teaspoon dried thyme or 2 sprigs fresh
        8 cups water
        2 cups dry, drinkable white wine
          Coarse kosher salt

Combine the fish, vegetables, herbs, water, and wine in a stockpot. Season lightly with salt. Bring to a simmer over medium-low heat. Skim the scum that rises to the surface as the liquid reaches a simmer. Keep skimming until no more scum rises, then simmer gently for an additional 15 minutes. Strain the fumet through a fine sieve, lined with damp paper towels or damp cheese cloth if necessary. Do not press the solids when straining or the liquid will be cloudy.

At the end of 30 minutes or so, all flavor contained within the fish bones and most of that in the vegetables will have dissipated into the liquid. Long simmering will not produce a better taste here; on the contrary, an unpleasant bitterness develops when fish fumet is cooked too long. If there is not enough flavor at the end of the cooking time, strain anyway, then reduce the fumet to a desirable taste level.

Shortcut Fumets

OPTION 1

        1½ cups bottled clam juice
          1 cup water
          1 cup dry white wine
          1 onion, chopped
          6 parsley stems

Simmer all ingredients together for about 30 minutes, allowing the liquid to reduce to 2 cups. Strain. Reduce to intensify the flavor if need be, but watch out for excessive saltiness.

OPTION 2

¾ cup dry white wine
¼ bottled clam juice
¼ cup water

Combine and use in place of fish fumet.

OPTION 3

Good homemade chicken stock can often replace fish fumet without deleterious results. Think of chicken stock as a neutral base or foundation that can be used with seafoods when necessary.

Mayonnaise

Makes 1 to 1½ cups.

Mayonnaise is not at all difficult to make. Home-made mayonnaise is so much better than anything that can be purchased in the grocery store, it is well worth the few minutes it takes to make.

2 to 3 tablespoons white wine vinegar
or lemon juice
Coarse kosher salt
Freshly ground white pepper
1 to 3 teaspoons Dijon mustard
2 egg yolks
1 to 1½ cups vegetable oil (a mixture of
salad oil and olive oil if
desired)

Blend the vinegar or lemon juice with salt, pepper, and mustard in a bowl (preferably one with a base smaller than the top edge) large enough to accommodate a balloon whisk. Add the egg yolks and whisk until thick and sticky. Begin adding the oil, drop by drop, whisking constantly all the while. When the mayonnaise begins to thicken, the oil may be added at a somewhat faster pace, but not too fast. Each addition should be thoroughly incorporated and invisible before adding the next. Continue until all the oil has been added; 1 cup oil will produce a thinner sauce than 1½ cups oil. Taste and adjust the seasonings, adding more vinegar or lemon juice if necessary. Mayonnaise should be stored, covered, in the warmest part of the refrigerator. It will keep for about 1 week.

PROCESSOR METHOD

Makes 1 to 1½ cups.

Process the initial ingredients as directed in the master recipe, but use 1 whole egg in place of the 2 egg yolks. Drizzle the oil through the feed tube, with the machine running, until all the oil is incorporated. Finish as with the master recipe.

VARIATIONS

Watercress Mayonnaise
To the basic Mayonnaise recipe, add ½ cup minced watercress, 2 teaspoons minced green onion, 2 teaspoons minced fresh dill (or ½ teaspoon dried dill), and 1 teaspoon lemon juice.

Green Mayonnaise
To the basic Mayonnaise recipe, add 1 tablespoon minced parsley and 1½ teaspoons each minced fresh chives, tarragon, and dill.

Garlic Mayonnaise
To the basic Mayonnaise recipe, add 2 cloves garlic minced and extra drops of lemon juice.

Dill Mayonnaise
To the basic Mayonnaise recipe, add 2 tablespoons sour cream, 2 tablespoons fresh minced dill, 1½ teaspoons Dijon mustard, ½ teaspoon anchovy paste, and 1 clove garlic minced.

Green Onion Mayonnaise
To the basic mayonnaise recipe, add 4 to 6 tablespoons minced green onion and 4 teaspoons minced parsley.

Basil or Mint Mayonnaise
To the basic Mayonnaise recipe, add 4 to 6 tablespoons fresh minced basil or 6 to 8 tablespoons fresh minced mint.

Pesto Mayonnaise
To the basic Mayonnaise recipe, add 1 to 3 tablespoons pesto.

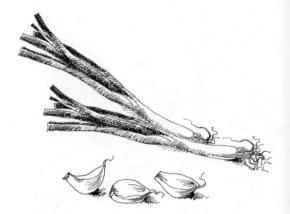

Rouille

Makes 1 cup.

Rouille is similar to aioli but crushed red peppers and roasted red bell pepper are added to the basic formula. (In recipes for both of these sauces white bread is sometimes listed among the ingredients. According to culinary doyenne Madeleine Kamman, the bread was used in the past to help begin the emulsification process. It hardly seems necessary today. For the modern cook, the processor provides the little extra help that the bread once gave.) Rouille is the traditional accompaniment to another of southern France's culinary treasures, bouillabaisse.

> 1 large red bell pepper, roasted, skinned, cored, and seeded, or ¼ cup canned pimiento, drained
> 4 cloves garlic, mashed and minced
> ½ to 1 teaspoon crushed red pepper
> 1 tablespoon white wine vinegar
> Coarse kosher salt
> Freshly ground white pepper
> 2 egg yolks
> 1 cup light olive oil

Purée the red bell pepper and garlic with the crushed red pepper, vinegar, salt, and pepper. Add the egg yolks and whisk until thick and sticky. Add the olive oil, drop by drop, whisk-ing constantly, until all of the oil is incorporated and the sauce has thickened. Taste and adjust the flavor with additional salt, pepper, and drops of lemon juice, if needed.

PROCESSOR METHOD

Use 1 whole egg in place of the 2 egg yolks and proceed as outlined in the master recipe, using the steel blade in the processor.

Short-Crust Pastry

This recipe yields enough dough for an 8- to 9-inch shallow tart pan with a removable bottom or a pie pan of the regular depth. Increase the proportions in ½ cup increments for larger pans.

There is really nothing easier than making a good pastry crust. For some reason though, the very word pastry evokes shudders from otherwise competent cooks. It seems that everyone has, at one time or another, had trouble with this basic dough. A description of what actually happens in pastry making may take out some of the mystery and, I hope, some of the fear as well.

There are only a few ingredients to consider; normally just flour, butter, and water—perhaps a little salt or sugar as well. First the flour is mixed with the butter in a procedure called sabler or to reduce to sand. The object is to coat tiny particles of flour with tiny particles of butter—to make a combination that looks like coarse cornmeal. This process is important to the final outcome of the crust because the butter shields some of the flour particles from the liquid that is to be added next and, by so doing, prevents the gluten within that portion of the flour from becoming activated. (Later on the same butter prevents the activated portion of the gluten from producing long connective strands.) The overdevelopment of gluten—the elastic network of proteins contained within the flour—is what makes a pastry tough. Besides liquid, warmth and manipulation both encourage the development of gluten and should thus be minimized as much as possible.

Next a small quantity of liquid is added to activate the unprotected (unbuttered) gluten proteins in the flour and give the dough enough cohesiveness to be rolled out easily. (If too much liquid is used, no amount of butter can prevent it from being absorbed by the flour, producing a tight network of gluten threads that will spell disaster for the pastry. If too little liquid is used, the dough will not hold its shape during rolling; it will be dry, crumbly, and will tear easily once rolled.) Note: Salt (and the sugar in Sweet Short-Crust Pastry) may be dissolved in the water. Many fine cooks prefer to do it this way.

Lastly, the dough is gathered quickly into a ball, flattened, covered with plastic wrap, and refrigerated to set the butter and relax the gluten. Short-crust pastry should (except in the case of double-crust or lattice-top pies, turnovers, or casings for pâtés, etc.) be partially or fully prebaked so that it will not absorb wet fillings as readily. Because of the butter content of this pastry, prebaked crusts need to be "baked blind" (lined with foil and filled with pie weights—see page 351) to keep the sides from collapsing.

There you have it. There is nothing terribly difficult at all—just a few simple precautions to be aware of. Here then is the basic recipe with a few more details.

PROPORTIONS PER CUP OF FLOUR
    1 cup flour
    ¼ teaspoon salt

4 tablespoons chilled, unsalted butter, cut into chunks

2 tablespoons chilled shortening, cut into chunks

3 tablespoons ice water, approximately

Blend the flour and salt together in a bowl. Add the chunks of butter and shortening evenly over the top of the flour.

With the fingertips pick up a bit of the flour and fat and rub lightly between the thumb and first two fingers—lift and rub, lift and rub, sifting occasionally through the fingers (or use a pastry blender)—to "reduce the mixture to sand." The mixture should resemble coarse cornmeal when it is finished; no large particles of butter should be distinguishable. (Do not use the palms of the hands, which are too warm, and be sure the butter and shortening are well chilled.)

Sprinkle on the water, a little at a time, and gather the dough up quickly and lightly into a ball with your hands. Add only enough water so that the dough forms a cohesive mass. It should not feel wet. (Remember: Manipulation activates the gluten. Do not overhandle.)

Flatten the dough between sheets of plastic wrap, seal, and refrigerate for at least an hour to relax the gluten and set the butter. (The dough may be kept under refrigeration for 2 to 3 days.)

Roll out on a floured board (Formica is fine) or, for real ease, on a floured pastry cloth to the desired thickness—somewhere between ⅛

to ¼ inch—and large enough to line an 8- or 9-inch tart pan.

Using a sharp knife, cut around the outside of the pastry to remove the jagged edges. (If left, these will cause the pastry to tear when you pick it up.) With a soft brush remove any excess flour from the pastry. Fold the pastry in half and carefully position it over the tart pan (no need to butter the pan). Unfold, carefully easing the pastry into the corners of the pan.

Pat in place and cut the pastry evenly ½ an inch larger all around than the diameter of the pan. Fold this extra ½ inch to the outside and press. This should give you a reinforced edge, a little higher than the sides of the pan, to work with. For a fancy fluted edge, crimp the pastry between the thumb and forefinger of one hand and the forefinger of the other, evenly all the way around. For a more delicate edge that will not get left behind on your guests' plates, push the reinforced edge down just a bit and trim off the excess even with the edge of the tart pan. Now use your fingers to push the edge back up a little so that it follows the indentations of the pan and extends a ¼ inch or so higher than the pan edge.

Prick the shell evenly with a sharp fork. (These holes will close up as the pastry bakes. They are necessary for the release of steam.) Refrigerate if at all possible for 15 to 30 minutes (or freeze briefly) to reset the butter, relax the gluten, and firm up the pastry so that it will not bend out of shape when the blind is inserted.

To prebake the shell, line the pastry carefully with foil (following the side curves) and fill the foil liner to at least the halfway mark with aluminum pie weights or dried beans (these may be used again and again indefinitely). Bake at 425° for 10 minutes, remove the liner with the pie weights (the "blind"), and continue baking for 4 minutes for a partially baked crust or for 10 minutes for a fully baked crust, for which the bottom should be completely set and the pastry beginning to color nicely. Remove from the oven and cool on a wire rack.

VARIATIONS (PER CUP OF FLOUR)

Sweet Short-Crust Pastry

Proceed as directed in the basic recipe for Short-Crust Pastry but decrease the salt by half and add 1 to 4 tablespoons finely granulated or powdered sugar to the flour. (The more sugar you add the more difficult the pastry will be to roll out. Do not try to roll it too thin.) Decrease the water just slightly.

Very Short Short-Crust Pastry (for basic or rich short-crust)

For people who hate to roll out pie crusts this makes a crumbly, melting tart shell that does not need to be rolled. Use as little water as possible and preferably none, to bind the pastry. Sprinkle the bits of loose dough onto the tart pan and press them into place with your fingertips, making sure to get the sides and bottom as even in thickness as possible. Work quickly and do not overwork the dough. Cut off the dough level with the edge of the tart pan. This procedure also works well with rich short-crust made with eggs; use a little less egg.

Short-Crust Pastry with Ground Nuts (for either basic or rich short-crust)

Replace ¼ cup of the flour with an equal amount of finely ground (but not oily) nuts. Use hazelnuts, walnuts, pecans, almonds, macadamia nuts, pine nuts, or even peanuts.

Short-Crust Pastry with Cheese

Add ¼ to ½ cup medium to hard grated cheese or a combination of cheeses to the flour and continue as in the basic recipe.

Alternate Grain Short-Crust Pastry

Replace ¼ to ½ cup of the wheat flour with another flour, meal, or the like—cornmeal, whole wheat flour, rye flour, or wheat germ. Dried herbs may also be used in moderation.

Cream Cheese Pastry

Blend 8 tablespoons unsalted butter and 4 ounces cream cheese, both at cool room temperature, with ¼ teaspoon salt until well mixed. Add 1 cup flour and mix quickly just until absorbed. If the dough is too soft and sticky, a little more flour may be necessary. Gather the dough into a ball, flatten between sheets of plastic wrap, and refrigerate for at least 2 hours before rolling. Continue as in the basic recipe. Good as a wrapper for appetizers.

Sour Cream Pastry

Substitute 6 tablespoons sour cream for the butter in the Cream Cheese Pastry and proceed as directed. Good as a wrapper for appetizers.

Rich Short-Crust Pastry

Makes one 8- to 9-inch pastry shell.

In this pastry so much sugar is used, in addition to egg, that the texture of the dough is dramatically different from that of regular and Sweet Short-Crust Pastry. The finished crust resembles a crisp, crumbly cookie and is perfect for dessert custards, cheesecakes, fresh berries, and the like. Special mixing procedures are called for to insure that the eggs, more viscous than water, are thoroughly and evenly incorporated into the flour. Note that the quantity of flour is an approximation; add enough to make a pliable, not too sticky dough.

PROPORTIONS PER CUP OF FLOUR

1 cup flour, approximately

2 egg yolks, slightly beaten

2 to 4 tablespoons very finely granulated or powdered sugar

4 tablespoons unsalted butter, chilled, cut into chunks, and left at room temperature for 10 minutes

2 tablespoons shortening, chilled, cut into chunks, and left at room temperature for 10 minutes

Measure 1 cup flour, remove 2 tablespoons for possible inclusion later, and mound the rest onto a countertop. Make a well in the middle of the flour and put the egg yolks, the sugar, the butter and the shortening into it.

With the tips of your fingers mash the fat, sugar, and egg yolk together until a homogeneous mass is obtained. This should be done quickly so that the fat remains cold.

Bit by bit, bring a little of the flour on top of the creamy butter mixture and cut through the entire mess (literally!) with the edge of a long-bladed spatula. Hold each end of the top of the spatula and chop-chop-chop through the mixture. Continue until all the flour has been used, adding more if necessary to achieve a cohesive mass that is not overly sticky.

Now we begin the process called *fraiser,* which is the final blending of fat and flour. Using the heel of the hand, smear small portions of the dough, one after the other, out and away from you. Gather the pieces of smeared dough up quickly into a ball, flatten it between sheets of plastic wrap, seal, and refrigerate for at least an hour.

In most other ways the pastry is shaped and baked according to the methods described in the basic Short-Crust Pastry recipe except one must remember that this pastry, because it has so much sugar and is stickier than usual, will be more difficult to handle. Do not attempt to do intricate shaping with this dough; the simpler the better. Also, this pastry browns rather easily. You may need to protect the edges with foil (an easy way to do this is to cut a circle a bit bigger than the tart pan and then remove the center, leaving a doughnut shape of foil that fits perfectly over the edges of the crust) during the final minutes of baking to keep them from overbrowning.

If you are having a terrible time of it, try rolling the dough out between two sheets of lightly floured plastic wrap. When you have the shape and thickness you want, remove one sheet of the plastic, lift the pastry and the remaining sheet into position over a tart pan, invert so that the plastic is on top, and ease the dough carefully into the pan. Strip away the plastic before finishing the edges. You may never want to roll this pastry any other way. This pastry may also be crumbled into the pan and patted into place. Be sure to get it an even depth everywhere.

VARIATIONS

Spicy Rich Short-Crust Pastry
To Rich Short-Crust Pastry add 1 teaspoon lemon or orange zest or a combination of both; ¼ teaspoon cinnamon and a pinch of cloves may be added. The additions are also good incorporated into Rich Short-Crust Pastry with Nuts.

Rich Short-Crust Pastry with Nuts
Replace ¼ cup of the flour with an equal amount of finely ground, but not oily, nuts. Use hazelnuts, walnuts, pecans, almonds, macadamia nuts, pine nuts, or even peanuts.

Pâte à Chou

Makes 15 to 20 small puffs or 10 large puffs.

Pâte à Chou or Cream Puff Pastry is probably the easiest pastry in the French repertoire, being just a very thick white sauce, or panade as it is called, into which eggs are beaten, one at a time, until a thick glossy paste is obtained. Two steps are required to make pâte à chou. The first is to cook the panade so as to swell the flour's starch partially, hasten some development of gluten, and distribute the fat throughout the paste. Cooked, the flour forms a thick, smooth, glossy emulsion; otherwise only a sticky mass incapable of puffing later in the oven would be formed. The second step is the addition of eggs to stabilize the stiff mixture. The eggs are the main source of leavening and moisture. To be effective, they should not be added when the mixture is either too hot or too cold—a temperature of 150 degrees is ideal.

Final measures are necessary to assure that the baked puffs remain crisp once they are taken from the oven. Because the center of a cream puff never cooks completely, it is important to allow the steam in the interior to escape before it makes the whole puff soggy. For small puffs, a narrow slit cut in the surface crust is enough; large puffs usually have to be split in half and the uncooked center should be removed.

½ cup water
4 tablespoons unsalted butter
¼ teaspoon salt
½ cup flour, sifted
2 to 3 eggs

Bring the water to a boil with the butter and salt. As soon as the butter melts, remove the saucepan from the heat and dump in the flour all at once. Beat vigorously with a wooden spoon until the mixture is smooth and pulls away from the sides of the pan to form a ball. Beat over low heat for 1 to 2 minutes to dry the paste a bit. It should form a cohesive mass and begin to film the bottom and sides of the pan. Do not cook longer or the butter will separate and appear on the surface.

Cool for 10 minutes or until the paste reaches 150°.

Beat the first two eggs, one at a time, into the paste, thoroughly incorporating the first before adding the next. Beat the remaining egg in a small bowl, then begin adding it to the paste in increments, until the paste has the right consistency, that is, is light enough to drop from a spoon with a little push, yet able to hold a rounded shape; you probably will not need all of the third egg. The paste is now ready to use for other recipes or to be baked as follows.

To make small puffs, fill a pastry bag, fitted with a ½-inch round tube opening, with the pâte à chou mixture, then pipe the paste onto buttered baking sheets, making the mounds about 1 inch in diameter and ½ inch high. Space the mounts 2 inches apart. Dip a small pastry brush into the remaining beaten egg and flatten each puff very slightly with the side of the brush. Be careful not to drip the egg down onto the baking sheet as this will keep the puff from rising properly.

Bake at 400° for 20 minutes. The puffs should double in size, turn golden brown, and be firm and crusty to the touch. Remove from the oven and slit each puff with the point of a paring knife. (If the puffs are larger, cut them in half and scoop out the centers.) Set in turned-off oven, leaving the door ajar, for 10 minutes to dry out or return to 400° oven for 3 to 5 minutes. Put on a wire rack to cool.

To make large puffs, use a ¾-inch round tube opening and pipe the paste into 2-inch mounds that stand 1 inch high. Bake at 425° for 20 minutes, then reduce the heat to 375° and bake for 10 to 15 minutes more, until doubled in size, golden brown, and firm and crusty to the touch. Remove them from the oven and make 1-inch slits in the side of each puff, or, if they are really large, cut them in half and scoop out the centers. Set in the turned-off oven, leaving the door ajar, for 10 minutes to dry out or return them to the 400° oven for 3 to 5 minutes. Test a puff when the drying-out time is up; if the center is still gooey, scoop it all out. Dry on a wire rack.

SWEET PÂTE À CHOU

Follow the recipe on the previous page but reduce the salt to a pinch and add 1 teaspoon sugar.

VARIATIONS

There is a lot you can do with basic Cream Puff Pastry to vary its taste and give it versatility in your cooking repertoire. Here are a few of the options:

Cheese Profiteroles

Add 1 cup grated Swiss cheese, a combination of Swiss and Parmesan cheeses, or any other flavorful, medium-firm to firm cheese to 2 cups *pâte à chou* and proceed as usual. These make lovely hors d'oeuvres.

Herb Profiteroles

Add 2 to 3 tablespoons fresh minced herbs of your choice to 2 cups *pâte à chou* and proceed as usual. These make an unusual garnish for soup.

Sweet Fried Profiteroles

Add 1 to 3 teaspoons sugar to basic *pâte à chou*, then deep-fry by teaspoonsful in corn oil heated to 325° until golden, about 5 to 8 minutes. Drain on paper towels and roll immediately in sieved powdered sugar. Eat right away. These are perfect for tea.

Handling Couscous Grains

Makes about 2 cups.

"A thousand tiny pellets of grain, light, separate, and tender, doused with a tagine, arranged into a pyramid, and then served upon a platter at the end of a meal—that is couscous, the Moroccan national dish." So says Paula Wolfert in her excellent book, Couscous and Other Good Food from Morocco. *Couscous may be prepared with semolina or with any number of other cracked grains, such as wheat, barley, millet, or corn. To keep the grains separate and light, a special steaming method, done with a two-part steamer called a* couscousière, *is used. Lacking this piece of equipment, a deep pot and colander (or steaming insert) will suffice as long as they fit together tightly. Couscous is usually cooked over a simmering stew (called a tagine) to add flavor to the grains, but boiling water can also be used. The following steps may seem a bit tedious to read through, but the actual preparation is not difficult.*

> 1 cup cracked wheat, corn, barley, whole millet, or couscous grains
> 1 tablespoon unsalted butter (optional)
> ½ teaspoon coarse salt

Washing and Drying: Using the grain of your choice, cover with cold water, toss a few times, and drain off the excess water. Dump the grains onto a buttered jelly-roll pan and smooth out in an even layer. Leave the grains to swell for 10 to 20 minutes. After 10 minutes rake through the grains with your fingers, keeping the grains as separate as possible.

First Steaming: Using a pot with a steaming insert, fill it with enough water to reach just below the insert making sure that it does not touch the water, and bring to a boil. Butter the inside of the steaming insert and add the grains to it a little at a time, rubbing the grains gently through your fingers to separate them. Steam *uncovered* for 20 minutes.

Second Drying: Remove the steaming insert and pour the grains back onto the buttered jelly-roll pan. (1 tablespoon or so of soft butter may be added at this point if you wish.) Sprinkle ½ cup of cold water over the grains along with ½ teaspoon salt. Separate the grains by lifting and stirring them gently with your fingers. Smooth the grains out and allow them to dry for at least 10 minutes. (If you are preparing the couscous in advance, let the grains dry at this point, covered with a damp cloth. The grains can wait for several hours if need be.)

Second Steaming: Pour the grains back into the steaming insert and steam *uncovered* for 20 minutes if the grains have dried for a short time or 30 minutes if they have been waiting longer. (The amount of cooked grain produced with this method will depend on the specific grain used, but will be approximately double the dried measurement.)

Fluff with a fork and serve; or cool and use cold in a salad.

Crème Fraîche

Makes 2 cups.

Make crème fraîche at least 1 day before you need to use it.

> 2 cups cream
> 2 tablespoons buttermilk or sour cream

Put the cream into a glass container and whisk in the buttermilk or sour cream. Cover with plastic wrap and leave out at room temperature until the culture thickens the cream. This can take anywhere from 8 to 24 hours, depending on the temperature of the room. A little warmth will speed up the process; too much will kill the bacterial culture responsible for thickening the cream. As soon as the cream has thickened properly, put it into the refrigerator to prevent it from becoming too sour.

Garam Masala

Makes about ¼ cup.

Garam masala *is a spice and herb blend used in Indian cuisine. There are hundreds, perhaps thousands, of these blends in India. This one is particularly fragrant.*

      15 green cardamom pods, husks
             removed
             2-inch stick cinnamon
      ¾ teaspoon whole cloves
       1 tablespoon black peppercorns
       2 tablespoons cumin seed
       2 tablespoons coriander seed

Roast all the ingredients in a hot, dry frying pan until they are fragrant but not burnt, about 2 minutes. Remove and let them cool. Put all the ingredients into a spice grinder and grind fine. Store in an airtight plastic bag or spice bottle.

Spice Blend

Makes about 2 tablespoons.

      2 teaspoons whole coriander seeds
      2 teaspoons whole allspice
      ½ teaspoon whole cardamom
      ⅛ teaspoon whole cloves
      1 teaspoon ground cinnamon
      1 teaspoon ground nutmeg

In a spice grinder or with a mortar and pestle, grind together the coriander, allspice, cardamom, and cloves. Stir in the ground cinnamon and nutmeg. Store in a tightly closed container.

Vinaigrettes

Among the more versatile of the French sauces, vinaigrette is useful for dishes other than salad. Often used in New American cooking with grilled, poached, or sautéed fish or chicken, it may also provide the sauce for hot pasta (if made with lemon juice rather than vinegar) as well as a more expected cold pasta salad and, instead of mayonnaise, for potato salad.

LEMON GARLIC VINAIGRETTE

Makes about ¾ cup.

- 2 tablespoons white wine vinegar
- 1 tablespoon lemon juice
- 1 teaspoon Dijon mustard
- 1 small clove garlic, minced
- ½ teaspoon coarse kosher salt
- 2 teaspoons brown sugar
- 4 tablespoons cold-pressed olive oil
- 4 tablespoons corn oil
  Freshly ground black pepper

Combine the vinegar, lemon juice, mustard, garlic, salt, and sugar in a small bowl. After dissolving the salt and sugar, whisk in the oils and pepper to taste.

HONEY LIME VINAIGRETTE

Makes about ¾ cup.

- 1 tablespoon white wine vinegar
- 2 tablespoons lime juice
- 1 small clove garlic, minced
- ½ teaspoon coarse kosher salt
- 1 tablespoon honey
- 8 tablespoons corn oil
  Freshly ground black pepper

Combine the vinegar, lime juice, garlic, salt, and honey in a small bowl. After dissolving the salt and sugar, whisk in the oil and pepper to taste.

MUSTARD GARLIC VINAIGRETTE

Makes about ½ cup.

- 2 tablespoons white wine vinegar
- 2 cloves garlic, minced
- 2 teaspoons Dijon mustard
- ½ teaspoon coarse kosher salt
- 3 tablespoons cold-pressed olive oil
- 3 tablespoons corn oil
  Freshly ground black pepper

Combine the vinegar, garlic, mustard, and salt in a small bowl. After dissolving the salt, whisk in the oils and black pepper to taste.

BURGUNDY VINAIGRETTE

Makes about ¾ cup.

  1½ tablespoons dry red wine
  1½ tablespoons red wine vinegar
  1 small clove garlic, minced
  1 teaspoon Dijon mustard
  ½ teaspoon coarse kosher salt
  2 teaspoons brown sugar
  ½ teaspoon Worcestershire sauce
  2 tablespoons tomato purée
  1 egg, lightly beaten
  2 tablespoons cold-pressed olive oil
  2 tablespoons corn oil

Whisk together the red wine, vinegar, garlic, mustard, salt, brown sugar, Worcestershire sauce, and tomato purée in a small bowl. After dissolving the salt, whisk in the egg and oils thoroughly.

ORIENTAL VINAIGRETTE

Makes about 1 cup.

  4 tablespoons rice wine vinegar
  2 teaspoons minced green onion
  ¼ teaspoon minced fresh ginger
  ¼ teaspoon minced garlic
  4 teaspoons brown sugar
  ½ teaspoon coarse kosher salt
  6 tablespoons corn oil
  2 tablespoons cold-pressed olive oil

Combine the vinegar, green onion, ginger, garlic, brown sugar, and salt in a small bowl. After dissolving the sugar and salt, whisk in the oils.

FRESH GINGER VINAIGRETTE

Makes about ½ cup.

  2 tablespoons rice wine vinegar
  ½ teaspoon coarse kosher salt
  1 teaspoon sugar
  1 teaspoon finely minced fresh ginger
  1 small clove garlic, minced
  6 tablespoons corn oil (or part corn oil
     and part cold-pressed olive oil)

Combine the vinegar, salt, sugar in a small bowl. After dissolving, add the ginger, garlic, and oil and whisk to blend.

HOT TOMATO VINAIGRETTE

Makes about 1½ cups.

  6 tablespoons cold-pressed olive oil
  ½ teaspoon crumbled oregano
  ½ teaspoon crumbled basil
  ⅛ teaspoon crushed red pepper flakes
  1 cup diced tomatoes
  2 tablespoons red wine vinegar
     Coarse kosher salt
     Freshly ground black pepper

Heat the olive oil in a skillet and add the oregano, basil, red pepper, and tomatoes. Cook quickly to reduce the moisture from the tomatoes by at least half. Add the vinegar, then salt and pepper to taste. Remove from the heat and use at once.

Sauce Beurre Blanc

Makes 1 cup.

Once the rage of French nouvelle cuisine, beurre blanc *or white butter sauce (which is warm butter held in suspension by a concentrated acidic reduction) has left an indelible mark on New American cooking. It tastes wonderful, is quick and easy to make, and lends itself to infinite variations. Because the sauce is highly unstable, it is usually served immediately. It can also be held in a warmed Thermos for 5 to 6 hours with no negative effect.*

> 3 tablespoons white wine vinegar
> 3 tablespoons dry white wine
>   Coarse kosher salt
>   Freshly ground white pepper
> 1 tablespoon finely chopped shallots
> 1 cup unsalted butter, in 1 tablespoon chunks
>   Lemon juice

Combine the vinegar, wine, salt, pepper, and shallots in a heavy-weight saucepan and reduce to 1 tablespoon. Take the saucepan off the heat for a moment to allow the reduction to cool slightly.

Add the chunks of butter all at one time. Stir with a wooden spoon over low heat to create an emulsion. Do not bring this sauce near a simmer or it will separate. Taste and adjust the seasonings, adding drops of lemon juice if more acidity is needed. The sauce is now ready to use; it may be strained or not, according to your preference. Use immediately or keep warm in a preheated, dry Thermos for up to 6 hours.

VARIATIONS

Lemon Beurre Blanc
Substitute lemon juice for vinegar in the recipe above.

Rosy Beurre Blanc
Using the above recipe, incorporate 2 tablespoons cream and 1 teaspoon tomato paste after the initial reduction. Reduce this mixture by one third. Finish the sauce with butter as outlined, adding 3 tablespoons of peeled, seeded, and diced tomato to the completed sauce.

Herb Butters

Herb-flavored butters are useful to have on hand and are easily made ahead. They keep very well in the freezer and make an almost instant, simple sauce for grilled fish or chicken. Do remember to bring them to room temperature before serving. The following recipes may be considered examples of the technique; almost any herb or combinations of herbs can be made up into butters.

PARSLEY MINT BUTTER

Makes a generous ¼ cup.

    3 tablespoons minced fresh mint
    3 tablespoons minced parsley
    4 tablespoons unsalted butter
    2 tablespoons lime juice
      Coarse kosher salt
      Freshly ground pepper

Blend the minced mint and parsley with the butter until smooth, then add the lime juice and incorporate. Season to taste with salt and pepper. Store in the refrigerator, well sealed in plastic wrap.

PARSLEY CHIVE BUTTER

Makes a generous ¼ cup.

    3 tablespoons minced fresh chives
    3 tablespoons minced fresh parsley
    4 tablespoons unsalted butter
    2 tablespoons lemon juice
      Coarse kosher salt
      Freshly ground black pepper

Blend the minced chives and parsley with the butter until smooth, then add the lemon juice and incorporate. Season to taste with salt and pepper. Store in the refrigerator, well sealed in plastic wrap.

CILANTRO BUTTER

Makes a generous ¼ cup.

    ¼ cup minced cilantro
    8 tablespoons unsalted butter
      Coarse kosher salt
      Freshly ground black pepper
      Cayenne pepper

Blend the minced cilantro with the butter until smooth, then season to taste with salt, pepper, and cayenne. Store in the refrigerator, well sealed in plastic wrap.

Grilling Tips

For the best grilled flavor possible, use wood charcoal alone or in combination with wood chips (which must first be soaked in cold water). Mesquite, alderwood, peachwood, and applewood are all excellent flavor producers.

Charcoal briquets vary widely in quality and are less desirable as a grilling medium, though they are so easily available it is always a temptation to use them. With briquets look out for the smell of petroleum (motor oil). It is often used to bind the pieces together and it doesn't always cook off before you are ready to barbecue. A greasy, smudged residue on your hands after touching one of these briquets is a good indication of the use of petroleum by-products in the charcoal.

Be sure to start your fire in plenty of time to ensure it is thoroughly active when you begin to grill. This will usually take 35 to 45 minutes; the coals should be covered with a coating of ash.

Your grill should be cleaned thoroughly after each use to prevent a buildup of heavy, off-flavored residues. Always brush the grill rack with oil before putting anything on it.

Fifteen to twenty briquets are plenty for a couple of chickens. Be sure to spread the coals out evenly before you begin to cook. The closer together the coals are spaced the hotter the fire will be.

Basic Egg Pasta

Makes about 1 pound.

> 1½ to 2 cups flour
> ½ teaspoon coarse salt
> 3 eggs
> 2 tablespoons coarse salt
> 1 tablespoon corn oil

Put 1½ cups flour and salt into a processor fitted with the steel knife. Add the eggs and process for 40 to 60 seconds, until the dough forms a ball. Stop the machine and test the dough for moisture. Add more flour if needed to make a pliable dough that is neither too moist nor too dry. The dough will break down into small crumbs and will probably not form a ball again in the processor. Test by pinching a bit of the dough together with your fingers; if it adheres to itself and does not feel wet, it is ready. Gather into a ball with your hands, knead for a few seconds, seal in plastic wrap, and let rest for 30 minutes.

Now you're going to need a pasta rolling machine. (You can attempt to do the rolling by hand with the help of the directions in *The Classic Italian Cookbook* by Marcella Hazan, but it is a laborious chore.) Clamp the pasta rolling machine securely to a tabletop. Take one fourth of the dough, flatten it with your hands, sprinkle it with flour, and run it through the rollers at the widest setting. Fold the dough in half and repeat, positioning the fold on the side before each run through the machine. Do this several times to smooth the dough and align it evenly. Continue dusting lightly with flour if the dough is damp. When the dough is smooth and pliable, begin diminishing the thickness of the rollers, one notch at a time, running the dough through twice with each change. Brush a little flour onto the dough and/or the roller blades if the dough begins to get sticky. About halfway to the thinnest setting you may notice that the dough is getting too long to handle easily; if so, cut it in half and proceed with one piece at a time. When the dough has reached the desired thinness, lay the sheet out on a clean towel to dry for 5 minutes. (Usually the thinnest setting on a pasta machine is too thin to be usable; stop at the setting just preceding this one.) Continue with the rest of the dough.

Before each sheet of pasta dries out too much (especially important when making ravioli and the like), run it through the cutting blade of the machine, or cut it by hand with a sharp knife. If appropriate to the pasta cut, shape each sheet of noodles into a loose twirl. Let dry on a clean towel or closely spaced wire rack.

If you plan to cook right away, let the noodles dry for 10 to 15 minutes first. Fresh pasta can also be frozen.

To cook, bring a large pot of water (1 gallon of water for every pound of pasta with 2 tablespoons coarse salt and 1 tablespoon oil added) to a full boil. Immerse the pasta all at once, stirring with a wooden fork to separate the strands. Put a lid on the pot and return to a boil as quickly as possible. Remove the lid and continue boiling until the pasta tests *al dente.* (To test the pasta, lift a strand out of the pot with a long-handled fork and take a bite. The pasta should be tender but at the same time retain some inner resistance to the teeth.) This can take as little time as 15 to 30 seconds after the boil returns with fresh pasta, to 7 minutes or longer with packaged dried pasta. Nothing is more disappointing than overcooked pasta, so watch closely.

Drain immediately into a colander and jerk up and down to force most of the water out of the pasta. Proceed as called for in the recipe, remembering that pasta must be quickly sauced and served to prevent it from cooling and becoming sticky. Always have the serving bowl and individual plates or pasta bowls heated and ready to go. (Have guests ready to go too!)

VARIATIONS

Since many of the following additions are to some degree moisture-laden, an extra measure of flour may be necessary to achieve the right dough consistency.

Speckled Herb Pasta

Add 2 tablespoons finely minced fresh herbs (either a single herb or a combination of herbs), for example, chives, green onion, mint, dill, tarragon, parsley, cilantro, watercress, thyme, oregano, rosemary, or sorrel, to the eggs and blend well. Continue as in the basic recipe.

Basil Pasta

Purée 1 cup packed basil leaves and add the eggs. Mix well and continue as in the basic recipe.

Beet Pasta

Add ½ cup puréed beets to the eggs, mix well, and continue as in the basic recipe.

Spinach Pasta

Add ½ pound fresh, chopped, cooked, and dried spinach (or 5 ounces frozen spinach, treated in the same way) to the eggs and continue as in the basic recipe.

Vegetable Pasta

Add ½ cup vegetable purée of choice to eggs and blend well. Continue as in the basic recipe.

Tomato Pasta

Add 2 to 3 tablespoons tomato paste to the eggs, mix well, and continue as in the basic recipe.

Shaping and Cooking Ravioli

Ravioli are shaped with two pieces of pasta cut into 1½-inch squares and laid one on top of the other to resemble little stuffed pillows. The edges are then sealed and decoratively edged with a ravioli crimper-cutter. A special two-piece ravioli mold makes shaping even easier as it provides uniform indentations for the filling.

To shape ravioli, roll the pasta as thinly as possible (without making it so thin that it will tear). Lay one sheet of pasta over the metal frame of a ravioli mold. Press down lightly with the plastic indentation template to create pockets for the filling. Spray the edges lightly with a fine mist of water. Fill immediately so that the pasta does not become too dry to adhere to itself. This is best accomplished with a pastry bag fitted with a ½-inch plain tip. Cover with a second sheet of pasta and press to seal. Run a rolling pin across the ravioli mold to finish sealing and separating the ravioli. Remove and leave to dry on a clean towel for at least a half hour before cooking.

To cook ravioli, add medium-small batches to a large quantity of gently boiling water for 8 to 10 minutes. When done remove from the water with a large slotted spoon or Chinese skimmer, gently combine with sauce, and serve in heated pasta bowls.

There will be scraps of dough left when making ravioli. Gather them together quickly as they occur and seal in plastic wrap. If necessary the scraps can be sprayed with a fine mist of water to moisten. Knead the scraps a bit, then put through the widest setting of the pasta rolling machine several times to form a cohesive dough. Do not worry if it looks like a mess the first few times through the rollers, the dough will cooperate if you are patient.

Crème Brulée

Serves 6.

Several references to Crème Brulée are made through-out this book. This is my basic recipe. Crème Brulée is very much like Crème Caramel except it is usually made with egg yolks instead of with whole eggs and with cream rather than milk. The other significant difference is that Crème Brulée is served in its baking dish with a crunchy burnt sugar topping rather than freestanding with a liquid caramel sauce.

2½ cups cream
1-inch length vanilla bean, split in
half lengthwise
6 egg yolks
½ cup sugar

TOPPING
½ cup brown sugar

Bring the cream and vanilla bean just to a boil in a deep saucepan. Watch that the cream does not boil over. Remove from the heat and let steep for 10 to 15 minutes. Combine the egg yolks and sugar with a whisk, but try not to create too much air. Add the warm milk and combine with a wooden spoon. Do not whisk or foam will form.

Pour the custard through a sieve into a but-tered 6-cup custard mold or into six individual 1-cup soufflé dishes. If there is any foam on the surface remove it with a spoon. (The foam has the texture of grit when it is cooked.) Put the mold or molds into a *bain marie* and pour boiling water halfway up the sides. Bake at 375° for 30 to 45 minutes for the large mold and for 20 to 30 minutes for the smaller ones. The custard should be set around the edges but still somewhat soft in the center. Cool and then chill.

When you are ready to serve, sieve the brown sugar over the top of the custard and broil about six inches from the heat to cara-melize. Serve immediately.

INDEX

Braised Halibut with,
42–43
Mustard, Mussels in, with
Julienne of Celery
Root, 298–299
Parmesan, Baked Halibut
with, 42
Pesto, 348
Sorrel, 88
Watercress, 348
See also Aioli
Mazza family, Seal Brand
cheeses of, *discussed,*
268
Meatballs, Mint, 87
Mediterranean
-Style, Braised Squid, 226
Tomato Sauce, Zucchini
and Eggplant with,
137–138
Melrose apple, *discussed,* 205
Mint
Aioli, 53
Herb-Marinated Grilled
Leg of Lamb with,
51–53
Basil Vinaigrette, 210
Chilled Mussels with,
84, 210
Breast of Chicken Stuffed
with Goat Cheese,
Basil, and, 129–130
Chili Chutneys, Fillet of
Trout with, 48–49
Cucumber Soup, Iced, with
Fresh, 110
Honey Vinaigrette, Shrimp
and Strawberry Salad
with, 33

Mayonnaise, 348
Braised Halibut with,
42–43
Meatballs, 87
Parsley Butter, 114, 362
Pilaf, 87
Relish, Fresh, 86–87
Rhubarb Sauce, 24
Salade Niçoise with, 87
Soufflé with Huckleberry
Sauce, 154–155
Tomato Salad with Creamy
Herb Dressing, 215
Misterly, Lora Lee, 269
Misterly, Rick, 269
Mitchell, Mike, 343
Monterey Jack, Polenta with
Mushroom Sauce,
Cream, and 331–332
Montrachet and Asparagus,
Fresh Pasta with, 21
Morels
discussed, 185–186
in Red Burgundy, 188
Mornay sauce, for Asparagus
Gratin, 20
Mount Capra cheeses,
discussed, 268
Mousse
Cranberry Ginger, 256–257
Hazelnut Praline, 341–342
Lemon, 151
Pumpkin and Rum, 260
Rhubarb, 25
Crimson, with
Strawberry-Gin Sauce,
63–64

Salmon
Boned Rainbow Trout
with, and Sauce *Beurre
Rouge,* 45–46
Smoked, Wild Rice and
Cornmeal Waffles
with, 30–31
Mozzarella, Hazelnut-Fried
Fresh, with Apple
Cider and Chives,
211–212
Muffin(s)
Basic Recipe for Perfect,
249–250
Cheddar and Bacon, 250
Cranberry Cornmeal, 250
Dried Oregon Cherry, 250
Hazelnut Butter, 251
Lemon Cardamom, Spicy,
251
Oat Bran and Apple, 251
Mushroom(s)
Chinese, 35
Fettuccini with Scallops,
Cream, and, 126–127
Sauce, Polenta with
Monterey Jack,
Cream, and, 331–332
Smoked Salmon, and
Cheddar, Tian of, 281
Stuffed, with Oregano, 87
See also Wild Mushroom(s)
Mussel(s)
Bouillabaisse, 304
Bourride, 302–304
Chilled, with Basil Mint
Vinaigrette, 84, 210
in Lemon Butter Sauce,
307